'WATCHING'

OVER CARLISLE

140 YEARS OF THE

CARLISLE CITY POLICE FORCE

1827 -1967

P3 Publications

ISBN-13: 978-0-9559017-6-8

Cover picture, 'Watching over Carlisle' - the Courts and surrounding area.
Photographed by the author on 31 July, 1999.

First Published in Great Britain
in July 2011 by P3 Publications
13 Beaver Road
Carlisle
Cumbria,
CA2 7PS

Typeset in Times Roman

Printed and bound in China by
Hong Kong Graphics and Printing Ltd.

www.p3publications.com

Contents

Be just and fear not;

Let all the ends thou aims't at be thy country's,
Thy God's and truth's; then if thou fallest, O Cromwell,
Thou falls't a blessed martyr!"

Shakespeare – King Henry VIII.
[Cardinal Wolsey to Thomas Cromwell, Earl of Essex, Secretary to the King and director of government policy].

*City Police insignia included the city's Coat of Arms and motto, most appropriate for a police force,
'Be just and fear not'.*

*The Arms used from 1885 [top] were not officially registered and were superseded
in 1924 by the currently used armorial bearings [bottom].*

Robert (Bob) Lowther
28 April 1938 - 26 April 2010

Acknowledgements

I am grateful to former Chief Constables of Cumbria Constabulary, Colin Phillips and Mike Baxter for allowing me access to police records and photographs and to the current Chief Constable, Craig Mackey, for his assistance and contribution to this publication.

I acknowledge the help of the staff at Cumbria Archives Office, The Castle, Carlisle and at Carlisle Library; Duncan Brodie, Curator, Greater Manchester Police Museum, who provided background information on Benjamin Batty, Carlisle's first Chief of Police, and Inspector Greg Alcorn of Edmonton Police Service, Alberta, Canada who traced and confirmed the presence of a former Chief Constable, George Hill, to his Force; Denis Perriam for sharing his historical knowledge and practical advice; former colleagues in the city police force and in Cumbria Constabulary, too numerous to mention individually here, for their stories and use of photographs and David Ramshaw, Publisher, Carlisle.

In particular, I wish to dedicate the book to my wife, Jennifer, always willing to lend a helping hand in its preparation and for her encouragement that kept me to the task.

oooOooo

Bibliography

The Police Service in Britain, HMSO 1965
Various study notes, The Police Staff College, Bramshill, Hampshire
Various study notes from GCE 'A' Level courses, [i] English Law and [ii] British Government and Politics, South East Derbyshire College, Heanor,
The Cumberland Evening News and Star
The Carlisle Journal
The Carlisle Patriot

oooOooo

Pictures

Cumbria Constabulary Museum [now closed]
Carlisle Corporation Octo-centenary celebrations booklet, 1958
HMSO Schools package, 'The story of our police' 1977
Tullie House Museum and Art Gallery, Carlisle
Carlisle Library
The Cumberland News
The Carlisle Journal
The Templeton Collection
The Mary Burgess Collection

Foreword

Mr Craig Mackey
Chief Constable of Cumbria

As Chief Constable of Cumbria Constabulary, it is a privilege to have been asked to write the foreword for this book. Until his untimely death in 2010, Bob Lowther continued to be a great friend and ally of the police. He worked tirelessly on behalf of all the retired officers who continue to live in the county and who continue to make the Constabulary feel like one big family.

The creation of Cumbria Constabulary, as we know it today, occurred over a period of time from 1856. Today it is recognised as one of the best performing Police Forces in the United Kingdom. This is despite the specific challenges faced in the County. The Force is the fifth largest in terms of geography, but one of the smallest in terms of police numbers. The total population of less than 500,000 is spread across often remote areas, with only a few conurbations of any size.

The largest of these, and the only city in the County, is that of Carlisle. As Bob's book explains in detail, the City of Carlisle has had a turbulent history and one that has required the presence of a strong and dependable police force at many times in the past. I have no doubt at all that the traditions and values established by the City of Carlisle Force continue to impact positively into today's service and the foundations for our current success were laid in the years prior to 1965.

Craig Mackey QPM
Chief Constable   April 2011

Preface

Retiring after a chequered thirty years police career serving in both rural areas and large cities, all of it spent in front-line operational roles, well over half in the detective branch, much of it at senior rank, caused quite a shock to the system - an overnight transition from leading a most active life with hardly enough hours in the day to, metaphorically, sitting twiddling my thumbs.

So here I was with time on my hands and back home in Carlisle where I began my police career. What was I going to do with it? The answer came when attending the weekly re-unions of the old city policemen as we reminisced and put the world to rights in the police club in Rickergate. Those sessions were good for the soul. With the help of the bold John Barleycorn, we would have a good laugh as we recalled experiences and exchanged tales, some serious, some humorous - even in the most serious of situations policemen find a funny side that helps to relieve tension. Often it would be said, "Someone should write a book about all this." Of course, many such books have been written elsewhere in the country, but we knew that no-one had carried out any in-depth research into our beloved old force - a big gap in our knowledge of it - and given our advancing years and dwindling numbers we couldn't see anyone stepping forward. When I galloped into the twentieth century and bought my own computer, not only was I considering what use I could put it to, but others had ideas too - a history of Carlisle City Police Force. And so, with a little bit of arm-twisting, a policeman would say persuasion, I embarked upon the project. I had no idea what I was taking on or what I might find, if anything at all back beyond our own service. I was, however, pleasantly surprised. There was much more material than I imagined. There was also much trawling to be done through ancient documents and newspapers to get at it, and many days without any end product, before I arrived at the finished article. I had no idea that it would take me so long to complete, one month, two maybe, but then it was a hobby, not a project for publication, save, I thought, for a few sheets of A4 to be circulated amongst a small group of former officers; and so I only worked at it occasionally. Now completed, a few years later, I hope that the following account provides not only a history of the Force but paints a fair picture of what life was like in the city and, in particular, for the men, and much later the women, who proudly trudged the cobbled streets of our fair old city in the uniform of the Carlisle City Police Force.

Unavoidably, there will be omissions, though I trust none too important, since force records are incomplete, almost non-existent, many lost after the amalgamation with Cumberland and Westmorland Constabulary in 1969 and, later, many more following local government re-organisation in 1974. I know of no photographs remaining of any officers serving prior to the early 1900s, unusual, when most county constabularies, at least, have a full complement of chief officer pictures going back to their origins in 1875. I would wager that there are numerous mementoes lying about in many homes in the city (maybe even further afield since local men were not able to join their home town forces until after WW2). I know of, and have seen one pristine 'Carlisle Police' helmet plate from the 1920s, cherished by the proud family of a former sergeant and I would love to know what happened to the painting of Britain's first black policeman, John Kent, that hung in the parlour of his home off Warwick Road, as the local press reported in his obituary notice. It would now be of national interest and probably worth a fortune. Where are the old photographs and uniforms that were stored in the Rickergate police station when I was a constable there? Items such as this should have been preserved as museum pieces. Certain chief officers must bear responsibility for disposing, almost criminally some would say, of records and memorabilia, effectively air-brushing the city police from memory. Rumour abounds that the much sought after silver helmet plates of the 1960s were ordered to be disposed of under a building in the course of construction at county police headquarters and that a JCB was used to excavate the hole before crushing and burying them. The few that remain, no doubt retained by the officers who wore them, have become rare, collector's items.

'WATCHING'
OVER CARLISLE

Picture from the website 'Learn history' shows Charlie Rouse, London's last Watchman,' wearing his watchcoat and carrying his cudgel, cutlass, rattle and oil lamp.

Carlisle's watchmen were similarly dressed and, apart from the cutlass, similarly equipped.

Watch
Watching
Watchman

Historically, the 'watch' refers to the body of men who patrolled the streets by night on the look-out for thieves, robbers and other criminals and who 'watched' to ensure that all was well. The Statute of Westminster, 1285, provided for the appointment of the first 'watchmen'.

Ward

'Ward' is an archaic term meaning 'guarding, defending'. [*Oxford Reference Dictionary*].

Watch and Ward

Watch was the term used to describe the ancient system of continuous vigilance by night and by day respectively.

Police/
Watch Committee

A civil force for maintaining law and order. The Municipal Corporations Act, 1835, empowered certain cities and boroughs to employ a 'police' under the supervision of a Corporation 'Watch Committee'. These committees remained the autonomous police authorities of every town that supported its own independent police force until the passing of the Police Act, 1964.

Constable

From the Latin 'comes stabuli' – 'officer of the stables'. Traditionally a great officer of state, an official of the royal household, a military commander and governor of a castle/fortress. Later the title of a parish officer and more recently a policeman. Every UK policeman, irrespective of rank, holds office as a 'constable'.

Introduction

As a state Britain is ancient, with ancient boundaries, ancient institutions such as the monarchy and parliament, and ancient customs. Dramatic or radical political changes have rarely occurred and progress to the present day has been evolutionary rather than revolutionary. There have been many instances of civil disobedience but a reasonably settled society has generally been democratic and law-abiding with a sense of civic duty and pride, fully recognising that the maintenance of the King's (Queen's) Peace is of paramount importance to good government. It is against this background that our police service has evolved. The service itself is a relatively modern institution, existing in something like its present form for little over 170 years, but its development can be traced back over 900 years. Unlike most states, Britain has never had a need for a national police force, for para-military style policing or for the universal arming of police officers. For centuries local communities have policed themselves. Society itself has from time immemorial made laws, many based on ancient customs, (common law), for its own regulation, protection and general well-being. Since these rules and regulations, echoing the wishes of the people, have been enforced by locally appointed officers, themselves answerable to the courts for any misbehaviour in office, the service is said to *'police by (public) consent.'*

Carlisle, too, is ancient, a Roman settlement almost 2000 years ago, with evidence that it existed perhaps centuries before then, and a cathedral city for 850 years having been granted civic independence by royal charter in 1158*. It was a corporate city in 1240, with a mayor as its head, dealing directly with the King. Unlike most of Britain, Carlisle has had a very turbulent past, centuries of warfare and strife with death and destruction ever present. It has passed to and fro between England and Scotland. The last time it fell was in November 1745 when the Scottish Prince Charles Edward Stuart, Bonnie Prince Charlie, and his Jacobite army took the city. It was regained for England by the Duke of Cumberland one month later with disastrous consequences for the Scots army. Thus peace came to the city. Just eighty years later, in order to preserve that peace, a number of respectable citizens concerned at the state of lawlessness in the city and its suburbs, perpetrated not by invading armies but by its own citizens, began steps to create a properly organized, professional and efficient police force. The first paid officers commenced duty on a temporary basis, in February, 1827. An Act of Parliament (7/8GeoIV LXXXXVI), known locally as the Carlisle Police Act, given royal assent on 14 June, 1827, provided statutory authority to a permanent force. The rest, as they say, is history.

---

*Picture shows the octo-centenary plaque in the Civic Centre unveiled by H.M. Queen Elizabeth II.

Chronology

*The placing of the principal events during the existence of the
Carlisle City Police Force into their contemporary history*

1748 - Bow Street Runners under Henry Fielding.

1760 - Death of George II - accession of George III.

1773 - Boston Tea party.

1776 - Declaration of American Independence.

1780 - Gordon Riots.

1781 - Surrender at Yorktown - American victory over British troops.

1789/1795 - French Revolution.

1792 - Coal gas used for lighting.

1793/1815 - Wars with France.

1799 - Napoleon seized power in France.

1800/1830 - rapid increase in population, especially in urban areas - Industrial revolution.

1801 - First British official census. Only 4 towns north of London with populations of over 50,000[18 by 1851]. Pop. Of Carlisle, 8,723 males, 10,216 females, total 18,939.

1805 - Battle of Trafalgar, Nelson defeats French and Spanish fleets.

1811 - Luddite disturbances in Nottinghamshire and Yorkshire.

1811 - Pop. of Carlisle, 10,077 males, 11,819 females, total 21,896.

1815 - Battle of Waterloo, Wellington defeats Napoleon bringing peace to Europe.

1815 - Over 200 capital crimes on the Statute Books.

1819 - Peterloo massacre.
  - Handloom weavers of Caldewgate rioted.
  - Gas street lighting introduced in Carlisle.

1820 - Death of George III, accession of George IV.

1821 - Death of Napoleon.
  - Population of Carlisle 12,820 males, 13,863 females, total 26,683.
  - First Temporary Police formed.

1821/1823 - Famine in Ireland.

1823/1853 -Canal from Carlisle to the Solway carrying freight and passengers, making city a busy port. [Regular sailings to Liverpool at a cost of 7 shillings [35p] for deck travel.

1825 - Stockton and Darlington Railway opened.

1826 - Shaddongate riots - 3 shot dead by the military.

1827 - February - Second Temporary police force started in Carlisle funded by public subscription. First Police Office housed in New Banks Lane.

June - Carlisle Police Act receives Royal Assent and a permanent police force begins operations on 13 July, 1827.

Benjamin Batty appointed Chief of Police.

1827 - New County Gaol opens in Carlisle.

1829 - London Metropolitan Police Force created by Home Secretary Robert Peel, commanded by two magistrates, retired Colonel Charles Rowan and lawyer Richard Mayne. First government financed police force in Britain.
  - Catholic emancipation.

1830 - Death of George IV, accession of William IV.

1830/1832 - Major cholera epidemic, started in Sunderland and spread like wildfire - 55,000 deaths. The biggest single problem in towns was that of public health.

1831 - Riots in rural areas against mechanisation of agriculture.

1831 - Robert Brown appointed Chief of Police.

1831 - Pop. of Carlisle, 15879 males, 17,093 females, total 32,972.

1832 - Capital punishment for horse-stealing and house-breaking abolished.

1832 - Reform Act, ridding country of 'rotten boroughs'. Qualification for voting remained 'ownership of property'. Carlisle had 2 MPs, Edinburgh, population. over 100,000 had just 1, Leeds and Manchester none at all.

1834 - Slavery abolished in the British Empire.

1834 - Parish workhouses instituted.

1834 - Transportation of the 'Tolpuddle martyrs', 6 Dorset labourers sentenced for practising secret union oaths.

1835 - Municipal Reform Act and Municipal Corporations Act become law. Over 200 corporations dissolved and replaced by 178 municipal boroughs. Municipal franchise granted to all ratepayers. Act provided for the first official municipal police forces funded by local authorities, but not obligatory. Act adopted by Carlisle City Council which indicated its intention of assuming control of the existing independent force. Prisons Act - first prisons inspectors appointed.

1836 - Railway reaches Carlisle [Carlisle and Newcastle line].

1836 - Dixon's chimney at 320' high completed and Shaddon Mill opened.

1837 - Death of William IV, accession of Victoria, aged 18 years.

1837 - Registration of births and deaths becomes compulsory.

1837 - 17 August. John Kent, son of a former slave in the West Indies, appointed constable in the Carlisle City Police Force - Britain's first black policeman.

1839 - Chartist riots across the country. City of London Police Force established. County Police Act allows magistrates to set up local police forces. Metropolitan Police boundaries extended to 15 mile radius of Charing Cross.

5

Chronology (continued)

1839 - John Graham appointed Chief of Police.

1840 - Penny post introduced. First detectives in Metpol.

1840 - First purpose built police headquarters opened on West Walls.

1841 - Sir Robert Peel became Prime Minister[1841/1846]. One of Carlisle's two M.P.s, Sir James Graham, considered to be Peel's closest councillor.

1841 - Constable Thomas Jardine murdered on duty in Greenmarket.

1841 - Pop. of Carlisle, 17,468 males, 18,691 females, total 36,159.

1841 - Cumberland Infirmary opened on Newtown Road, Carlisle.

1842 - Women and children forbidden to be employed underground in coal mines.

1844 - John Sabbage appointed Chief of Police.

1844/1845 - 5,000 miles of railway track laid - Maryport and Carlisle line opened.

1845 - Irish potato famine caused deaths of approx. 1 million people and led to large scale emigration to the USA and to England [the navvies, who helped build the canals and railways].

1846 - The Corn Laws abolished.

1847 - Carlisle Citadel Railway Station opened.

1848 - Public Health Act, and Regulations requiring all new buildings to have proper drainage and lavatories. Local authorities could levy a rate for the provision of clean water supplies, street cleaning and refuse collection.

1851 - Pop. of Carlisle, 20,138 males, 21,419 females, total 41,557.

1854/1856 - Crimean War.

1856 - The County and Borough Police Act made police forces obligatory in all counties and boroughs in England and Wales. Central Government provided a grant towards the expenses of all police forces subject to inspection to ensure efficiency. HMIs appointed to carry out the inspections.

1857 - County police forces established in Scotland.

1857 - George Edward Bent, appointed Chief Constable.

1861 - Outbreak of the American Civil War.

1861 and 1865 - Road Acts required all motor vehicles to be preceded by a person carrying a red warning flag [repealed 1896].

1862 - America abolishes slavery. William Charlton hanged for murder in Carlisle - the city's last public execution.

1865 - President Lincoln assassinated. Surrender of General Lee.

1867 - Transportation of criminals to Australia ended [after 451 cases that year]. British convicts still sent to Gibralter until 1875.

1869 - Suez Canal opened. 1870 - Education Act provided a system of education for the first time, but not necessarily free of charge.

1873 - Walter Hemingway appointed Chief Constable.

1876 - Battle of the Little Big Horn, Montana - General Custer's last stand.

1876 - Alexander Graham Bell invented the telephone.

1876 - George MacKay appointed Chief Constable.

1877 - County gaols come under government control.

1880/1881 - First Boer War.

1881 - Education compulsory for all 5/10 year olds.

1885 - [October] Robbery at Netherby Hall, near Carlisle and shooting of a county policeman at Kingstown, Carlisle. Constable Fortune of the City Police Force severely beaten and injured on the railway side in Wapping, Carlisle. Constable Byrnes of the county police shot and killed at Plumpton, to the south of the city. The offenders in each case, three London criminals, Rudge, Martin and Baker were arrested and hanged at Carlisle in February, 1886.

1888 - Local Government Act granted 61 towns county borough status.

1888 - County Councils Act created elected county councils.

1891- Free education.

1899/1902 - Second Boer War.

1901 - Death of Victoria, accession of Edward VII.

1904 - George Hill appointed Chief Constable.

1910 - Death of Edward VII, accession of George V.

1913 - Eric Herbert deSchmid appointed Chief Constable.

1914/1918 - First World War.

Creation of the Carlisle and District State Management Scheme. Prime Minister Lloyd George, fearing uprisings as in Ireland, nationalised the city's liquor trade "to prevent such drinking as renders workers unfit for

national service". [Munitions factories in the Carlisle area employed thousands of mainly Irish workers]. There were 100 pubs and 4 breweries in the city.

1926 - General Strike.

1928 - Archibald Kennedy Wilson appointed Chief Constable.

1929 - Andrew Alexander Johnston appointed Chief Constable.

1936 - Death of George V, accession and later abdication of Edward VII, accession of George VI.

1938 - William Henry Lakeman appointed Chief Constable.

1939/1945 - Second World War.

1941 - New Headquarters in Rickergate officially opened.

1946 - Police Act enforced compulsory amalgamations of several small police forces with their neighbouring counties.

1947 - Labour Government's nationalisation plans put into effect - coal mining, railways, road transport, steel.

1952 - Death of George VI, accession of Elizabeth II.

1960 - Royal Commission on the Police.

1961 - Frank Edgar Williamson appointed the 13th and last Chief Constable.

1963 - Carlisle City Watch Committee voluntarily agrees to the integration of the city and county police forces.

1964 - Police Act gave Home Secretary power to order compulsory amalgamations of forces. Number of forces reduced from 125 to 49 in England and Wales.

1964 - Frank Williamson appointed Chief Constable of the Cumberland and Westmorland Constabulary [jointly with the city force].

1965 - Constable George Russell shot and murdered on duty at Oxenholme in Westmorland. Colleagues also shot, Constable Alec Archibald severely wounded and Inspector Alf Harrison slightly injured.

1967 - Carlisle City Police Force ceased to exist on amalgamation with Cumberland and Westmorland Constabulary to form a new Cumbria Constabulary.

AN EARLY ATTEMPT TO ESTABLISH A POLICE FORCE IN THE CITY

WANTED,

SEVERAL Stout Active Men as POLICE OFFICERS for the City of CARLISLE and Neighbourhood. None need apply unless they can produce satisfactory recommendations as to Character. Candidates to leave their Names and Recommendations at the PUBLIC OFFICE, Carlisle, on FRIDAY the 12th Instant, and the Appointment will take place on the SATURDAY or Wednesday following.

By ORDER OF THE MAGISTRATES.

Public Office, Scotch-street,
January 4, 1821.

In January 1821, in the Town Hall, local magistrates met a deputation of citizens who were demanding firm action be taken to curb an increase in lawlessness in the city and district. They resolved to establish a 'public office' and to employ a number of police officers. They announced their decision in the local press and placed an advertisement for 'several stout active men' to be appointed without delay. Not every citizen welcomed the move and one, under the nom-de-plume *'Juventus'*, wrote to the Carlisle Patriot expressing his opposition, not only to the principle, but also to the cost of maintaining a police and to the names of city magistrates taking precedence over county justices in a published list of the scheme's supporters. A magistrate replied at some length, stating, inter alia,

'Why, surely the Mayor is the Chief Magistrate of Carlisle; and this is not only called 'the City Police' but is bone fide so - the County Magistrates having only a concurrent and not an original jurisdiction.'

'I shall merely observe, that if anything was wanting to convince every unprejudiced and disinterested person of the necessity of a Police Establishment in this populous and exposed City and neighbourhood, it may be found in the events of the past week. When attempts at assassination and robbery, by firearms, are made in our very streets, it is time that the magistracy and the inhabitants should be unanimous and on the alert; and that individuals should prefer the public good, to the gratification of a sordid love of self.'

[signed] ONE OF THE TOWN-HALL MEETING.

A temporary force had been appointed because, at the close of 1822, the Carlisle Journal stated that there was a call *"of carrying on an establishment of eight policemen which had been for the two proceeding years supported by subscription"*. However the City Council were not prepared either to fund an Act to form a permanent police force or to pay for the force itself. A further five years of argument and discussion were to pass before the City Council were finally forced to agree to supporting a permanent police force. This was due to the intervention of Sir Robert Peel.

Peel wrote to the Carlisle MP, Sir James Graham: *"I feel so much interested on public grounds in the establishment of an efficient police in Carlisle that I have no objection to take the opinion of law officers of the Crown as to the legal effect of the Charter in obliging the Corporation to maintain or contribute to the maintenance of the police."* This did the trick and in 1827 Carlisle finally established a permanent police force.

Judge's Escorts

Cumberland Assizes, held biannually in the Citadel Courthouses, were traditionally opened amid pomp and ceremony. Before the commencement of court business, HM judges, heralded by military trumpeters, and other members of the legal profession attended a service in Carlisle Cathedral, after which the Judge's carriage was accompanied along English Street to the Citadel by an escort of city foot patrolmen. With the coming of the motor car, Judges were escorted to and from their lodgings in the city by a traffic patrol car each time they attended court.

The photograph on the right, taken c1902, shows the Judge's carriage leaving his lodgings which were then in Lowther Street, now the premises of the Royal Bank of Scotland. The premises have changed little in outer appearance over the century and are easily recognisable in the picture. Later the Judges' lodgings moved to Warwick Road and then to St Ann's Hill.

This photograph shows an escort of a sergeant and four constables outside the cathedral on 8 June 1915, this being the first time mechanised transport was used in the city to carry a Judge. The car is a new Daimler recently purchased and owned by the High Sheriff of Cumberland.

This photograph, taken outside the cathedral in 1956, shows an escort of from the left:
two motor patrolmen, PC Joe Richardson and 'Big' John Brown, one sergeant, Harold Joffre Robinson and six constables.

The six constables are:
Gerald Salkeld, Bill Lowther [my big brother], Ken Grainger, Jimmy Dunn, Norman Robinson and 'the other' John [Singleton] Brown.

Punch's drawing in 1847 depicted a collection of police mementoes preserved for a hundred years. If only the chief officers of Carlisle and Cumbria had had such foresight!!

A HUNDRED YEARS HENCE.—A ROOM IN THE STYLE OF THE NINETEENTH CENTURY
[*Punch*, Vol. XII, 1847

Part One

From 'Watching' to the establishment of the city police force

Policing in England is founded on ancient custom and since time immemorial has been based on the principle of 'collective responsibility' or public co-operation. As far back as the 6th Century there was an obligation on parish communities to police themselves and to unite against evildoers. Every male, upon reaching twelve years of age, had a duty to act if he witnessed the commission of a crime and was duty bound to raise a 'hue and cry' and to join in the chase to arrest the offender. All of the group were fined for any neglect of duty by a single member. They delivered miscreants to the local 'moot' court for minor breaches of the law. Serious matters were passed up to the county shire-reeve (sheriff), whose duty it was to ensure that the King's Peace was maintained. He had authority to call out all the available men in the shire, if necessary, to pursue felons. The Normans retained and reinforced these Anglo-Saxon customs. Carlisle, an ancient city with a history dating back over 900 years, would be compelled to adopt such a system of policing. Towards the end of the 12th Century, the sheriff's authority was taken over by the lords of the manors. The high-ranking office of 'constable' * was introduced, his duty to keep the King's Peace 'exercising his powers under common law as a person paid to perform, as a matter of duty, acts which if he were so minded he might have done voluntarily.**

In 1158, Henry II granted the city its first Royal Charter and numerous others followed for, amongst other benefits, 'its defence and preservation, as well as against public enemies as against robbers and plunderers.'

The Statute of Winchester in 1285, an Act that provided for **'Watching'** *** and keeping of the King's Peace' in towns influenced the system of policing in England for some 600 years and firmly established the principle of 'local responsibility' (community policing) in the following terms:

'And the King commandeth, That from henceforth all Towns be kept as it hath been used in Times passed, That is, to wit, from the Day of Ascension unto the Day of Saint Michael; in every City Six Men shall keep at every Gate; in every Borough Twelve Men; in every Town Six or Four; according to the Number of the Inhabitants of the Town; and shall watch the town continually all Night, from the Sun setting to the Sun rising.

---

* *A term, or rank, used by the Normans in a military context - a title used variously to name a high officer of a royal or noble household, a warden or governor of a royal castle or fortified town, a high constable of a hundred or shire down to a petty constable of a parish..*

**Royal Commission on Police Powers and Procedure, 1929.*

****See introductory pages, ibid, and title of this publication.*

And if any Stranger do pass by them, he shall be arrested until Morning; and if no Suspicion be found, he shall go quit; and if they find Cause or Suspicion, they shall forthwith deliver him to the Sheriff, and the Sheriff may receive him without Damage, and shall keep him safely, until he be delivered in due Manner'.

The authorities in Carlisle were under an obligation to enforce the Act, under the terms of which every man was to maintain the King's Peace and had the power to arrest those who did not. A **Watch**[*] of unpaid men, selected on a rota basis from all the honest men of the town, was required to be placed nightly at every gate of the town with an obligation, if offenders were discovered, to raise the 'hue and cry' in order to give chase and arrest them. Every male between the ages of 15 and 60 was compelled to keep at home, arms for use in maintaining the peace. It was the constable's duty to check and examine those arms for serviceability.

A Charter granted by Charles I in 1637 provided for 'the good government of the City and the preservation of the Peace' stating in its preamble,

'and the said Charter authorizes and directs the election of the Mayor, Aldermen and Council and gives them various powers of making and enforcing Bye-laws in the City; and likewise directs the election of a Recorder, Town Clerk, two Bailiffs, two Coroners, a Sword Bearer and three Sergeants at Mace.'

The Mayor and two Aldermen together with the Recorder were appointed Justices of the Peace. The Royal Sword was to be carried before them as a symbol of their jurisdiction and the Sergeants at Mace were to carry maces of gold or silver adorned with the arms of England to indicate that the Mayor had certain Royal powers. In ancient times, the Corporation engaged a Watch, for protecting the city 'against freebooters and robbers' with which it was well populated. The watchmen called the night curfew at eight or nine o'clock and the morning rouse at four or five o'clock. Later, it employed, in addition to the chartered appointments, officers who were, effectively, police officers, namely a High Constable and six Halbertmen or Beadles. They were equipped and paid regular salaries entirely from Corporation funds, raised by tolls, and at no cost to the citizens. They were, apparently, sufficiently able to provide a satisfactory policing service but the Corporation, finding their upkeep too costly, replaced them with two 'common bailiffs or constables.' The 17th Century Beadles were each paid £1.6s.8d [£1.33] per annum, as were the city's Bellman [Town Crier] and gaolers, whilst the sword-bearer got £6.13s.4d [£6.66]. The Sword-bearer, mace sergeants and beadles, duties that were carried out by city policemen until relatively recent times, wore the city's livery. The Chamberlain's accounts indicate that one particular Alderman normally won the contract to supply the uniforms.

In the early 18th Century, local manorial courts and later Justices of the Peace appointed constables to act in towns and parishes whilst, additionally, in some places, the provisions of the Statute of Winchester still applied. These long-standing arrangements became discredited with the coming of the Industrial Revolution.

Nationwide, a rapid growth in population in urban areas, without a corresponding improvement in infrastructure, resulted in living conditions that were indescribably squalid. Mechanisation of manufacturing processes led to wholesale unemployment. Levels of crime and lawlessness increased and became intolerable. Those required to perform watch duties, who could ill afford to neglect their own livelihoods for the unpaid business of law enforcement, began to pay others to deputise for them. Then deputies themselves paid for deputies until only the old and infirm and those least suited to the task were left carrying out the duties. They were unfit for purpose, the targets of scorn.

Whilst desperation was behind some crimes there is no doubt that footpads took full advantage of the prevailing conditions knowing that without a police there was little likelihood of capture and conviction. Criminal activity was rampant and the government lacked either the ability or the determination, or both, to effectively tackle the situation. Harsh penalties imposed on offenders were considered to be the best deterrent. In 1819, over 200 offences were punishable by death.

---

[*] *See introductory pages, ibid.*

Locally, over the years, the Corporation seemed quite indifferent to the worries and concerns of citizens. There were talks about preventing unlawful activity, but only half-hearted attempts at finding a real and lasting solution. The Cumberland Pacquet (28 May 1788) recorded that there had never been a regular police force in the city, but that in 1777 it had been announced, *'Several attempts having been lately made to break into some of the capital houses in Carlisle, the Corporation have agreed to give £20 a year for a night-watch, which we hear will be established next winter.'* On 7 May 1788, the Pacquet reported that the magistrates had appointed constables to patrol the streets during the times of divine service, *'to apprehend all vagrants and idle people who shall be found profaning the day or neglecting the duties of it.'* The arrangement, quote, *'which reflects real credit on their police'* was explained. *'The city is divided into districts, through each of which two constables and two principal inhabitants, who take it by rotation, patrol the streets from ten o'clock in the morning till one; and from three till five in the afternoon; during which hours the doors of all the inns and public houses are kept shut; the patrol having first visited them to see that no person is tippling in them. So much respect is paid to this regulation that during these hours no person is seen in the streets but those who are going to, or returning from, some place of worship.'* Lack of funding led to the discontinuation of the patrols. Consideration was given to the establishment of a regular watch in 1791 but there is no evidence that it came to fruition. In January of that year, the 'Pacquet' reported *'attacks upon two houses in St. Cuthbert's Lane, conducted in the most audacious manner.'* Two men, seen trying keys in the doors of several houses which at the time were occupied by the residents, were disturbed by Dr. Heysham* who *'threw up the sash of his window and, presenting a musket, threatened to fire if they did not instantly depart; on this, they thought it proper to make off.'* In 1811, five beadles, also employed as scavengers, were engaged by Corporation whilst the magistrates employed eight constables between 1821 and 1823. They had been considered relatively successful but their services were dispensed with due to a lack of subscriptions and the absence of any determination on the part of the authorities to obtain an Act of Parliament. Peacekeeping, so far as the Corporation was concerned, could still be done on the cheap. In times of, and usually in response to, an emergency, householders could be sworn as unpaid special constables and if they were unable to solve the problem a magistrate was empowered to call out the military. Carlisle being a garrison city, they experienced no difficulty in quickly procuring military aid. Policing in the town was haphazard and, in short, a shambles. There were too few peacekeepers for a population of 20,000 even if, generally, Carlisle had been a law-abiding place which, clearly, it was not. The parish constables or beadles often lacked the ability even to execute a warrant.

By the end of the century, peacekeeping methods were further tested by a new phenomenon, serious rioting and public disorder which reached new heights of violence and intensity, inflamed by public dissatisfaction with religious, political and economic issues. In London, the Gordon riots in June 1780 are said to have resulted in up to seven hundred deaths, whilst in Manchester, in the so-called Peterloo riots in August 1819, eleven were killed and over four hundred injured. The law officers of the day were simply overwhelmed by the enormity of the rioting crowds. It is not surprising, therefore, that the military were frequently called to restore order as ancient 'policing' systems collapsed.

In Carlisle, in January, 1827, the Journal reported, *'There are two constables, Barnes and Mullinder. This for a population of 15,000, one fourth of whom consist of poor Irish out of employment. There is no lock-up house in the place, so that even if they were disposed to apprehend malefactors or reputed thieves, they have no means of lodging them in any temporary prison for security. The governor of the gaol will not, can not by law, receive them without a warrant that cannot in many instances be obtained till, by the escape of the offenders, it has ceased to be of use.'* Later in the same month, the paper commented, 'It is admitted that Carlisle is without a police.

Early peacekeeping in the city was succinctly summed up by Mr. J.H. Minns, Vice Chairman of the Watch Committee, during the opening ceremony of the Rickergate Police Headquarters in April, 1941:
"This ancient City of Carlisle has seen many changes since the boom of the evening gun from the castle warned those who were leaving or those entertaining that the gates were about to close at sunset, and once

---

* *Magistrate and later a Police Commissioner.*

they swung on their creaking hinges, and the locks and bolts in their sockets, they remained closed until sunrise the following morning. In medieval times, if a crime of any description was committed and the citizens failed in their efforts to catch the criminal, they were fined for neglect of duty. In Tudor and Stuart days, the city was patrolled at night by watchmen, called 'Charlies', old men shuffled about the streets and lanes carrying a candle stable lantern, a rattle and a stick, and through the night calling out such phrases as 'Past twelve o' clock - fine moonlight night - all's well,' even if a murder had been committed in the next lane."

19th Century Carlisle

It is of interest to know what kind of place Carlisle was at the beginning of the 19th Century, for it was the prevailing economic, social and living conditions then that led to organised policing of the city. Just fifty years after its restoration as an English city, following its capture by Bonnie Prince Charlie's Jacobite army, Carlisle was again in turmoil, but this time invading armies were not the cause. The city was suffering from problems common in other developing northern towns and cities - the adverse effects of the industrial revolution. In particular, the high incidences of criminal activity and general lawlessness, protests and demonstrations were far beyond the capacity of the few 'peacekeepers' who were then employed.

An important centre on the stagecoach routes, Carlisle was a compact, walled city whose population, in the first half of the century almost trebled in size. From the census returns it can be ascertained that the figures for the city, that is the parishes of St.Cuthberts and St. Marys, increased from 10,712 in 1801 to 28,567 in 1851. If the suburbs of Stanwix, Dalston and Burgh are included, the returns show 18,939 residents in 1801, rising by 1851, to 41,557.

Jollie's Directory, in 1811, recorded that the Corporation consisted of *'a Mayor, eleven Aldermen, two Bailiffs, two Coroners and a Common Council of twenty-four 'capital citizens'.* It was a closed shop - upon the death of any, the others chose a replacement. They engaged three Sergeants at Mace* and, by this time, five Beadles, or town scavengers** who wore the corporate livery of the city, *'brown, turned up with red'* and their appointments were generally for life. The Sergeants acted as Bailiffs to the Mayor's Court, executing summonses and writs for debt. Work had begun on the construction of new Court Houses on the site of the Citadel. The county gaol, wretched and constantly damp, and was described

The Scotch Gate and the city debtors gaol.

at the time as *'much out of repair but plans for a new building are well advanced. It is a mean edifice. There is no furniture belonging to the prison but what is found by the unfortunate persons confined there, who are allowed merely straw for their beds.'* An Act of 1804 for lighting, footpaths, etc, had been adopted, and it was claimed that *'not a town or city in the Kingdom is better regulated in this respect.'* The city had two fire engines, but no firemen - the keys, to gain access to the engines, were kept by Mr. Thomas Thompson at the Turks Head public house.

---

* *Re-iterating the position in 1881, the Town Clerk, addressing the Town Council, quoted from the Royal Charters and said that Carlisle's own Bailiffs were appointed to exercise jurisdiction within the city independent of the county sheriff. Carlisle was in all but name a county itself. Supporting his recommendations, the Council appointed the Chief Constable and his deputy City Bailiffs and instructed that two senior police sergeants should be appointed Sword Bearer and Mace Bearer, three others to be Sergeants at Mace, the senior of them to be the Mayor's Sergeant. All were to carry small silver maces on ceremonial occasions.*

** *Street cleaners.*

Pigot's Directory, 1828-29, recorded, inter alia, that Carlisle's *'municipal government is vested partly in Commissioners of Police under an Act obtained in 1827 and partly by a Corporation as old as Henry II. Assizes for the county are held here twice a year, County Quarter Sessions at Easter and Midsummer and Courts of the Mayor and Bailiffs sit every Monday to try actions for debt. A court of sessions is held four*

times per year before the Mayor and two senior Aldermen on the day preceding the County Sessions and the Dean and Chapter and the Duke of Devonshire hold Courts Leet and Baron in the suburbs for their respective manors. The city returns two members to Parliament; the right of voting is with freemen who number about 800, their freedom being acquired by birth and servitude. The Mayor is the returning officer. The Town Hall has two spacious apartments, one used by the Corporation for transacting all city business, the other for holding the Mayor's Court, electing MPs for the city and the holding of the Court of Assize.'

The Town Hall in 1790. The building housed the Quarter sessions, Police and Magistrates Court until the Rickergate Court-house was opened in 1941. The First Police commissioners and later the Watch Committee held meetings here.

Unique Survivor: The uniform jacket of a Sergeant at Mace discovered in a Carlisle attic in 1994. It had lain untouched since frock coats were abandoned in 1920.

(Modelled by Denis Perriam at Tullie House Museum).

Carlisle was heavily involved in the textile industry, cotton spinning and weaving, (ginghams and checks), calico printing and the manufacture of a much-exported cotton twist being the most important. There were extensive dyeworks. Weaving was undertaken by many handloom weavers working from their homes in Caldewgate and Shaddongate*. Carr and Company, biscuit manufacturers, now part of McVitie's, and Hudson Scott's, tin box makers, later the main force behind the nationwide Metal Box Company, began in Carlisle in 1831. Superior quality hats were made in the city and there were three large iron foundries. The building of Dixon's chimney (320 feet high and reputedly, at the time, the tallest chimney in Europe) was completed in 1836 and Shaddon Mill opened. Cowans Sheldon, engineers and cranemakers opened in 1846 and two years later, what was to become an international, and one of the country's biggest building and civil engineering companies, Messrs. John Laing and Son, Limited, my only other employer, was created in the city. John Laing's brother, David Laing, a coal merchant, was one time chairman of the city's Watch Committee. Between 1823 and 1853, Carlisle was a busy port, for the conveyance of both passengers and cargoes, linked to the sea by a ship canal to Port Carlisle. Some shipbuilding took place in Canal Basin in Caldewgate. 'The City', the first ship ever built here and launched in October,1825, was lost at sea sailing from Dublin to Glasgow with a cargo of barley in December, 1825, the crew, mostly from Annan, perishing. Carlisle became a very important railway city. The railway arrived in 1836 with the opening of the western end of the Newcastle and Carlisle Railway operating from its station in London Road. The line was completed in 1838, and was followed by the Maryport and Carlisle Railway with a station in Crown Street. Citadel Station was opened in 1847 as a stopping place on the main west coast England to Scotland route, later becoming the city's only station, servicing seven railway companies.

---

* The Carlisle Journal, looking back in 1882, reported that some 5,000 hand-loom weavers were employed in Caldewgate.

Parliamentary elections were frequent, with no fewer than fifteen general elections and six by-elections between 1802 and 1852. In 1827, the city's members were Sir James Graham, later to become a Home Secretary, and Sir Philip Musgrave, who died later the same year. By contrast, Edinburgh, with a population in excess of 100,000, sent only one member, chosen by just thirty-three electors. Carlisle's Corporation governed locally. It is hardly surprising that the inhabitants of the city felt aggrieved, in that they were neither truly represented in Parliament nor had they a voice in municipal matters.

There was a prima-facie case to argue that in the early part of the 19th Century, Carlisle was a thriving, successful, progressive place but just below the surface was a ground swell of unrest, especially amongst the poorer classes in the Caldewgate and Shaddongate areas, unrest that, in 1812 and again in 1826, was to manifest itself in a most dramatic and tragic way.

Shot and killed by the military
Poverty-stricken and hungry, the citizens could, perhaps, be forgiven for resorting to desperate, including criminal, means while the local authority and city merchants seemed insensitive to their needs. At the beginning of April, 1812, shipping near Sandsfield and warehouses in Dalston were attacked and food contents stolen. On Saturday 4 April, bread corn in the city quickly sold out leaving many without food. Two days later, with families at the point of starvation, huge quantities of grain were moved from the city for export through the nearby port of Sandsfield. Cartloads were seized by locals. Magistrates and the military were summoned to the scene and the stolen grain was recovered. At 7pm, soldiers of the 55th Regiment marched, triumphantly, into the city centre drums beating. One woman threw a stone at an officer. Sword drawn, he pursued her whilst another officer struck out with his sword at a young boy, exacerbating an already tense situation. The soldiers were dismissed in the Market Place, whereupon the crowd began to stone the officers. Drums beat again, recalling the soldiers to arms. The Riot Act was read and the streets were cleared by soldiers with fixed bayonets. Thirty-eight citizens were arrested and marched off to the county gaol. Afterwards, there was criticism because no constables were called to deal with the disorder. Had they been summoned, they probably could not have coped with such an inflammatory situation. By 7.30pm, a crowd, thousands in number, had gathered in the Market Place, many simply out of curiosity and unaware of the Riot Act proclamation. A magistrate met up with the soldiers, and the stoning began once again. He ordered them to fire in all directions. The crowd, at first, believed the soldiers were firing blanks. They were not and *'one poor, unoffending woman in an advanced stage of pregnancy,'* the wife of a soldier of the 55th who was at the time at Sandsfield, was shot and killed. A verdict of 'accidental death' was recorded by the coroner, and on the Wednesday following the occurrence, the city magistrates entertained the officers of the 55th in appreciation of *'the way they had preserved the Peace'.* Such was law and order, 1812 style!

On Tuesday 21 April, city magistrates addressed a gathering of townspeople outside the Town Hall, telling them there was no need for them to steal since they could apply for parochial aid. That would have entailed giving up their children as *'parish apprentices,'* a totally unacceptable option, the feeling being that they would rather suffer hardships than be parted from their children. Threats were shouted from the crowd and the militia were called. The soldiers marched eighteen miles from Penrith. Surely the crowds had dispersed by the time of their arrival in the city. Meanwhile, firearms were stolen in Denton Holme and about a dozen men, with faces blackened, attacked a watchman at a factory in the area.

The city's better off increasingly became victims of a tide of rising crime, the perpetrators often operating in small gangs, some in possession of firearms or other offensive weapons. It was not uncommon for decent people to arm themselves in self-defence, and there seemed to be no compunction about using their weapons to scare off criminals. Why did they have to take the law into their own hands? The answer may lie in a letter* written in 1826 by the Town Mayor, William Hodgson, addressed to Lord Lonsdale, *'There are only two constables in the city kept and paid by the Corporation, and five parish constables none of which latter are ever effective, being changed annually and only useful in parish matters.'* Sir Philip Musgrave, MP, also wrote to the noble gentleman in June 1826, *'The civil power at Carlisle is so ridiculously inefficient that*

_____

* County Record Office document.

it can give no protection to anyone.' In another letter to Lord Lonsdale one week later, he said, *'I think the inhabitants of Carlisle must now be convinced of the necessity of establishing a more efficient police in their city if they value their lives and properties which appear to be far from secure under the present order of things.'*

Surprisingly, however, given the prevailing crime and public order situations, there was still considerable opposition from all quarters to a professional police force. Local newspapers tended to advise against the idea whilst, throughout the land, public feelings ran high against such proposals. The very word 'police', of French origin, was new to England and conjured up images of the dreaded French military body that, on behalf of the government, insidiously encroached into their countrymen's lives (a bit like our government does today, perhaps?)

The English Gate and the City's Old Gaol on the right.

Englishmen enjoyed and jealously protected their freedom, while villains, of course, could see their evil ways being severely curtailed. Some contemporary newspaper reports give an idea of the opposition faced. On 7 January 1826, the Journal observed, *'It cannot have escaped any person's observations that a police establishment is an evil in itself and it is to be submitted to as the less of two evils .... the inconveniences are particularly experienced in small towns like this .... the men employed as constables, by coming into frequent contact with the magistrates, necessarily become a kind of humble friends of theirs and obtain an influence which they are certain to abuse.'* Another paper reported, *'On Monday and Wednesday night, a great many windows were broken in Caldewgate, Fisher Street and Scotch Street. Two gentlemen, victims in Caldewgate, are supposed to have joined the association for the prosecution of offenders. They replied sharply to the stones, some of them large, by a discharge of small shot the effect of which is not known.'* The Patriot reported *'mobs in the city',* one attacking gentlemen and their property for *'rendering themselves obnoxious' by being members of a group formed to ensure the prosecution of offenders'* (those who were - clearly not so secretly - planning to create an organised police for the city). Probably the most disturbing report read, *'On Wednesday afternoon, Mr.McCutcheon of Caldewgate, was violently assaulted, for having joined the association. A party from the Free City (Shaddongate) were themselves engaged in fisticuffs when they recognised him and assailed him with stones and brickbats. As he got up, one of the gang knocked him down with a severe blow to the head, and they all stoned him again. Mr. McCutcheon suffered severe head injuries. Knowing two of the assailants he applied to the magistrates for a warrant for their arrest. He was refused because "the whole of our constabulary force would be insufficient to execute it.'*

There was no end, it seemed, to the suffering of a population who were having, somehow, to exist on low pay with the constant fear of redundancy; some, of course, had already lost their livelihoods, had no income and were dependent upon the charity of friends and neighbours. High living costs, due mainly to the harsh effects of the Corn Laws, caused untold poverty, hardship and general dissatisfaction. *'It is with pain that we are obliged to allude to the truly wretched state of the poorer classes now existing on a frail and precarious subsistence in Carlisle and its vicinity - literally starving,'* reported the Carlisle Journal in February 1826, as the newspaper appealed to the more fortunate to help relieve the suffering. By April, it was reporting *'Misery and distress are making rapid strides amongst the families of the operative manufacturers of our good city. Wretchedness is daily increasing and many poor families are nearly destitute of the necessities of life.'*

What could the dispirited citizens do themselves to counteract this appalling situation? Well, a number of influential lawyers, clergymen and businessmen held a series of meetings to consider this very question. They put together suggestions to be included in a proposed bill to be placed before parliament, but, before they could act, they were overtaken by events. In June 1826, rioting by the city's weavers resulted in a violent confrontation with authority and the loss, in horrific circumstances, of three innocent lives. Caldewgate, and in particular Shaddongate, was in a state of anarchy. The reputation of the city had sunk to its nadir.

Rioting and deaths in Shaddongate

A General Election was held in June 1826. The candidates for Carlisle were Sir James Graham, Sir Philip Musgrave and Mr. James, the latter, after the dreadful events described below, refusing to have anything more to do with electioneering in the city. Sir Philip arrived in Carlisle on Monday, 5 June and immediately began campaigning in the city centre. Next day, at 11am, accompanied by a few friends, he went to canvas a freeman in Shaddongate, an area inhabited mainly by destitute, mostly Irish, hand-loom weavers. In a shop at Milburn's Buildings, he was quickly surrounded by a number of the locals (they, of course, did not have the franchise) and was questioned as to his views on parliamentary reform, the Corn Laws and other controversial issues. The stringent Corn Laws that were causing so much hardship throughout the land and universal suffrage were their chief concerns. The gathering was not impressed with Sir Philip's responses but there were no ill-feelings and Sir, Philip left the premises.

The' dam' or mill-race between Shaddongate (on left of picture) and Brewery Row cottages (now demolished). Caldew Bridge top left.

Shaddongate, March 2009. Picture taken from opposite Queen Street, looking along the mill-race towards the site of Brewery Row and Caldew Bridge.

As he did so he discovered that whilst he had been inside the shop a large crowd, weavers, their wives and children, had gathered in the street outside. They began to stone him and his party so vigorously that, for their very survival, all but a couple of them took shelter in a nearby house where they remained under siege for several hours. Somehow, the others had managed to escape the area into the city where they alerted the Mayor as to Sir Philip's predicament. Sir Philip was severely bruised whilst two of his companions had been struck on the head with *'immense stones'*. A number of parish constables, in attendance with the MP, were thrown into the waters of the dam.

There was considerable tension in the town as 300 special constables were sworn in by the Magistrates. Led by the Mayor, Thomas Blamire, and a County Magistrate, Richard Ferguson, they all proceeded to Shaddongate. But the mob had also greatly increased and had ready a plentiful supply of cobble-stones taken from the river nearby. The Mayor read the Riot Act and ordered the mob to disperse, but, instead, his words had the opposite effect and were the signal for them to advance on and to brutally stone his party. The Caldewgate (parish) constables, Barnes, who suffered serious injury, and Mullender stood firm, but the vast majority of the specials took to their heels. The fleeing 'lawmen' were ambushed by the rioters near Caldew Bridge causing them to disperse in all directions. About a dozen of the remaining specials, as well as the Mayor himself, were compelled to take refuge in houses where they barricaded themselves inside against the efforts of the mob to reach them. Ferguson the magistrate escaped to the city centre.

At 3pm, a detachment of the 55th Regiment of foot, consisting, according to the press, of *'unskilled, inexperienced and indisciplined lads'*, about 120 in number, and a group of artillerymen, all with fixed bayonets, marched into Shaddongate to rescue Sir Philip. Mr. Ferguson and a number of the

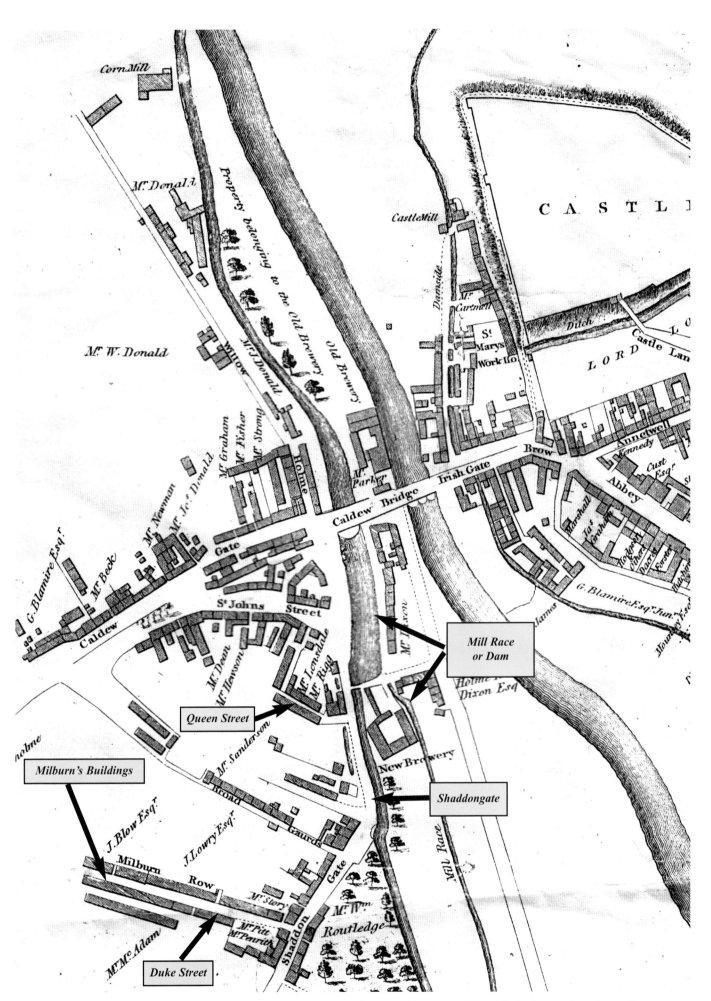

*Map of Shaddongate area [1865] scene of the 1826 rioting showing Milburn's Buildings, parallel with Duke Street, where the troubles started.
Mr. Story's house, where Sir Philip Musgrave was given refuge, is on the corner. The Mill Race or 'Dam' into which a number of constables
were thrown, flows through Shaddon Works and past the New Brewery. Queen Street is where Robert Noble was shot by the military.*

'special' constables accompanied them. As they neared the New Brewery, they were subjected to a ferocious stoning and several of the soldiers received injuries. Women were seen running around, their aprons full of stones, replenishing their menfolk's ammunition. The stoning was unremitting, and the soldiers, who had broken ranks, now formed up in close order with a wall at their backs facing the mob. With fixed bayonets and drawn swords they began a charge towards Queen Street and the roadway was quickly cleared, but the stoning persisted. With their lives considered to be in danger, they were ordered to fire, which they did. One shot pierced the shuttered window of a house used as a schoolroom, and struck a 14 year-old girl, Isabella Pattinson, in the head. A young woman, Mary Birrell, was standing near her front door, key in hand, looking for her brother when she was shot in the head. Robert Noble, a young father, was seeking his children when he was hit in the chest. All three died later the same day. A 15 years old boy named Skinner was shot in the foot. A few others had narrow escapes as shots passed through their clothing. The mob quickly dispersed and Sir Philip was rescued, after three hours 'in captivity' and escorted back into the city. En-route, the soldiers were met by a strong body of Dragoon Guards heading towards Shaddongate, and at that point, it was realised that Mayor Blamire was still confined to the house where he had sought refuge. The Guards proceeded to the premises and rescued the badly bruised official.

Shaddongate today

View from Caldew Bridge. The 'Dam' is on the left.

Shaddongate viewed from Dalston Road.

That was not to be the end of his suffering during the election campaign. On Election Day, Friday, 9 June, three days after the riots, a huge crowd congregated at the Town Hall, the venue of the poll. Sir Philip Musgrave, very wisely, stayed away for fear of inciting more violence. Mayor Blamire was present as Returning Officer. Soldiers were ordered to be on stand-by to prevent further troubles, but they were given instructions not to enter the city centre unless ordered to do so by the magistrates. It seems that a single officer, in his scarlet uniform, did venture into town, perhaps to carry out a recce. News of his presence spread, and the crowd became excited, fearing a full turn-out of troops. There were cries of 'Shaddongate Butchers.' Some of the mobsters gained entry to the Town Hall intending to seize the Mayor and throw him out of the window. They leapt upon his table, screamed insults and spat in his face. They accused him of calling out the military to Shaddongate, an allegation he strenuously denied. Determined efforts to get at him were fought off by the few strong men present to protect him. The Mayor, who had not been in good health, was taken ill. With extreme difficulty he was removed from the Town Hall and carried through the hostile crowd to the Coffee House (Crown and Mitre Hotel) for urgent medical attention. Clearly, he was unable to continue as Returning Officer and the poll had to be abandoned, as a consequence of which a number of citizens were denied their legal right to cast a vote.

Before leaving the Town Hall, the Mayor, *'under duress, seriously ill and his life in imminent danger,'* signed an order the effect of which was to ensure that the military presence was stationed at least four miles from the city. As he was carried off, one man shouted *'The Mayor deserves to be hanged,'* while another cried out, *'Neck him, neck him.'* His doctor said death would have resulted had the Mayor remained in the Town Hall for another ten minutes. As it was, he remained seriously ill for several days.

'We wonder what the rest of the Kingdom think of us' queried the Carlisle Patriot in its 16 June edition. *'We figure in all the journals of the Empire, nay, in the French journals likewise, as the perfect examples of savage turbulence in His Majesty's goodly island of Great Britain. Do we or do we not deserve the character? One of the London papers censures the magistrates for calling out the military. But let no false reasoner attempt to shift the blame from those to whom it belongs to those who do not merit it. The blood of the sufferers is on the heads of the originators of the riot and not on those who quelled it'.*

Shaddongate today

Queen Street viewed from Shaddongate.

Shaddongate and Dixon's Mill viewed from Paddy's Market.

The Joiners Arms, or 'Blue Lugs' as it is known locally, in Bridge Street, Caldewgate, where the inquests into the deaths of the Shaddongate victims were held. (pictured March 2009).

As was to be expected, there was outrage throughout the land at the occurrences in Carlisle. Many questions were asked about the handling of the events in Shaddongate. Why were raw recruits used instead of the experienced cavalry, who would have quelled the rioting speedily and most likely without bloodshed? But would they have been able to do that given the ferocity and determination of this particular mob? Why was live ammunition used and not blanks, which would have been sufficient to send the rioters scattering? There was a suggestion that perhaps the crowd could have been persuaded to disperse *'with the application of a barrel of ale'.* Caldewgate / Shaddongate was well known as a volatile district of the city. Why did the unpopular Sir Philip expose himself to the possibility of attack by entering such an area, where he could hardly have expected the residents to welcome him with open arms. Surely he knew his Government's policies were manifestly unpopular with the poorer classes of society everywhere, not just in Carlisle, a city which at the time was known throughout the land for the depressed state of its inhabitants. It seems he went to canvas a single freeman in this heavily populated area, an area where few of the residents were allowed to cast a vote. The danger signals, surely, were there for him to see, and a person of his intellect and standing ought to have anticipated the mood of the people. As there was no civil power of any consequence to prevent such an incident, and as neither the Magistrates nor the Mayor and Corporation could have guaranteed his safety, he was somewhat foolhardy to venture into the district without first taking adequate steps to protect himself.

At the inquests into the deaths of the two females, held in the Joiner's Arms, a surgeon, present at the scene, told the Coroner how he had witnessed the mob attack the military and special constables with missiles and how the soldiers, responding, rushed into them with bayonets fixed. He saw a soldier fire his musket and he estimated about twenty shots were fired. The child Isabella Pattinson had not been a

19

scholar at the school but, ironically, had been taken inside to escape the troubles in the streets. Evidence was given that a Constable Morley gave the soldiers orders to shoot and that they did so, firing into houses and into the buildings of Irving the Clogger and the school.

A Royal Artillery captain said he was with the Mayor, when, in his capacity as a magistrate, he, the Mayor, read the Riot Act. Assuming that the 300 special constables present would assist, the captain said he had advised the Mayor to rush the mob. The constables however stood idly by.

The officer said he then went to the castle for reinforcements, and that when he returned he was told that the Mayor had been taken prisoner by the rioters and that there were fears for his life. Unlike in London and other places where there had been serious rioting, there was no other magistrate present in Shaddongate to instruct the military. Since the military had no mandate to become involved in a civil matter, there was hesitation and considerable confusion. Eventually another magistrate did arrive. However he ignored the captain's repeated requests for authority to disperse the crowd until the captain himself was struck by a stone, whereupon the magistrate gave orders to fire on the demonstrators. The captain said he cried out *"For God's sake fire high and do no harm"*. He then chased down Queen Street after the man who had stoned him and when he returned Sir Philip had been freed. The Coroner, summing up, said that the soldiers were justified in shooting in consequence of the Riot Act having been read, but, he added, in the jurors' opinion *"the soldiers continued to fire in an indiscreet and inconsiderate manner, and particularly into private homes, when the need to do so seemed to have ceased."*

How could the shooting of the two females, one a child, be warranted? They were unfortunate to find themselves caught up in the riot, but that did not justify their shooting. Further, since no evidence was introduced to show that the deceased Robert Noble was a participant in the unlawful disturbance, his killing could hardly have been justified. The military may well have claimed that his shooting was accidental, and that might have been offered as a defence in a criminal trial, but since the victim was shot twice, *'accident'* seems unlikely. If the person inflicting the fatal shot could have been identified, and there were suggestions that he could have been, then, surely, a charge against that person of murder or manslaughter should, at least, have been considered. The Coroner clearly thought otherwise. There were allegations that a named parish constable instructed the military to open fire. Apparently, those claims were summarily dismissed. I would have thought that a markedly different investigation, and verdict, would follow today in the wake of a similar incident occurring. However, in 2008, the London Coroner's findings were not dissimilar following the police killing of the unfortunate Brazilian man, Jean Charles de Menezes[*], shot when he was mistaken for a terrorist. An inquest into the death of Robert Noble raised an interesting legal argument. It was reported that the deceased had initially been shot in the heel as a consequence of which he could not quit the scene quickly enough before he was shot again receiving mortal injuries. A surgeon intended to depose that, when he had attended to the injured man's wounds, he told Noble that *"he had but a short time to live"* and that he had then questioned him as to his version of the events leading to his injuries and had recorded his answers. Controversially, the Coroner disallowed the introduction of the evidence since it had not been gathered by an authorised person. *'Who were authorised persons?'* one might ask, and from where did they derive their authority? What would have been the odds on an 'authorised' person being present in Shaddongate in this particular case? A *'dying declaration'* is a written or oral statement made by a person, knowing that he was on the point of death, concerning the cause of his injuries. Albeit hearsay evidence, it would normally be admissible in cases of murder and manslaughter provided that, as in this case, the evidence was gleaned at *'first hand.'*

What can be said of the 'policing' of this event? Well nothing in its favour. The few constables escorting the MP into Shaddongate were no match for the crowd and when disorder erupted, which must surely have been anticipated even if not to the extent to which it developed, they were thrown into the dam. Those 300 or so special constables, almost all of whom were citizen ratepayers who had hastily been sworn in, sent to quell the rioting had had no training for such a contingency, an occurrence which, by all accounts, would have tested the ability and professionalism of today's police.

---

[*] He was shot eight times at point-blank range and police admitted a number of mistakes had been made, yet the Coroner declared that he could not return a verdict of 'unlawful killing.' Critics have argued that the inquest was a whitewash.

Few of them were volunteers as today's special constables are. Many were, understandably, fearful for their safety going into the *'lion's den'* that was Shaddongate. Despite their numbers, without the support of armed soldiers, they, too, would have been overwhelmed and *'roughed up'* by the mob. In the event, the magistracy panicked and the soldiers over-reacted.

As far as can be ascertained little or no action was taken to bring any of the rioters to justice. Yet, the inadequacy of the existing civil power and the deaths of innocent persons were still, apparently, insufficient reason to stir the local authorities into remedial action. The magistrates sat on the fence, whilst the Corporation denied any liability on their part to maintain a police. Such intransigence, dereliction of duty, it seems, could be excused on the basis of cost, but such bungling always sends out the wrong signals to mischief-makers and brings the whole system of law and order into disrepute. One might have expected these tragic events to have brought about a marked improvement in public behaviour and to have stirred the Corporation into taking remedial action. Not so. In the absence of any positive measures and of a permanent police force, the wickedness and defiance of authority continued apace.

LAYING DOWN THE LAW

Special Constable. 'NOW MIND, YOU KNOW - IF I KILL YOU , IT'S NOTHING; BUT IF YOU KILL ME, BY JINGO, IT'S MURDER'

[Punch, Vol . XIV, p 172, 1848]

A Punch cartoon in 1848 depicted, and mocked, the deployment of Special Constables in riot situations in London. Apart from the scale of the operations, the situation was very much the same in Shaddongate where the out-numbered, untrained and ill-appointed Specials took flight as soon as violence erupted.

Peel's police

Loughborough University , MCCCJ.

Sir Robert, Peel
Home Secretary 1822-1827, 1828-1830.
Prime Minister 1834-1835, 1841-1846.

Peel was directly involved in the creation of a modern police force in Carlisle in 1827.

"I feel so much interested, on public grounds, in the establishment of an efficient Police in the City of Carlisle".

"If the inhabitants will not, or cannot, agree among themselves, I will do that for them which the King's Peace requires - establish in the city and suburbs an efficient police".

On 24 November, 1999, an engraved portrait of Sir Robert (not the original shown left) that had been handed down through generations of the family, was presented to Cumbria Police by Annie Peel, a descendant, who had decided that it should be displayed at Carlisle Police Station.

Robert Peel became Home Secretary in 1822, setting out with a vision of paid, uniformed, professional police forces patrolling the streets, whose primary aim would be the prevention of crime rather than, as hitherto, chasing offenders after the commission of crimes. *'The primary object of an efficient police force is the prevention of crime,'* he said, *'the next, the detection and punishment of offenders if crime is committed. To this end all the efforts of the police must be directed. The protection of life and property, the preservation of public tranquility and the absence of crime will alone prove whether these efforts have been successful and whether the objects for which the police have been appointed have been successful.'*

His police would be fit, able-bodied disciplined men and their very presence would be a deterrent to criminal activity. They would be selected to represent the widest range of society and were not to be appointed because they had been placed by influential people. For him, London, understandably, was a priority but it was not until 1829 that the capital's Metropolitan Police Force, a body of over 2,000 men, took to the streets. Since the establishment of a police service was not universally welcomed, Peel had to overcome many obstacles along the way. *"It has given me, from first to last, more trouble than anything I ever undertook,"* he said. His definition of what constituted a successful police was augmented by the first Metropolitan Police Commissioners[*] who emphasized the importance of prevention. Policing would be better served by this, they said, than by the detection and punishment of the offender after he has succeeded in committing the crime. Their instruction added that *'this should constantly be kept in mind by every member of the police force as the guide for his own conduct. Officers and constables should endeavour to distinguish themselves by such vigilance and activity as may render it extremely difficult for anyone to commit a crime within that portion of the town within their charge. When in any Division offences are frequently committed, there must be reason to suspect that the police is not in that Division properly conducted. The absence of crime will be considered the best proof of the complete efficiency of the Force.'*

oooOooo

Naturally, as Home Secretary, Peel was taking careful note of the events in Shaddongate in June 1826. Such rebellious behaviour could not be overlooked. It proved to be the catalyst for the creation of an organisation in Carlisle then almost unknown anywhere in mainland Britain - a statutory, full-time, paid, professional police force commensurate with Peel's formula. Within months such a body followed at the behest of local citizens, but with no little prompting from the Home Secretary himself and not before much more criminality.

As the year 1826 drew to a close the city was beset with civil unrest and lawlessness. What a truly awful place it must have been. *'On Tuesday evening, 13 November 1826, Nicholson, the Caldewgate constable, had his thumb bitten off just above the first joint, in a scuffle with a drunken pensioner whom he was in the act of arresting for creating a riot at the house of the parish officer who had refused him an advance on his pension, which he required for drink.'* Villages close to town did not escape. *Postman William Burgess, carrying the mail to Wigton, reached the windmill at Cardewlees when he was attacked by four armed men. They demanded that he hand over the mail. "I'd sooner give you the contents of the barrel" said the postman. Two of the robbers made to attack him on his horse, whereupon he fired his pistol and shot one attacker before leaping over the hedge and galloping off. There was further exchange of fire. It is not known if the postman's shot proved fatal, but at daylight, blood was found at the scene on the snow covered ground.'* *'At Burgh, on Saturday morning, a shot was fired at some depredators. Blood was traced to Kirkandrews. A nightly Watch has now been placed on Burgh, Kirkandrews, Beaumont and Dalston and the watchers have been plentifully provided with firearms'* *'Carlisle remains in the same state of depravity and alarm. There is no diminution in the list of nightly depredations. John Rayson of Aglionby, on his way home, was attacked and robbed by a gang of men near St. Cuthberts Lane. Mr. Blamire of Dalston, was also returning home when he was confronted "by a number of footpads" as he crossed Wigton Road. Mr. Blamire escaped by firing several shots at them.* Christmas arrived - a time of peace and goodwill? Hardly that - *'as soon as the clock struck twelve, a great number of idle and disorderly fellows assembled at the Market Cross, and there, amid a noise that kept the whole neighbourhood in alarm, they kindled a huge bonfire by way of celebrating the dawn of Christmas Day, and in order to feed the fire they committed a great number of*

---

[*] Two police chiefs [Commissioners] were appointed by Peel to lead the Metropolitan Police, 46 year-old retired Lt. Colonel Charles Rowan and lawyer Richard Mayne, 34 years.

depredations, tearing down spouts, window shutters and doors. They broke into timber yards and other enclosed places for combustible matter. At one time, they actually had on the fire a stage-coach, which they had taken from outside the King's Arms Inn, and a carrier's cart. Some among them thought this was taking things too far and that it was dangerous, and so the vehicles were let off with just a scorching. Firebrands were thrown in great profusion, against windows of adjoining houses and some onto the roofs. The residents were too alarmed to go to bed, and sat, guarding their properties until daylight.'

'Never in the memory of man were crimes so abundant in the north of England as they are now in the neighbourhood of Carlisle. The current talk of the day is 'robbery, robbery, robbery,' recorded the Journal. Carlisle's ancient, cost-free watch system and what few peacekeeping initiatives existed in the rural areas were ill-prepared to meet these challenges.

At the end of the year, the newspaper desperately appealed to the townsfolk - *'It is time the people should rouse themselves. It is the duty of the people of Carlisle to teach the magistrates that there is a higher tribunal to appeal to if the town becomes depraved from evident misrule and official neglect. We earnestly implore that the people of Carlisle would ponder well upon the present consequences of their inactivity and consider upon the fearful future unless some decisive measures be adopted to give security for the lives and properties of the residents of the city and neighbouring parishes. We cannot give room in our columns to recount the numerous acts of atrocity which have been committed during the week, but, we demand," Is there a man in Carlisle that dares venture at night a quarter of a mile from the city [centre] without trembling?" We feel assured there is not. In passing we beg to call the readers attention to a remark which issued from the Patriot last week - "He did not get a warrant because the whole of our constabulary force would be insufficient to execute it." Now the robbers carry firearms and the lives of men themselves become in danger. This is a most deplorable fact, yet, without a speedy and effectual intervention, who can insure us against the consequences of a still further increase in crime which becomes more deadly as it advances?'*

As the paper went to press, those city gentlemen who had met, before the Shaddongate killings, to discuss the policing issue, stepped up their deliberations. Their objective was to secure, through the city's MPs, a parliamentary bill in order to attain legal support for a new force. The first open meeting of this association of local citizens was convened in the Coffee House (Crown and Mitre) on Tuesday 2 January, 1827. A specially invited limited number of prominent citizens were summoned by anonymous circular but their numbers were swollen by many more interested parties representing all classes of the population. Mr. Henry Pearson, a solicitor, who seems to have been the instigator of the movement, proposed that the Reverend W. Rees, Curate of St. Mary's, take the chair. The reverend gentleman opened the meeting, outlined its purpose, namely to create a city police, and hoped that everyone present would have opportunity to express his views. Mr. Pearson outlined the sentiments of a number of gentlemen present, as discussed at a previous, privately held meeting. He informed the congregation that Home Secretary Robert Peel and the city's two MPs had held discussions about the problems, and it was clear to Mr. Pearson and his party that it was Peel's intention to introduce legislation to bring into being a police force for the city and its suburbs irrespective of the views of the Corporation or citizens. It was clear that the Committee would have to press ahead without the Corporation and it suggested to the meeting that if the ancient organisation of one high constable, filled by an efficient person, with six active halbertmen were to be re-established, and if, at the same time, they were to be joined by a number of suitable night-watchmen, they would constitute a sufficient police for the city and suburbs. The Committee felt it needed to establish that *'by reason of the increase in trade, manufacturing and population of the city, together with the discontinuance of the ancient Corporation Police, disturbances and crime had greatly increased, so alarming the citizens that in the absence of any lead from the Corporation',* the Committee had themselves been forced to confront the issues and seek solutions. Despite the Corporation having ample revenues to meet the entire costs of a police, raised mainly from the tolls on goods carried into and out of the city, and, since the suburbs were almost as large as, and even more in need of a police force than the city itself, the Committee was mindful that a force for the city and suburbs should not be financed from city revenues alone, but that an equal measure of the expense should be borne by the inhabitants. The meeting formally elected a Committee (details at Appendix 'A') to act on behalf of the citizens in negotiations to bring about the proposed police force. Those selected were warned to give the matter their undivided attention since there were very powerful interests in the city opposed to them, including the magistrates and the Corporation. However, it was earnestly hoped that consensus with the Corporation could still be reached, for, as the Patriot recorded, *'Mr. Peel has intimated, in express terms, that if the inhabitants will not, or cannot agree among themselves, he will do that for them which the King's Peace requires - establish in the city and suburbs an efficient police.'* Mr. Dobinson said the inhabitants should not relax their vigilance but he believed that the interests of the town were safe in the hands of the committee. *'The most perfect order and decorum were observed throughout'* declared the Carlisle Journal. *'There were no irritating expressions - all seemed actuated by a sincere desire to settle the question by negotiation'.*

Meanwhile, the New Year saw the city's reputation take a bashing in the national press. The Morning Chronicle reported that *'Carlisle, with a population of between eighteen and twenty thousand inhabitants, has become a den of thieves and her streets the resort of ruffians and highwaymen.'* The Carlisle Patriot firmly placed the blame upon the Corporation and the magistrates. One journalist said Carlisle was *'a second Ireland.'* The Carlisle Journal disagreed but pointed out that amongst those who had brought such a bad reputation upon the city, there were, indeed, many Irishmen. The Patriot recorded that many people in the land, influenced by exaggerated newspaper reports, saw the citizens of Carlisle as *'little better than the inhabitants of the desert, or as worthy companions for the night-roving patriots of the south-west of Ireland.'* The Carlisle Journal denied that it had labelled the Irish weavers of Carlisle, as a whole, a *'depraved and abandoned gang of lawless villains.'* Just the same, it was taken to task by the Dublin Evening Post, reputedly one of the most liberal newspapers in the British Empire. The editor, evidently upset at such a slur on his fellow countrymen, wrote: *"The remotest towns in Ireland, the most miserable and secluded villages, do not contain an organised band of burglars and robbers. But that Carlisle, the shire town of Cumberland, in former days the bulwark against the Scottish robbers, the city more celebrated, perhaps, than any in England, that 'merrie Carlisle' should, in the 19th Century, with its mayor and burgesses, its police and its military, its garrison, and, above all, its bible schools, that Carlisle, in which the light of the pure reformed faith hath shone with such surpassing brightness for nearly three centuries, which has joined, like its neighbours, in the march of intellect, should contain gangs of several hundred robbers who continue to sleep all day and sally out to commit robberies at night, is a thing we would not believe except on the authority of a journal published on the spot. Live they in a Christian land? Is this England? Is this Cumberland, from which we import land stewards and the system that improved agriculture, and itinerant parsons?"*

Sir James Graham, Bt., wrote to Mr. Home Secretary Robert Peel in March, 1827 explaining the Corporation's reluctance to support or finance the police force. He invited his opinion as to whether the Corporation was legally liable to contribute, and if so, in what proportion. The Home Secretary replied that he would not be a party to any legal proceedings to test liability or to enforce the Corporation's support, but he left it open to the parties involved to make application to the Attorney General with such proceedings in mind. He added that it would be a much better course, to save both expense and delay, and that it would be in the best interests of the City of Carlisle, if an amicable understanding could be reached between the citizens and the Corporation. He advised that the parties mutually consent to an arrangement in virtue of which an efficient police force should be constituted in the city.

At the beginning of April 1827, by which time a second Temporary Police was in place, Sir James addressed Parliament at length on the killing of the three innocent citizens in Shaddongate, and seizing the opportunity, he pressed for the *'placing of a police on a more efficient footing.'* Referring to the Bill (Carlisle Police Bill) now before Parliament, he said, *"To this Bill the Corporation of Carlisle, the very parties who had resorted to military force on the occasion complained of, were now raising every opposition in their power to impede its progress."* He called on the honourable gentleman, the Secretary of State for the Home Department, Robert Peel, *"to give his support in carrying that measure."* In his response, Peel commented, *"It was consequent on Carlisle being a garrison town that it had been so long without an efficient police."* A strange response considering that there were few, if any, organised and efficient police anywhere in the country at that time. Peel not only supported the idea of a properly organised force for the city, as a matter of some urgency, he made clear that he would enforce its formation. In a letter dated 18 January, 1827, to Sir James, he wrote, *'I feel so much interested, on public grounds, in the establishment of an efficient Police in the City of Carlisle, that I shall have no objection to take the opinion of the Law Officers of the Crown as to the legal effect of the Charter in obliging the Corporation of Carlisle to maintain or contribute to the maintenance of the Police'.*

Had it not been for the intervention of the local citizens' committee, Carlisle City police force might well have been Peel's first English constabulary. In 1959, his definition, 130 years earlier, of what constituted an efficient police formed the basis of one of the first lectures to my recruit training class at the District Police Training Centre at Warrington. We were required to commit his words to memory and often asked to repeat them during the course. There was no room for doubt as to what the service expected of us. Peel's principles had stood the test of time.

oooOooo

A new police for the city

In January 1827, after several meetings and discussions with the local authority, the citizens committee themselves set on a temporary police at an estimated first year cost of some £700, paid for by voluntary subscriptions. By June it had secured the passage of a Bill through Parliament - the Bill for which Sir

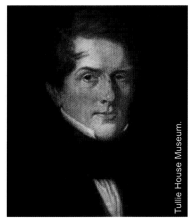

Tullie House Museum.

George Gill Mounsey, Chairman of the city's first Watch Committee.

James Graham had canvassed Peel's support. On 13 July, under the provisions of a Police Act, fifty Commissioners of Police took office, from whom a Watch Committee chaired by Mr. George Gill Mounsey was elected. Twenty-two officers, including a chief, were sworn-in as constables. The Act enabled the Commissioners to levy a Police Rate to finance the new permanent establishment.

Peel (not yet Sir Robert) was already credited with setting up the 'Irish Constabulary' in Dublin (Britain's first professional police force) and had made determined, but, as yet, unsuccessful, attempts to create a London Metropolitan Police. In an endorsement of the Fielding brothers' * work, he was encouraging towns and cities to adopt preventive policing with officers visible, in uniform, on the streets, as a deterrent to the many criminals then operating. He was not, however, making much headway and there were no

organised mainland forces of the type he envisaged. It being the case that Peel himself had targeted Carlisle in particular for such a force, the easiest solution for the local population would have been to stand by and wait for him to take the lead. However, the problem was that if he had imposed his will on the city and its suburbs, it was likely that the numbers of police and their costs would not have been negotiable and may have been beyond the means of the local authority and especially, of the citizens, who already had to meet punitive taxes from their meagre incomes. It is fair to comment that there was no financial help available, as there is today, from central government for the purposes of supporting a police force. *"Mr. Peel will step in,"* said the Patriot, *"and we cannot expect him to be scrupulous as to the cost, present or future. His object and duty are to preserve the King's Peace, and experience teaches us that he is not easily set aside."* It was known to the Committee that the Mayor had acknowledged the necessity of an efficient police and that the Corporation had corresponded with Peel accepting some responsibility for forming, but denying any liability for the expense of maintaining, such a body. The Committee, on the other hand, held the firm opinion that under the provisions of the city's Charters the Corporation was under an obligation to maintain the King's Peace and that they had abdicated their responsibilities to such an extent that the unruliness in the city had become intolerable. Something needed to be done, and done quickly. The Committee resolved to put the utmost pressure on the Corporation to create, maintain and finance an efficient city police force. Accordingly, the Committee addressed a letter to the Mayor, its purport being to seek consensus and render unnecessary the need to legally, and thereby expensively, test the Corporation's liability. The reply they received stated that, *"the Corporation is equally impressed (as the Committee) with the necessity of immediate measures for preserving the peace of the city and will contribute towards the expense."* But since the Committee's claim, that in its opinion the Corporation was bound by ancient Charter to maintain a police, was not conceded, the Corporation refused to pledge any specific proportion of the expense, in the following words,

---

* Sir John Fielding, the blind Bow Street magistrate, and Henry Fielding, each credited with forming the famous 'Bow Street Runners' and introducing the 'Weekly Pursuit', forerunner of today's 'Police Gazette'.

'The Corporation, at the same time, wish it to be distinctly understood, that they do not admit to any liability on their part to maintain a police within the city, and that any contribution they may deem proper to make will be made gratuitously, and not in discharge of any obligation imposed upon the Corporation.'

On 25 January 1827, in a written communication, the Committee formally asked a second time if the Corporation was prepared to contribute one half of the total costs of the proposed police establishment. The request received short shrift, the response being to give public notice of a Bill that the Corporation itself was promoting, *'that in consequence of an increase in trade and population in Carlisle, it is necessary to have a well regulated police, and that the Mayor and Corporation are, in virtue of their various charters, liable to maintain an efficient police within the city.'*

On the face of it a U-turn, with full acknowledgement of its responsibility for providing and financing a constabulary force, the Corporation now appeared to be accepting, even hi-jacking, the Committee's proposals. In fact, citizens saw this simply as a ploy to obstruct the passage of the independent Bill and to delay the Corporation's enforced involvement and pecuniary liability in the project. Further, the Corporation having been seriously challenged by the determination of the Committee to establish a police with or without its blessing, it was judged to be an attempt by the Corporation to deprive the public at large from serving as police commissioners. The Carlisle Journal, no doubt in a show of political partisanship, railed against the local authority, and in particular against the Mayor's lavish lifestyle at the ratepayers' expense, commenting, *'The time is fast approaching when the Corporation will be totally isolated in this city,"* it said. *"We believe that matters are now in train for having it decided what are the purposes to which the Corporation revenues are legally applied; if they are not applicable to the maintenance of a police, to what are they applicable? Is it pretended that the Corporation may, at its discretion, apply the funds to any purpose they choose? The Charter gives them no such power. We would have him [the Mayor] maintain an efficient, well-regulated civil power to enable him to exert his authority for the good government and peace of the city. Without this, we contend that his power and authorities are a dead letter. They were, in fact, a dead letter at the election. He was no longer Mayor of Carlisle, but in name. He was driven out of his own Hall and the dignity of his office utterly prostrated and trampled on by a mob.'*

The first year's running costs of the proposed police establishment was estimated to be £700, a negligible sum when compared to the £9,000 which Carlisle Corporation was alleged, in one local newspaper, to have spent on three pictures in May 1826, just one month before the Shaddongate riots. What, one might ask, were the council's priorities?

Faced with the Corporation's intransigence, the Committee proceeded alone. They despatched a *'memorial'* to Home Secretary Peel, signed by a large number of citizens. Mr. Mounsey, solicitor, was engaged to solicit the Bill through Parliament, its principle objective being to obtain statutory authority for a permanent, professional police for the city. They appointed a temporary police* and instituted a public subscription raising the sum of two hundred pounds, sufficient to support the force for about three months. The Mayor was reported to have contributed one guinea (£1.05) towards it from his own pocket and, eventually, the Corporation grudgingly contributed £21, but only after the intervention of Peel. Premises, owned by a local businessman named Barwise, were leased for use as an office at a quarterly rental of £13.10s.0d (£13.50). Situated in New Bank Lane, (sometimes known as Theatre Lane), an alley that ran between English Street and Blackfriars Street. The building location was in an area presently covered by the House of Fraser store. The street sign, *'New Bank Lane',* is still visible at the rear entrance to the store in Blackfriars Street. Additionally, the Committee successfully applied to the Corporation for the use of the old Guardhouse in the marketplace as a lock-up for offenders taken into custody and as a place of rendezvous for the patrolling watchmen. The Corporation granted the use of a room in the Town Hall for the meetings of the Committee. Pigot's Directory of the city in 1829 recorded that the police office was in English Street, meaning the force was housed in New Bank Lane, until a purpose built police station was opened in West Walls in 1841. A temporary police force was up and running but the Committee's battles with the Corporation and the magistrates were far from over. The County Magistrates, led by the Rev. Mr. Fletcher (the city's only magistrate, by reason of his office, was the Mayor) wrote to the Home Secretary,

---

* For names of the first city police officers see Appendix 'A'.

Clockwise from top left, the New Bank Lane street sign on the House of Fraser Store in Blackfriars Street, Carlisle Cross and the Old Guardhouse that stood in English Street and New Bank Lane, between the Gray Goat Hotel and Wright's premises in English Street.

attempting to excuse their own deficiencies. They had, they said, engaged eight police officers in the city in 1821, but the fees for their upkeep fell very far short of their cost and when the funds were exhausted in 1823 they had been obliged to discharge the officers. In fairness to them, they had no means, officially, of raising the expenses of a police force, and were dependent upon voluntary subscriptions for the purpose. The Corporation had allowed the magistrates to meet in the Town Hall for policing purposes, but *'the numbers of magistrates declined due to death and other causes'* and, they claimed, in any event *'the police did not have the support of the inhabitants'* * They complained that they had not been consulted about the proposed independent Bill, and that an officer from Manchester had been engaged and a nightly Watch established, *'the numbers and names of whom had never been communicated to the magistrates, nor even to the mayor.'* They, rightly, accepted some liability for ineffectiveness, and they offered to withdraw from the city altogether, saying they, *'would prefer to close our office rather than allow a feeling of opposition to be kept up and subject ourselves to the insults we have repeatedly experienced.'* It was, of course, out of the question that the Magistrates should relinquish office and desert the city, and Peel urged them to immediately discuss the situation with the local Members of Parliament.

The Corporation, meanwhile, succumbed to the wishes of the Home Secretary to support the creation of a police, though not without some reluctance. The Town Clerk, Mr. Nanson, begrudgingly enclosing a cheque for twenty guineas (£21), wrote to the (independent) Police Committee on 20 March 1827:

---

* There was, of course, some truth in this statement applied nationwide, but little evidence, apart from the Corporation's stance, locally.

'Sir,

The requisition of yourself and other gentlemen relative to a temporary police has been this day submitted by the Mayor to the Corporation in council and I am directed to inform you that, in their opinion, the proceedings of the police committee ought, in the first instance, to have been communicated to the Mayor and other Magistrates who assemble at the public office, and the Magistrates ought also to have been consulted by the committee upon any arrangements deemed necessary for the preservation of the peace. The Corporation have, however, notwithstanding their disapproval of the manner in which the proceedings of the committee have been conducted, directed their Chamberlain to pay the sum of twenty guineas as a contribution from the Corporation towards the maintenance of a temporary police.'

The Chairman of the Police Committee, Rev. W. Rees, accepting the donation, but clearly irritated by the tone of this letter, responded on 22 March;

Sir,

I had the honour of submitting your letter of the 20th to the Police Committee this morning, by whom I am directed to acknowledge the contribution ordered by the Corporation. I am further directed to explain through you to the Corporation a misapprehension which, from the tenor of your letter, they appear to labour under. So far from its being the case that the magistrates at the public office were not previously consulted, the fact is that the first step taken was an application by several respectable individuals who waited on them with a request that they would adopt immediate and efficient measures to preserve the public peace and repress the riotous proceedings which had then reached such an alarming height that neither the lives nor property of the peaceable were considered safe. It was not till they found this request neglected, and had lost all hope of seeing the lead in a measure of such general importance taken by those in whom the authority, and in their view of the case the duty of attending to the public welfare, was vested, that the committee, assembled in the first instance for another purpose, found themselves imperiously called upon by the urgency of the case and the general voice of the town to attempt establishing a police body, as it now stands, being thus forced into undertaking a most serious responsibility, or suffering the town to remain in a general state of terror and danger from the depredations which were hourly committed. Influenced by the knowledge that the above mentioned application to the magistrates at the public office had not received the attention which they considered it merited, they naturally looked out for others from whom they might hope to obtain more active and efficient aid. Finding these suspicions well grounded, they, unanimously, as well as the other inhabitants of the town, lent the measures proposed that full support and assistance which was necessary to overcome the evil, and which they would have felt equal pleasure in affording the magistrates at the public office if called upon for the same purpose. The Committee, fully sensible of the responsibility of their situation, can only congratulate themselves that the police establishment has, in so short a period, answered the desired end even beyond their most sanguine expectations, in restoring peace and good order in the city and suburbs, and that they have so discharged the trust confided in them as to have obtained the approbation and confidence of the inhabitants generally.

A permanent police force

On 14 June 1827, an Act for Watching, Regulating and Improving the City of Carlisle and its suburbs, became law [7/8 George IV, LXXXVI]. Commonly referred to, locally, as the 'Police Act' or the 'Carlisle Police Act', Sections 4 and 5 provided for the appointment, by election, of fifty Commissioners of Police, to hold office for three years, alongside the Mayor, Recorder, Alderman, Dean and Prebendaries. There is no evidence that any person other than the commissioners actually did become involved in the running of the police, in fact, quite the contrary. Section 8 laid down that all had to swear an oath that he would truly and impartially execute and perform all and every the powers reposed in him under the Act. Section 9 ordered that the Commissioners, at least nine in number, were to meet on the last Thursday in June 1827, to put the Act into execution. Section 21 empowered the Commissioners:

'to appoint such a number of able-bodied men to be employed as watchmen or patrols, either on foot or on horseback, or as beadles to act as well as for the day as for the night, as the Commissioners shall judge necessary, and, from time to time, to make orders and regulations for the conduct of these officers, and grant rewards or allowances to them, or to any persons assisting them, who may be disabled or hurt in the execution of their duty.

Ballot box for the parish of Caldewgate.

Every watchman, patrol or beadle found guilty of neglect is liable to forfeit a sum not exceeding forty shillings.'

More details of the Carlisle Police Act can be found at Appendix 'B.'

On Thursday, 28 June 1827, balloting took place in the vestry rooms of the various parishes of the city for the election of the fifty Commissioners. Apathy was the order of the day, as only about one third of those competent to vote did so. Next day, the chairmen, inspectors and clerks of the parishes attended the Town Hall with their ballot boxes before the Mayor and assessors. Details of those elected are shown at Appendix 'C.' The Carlisle Journal commented, *'It shows the popularity of our city corporation when its agent, Nanson, only obtained two votes.'*

The first meeting of Commissioners, over forty of them, took place on Friday the 13th (what a day to start any sort of business, let alone a police force) July 1827, with Dr. Heysham in the chair. James Willoughby was appointed Clerk at an annual salary of £26. John Forster, Jnr., accepted the position of Treasurer without salary. The appointments of a Superintendent at a weekly salary of £1.10s.0d (£1.50) and 21 officers (Appendix D') at an average pay of twelve shillings (60p) were confirmed. All were sworn before John Heysham, JP, to act as constables for the City of Carlisle and suburbs thereof. The men worked long hours and had no rest days or annual leave entitlements. A Watch Committee of twelve Commissioners was appointed (Appendix 'C') to see that the orders of the full Commission were carried into effect and to attend to the general management of the police. The general feeling at the meeting was summed up in the following words. *'We are quite sure that we shall for the future have a well regulated and efficient civil power in the city and suburbs without experiencing any very heavy addition to our present taxation.'*

The Police Act authorised the Commissioners to set a rate to cover the costs of general police services. Any special duties performed by the men, that is to say any carried out for persons or organisations other than the Commissioners, were charged and the proceeds shared between the men in such a manner that the Superintendent always received double that of the other officers (I should think so, too!). A proportion of all fines imposed by the Magistrates against informations (summonses) laid by the watchmen and beadles was recoverable by the Commissioners. Outgoings included salaries at an average of £13 per week (in total) and rent for the police office at £13.10s.0d per quarter. The Watch Committee contracted Mr. Halstead (an Alderman) to supply eighteen uniform coats, numbered, at a cost of £1.5s.0d each (£1.25p), a Mr. Jefferson was asked to supply 20 rattles at 1/6d (7fi p) each but by far the largest expense, and the one that presented the greatest difficulty, was the legal cost of soliciting the Police Bill through Parliament. City solicitor Mr. Mounsey's fee for his services was £400. Having examined and approved the charges, the Commissioners set about looking at ways of raising the monies. Two of their own body came to the rescue, solicitors Silas Saul and John Blow, each lending the authority £200 repayable at 4fi% p.a. Set against the expense of creating an organised force, the Corporation's contribution of twenty guineas was miserly in the extreme.

Rattles were the only means the constables had of raising an alarm or summoning assistance.

In its 140 year history, the Force was commanded by thirteen Chief Officers. What follows is an account of some of the events that took place during each chief's tenure, and a look at life in the Carlisle City Police Force, from the days of the undisciplined watchmen to the professional force that existed at the date of its demise - the politics, tragedies, comedy and all of the other multifarious incidents that make up the rich tapestry of life that is the police service.

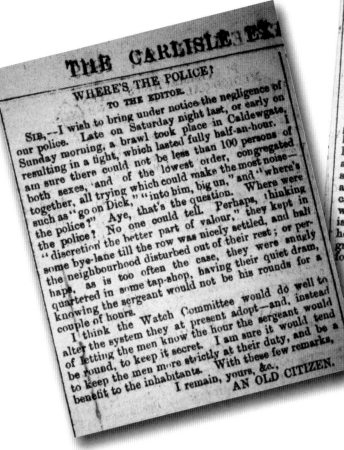

THE CARLISLE EX[...]

WHERE'S THE POLICE?

TO THE EDITOR.

SIR,—I wish to bring under notice the negligence of our police. Late on Saturday night last, or early on Sunday morning, a brawl took place in Caldewgate, resulting in a fight, which lasted fully half-an-hour. I am sure there could not be less than 100 persons of both sexes, and of the lowest order, congregated together, all trying which could make the most noise—such as "go on Dick," "into him, big un," and "where's the police?" Aye, that's the question. Where were the police? No one could tell. Perhaps, thinking "discretion the better part of valour," they kept in some bye-lane till the row was nicely settled, and half the neighbourhood disturbed out of their rest; or perhaps, as is too often the case, they were snugly quartered in some tap-shop, having their quiet dram, knowing the sergeant would not be his rounds for a couple of hours.

I think the Watch Committee would do well to alter the system they at present adopt—and, instead of letting the men know the hour the sergeant would be round, to keep it secret. I am sure it would tend to keep the men more strictly at their duty, and be a benefit to the inhabitants. With these few remarks, I remain, yours, &c.,

AN OLD CITIZEN.

WHERE'S THE POLICE?

TO THE EDITOR.

"Lo! they come! they come!
Here we are! here we are!"

SIR,—An Old Citizen, who is a ready writer of sarcasms and falsehoods, has made a very spiteful and malicious attack on the police, in his letter which appeared in the *Examiner* of Tuesday last. Our learned friend flatters himself that he is possessed of rare abilities when he assumes to dictate to the Watch Committee—he displays a good deal of self-conceit and witticism in laying down his golden rule for the good government of the force; but why does he not sign his own name like an honest man, and not use aliases like rogues and vagabonds? He makes a sweeping assertion, that the officers skulk in public houses instead of attending to their duty. If he had been as honest as he is malicious, he would have mentioned individual cases, and not have condemned the whole force for what he cannot know of his own knowledge, unless he is in the habit of frequenting such places at untimely hours; and even then his charge would be utterly groundless, as applied indiscriminately to the police force.—Yours respectfully,

A CITY POLICE OFFICER.

Carlisle, Sept. 28, 1859.

From the Carlisle Examiner, September 1859. 'Old Citizens' were in the habit of carping about the police in those days, too.

Part Two

The Chief Constables

1	Benjamin BATTY (*)	03.02.1827	to	09.03.1831
2	Robert BROWN (*)	10.03.1831	to	16.10.1839
3	John GRAHAM (*)	17.10.1839	to	26.09.1844
4	John SABBAGE (*)	27.09.1844	to	21.01.1857
5	George Edward BENT (**)	22.01.1857	to	17.07.1873
6	Walter HEMINGWAY	01.08.1873	to	03.08.1876
7	George MacKAY	19.08.1876	to	11.08.1904
8	George HILL (***)	12.08.1904	to	07.01.1913
9	Eric Herbert deSCHMID (****)	02.05.1913	to	30.11.1928
10	Archibald Kennedy WILSON	01.12.1928	to	30.11.1929
11	Andrew Alexander JOHNSTON	01.12.1929	to	31.08.1938
12	William Henry LAKEMAN	01.09.1938	to	15.11.1961
13	Frank Edgar WILLIAMSON	16.11.1961	to	31.03.1967

(*)   Appointed Chief Officer in the rank of Superintendent.
(**)   Ditto, but title changed to Chief Constable, October 1857.
(***)   Supt. ECKFORD was Acting Chief Constable Jan to May 1913.
(****)   Changed surname to SPENCE.

George MacKay served for the longest period, 28 years, whilst Archibald Kennedy Wilson stayed for just twelve months.

Benjamin Batty, the first chief, was dismissed.

George Edward Bent, who died at the age of 49 years, just seventeen days after resigning due to ill-health, was fortunate to survive a call for his resignation.

George Hill left through ill-health but under a cloud. He 'reappeared' as a Chief Constable in Canada.

Andrew Alexander Johnston retired through sickness in the midst of spurious allegations and rumour.

Walter Hemingway was successfully sued for slander. His actions on another occasion resulted in the resignations of all but two of the Watch Committee.

Two had previously been chief constables, George Hill at Kilmarnock and Eric Herbert deSchmid, who changed his surname to Spence after the First World War, at Exeter City. The first and the last chiefs came from Manchester, while four had previous service in London's Metropolitan Police. Two, what would be unusual appointments nowadays, came from Scottish forces. Four moved on to command larger forces;

John Sabbage to Newcastle City, Walter Hemingway to Cardiff City, Archibald Kennedy Wilson to Plymouth City and later to Liverpool City, and Frank Edgar Williamson to Cumberland, Westmorland and Carlisle, later Cumbria. Mr. Williamson was appointed H.M. Inspector of Constabulary for Crime, the first, and only, such appointment in the United Kingdom.

Superintendent Peter Eckford served as Acting Chief Constable for five months after the departure of George Hill, and Chief Inspector J. Walker similarly acted for three months following Andrew Alexander Johnston's untimely retirement.

None of the thirteen chief officers joined and climbed through each of the ranks of the city force, though two, John Graham and Andrew Alexander Johnston, who had begun their careers elsewhere, were appointed to the top post from within.

Only three retired naturally (from the city police) on completion of their service.

An at-a-glance summary of the chief constables' careers can be found at Appendix 'F'.

Benjamin Batty, Superintendent (Chief Officer)
3 February 1827 to 9 March 1831.

'An Act of Parliament police cannot now be avoided' claimed the Journal as, on Wednesday, 31 January, 1827, the (Police) Committee set on duty, in all parts of the City of Carlisle and its suburbs, a force comprising twenty-one 'stout' men, sworn-in as constables. Mr. Benjamin Batty was appointed in the rank of Superintendent to lead the force. He took up his duties on Saturday, 3 February 1827. The arrangements were temporary pending the grant of statutory authority.

"Welcome, Mr. Batty, to Caudagate!" And, for his first visit to the so-called *'Free City,'* as Caldewgate had become known, what a very special, hair-raising, reception he had. On Tuesday, 6 February, he and George Palmer, a constable, set off to survey the area. When they reached Millburn's Buildings in Shaddongate, they were stoned by several boys. Mr. Batty, who had already been nicknamed the *'Manchester Trotter'* by the people of Shaddongate, turned to them, and seeing them ready to throw more missiles, asked them to desist, *"for"*, he said, *"we have only come to look at the place, nothing more."* A mob gathered and the two policemen were further stoned, Palmer receiving considerable injuries from several severe blows to his head and body. A grocer, Mr. Storey, took them into his home where they barricaded themselves inside. The mob had quickly swollen into the hundreds. News of the attack and siege spread. For a couple of hours the town came to a standstill as thousands of spectators gathered in West Walls and Annetwell Street, Irishgate Brow and on Caldew Bridge. Eight constables set off to rescue their colleagues but they, too, were met by volleys of stones thrown by hundreds of Shaddongate's residents. For them to have attempted to proceed further would have been madness, almost suicidal. They returned to the police office and reported the impossibility of their being of any help to the two *'captive'* officers. They had been simply overwhelmed by numbers. Events of the previous June in Shaddongate must have exercised the minds of both those in authority and rioter alike. The military were called out from the castle. A party of the 5th Dragoon Guards, swords drawn, followed by a detachment of the 90th Foot Regiment, weapons in readiness, and a group of artillerymen, the whole under the command of Colonel Birrell of the 90th, proceeded, as both the Carlisle Journal and Carlisle Patriot reported *'in fearful array into Shaddongate, and the moment the crowd found this determined course, they fled.'* Mr. Batty and Palmer were rescued from their predicament. In defiance of authority, the mob hoisted a makeshift flag over Millburn's Buildings to commemorate what they considered to be their *'victory over the police.'* They held a meeting and resolved to stand by one another to resist all attacks upon them, *'attacks'* meaning any attempt to enforce the law or interference in their community by law-enforcement officers. They determined to allow no *'watchmen' within the limits of the 'Free City'* and to oppose the Corporation's plans to install gas lighting in the area. If he had not previously realised the enormity of his task of bringing order to the city, after this incident the new chief could have been in little doubt. A military presence of nine privates, a sergeant, a corporal and a bugleman took up position in Caldewgate nightly to maintain the peace. Warrants for the arrest of the ringleaders were not executed because of the *'insufficiency of the civil force.'*

The Journal which had campaigned for an efficient, able police force, harangued the Magistrates, the Mayor and Corporation for their lack of support, and suggested that they, the newspaper, had predicted what would happen in consequence of official indifference to the lawlessness of the city. The paper concluded that the new Watch Committee *'had taken upon themselves the most fearful responsibility of controlling a police,'* whilst the Corporation had become a 'complete nonentity.' On Friday and Saturday, 9 and 10 February, some two hundred householders were sworn in as special constables to raid Shaddongate and capture the ringleaders concerned in the disturbance. Military support was arranged to surround the area to prevent escapes, the troops all armed with thirty to forty rounds of ball cartridge. A bugleman accompanied them, his task, if required, to signal and call to the scene the remainder of the infantrymen under arms in the castle. At least a dozen rioters were arrested. Meanwhile, it had been reported in Penrith that Mr. Batty had been hanged from a lamp post by the mob. By the time of their next edition the Journal reported, *'When our paper last went to press the whole town was in one grand state of confusion. Robbers, rebels, police, special constables, military, prisoners were the order of the day. Now, never was a town more quiet - we have not heard so much as a common insult being offered during the week. This wonderful transition from a state of absolute anarchy to the utmost tranquility has been effected by the town rising to take into their own hands what ought to have been the duty of the Corporation.'*

The follow-up enquiries to the riot were a shambles. The evidence gathered in support of the charges was of poor quality and most, if not all, of those arrested escaped conviction. However, all of the prisoners, whether or not found guilty, were cautioned as to their future conduct. *"Everyone in the neighbourhood of the riots is to be narrowly watched, and they will rue the consequences if found in any mischief"* warned the Magistrate. One beneficial consequence of the raids was the flight from the city of a good number of the troublemakers. One local paper reported, *'A regular watch is now established in the place, so lately the emporium of determined rebels and robbers. We understand nearly a hundred fellows have absconded'.* There were some amusing accounts of the court proceedings (see examples above). Another paper denied a story circulating in the town that it had condemned *'the weavers of Caldewgate in the whole as a depraved and abandoned gang of lawless villains.'*

The local press, reporting that Mr. Batty came highly recommended by a Mr. Lavender, stated that he was an experienced policeman who had gained *'superior tact in the manoeuvrings of police government,'* adding that he would be *'one who would quickly get to grips with the criminal element in the city without adopting an over-zealous, overbearing attitude towards the citizens generally.'* That was a rather over-optimistic prediction, as his first experience of Caldewgate palpably illustrated - quite the reverse happened as the local baddies provided him with a demonstration of their infamy. Surprisingly, given the significance of the role he was to undertake, apart from those few words in the Journal, there is, locally, no antecedent history of Mr. Batty and no record as to how he was selected or if others were in the frame for the job. I am grateful to Mr. Duncan Broady, Curator of Greater Manchester Police Museum for filling a few of the gaps. It appears that the Manor of Manchester appointed two Constables annually. As in other townships, their's was

Carlisle Journal of 17 February 1827 reporting on the prosecution of two rioters.

IT'S A FALSITY!

Thomas Matthews, charged by Watchman William Corrigan [of whom pretty stories were told] with having threatened to shoot him. "God Bless me," said the prisoner, "I never did such a thing in my life," and as further proof he added an oath or two. This would not do, for Mary Hastings, the wife of a weaver from Shaddongate, swore to his having said, "Corrigan ought to have his brains blown out." "Oh shame, said our immaculate hero, "its a falsity. I do declare it is. I never used violence in my life, not to no-one. "Oh, it's a falsity." He was found 'not guilty'.

A POUND FROM THE POOR BOX

Bernard Rowan was next. An Irishman, all tattered and torn, never was a man more innocent, that is according to his own account. He was one of the gentry taken up at Raffles by Mr Armstrong.. "Och, " he said, "please your Honour. I never threw a stone in my life. I've been here, Sir, a twelvemonth last September and I'm not married and earned seven shillings a week, worked eighteen hours a day and two shillings out of that to me landlord and tuppence in the shilling for the winder, and I've always been innocent of everthing of this kind, Sir. Please your Honour, och Sir, I'm as innocent as the babe unborn." Asked what made him fly Shaddongate, he said, "The people told us the innocent as well as the guilty were to be taken, and that was the reason. I've always conducted myself with such rectitude. I know I look like a pickpocket, but I can't help that." Asked who put up the flag of defiance, he declared it was because there were no watchmen and he had never been to a town of any consequence without them. There being no evidence sufficient to convict, the prisoner was told he was free to go. "Well then, as I'm discharged maybe you'll spare a little charity for me?" he asked. He was told to walk, with a severe reprimand for his insolence.

an important but unpaid civic role. Each October, the Constables, acting under the auspices of the Manorial Court Leet, appointed a paid Deputy Constable and four paid beadles whose task it was to maintain law and order in the community (just five officers for Manchester!). One such Deputy, appointed in 1821, was the above Stephen Lavender, one of the original Bow Street Runners in London in which capacity he had gained considerable 'policing' experience. Benjamin Batty (or Battye as records sometimes showed) was one of his beadles, first appointed also in 1821 and having been retained annually until his move to Carlisle. The Court Leet Records in Manchester show that the Lord of the Manor had absolute authority over the town's markets and that most offences coming before the court fell under the general headings of using defective weights and measures, unlawful sales of meat, chimney fires, failing to fence land and/or cellar steps, failing to keep walls and bridges in good repair and offences relating to the cleanliness of streets, privies and pigsties, the very sort of nuisances Mr. Batty would have to deal with in Carlisle, in addition, of course, to the problems of crime and disorder. The Chief was provided with a house in Kings Arms Lane. leased for five years from Mr. E. W. Thurnam.*

When he took up his duties he was directed around the city by George Palmer, quote, 'the constable', the same officer who accompanied him on his ill-fated, first excursion into Caldewgate. Together they organized the town into fifteen 'beats' on each of which, initially, the watchmen stood or remained close to strategic points keeping watch and calling out the hour. The day-officers were given a separate patrol pattern. Significantly, Palmer was not one of the officers sworn into the new force. A Benjamin Lee and Christopher Daly were also operating in the city as 'day-officers'**. Two constables, Barnes and Joseph Mullender were working the Caldewgate parish. There is no evidence available of any conflict of interests between these law officers and the new police, save that a Joseph Mullinder, who may, or may not, have been the constable of the same name, is recorded in Watch Committee minutes after being charged in November, 1830, with an assault on Chief Batty.

Superintendent Batty did not enjoy operational autonomy as do present-day chief constables, the Police Commissioners being very much involved in deciding what duties should, or should not, be undertaken. His was a hands-on role and there is ample evidence that he was out and about in the city making arrests,[+] cautioning licensees for keeping late hours, etc. The Chief's principal responsibility was the supervision of his officers, directing and controlling their work and maintaining discipline, the latter apparently being no small task judging by the numbers of defaulting officers reported to the Watch Committee for punishment.

Discipline in the force was generally poor. Initially, the men's working methods carried on from the ancient system of 'watch and ward'. Standing at fixed points during the night-time, apart from being boring and sleep inducing, cannot have been the most effective use of manpower since there must have been areas out of the men's sight and consequently unprotected. A number of those appointed let the side down badly, some being found absent from, or asleep at, their posts, whilst drunkenness was a major problem. Several were dismissed, others suspended without pay, for being found drunk and incapable of properly performing their duties.

New Beat System	
FIRST DISTRICT	SECOND DISTRICT
First Round [2 hours]	First Round [1 hour]
Rosemary Lane	Kings Arms Lane
West Walls	Lowther Street
Irish Brow	The Crescent
Caldew Bridge	Botchergate
Shaddongate	English Street
Milburn's Buildings	Police Office
Queen Street or	Second Round [1 hour]
Broadguards	Fergusons Lane
Caldcotes	Blackfriars Street
Caldewgate	Collier Lane
Willow Holme	Browns Lane
Abbey Street	Robert Street
Paternoster Row	Water Lane
Castle Street	Caldew Brow
Police Office	Police Office
Second Round[1 hour]	Third Round [1 hour]
Castle Street	Scotch Street
Annetwell Street	Tower Street
Finkle Street	Rickergate
Fisher Street	Eden Street or George Street
Greenmarket	Drovers Lane
Police Office	Jollies Buildings
Third Round [1 hour]	Lowther Street
Sally Port	Kings Arms lane
West Walls to the Gaol	Police Office
Damside to Sally Port	
Police Office	

* Grigg's 'Principal Inhabitants of Cumberland and Westmorland' shows Mr Batty living at King's Arms Lane.
** Since none of them were appointed under the new Act, which did not dispense with previous ancient custom, it seems they were probably the Corporation's bailiffs or parish constables in office at the time that the Act came into force.
+ for which he was able to claim expenses.

After-hours drinking was, generally, prevalent amongst the population, with some officers not only turning a blind-eye to, but actively encouraging, the practice. A number of licensees were summoned for keeping late hours, for harbouring police officers on their premises and for supplying them with drink. It is evident that Mr. Batty spent considerable time supervising during the night-time in addition to his many daytime duties. Not unreasonably, in the circumstances, he applied for an increase in salary and on 8 February, 1828, he was granted a raise of six shillings to a total of 36 shillings a week. Despite their transgressions, the new police appeared to be effective in restoring some order to the city.

They didn't have it all their own way, however, and there remained some opposition to their activities. On 28 September, 1827, a warrant was sworn against a Mr. Gorman for assaulting PC John Hewson, the first recorded assault upon a police officer in Carlisle. A Captain Slade and Doctor Blake were prosecuted for assaulting PC John Wright and others a fortnight later.

Mr. Batty arranged for his two day officers to be on duty at half past seven in the morning during the summer months[*] and eight o'clock during the winter. They alternated their duties so that at all times one was in the office, the other out on foot patrol. Both were required to be in the office until midnight on Saturdays – very long hours for a paltry wage.

On 16 May 1828 prescribed foot-beats were introduced *'for the purposes of day officers performing their duties in a more regular and efficient manner. It is directed that the city and suburbs be divided into districts and rounds and be patrolled within the times specified.'* A short while later, the Police Commissioners resolved that *"the Superintendent shall appoint an officer to take charge of each district, and from time to time shall remove them from one district to another as required, but in no instance shall he allow an officer to remain on one and the same district for a longer period than seven days at one time."* [**]

Mr. Batty further instructed that officers should not patrol the same rounds at the same times on successive days, but otherwise they were free to select the order in which they would patrol their allocated district provided that the whole city was covered each day[+]. They could decide themselves to patrol together if circumstances demanded. Officers were directed to *'use their utmost endeavours at all times, and especially when on patrol, to obtain a correct knowledge of all persons who are of disorderly or suspicious character, and to detect offences against the regulations of the Carlisle Police Act.'* They were required to sign on and off duty and record their duty movements in a *'journal'* [++] provided for the purpose. Mr. Batty had to write in the journal the name of a day-officer who would take charge of the Force in his absence. The Chief had no recognised deputy therefore either of the two daymen[*+] would be nominated to take control in his absence. As these new instructions took effect, the day officers hours of duty were extended so that they commenced at 7am in the summer and 8am in the winter whilst their Saturday tours were stretched to 2am (Sunday morning). They were to be at the beck and call of the superintendent even outside of their normal hours. There was no extra remuneration for them for the *'privilege'* of working such unsocial hours.

Of the city's new police force, the compiler of the 'History, Directory and Gazetteer of the Counties of Cumberland and Westmorland' wrote, in 1829, *'so successful have been his (Mr. Batty's) efforts, that Carlisle now ranks as one of the most peaceable cities in the kingdom, though Mr. Batty and the officers under him met with serious resistance from the Irish, Scotch and other weavers in Shaddongate unused to the interference of an effective police. The officers have since exercised their functions without opposition, and peace and property are now as well preserved here as in any other place in his Majesty's dominions.'*

---

[*] *March to September.*
[**] *This was an arrangement that, generally, existed until unit beat policing was introduced in 1963.*
[+] *Ditto.*
[++] *A Journal still so named and used in much the same way, was kept in the CID office and completed by detectives until amalgamation in 1967.*
[*+] *who were senior in status to and received slightly more remuneration than the watchmen.*

The road over Caldew Bridge into Bridge Street, Caldewgate, March 2009.

The writer's comments were somewhat premature, for in the face of serious opposition from the troublesome elements of Caldewgate, the Force was yet again to be stretched beyond its capabilities.

Anxiety over the competence and effectiveness of the magistrates raised its head in November, 1830. The Police Commissioners reported to Sir Robert Peel, * via the city's Member of Parliament, Sir James Graham: *'For some nights past the city has been visited by a large assemblage of people from the suburbs, parading the streets with torches, flags and inflammatory placards, and creating in the minds of the peaceable inhabitants great apprehension. Although the Commissioners of Police, and indeed the townsmen, had for some years past obtained an Act of Parliament [Carlisle Police Act] and organised an adequate and respectable police force, yet they felt they were paralysed by the inadequacy of the magistrates of the city. The magistrates, to whom recourse must be had in case of emergency, consist at this moment of the Mayor, one senior Alderman and one County Magistrate. The Mayor, an elderly clergyman, is not resident in the city; the others are of advanced age and infirmity, altogether unequal to their duties and lacking the confidence of the Commissioners.'* They added that *'the situation exists not for the lack of suitably qualified gentlemen....'* Sir James sought Peel's support for the appointment of active resident magistrates for the city. Two weeks later, before any remedial action could be taken, the Commissioners' worst fears were realised.

The Watch Committee minutes dated 2 December 1830 record a letter from Peel, alerted by Lord Melbourne[+], in connection with a number of wilfully started fires in the city where mobs had driven away the police fire-fighters. He demanded to know the circumstances and, writing to the Mayor, asked what was being done to assist fire-fighters and what steps were being taken to secure the peace in the city. Questions asked by such 'big guns' needed urgent attention and full explanations. It fell to Superintendent Batty to provide the answers. He reported that the incidents had been witnessed by a number of the Police Commissioners. He told the Committee that at 9.30pm, on Thursday, 30 November, 1830, police had been told that two stacks were ablaze, one in Caldewgate and one in Willow Holme. A fire engine was despatched to Willow Holme. Mr. Batty and two officers took another to Caldewgate, where they found that the fire there had too great a hold and was in danger of spreading to other stacks. He asked for assistance from onlookers to move the engine into a better position, *'but found determined opposition from the mob.'* The engine was moved but the obstruction continued. Hooligans cut the water hoses and stoned the fire-fighters and those assisting them. The officer working the engine was knocked senseless by a missile. All except Mr. Batty and

---

* *Now Sir Robert, having inherited his father's fortune in May 1830, but out of office after the defeat of the Duke of Wellington's government.*

+ *Home Secretary and a future Prime Minister.*

one officer were driven away. The mob threw fire-fighting equipment onto the blaze and called out for an attack on Mr. Batty. How he must have 'loved' Caldewgate! The Chief managed to gather together a strong body of police and residents before venturing to recover the fire engine. With the stacks completely destroyed, the mob dispersed. At Willow Holme, the picture was much the same – officers were attacked and water pumps were choked with gravel to prevent them operating. It was reported that there were no magistrates available in the city, *the two were utterly incapacitated by advanced years and ill-health.'*

As a consequence, the Police Commissioners could not avail themselves of special constables. Warrants were subsequently issued against five known offenders and one was captured. Mobsters joined together to prevent any further arrests. On the following Saturday morning, magistrates, police, special constables and a military unit went into Caldewgate where they took another prisoner. No other offenders were found. Mr. Batty told the Commissioners that the police were inadequate because a number of those on duty at the time the fires were reported were at home preparing themselves for the night-shift, and that the two fires, being simultaneous and a mile apart, had caused division of available manpower. Further, upon receipt of the fire reports, he had no reason to suspect that they were other than accidental, in which case, he said, he believed that persons present at the scenes would assist. A third stack fire had occurred at about the same time some five miles distant. The Commissioners, being most concerned, demanded that *'as a measure of absolute necessity a body of cavalry should be stationed in Carlisle for the preservation of the public peace.'* They wrote in reply to Lord Melbourne's complaint: *'...the city is now in a state of tranquility and the weavers have returned to their usual employment neglected for the past fortnight. The Commissioners expect they have laid aside all idea of further violence. None of the incendiaries have been apprehended * but officers sent in search of them have returned, having left proper descriptions of them at Dumfries, Langholm, Preston, Cockermouth and the immediate towns through which there is any probability of their passing, so that we entertain strong hopes of their being speedily captured.'* One wonders how long it took officers, in 1830, to undertake the Preston trip, some 90 miles distant, and what facilities, police or otherwise, existed to help them trace, arrest and return any offenders to Carlisle [+]. The Commissioners authorised replacement of the fire-fighting equipment and acquired helmets for the protection of the men. The Magistrates directed that 300 staves should be made available to the special constables. They also recommended the employment of twenty-five Specials, to be paid daily wages, whilst the city remained troublesome. The Commissioners did not object provided they worked under the control and directions of Mr. Batty and that their wages were not paid from police rates.

Benjamin Batty, when he accepted office, could surely never have anticipated the nature of the formidable task he was about to undertake. As if organising and leading a new, professional police body was not taxing enough, he had also to rid the city of its dreadful reputation and bring under control and to justice its criminal elements and rabble-rousers, each with larger numbers than his establishment enjoyed and each with a propensity for extreme violence and disorder. However, he seems always to have led from the front, and was at the scene of most incidents requiring police attention. Leaving apart the Commissioners, who were new to the business themselves, he had little or no support from those in authority in the city. Nevertheless, looking back now, there is no doubt that this first chief laid solid foundations for the efficient policing of Carlisle, and that some of his innovations certainly stood the test of time.

Old records show that Mr. Batty not only enforced the criminal law but, also, that he was not averse to imposing strict discipline upon his own men. He had a regular turnover of personnel as a consequence. His man-management skills were somewhat questionable and maybe not dissimilar to those of a chief constable that I worked under in Carlisle. He seems to have had a knack of irritating his staff and causing discontent. It was to prove to be his Achilles' heel and it brought about his downfall. Since he was not afraid to take others to task for neglecting their duties or for other disciplinary breaches as the following examples illustrate, it would have been prudent of him to make sure he was 'fireproof' himself. He clearly was not. Some examples of the conflict *'in the office'* are shown on the next page:

---

* *Those arrested must have been released without charge.*
+ *Further research shows that in 1810 there were just three policemen in Preston who were paid £3 per week. In 1832, the force consisted of six officers and it wa thought fitting that they should be presented with a uniform, having carried out their duties in ordinary clothes up to then. So precious were the new uniforms that the officers were ilnstructed to wear them only on Sundays.*

* 16 May 1828 – John Hewson, a watchman, was discharged from the force for using insulting language to his superintendent.
* 23 May 1828 – William Corrigan, a day officer, was reduced in rank to night-watchman for insolence to Mr. Batty.
* 25 November 1830 – A Joseph Mullender was summonsed before the magistrates for assaulting Mr. Batty in the execution of his duty. The circumstances of the offence are not known, but there was in the city at that time a Parish Constable Joseph Mullinder, who was not a member of the new police but who would probably have been appointed under ancient custom and who would almost certainly have come into contact with Mr. Batty. He may well have been the man who assaulted the Chief. there can't have been too many Joseph Mullinders in the town.

In January, 1831, day officer, Joseph Nixson, complained to the Police Commissioners about the Chief's conduct and a sub-committee was formed to investigate. It concluded:

* that there had been frequent disputes between the officers and their superintendent;
* that there had been mutual allegations of improper conduct;
* that the business of the police office was improperly managed because of frequent bickerings between Mr. Batty and his staff;
* that Mr. Batty had shown favouritism towards certain officers to the injury of the establishment;
* (negligence, in that) although most of his men were present in Caldewgate during recent rioting when haystacks were criminally burned and the fire engines and equipment criminally damaged, no police officers had identified any offender;
* that he had neglected, or refused, to give necessary orders to officers on duty and then complained against them for neglect;
* that he had neglected his own duty by leaving his wife to parade the night-shift and to direct them to their duties for the night.

There were a number of other charges against Mr. Batty which were not made public. The Commissioners found that they had no alternative other than to dismiss him and on 13 January, 1831, he was given two months notice to quit. Having regard to the nature of the allegations, it is surprising that he was allowed any notice at all. On 10 February, Mr. Batty was ordered to return the swords held by the police to the storekeeper at Carlisle Castle. One month later he was ordered to give up full possession of his house, he was paid the balance of outstanding expenses and he was given ten shillings for a pair of handcuffs that he had brought with him from Manchester. Mr. Batty left the Force on 9 March 1831. Both local newspapers carried a formal notice from the Commissioners that all future communications for the police force should be addressed not to Mr. Batty but to Mr. Brown, a new chief. Quite an ignominious ending for a man who arrived in the city with so much respect and promise, and who had done some sterling work to ensure the new force successfully got off the ground. The Carlisle Patriot of 15 January, 1831 expressed its admiration for the man and its view that the decision to dispense with his services was probably politically motivated. There had been, it reported, 'unfriendly' feelings between the Commissioners and the Chief, and they had been at odds over the policing of some instances of serious disorder in the city. However, the paper stated, *the town will certainly deplore the loss of the best informed and most active police officer whom it has ever had the advantage of possessing. From the very high recommendations which Mr. Batty will carry with him from the magistracy we have no doubt that his valuable services will soon be retained elsewhere, and, perhaps, under happier circumstances.'*

Benjamin Batty's services were, indeed, quickly retained. The Court Leet records in Manchester again come to the rescue and show that he was re-engaged as a beadle in 1831, a matter of weeks after leaving Carlisle and that he remained in office until stepping down in October, 1833. It is not known what he chose to do after that time. With his experience he would have had no difficulty acquiring another senior police position in one of the many peacekeeping bodies being formed at about this time. As a matter of interest, Manchester Borough (City) Police Force was not formed until 1839.

A few odds and ends from Chief Batty's days

1827
Jul 13 – [1] Each market day, the chief, his 2 day-men and 6 watchmen shall attend for keeping order, preventing misdemeanours and felonies, WITHOUT ANY ADDITIONAL PAY. [2] A Mr. Scott fined 10 shillings, five of which was awarded to the reporting officer, James Nixson.

Jul 27 – 1000 copies of the following clauses of the Police Act printed by Charles Thurnam at a cost of 38 shillings [£1.90p], and distributed in the city – [a]the enjoining of watchmen to apprehend offenders [power to arrest]; [b]the duties of beadles in the day-time; [c]the penalty for assaulting watchmen and beadles, for obstruction and other street nuisances and for removal of slaughter-houses, etc.

Oct 19 – Mr. Batty instructed not to assist the Mayor and Corporation without the consent of the Police Commissioners.

Nov 2 – Collectors of the Police Rates instructed to call upon the occupiers of tenements let for less than £10 per annum. to demand the rates and, in case of refusal, to enforce payment as prescribed by the [Carlisle] Police Act.

1828
Feb 28 – Mr. Batty authorised to purchased 3 pairs of handcuffs and 2 sets of leg-locks.

Nov 25 – Watchmen James Siddon and John Bird suspended for one week for allowing a prisoner, Tweddle, to escape [N.B. John Bird was appointed Chief Constable of Barnard Castle in 1839].

Dec 2 – Dean Hodgson seeks release from liability for police rate in respect of properties in the Abbey – his offer of 12 guineas [£12.12s.] per annum was accepted in lieu.

1830
Dec 2 – Memo from Police Commissioners – "The watchmen have been careless in trimming their lamps, thus wasting oil." Ordered " that every morning when they leave their beats they place their oil boxes in the engine house [fire-station] and take their lamps home to clean. The Day-officer, after he has cleaned the office, shall trim all the lamps and make them ready for the watchmen. A padlock will be fitted to the oilcan, and the Day-officer shall have sole keeping of the oil and wick." The good old days!

Robert Brown, Superintendent (Chief Officer)
10 March, 1831 to 16 October, 1839.

Like Mr. Batty before him, Chief Brown had a ghastly experience at the outset of his tenure of office, narrowly escaping death. At 4am, *(yes, there were two 4 o'clocks in a chief's working day in 1831)*, on Wednesday 29 June 1831, just three months into the job, Mr. Brown was carrying out checks of Scottish coaches leaving the city. He had in his possession a warrant for the arrest for felony of a Thomas Clarke, a horse-dealer, of Edinburgh and enquiries had revealed the offender to be in Carlisle. Mr. Brown eventually found the felon in a coach outside the Blue Bell Inn in Scotch Street. There was an altercation, during which another police officer, Lloyd, joined his Chief. Lloyd was pushed aside by the coachman, who tried to close the coach door before climbing into his seat and setting off, ignoring the police calls to stop. Lloyd held the door open whilst the Chief grabbed Clarke and began to drag him from the coach. The coachman drove off furiously, at the same time striking at the police officers with his whip. Mr. Brown was thrown face down into the roadway and the lead wheel of the coach ran over his shoulder and grazed the side of his head. The felon escaped. Mr. Brown lost the use of his arm and was confined to bed. The Patriot commented, *'Had the wheel passed an inch nearer Mr. Brown's head, he would inevitably have been killed on the spot.'*

oooOooo

Within two weeks of dismissing Mr. Batty, the Watch Committee had, somehow, found his successor. As in the case of Mr. Batty, no advertisement for the post appeared in the newspapers and there is no record, not even in the Watch Committee minutes, as to how he was chosen. Apart from the announcement that Robert Brown was a turn-key in the city's gaol when he was appointed Superintendent and Chief of Police at a Watch Committee meeting on 27 January 1831, no antecedent history of the man is available today. Mr. Brown also took charge of the city's fire-fighting service. His starting salary was 30 shillings (£1.50p) a week and he had the occupancy of the Superintendent's house free of rent and rates. The new chief does not appear to have had any policing experience to offer, but, given the nature of some of the menial tasks he was expected to carry out, perhaps he hardly needed any. More nuisances than crimes were policed and prosecuted as could be seen in the local newspaper, the Carlisle Patriot carried a brief two line report of Mr. Brown's arrival in office and continued in the next sentence, *'We are told that the Police Commissioners have determined in future to put a stop to sweeps shaking their soot bags in the street.'* Very proper, too, but hardly a duty of a Chief Constable! Mr. Brown was chief in name only; the Commissioners, with no more experience than he had, ruled the roost.

At the time of Mr. Brown's appointment the Metropolitan Police Force had been up and running for two years. In May, 1832, he took nine days away from the city to look at London's policing methods. He no doubt had his eyes opened whilst there, but there is no evidence that he brought back any new ideas – the force, it seems, continued as before. Almost certainly the Watch Committee would never have allowed him to make changes of his own volition. It made the decisions, operational, administrative and regarding prosecutions, whilst the chief was left to supervise the rank and file in much the same way as a sergeant would today, except that he was required to work all hours. Such was the lack of the chief's independence to manage, that almost four years after his appointment, he had to obtain the authority of his Watch Committee to *"get a nail put up in the police office to hang the police staves upon!"*

Brown's early years in the police force were at a time of some considerable national, political upheaval. In 1832, the Reform Act redistributed many parliamentary constituencies from the 'rotten boroughs' to the industrial towns and extended the vote to all males over 21 years old who were the owners of property with a rent of £10 per year - in effect, to the middle classes of society. This was followed in 1835 by the passing of the Municipal Corporations Act, which swept away over two hundred town councils replacing them with 178 new municipal (corporate) boroughs (of which one was Carlisle) with a common form of local government open to public scrutiny. It also granted the municipal franchise to all ratepayers. For the first time Town Councillors were elected by the citizens and eight new members took office, seven Liberals and one Tory, the latter being a former Town Chamberlain. Most importantly, so far as related to law and order, the Act empowered, but did not make mandatory, each new borough to form its own police force under the control of a Watch Committee. Only about half did so. In spite of all the political conflict that had gone before, the new Carlisle Corporation readily adopted the measures from the earliest opportunity. A municipal police force began operations on 1 January 1836.

Carlisle, of course, had had the benefit of a well established police force for almost nine years by the time the Act became effective. This gave rise to some uncertainty within the Corporation as to how the existing police authority would respond to being replaced. After all, the city's Corporation had, up to that time, been quite content to allow an independent body to finance and run the city's police, contributing little in terms of assistance and even less in financial support. The fears proved groundless, for a smooth transition of power was already being planned by the existing Commissioners. The two bodies co-operated as never before, the Corporation even asking the Commissioners to retain control of the Force until such time as the Corporation had a new municipal Watch Committee in place. At a meeting on the 4 January, 1836, the Commissioners resolved:

> *(1) that the Police Committee room, the public office, the lock-up and all the apartments connected therewith and thereto belonging, now in the occupation of the Superintendent, and also the fire engine house with the fire engines, buckets, and all other implements and utensils, and likewise the watch coats, lanterns, rattles and all the staves, accoutrements and all other necessaries provided for the Superintendent and day and night watchmen shall, upon demand, be given up to the Watch Committee appointed for the Borough of Carlisle under the Municipal Reform Act (Municipal Corporations Act). And that the Superintendent is hereby authorised and directed so to do accordingly.*

> *(2) that the Banking and Pass Books kept by the Establishment with Mr. John Forster, their Treasurer, shall also, upon the like demand, be given up to the said Committee to enable them to receive the balance due from the said Treasurer, and that James Willoughby, the Clerk, is hereby authorised and directed to give up the said Banking and Pass Books accordingly, together with all the rate books and other books, accounts, papers and writings whatsoever belonging to this Establishment.*

oooOooo

Like his predecessor, Chief Brown's was a hands-on operational role and there is evidence to show he was much involved in day-to-day policing incidents. At the County Sessions on Tuesday, 5 January, 1836, he gave evidence in the prosecution of William Johnston, aged 35 years, of Upperby, Carlisle, for stealing four geese from Walby, not a *'federal'* offence by today's standards, but one for which the accused, a first offender, was transported for seven years. At the same court, he deposed in the case of a gang of young men charged with *robbing*[*] (sic) Mr. Jackson's house at Etterby Scaur. The men, James Wood (20), Samuel Murray (19), John Smith (18), John McKay (18) and Edward Black (20), pleaded guilty and were sentenced to transportation for seven years. John Wilson, (17) was charged with stealing clothing and two bacon hams. Mr. Brown proved that the prisoner had been present at the robbery with the gang. The other accused corroborated Wilson's testimony that this was the first time he had been out with them and that he had not entered the house. Nevertheless, Wilson was also transported for seven years. Seven local criminals out of circulation for seven years, perhaps for ever; not a bad day's work from the Chief! Are there any Chief Officers out there today who could lay claim to putting away seven criminals in a day in their service, let alone whilst serving in the rank? Some would suggest few have put away seven criminals in their entire careers!

A Corporation Watch Committee of fifteen members, including six former Commissioners, was formed on 13 January and held its first meeting proper in the police office on 18 January 1836. The Chairman was the Mayor, George Gill Mounsey. James Willoughby was appointed Clerk. The City Treasurer took responsibility for the finances. The incumbent chief Robert Brown was to continue in office, and for the first time, the chief was to have a recognised deputy.

Few of the original (1827) policemen had survived in office, research showing that just two could be positively identified with the possibility of a further two [+]. (four out of the original twenty-one). There is no evidence to suggest that the Corporation did other than take over the existing body of police officers, (Appendix 'G') though it did promulgate its own rules, shown here, for the good governance of the Force.

- ◆ All fees received by, or due to, any officer to be paid to the Clerk.
- ◆ All allowances due to officers for attending as witnesses in criminal trials to be paid to the Clerk;
- ◆ Out of these monies, the Watch Committee may reward those officers who distinguish themselves by activity; balance to the Treasurer;
- ◆ A Superintendent and two day-officers appointed to keep the peace during the day;
- ◆ An officer, to be called the Night-Constable, to be appointed to superintend the night-watchmen and to take bail for the appearance of prisoners before a magistrate, such Night-Constable to rank next to the Superintendent;
- ◆ For the purpose of watching the town during the night, it shall be divided into sections, each to have a certain number of men, one of whom, alternatively shall rest while the remainder are patrolling the whole of the section. The stand, or resting place to be in that part of the section best adapted for maintaining a communication through the town;
- ◆ A sub-committee appointed to divide the town into sections and decide on the number of officers required;
- ◆ The practice of calling time to be discontinued;
- ◆ Two men, to be taken in rotation from the whole number, required to come on duty at dusk to assist the day-men in patrolling the streets during the dark part of the evening;
- ◆ Watchmen not allowed on any account to wear clogs whilst on duty;
- ◆ Superintendent, Night-Constable and day-men to wear a uniform;
- ◆ Robert Brown appointed Superintendent of Police for the Borough of Carlisle;
- ◆ A Night-Constable be advertised for in the Carlisle papers, and also in a Manchester, Liverpool and Glasgow paper – applicants to send in testimonials of character and the terms upon which they will do the duties, on or before 15 February.

At a meeting on 22 January 1836, the Watch Committee were informed that the city had been divided into four sections, each to be patrolled by three men under a Night-Constable.

---

[*] *Robbery is an offence committed against a person and involves the use of threats of force against the victim in order to complete the theft. Robbery cannot be committed against a building.*

[+] *The acccuracy of some records is dubious, e.g. through spelling errors.*

The Carlisle Journal reported on 16 January that the new Town Council was making good progress and, on its old hobby-horse, it asked how much had been spent on the Mayor and Corporation's lavish life-style at public expense, adding, *'We are glad to perceive that feasting at the public cost is to be entirely abolished.'* One week later it reported that the total annual income to Borough funds amounted to £1835, that the expenditure on salaries, etc., was £900, therefore *'leaving for the purposes of the police £935. This is certainly a cheering account. It will enable the Council to maintain an excellent police establishment without the cost of one farthing to the inhabitants. The cost of the police last year (1835) was £717 and the average cost for the eight years it has been in existence has been about £800 per annum. The Council will thus have at its disposal about £100 a year for public improvements.'* If only it were that simple. The newspaper alleged that for at least eight years past the old Corporation had spent, *"for no useful purpose whatever, from £700 to £1,000 per annum. Whilst they were wasting these funds, the inhabitants of the city were called upon to maintain, at great cost, a police establishment which was the pecuniary duty of the Corporation to provide. Whilst these men were squandering the money the poorest and most helpless of the people were compelled to contribute part of their miserable earnings, in fact, a part of the food for their children, towards the maintenance of the peace of the city. Can the English language furnish a word sufficiently expressive of the depth of scorn with which their actions must be viewed by every man with the slightest pretensions to correct moral feeling.'*

At a public dinner to celebrate the first publicly elected Mayor of Carlisle, Mr. George Gill Mounsey, (Chairman of the Watch Committee), it was said that it was ancient custom for the Mayor to treat his private friends, etc., from public funds but the new council was determined to manage differently - *"the funds could not pay for both feasts and policemen."* But the old Corporation would not go away without a fight. William Hodgson, formally a senior Alderman had been paid £25 a year in office, and now, having been deprived of that income, he claimed compensation, in the sum of £250, from the new council. Old habits die hard! The Corporation resolved that, since he was removed from office by the Municipal Corporations Act and not by the new council, *"If he has to get compensation, let him do so through the courts!"*

On 4 February 1836, at a meeting of the new Watch Committee, the former Commissioners handed over their books, showing a credit balance of £380.18s.0d, thus ending their association with the city police and their role becoming redundant in the process. Whilst the task of 'civilising' the city was not yet complete, they had given sterling service to the community and could be justifiably be proud of their achievement in establishing a professional police force in Carlisle. Notice to quit was given to four serving watchmen when the new Committee reduced the strength of the force establishment. Three of them were re-deployed as scavengers to be called upon as and when required, and to fill any vacancies occurring on the regular establishment. Jonathan Fisher, late of the Royal Artillery, was appointed *'captain of the night-watch'*, and effectively deputy chief of police, taking up his duties on Thursday, 18 February. Chief Officer Brown was appointed Billet-master and Markets Superintendent for the city.

What was the Force like at this time? An examination of early records suggests that the quality of the patrolmen was suspect. They show a catalogue of disciplinary hearings, before either the Chief Officer or the Watch Committee, for a range of indiscretions from neglect or being found asleep to the most common of all, being drunk on duty. There were many physical attacks on the officers, but there is some evidence that they could *'dish it out'* themselves too. Considering the aggravation they experienced, the very low pay, the extremely long hours of duty without rest-days, and the insistence on them having to reside in some of the worst areas of the city, it is a wonder that anyone took the job. Officers were usually selected from a pool of reserves employed as 'scavengers'*, or street cleaners. Not so odd really, since the Chief of Police was also responsible for street cleaning as well as billets and markets. Occasionally, notices were posted on public buildings or an advertisement appeared in the local press requesting anyone interested in becoming a police officer to report to the police station at a specific time and date, usually only a couple of days notice being given. There are no records of how many actually did apply, but there seemed to be no shortage of recruits. What qualities were sought in potential officers? The adverts gave no indication. Candidates were simply asked to bring along testimonials as to character and be prepared to commence duties immediately.

---

* *Street cleaners, [The Chief Constable was also responsible for the cleanliness of the streets].*

Obviously they were expected to have the ability to read and write, but there is no evidence of educational examination or medical checks having taken place. It was normal for the Watch Committee to be informed of new recruits and for it to confirm appointment. This was, in fact, a legal requirement in city and borough forces until the passing of the Police Act of 1964. Frequent dismissals led to quite a turnover of manpower that persisted for a number of years. Some men moved on to other forces as they were being established, a few of them as chief or senior officers. Few stayed long enough in the city force to acquire much experience in those early days. Neither the Chief Officer, Robert Brown, nor his deputy, Jonathan Fisher, had previous policing experience, the Chief coming from the prison service, the deputy from the army – the blind leading the blind!

Nevertheless, theirs was a hands-on job, and their working hours just as long and arduous as those of the men. Though they were able to maintain the peace better than their forebears, and recognising that they laid some solid foundations for future policing, the city police force of the 1830's bore little resemblance to the professional service at its demise in the 1960s.

Carlisle

1835
As it was about the time of the formation of the city police.

© *Paintings from the collection of Tullie House Museum and Art Gallery, Carlisle.*

William Henry Nutter [1819 - 1872].

POLICE OFFICERS.

ANY PERSON desirous of being appointed on the CARLISLE POLICE ESTABLISHMENT, is desired to apply Personally, with Testimonials of character, to Mr. SABBAGE, the Superintendent, at the POLICE OFFICE, on or before THURSDAY next, and to attend at the Meeting of the Watch Committee, at Seven o'Clock on the Evening of that Day.

The Wages of an Officer are 15s., 17s., and 18s. per week, and uniform Clothing.

Carlisle Police Office, 4th Sept., 1856.

Top left: Carlisle Market Place from the South, 1835 (looking towards Scotch Street).
Bottom: Carlisle Market Cross from the Town Hall.   *Top right: Glover's Row, Carlisle 1835 (Cathedral in background).*

John Kent - Britain's first black policeman

On 17 August 1837, some twenty months after the new police authority took office, it confirmed a unique appointment to the force, one that attracted little publicity at the time but which became 'news' almost fifty years later and sensational news in more recent years – that of John Kent. John was, almost certainly, Britain's first black police officer. Though there were Watch Committee records of John's service in the city police, the first indication that he was an officer of Afro-Caribbean origin appeared in his obituary notices in the local newspapers.

John Kent passed away on Monday, 19 July 1886, at his home in Henry Street (Warwick Road), Carlisle. He was interred in Carlisle Cemetery, where his recorded age is shown as 88. 'Black Kent is dead,' announced the 'Carlisle Journal,' adding that it was 'an announcement which would have had much more significance forty years ago than it has today.' – 'Death of a Carlisle Noteable' stated the Carlisle Patriot. 'Yesterday,' the article read, 'there were interred at the Carlisle Cemetery the mortal remains of one of the oldest and best known inhabitants of this city, John Kent, popularly known as 'Black Kent,' he being of negro descent.'

A black person would have been an extremely rare sight in Carlisle in 1886, even more so in 1837. When I served in the city police in the 1960s, it would have been possible to count the ethnic population on one's fingers. A black policeman, then, would certainly have turned heads. How, then, did John Kent appear on the Carlisle scene?

In the late 18th Century, Thomas Kent, a black African, was transported from his homeland to the plantations of the West Indies, a victim of the slave trade. He arrived in England from the Caribbean and landed in Whitehaven. His surname came from a Jamaican plantation owner when his real name was Jubal. He was a servant at Calder Abbey and after seven or eight years he went to sea before returning to Carlisle where he married a Cumbrian girl. They had ten children, one of whom a son, John Kent, was born at the family home at Low Hesket, Carlisle, sometime between 1795 and 1805. John, who never knew his precise date of birth, grew up in the area and married a girl from Longtown.

'In his prime' claimed the 'Cumberland Pacquet' newspaper, 'John Kent was a big powerful man.' The Patriot' reporting that at one time he had been employed laying pavements in the city, said, 'Crowds gathered to watch the tremendous blows dealt with his pavior's beater.' There can be little doubt that an added 'attraction' was the fact that John was 'as black as ebony.' Judging from detailed obituaries of the man printed in the local newspapers, John was a popular and well-respected police officer in the early days of the police. The paper continued, 'Then 'Black Kent' was a policeman in the Carlisle City Police Force and one of the first appointments under Sir Robert Peel's Act*, and the 'Black Douglas+' was not a greater terror in his time to the children (of Carlisle) forty years ago. Many of those children, now in middle age, will remember distinctly the figure of the man of colour in his policeman's swallow-tail with a shiny leather crowned top hat on his head and a stout oaken walking-stick in his hand, and upon bright summer days,

---

* The municipal Corporation Act.

+ Sir James Douglas, 1286-1330, champion of Robert Bruce, was known as 'Black Douglas' by the English Borderers to whom he became a figure of dread.

a pair of regulation 'ducks' replacing the ordinary trousers of blue cloth.'

The newspaper commented that hundreds of Carlisle men, well past middle age, have *'vivid recollections of the big, black policeman'*. So unusual was the sight of any black person in the city at that time, let alone a policeman, that *"Black Kent's coming"* became a household term used to frighten mischievous children into behaving themselves. *'But the imputation was ill-deserved. 'Black Kent' in the flesh and seen face-to-face was a quiet, inoffensive man with a positive fondness for the children who were brought up to regard him as an ogre. Having served the city for many years as a policeman, one of the original 'Bobbies', he entered the service of the London and North Western Railway Company and in that service he ended his days this week as an attendant at one of the waiting-rooms at Citadel station'.* He was then an old man of 88 years of age [or 91, according to Kent himself].

Watch Committee records show that John Kent was appointed a supernumerary (probationer) constable in the Carlisle City Police Force on 17 August 1837 and that he was confirmed in office as a permanent constable on 26 October following. He had had some relevant experience of policing, as an appointee of the county magistrates in Maryport. Giving evidence in August, 1841 at Carlisle Assizes at the trial of several rioters (a riot during which a city policeman was murdered) he opened by saying, *"I have been a policeman for seven years, two or three in Maryport, the rest in Carlisle."* He was 'promoted' to day-constable on 16 May 1839.

He lived at several addresses in the city, the last in Henry Street (Warwick Road). There stated the newspapers,

An impression of John Kent, Britain's first black policeman, taken from an original painting by Mark Custerson hanging at Cumbria Police Headquarters, Carleton Hall, Penrith. The constable on the left is wearing the summer uniform of the city police.

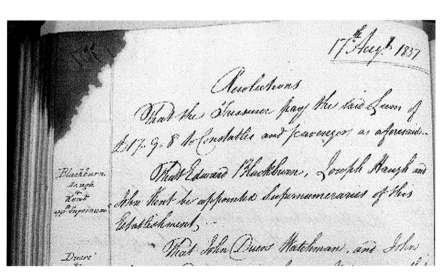

Early policeman's summer uniform.

hanging on the wall in his home, he proudly displayed a portrait of himself in the uniform of the Mayor's Sergeant *, an appointment he held for a number of years while serving in the city force.

John was proud of his police service and like all policemen he liked to reminisce about his experiences. It appears he had plenty to talk about. According to the newspapers, one of his earliest arrests, evidently before he was appointed to the Force in Carlisle, was that of two hotel 'coiners'. He'd tell of how he captured one and chained him to the fire-grate in his own home before placing an empty pistol on the table and telling his wife to shoot the man if he so much as attempted to escape. He then went off and caught the other offender. On another occasion, he arrested a man for a robbery committed near Wigton. In order to put the offender off his guard, he feigned drunkenness, (not too difficult a task for our hero!) *'but the villain was soon to discover that what he supposed to be a staggering inebriate was in fact a stalwart guardian of the peace with all his senses about him.'*

A Coroner's inquest into the death of 17 year old James Donaghue, a potter,** in March 1839, was told how the youth had been playing with others on planks of wood floating in the timber dock on the canal in Caldewgate when PC Kent, patrolling the canal basin,[+] came upon the scene. Clearly the boys should not have been there and in their hurry to escape the officer's attention they made to jump ashore. Unfortunately Donaghue overbalanced and fell into the water where he remained submerged for some five minutes. Constable Kent and a sailor managed to raise the youth from the bottom of the canal and after a short time he appeared to be

Carlisle Canal Basin in 1823, from a painting by William Brown
© Tullie House Museum and Art Gallery, Carlisle.

none the worse for his ordeal and was able to talk with them. Three hours later the lad died after suffering violent chest pains and bleeding from his mouth and nose. Some criticism of the authorities for not taking adequate steps to prevent children from entering and playing in the canal basin ensued, but there was no recognition for the two men who rescued the youth from the canal bed.

A couple of months later, and again in Caldewgate, an officer, called to a disturbance, was threatened by three men armed with a blunderbuss and daggers. PCs Kent and Ruddick together with Sergeant John Bird, arrived on the scene and arrested the offenders. Life in the Force wasn't all rosy for PC Kent. He clashed with at least one colleague and had several *'brushes'* with authority to recall. In 1838 he was suspended without pay for two nights in January for neglect of duty whilst in November he and a colleague, Thomas Hetherington, had unpleasant exchanges. That resulted in both being formally cautioned by the Watch Committee. Kent had alleged the use of *'intemperate language'* towards him while he was searching a prisoner and Hetherington, a week later, counter-claimed that Kent had behaved improperly towards him.

In August 1843, the city's Mayor made a complaint against him for failing to pay for a horse and cart which he had commandeered to convey two prisoners to the city lock-up from Rosley, some twelve miles from Carlisle.

---

* *A civic role, escorting the Mayor and Corporation on ceremonial occasions.*

** *Potters - a generic name used in Carlisle to describe the large group from Caldewgate, mainly of Irish origin, of general dealers, such as rag and bone men, scrap metal dealers and scissor grinders, who plied their trade around the streets from horses and carts, barrows, etc..*

[+] *Carlisle was a busy port with access to the sea via the Carlisle Canal. The Canal Company engaged and paid for city police officers to patrol the Basin, particularly at night.*

How was the policeman, acting alone, expected to take two men to the lock-up so far away, one might ask? And was he really expected to have paid the owner of the cart from his own pocket?

Surely, instead of complaining, the Mayor should have been commending the constable for his zeal and initiative. There is no report as to how this issue was resolved and no record of any disciplinary or other action being taken against PC Kent.

Drunkenness was always a problem amongst old policemen and it was one to which PC Kent succumbed. On 18 May 1844 he again came to the notice of the Watch Committee. Together with Hetherington, now a sergeant, and other officers he attended a fire* at Naworth Castle, seat of the Earl of Carlisle. Afterwards, a Sheriff's Officer complained that the officers were under the influence of drink at the time. An investigation showed that they had been drinking in Carlisle before responding to the fire call. The Committee was anxious not to undermine the sergeant's authority and dealt with him by way of a verbal caution. Records do not show how the case against PC Kent was concluded, but it would be reasonable to expect that he, too, would have been cautioned. Perhaps he was. However, on 30 May 1844, just a week after the complaint was received, he was suspended by the Watch Committee for one month without any pay for being drunk on duty. Did the Committee deem it necessary to deal more severely with him, or was this a second drinking offence within a matter of days? It appears to have been a particularly harsh penalty when usually, at that time, one week's suspension seemed to be the norm for such a transgression. One assumes there must have been aggravating circumstances, though it is fair to comment that on the odd occasion officers were dismissed the first time they offended. Records show that on 6 June, while still under suspension, PC Kent, ironically, received a reward of five shillings for his work at the Naworth fire scene.

Some three months later, in September 1844, John Sabbage was appointed Chief Constable of Carlisle and he was clearly concerned about indiscipline and about drinking in particular. He very soon introduced new rules and regulations for the conduct of his men and posted notices in the station warning them against being found drunk on duty and of the consequences they could expect if his orders were disregarded. A few days prior to the new chief's arrival, John Kent was disciplined for being late for duty on two successive days. The Chief Constable dismissed the charges with the officer's agreement to refund the wages he had received for the time worked. Whether or not drink played its part on those occasions is not known. Two months down the line, on 6 December 1844, Kent reported for duty at 9pm in an intoxicated state. He was once again taken before the Watch Committee and, probably on the new chief's recommendation and having regard to his recent poor disciplinary record and the warning that the Force, generally, had been given, his services were dispensed with. He left on 12 December 1844 after little over seven years service, an ignominious end to his career.

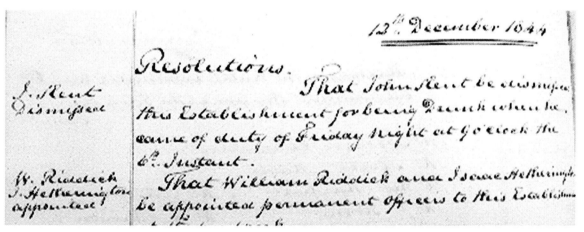

Entry in Watch Committee Minute Book recording the dismissal of PC Kent from the Force.

After leaving the police, John became a *'very confidential servant of the company constructing the main west-coast railway through Carlisle and was entrusted with important work.'* In the 1851 census he is a railway policeman, which meant at that time a signalman.

---

* *The City Police also performed fire brigade duties. A fire station was attached to the Police Office in New Bank Lane but moved to purpose built premises on West Walls in 1836.*

A contributor to the *'LNWR Gazette'* reminiscing about Kent the railwayman, described him as 'being as black as ebony.' The writer had known Mr. Kent for many years and remembered him as a city policeman. The Carlisle Patriot recalled a humorous story about signalman John Kent. *'The youthful Prince of Wales, passing through Carlisle shortly after the publication of Mrs. Stowe's 'Uncle Tom's Cabin', saw John in the signal box and asked his attendants if that was Uncle Tom in his cabin.'* There could be some truth in what may be regarded a myth, the Prince of Wales was visiting Carlisle at this time.

The last seven or eight years of John's life were spent as an attendant in the First Class Waiting Room in Carlisle Station where *'his civility and unvarying good humour made him a favourite with everyone, while his strict attention to duty commended him to his employers.'* He was there, as usual, until a couple of days before his death. John Kent had, quite literally, worked all of his very long life. He was a truly remarkable character.

It has been generally accepted that the first black police officer in the UK was appointed in Birmingham in 1961 [*]. However, the

CROWN STREET CABIN No.7

Kent's Cabin, the signal box at citadel Station, which Edward VII, when a boy, had referred to as 'Uncle Tom's Cabin'.

existence of a record of PC Kent's police service in Carlisle some one hundred and thirty years earlier is a clear indication that he holds that title. Since there were few municipal police forces and no county forces, the appointment in 1837 of a black man of West Indian descent to the office of constable was almost certainly without precedent. My enquiries of the Home Office and of the National Co-ordinator of the Black Police Association have failed to indicate otherwise. Therefore, in the unlikely event that the contrary can be established, the Carlisle City Force can justifiably claim the distinction of recruiting the first black officer to serve in a British police force.

In 2006, the BBC produced a television programme, 'The Hidden Slave Trail,' in which it looked at former slaves and their descendants in Britain. John Kent was featured. A remarkable result of the BBC's, investigations was the tracing, over two centuries later, of descendants of John Kent still living in the Carlisle area and hardly a stone's-throw from his birthplace. None of them show any trace of their ethnic ancestry or were aware of their now famous forebear.

The unmarked grave of John Kent in Carlisle Cemetary

The most telling reaction on being told was, *"Well, fancy having a policeman in the family!"* Now, understandably, that is something one doesn't want to admit!

Benjamin Batty, the first chief officer, was dismissed after complaints by his subordinates had been upheld by the Watch Committee. Brown, himself, was hauled before a Watch Committee meeting on 24 December, 1838 after PC William Kellon, dismissed for neglect of duty, (absent from his beat for an hour and ten minutes the previous day – swift justice!) retaliated by complaining about the Chief's conduct towards him. The minutes recorded that the Chief had his knuckles rapped - *'this Committee highly disapproves of the expressions used by him Sunday last towards William Kellon, a Watchman, relative to his religious professions, and they direct that he pay more strict attention in future to the first article in the instructions to the Superintendent.'* The Committee added that, in future, whenever an officer was guilty of insubordination, he should be reported immediately to the Committee which would support the Superintendent in maintaining discipline, *'but it cannot permit harsh or taunting language to be used.'*

---

[*] *Cumberland News 15 Sep. 1961 - a number of candidates applying for police vacancies in Birmingham were said to be 'black'. At the time this was thought to be the first time a black person was appointed to the service.*

In January 1839, the city magistrates wrote to the Watch Committee, *'The undersigned magistrates for the Borough of Carlisle, being clearly of the opinion that it would add most materially to the efficiency, as well as respectability, of the police establishment if the night patrols were clothed in the same uniform as the day-police when on duty at the magistrates' office, patrolling the streets on Saturdays and Sundays, and also when called out upon any public occasion, they, in consequence, strongly recommend this subject to the serious consideration of the Watch Committee and they further beg to state, that in order to carry this very desirable object into immediate execution, they will contribute, out of the fees of their office, the sum of twenty-five pounds.'*

An early City Police uniform.

from Cumbria Police Museum (now closed).

The Force had worn a uniform since its formation in 1827, but those of the day-officers had always been of better quality. The Watch Committee estimated the cost to equip every officer in accordance with the magistrates' wishes would be £60 and that the uniforms would last for five years. The Committee, avariciously, was happy to accept the proposal provided that the offer was increased to £30 and that a further contribution would be forthcoming when the clothing was due for renewal. It added, *'When in uniform [the men] should also be clean in person. If dirty or slovenly, they shall be fined by the Committee. They will be responsible for the good care (of the uniform) otherwise they will be charged the costs of damage.'*

The Chief Officer's Annual Report of that year, recording the introduction of the uniforms, acknowledged the magistrates' £30 contribution, and went on, *'The adoption of the uniform has not only greatly improved the appearance of the men but has proved highly beneficial to the public by the police officers being at once known.'*

It also had another important effect – since all of the men were in uniform, there was no reason why the day and night patrols could not be amalgamated. Mr. Brown recommended accordingly. Further, in May, when a vacancy occurred for a day-officer, it was filled by night-officers on rotation, one week at a time, so as to make them acquainted with a greater range of police duties to the mutual benefit of the men and the establishment. The Watch Committee accepted the Chief's recommendation, at the same time reducing the number of officers on duty during the night-time and correspondingly increasing the day patrols which thus proved effective in the prevention and detection of crimes and other irregularities in the daylight hours.

oooOooo

Plans for the Force to move

When the Corporation assumed control of the Force, it was already clear that purpose built accommodation would have to be provided to house it. In February 1839, Captain Williams, the Inspector of Prisons, condemned the city's lock-ups as *'wholly unfit, ill-ventilated, without light, no yards or outside conveniences, no separation of prisoners, quite insufficient for so populous a town.'* It is worthy of note that the Main Guard in the Market Place was built in 1649 from stone removed from the cathedral by the parliamentary administration. It was in the hands of the Board of Ordnance for use by soldiers as a military store and, in 1794, was described as *'a very great nuisance that hurts the view of the principal streets.'* When acquired by the Corporation in 1826 it became the first lock-up for the new police. The acquisition appears to have set the pattern for future, poorly-planned, police accommodation.

On 25 May 1839, local newspapers published a notice of the Corporation's intention to construct a new, purpose- built police station and sought suggestions for the scheme:

There were many responses, *'some possessing great architectural beauty calculated to add greatly to the appearance of the city'* and estimated costs varied considerably.

To Architects, Builders and Others,
Intended New Police Office and Lock-up House

The Corporation of Carlisle hereby offer a premium of ten guineas for the best plan and specification of a Police Office and Lock-up House to be approved by the Inspector of Prisons.

The building must contain12/14 separate cells with airy grounds or yards, a magistrates' office with retiring rooom adjoining, one room for the convenience of witnesses, etc., an apartment for the Watch Committee to accommodate 20 members, an office and suitable rooms for the Superintendent of Police as well as rooms for day-officers.

The Inspector of Prisons approved a plan by Messrs. Scott and Moffat estimated to cost at most £1,500 built on a level site, more if constructed on the more difficult Corporation-owned gardens in West Walls. The Inspector wrote:

London, Sept 21st, 1839.

> *Sir,*
> *I have seen Mr. Scott upon the subject of proposed lock-ups. I beg very strenuously to recommend the Town Council that the size of the cells should not be diminished but remain as at first intended. A great advantage will be derived from having suitable places where refractory apprentices or disorderly youths may be locked up for a few hours instead of sending them to gaol, which, with all that can be done, is but too often more likely to diminish than increase the terror their previous imagination had invested it with. A prison should be made use of as a last resort. Unfortunately, for the want of other means, it is but too often the first.*
>
> *I fully concur with you in your opinion upon the advantage of concentrating the police force and all such appurtenances to them as fire-engines, etc. Much efficiency would be lost if it were otherwise. Much, however, will depend upon the situation selected, which should be well known, central, with easy access and egress. The Market Place appears to offer every advantage.*
>
> *[signed] William J.N.O. Williams,*
> *Inspector of Prisons.*

A suitable plot of land was available close to the Market Place though it was not the Corporation's first choice for a police office. Objections on the grounds of cost also began to surface. Alderman Richardson saw no need for a magistrates' office since there already was one and *"it was a great objection to incur additional expense for that purpose."* Alderman Ross agreed that the present buildings were disgraceful *"but the new ones need no ornament. Police lock-ups are not any credit to a town nor something people ought to boast of or take a pride in and the less they were brought before the public eye the better."* He was opposed to anything other than a decent house for the superintendent and secure accommodation for the temporary confinement of prisoners. In his view the plans were far too ambitious. *"It was an elevation for a palace, not a prison."* The Mayor disagreed, but he fought a losing battle, the Town Council rejecting the plans but agreeing to pay the architect the costs of their preparation.

A few months later, in February 1840, a plan was approved by the council. Mr. John Hodgson's design, drawn in pencil to save costs (on the back of a 'fag' packet, I wonder?) was accepted and he would oversee its construction for 3fi% of the total building costs. But there was still criticism and objections within the Corporation. *"It is not necessary to have fine turrets, lofty towers and battlemented walls,"* said one member, *"Not necessary to spend four or five thousand pounds on a building designed for the reception of a few disorderly persons for a few hours; we have a gaol sufficiently large and commodious for all prisoners,"* added another. Hodgson's plan was cheap at just £1,000 but the building would be austere. It would have just six cells, two exercise yards, one for male and one for female prisoners, a superintendent's house, a Watch Committee room, a muster room for the police force, a small charge office and a room for the policemen's clothing and for the storage of stolen and prisoners' property. The building, constructed in red sandstone, would be built in the Corporation gardens in West Walls, opposite the Grammar School. Proper plans could be drawn and work started immediately. The Mayor said he did not need to remind the Watch Committee of the necessity of such a building, *"the present lock-ups being unfit to confine human beings in!"*

The financing of the new premises was discussed by the council. The Mayor suggested a mortgage. Alderman Steel said the Corporation possessed ten railway shares that were now at a premium and that if they were sold the monies could be raised at once. Another alderman suggested selling the City Mills. As the discussions continued, construction work began. Seven months later, when the building was almost completed, the council agreed to install a form of central heating together with gas lighting, gave its consent to paving the front of the premises with Lazonby sandstone flags and sought permission of the Lighting Committee for a gas lamp to be hung above the main entrance.

oooOooo

The magistrates and police authority clashed yet again in May 1839, but this time the authority was the Corporation Watch Committee and not the independent commissioners. The magistrates instructed Sir William Follett, a barrister, to challenge the City Council on the powers and authority of its Watch Committee. The Justices clearly were of the opinion that their responsibilities for maintaining the Queen's Peace included a major say in the constitution and organization of the city police force and they could not accept otherwise. They did, indeed, have a responsibility in rural areas where they were instrumental in appointing and organizing the parish constables, since, at that time, there were no county police forces. In law, however, that was not the case in the new boroughs, where the Town Councils, through their Watch Committees, held sway*. The Chairman of the Magistrates wrote stating that Sir William was of the view that the Committee was not responsible for law and order nor for maintaining the peace of the city; further, he would argue, the Committee had no authority to interfere with or to decide upon what complaints should be brought before the magistrates.** Accordingly, the magistrates had instructed the city's police chief to lay all complaints before them in future, as well as reporting to them on the efficiency of the force. The writer continued, *'The magistrates hope and trust that the Watch Committee will use their best endeavours to make the police of this Borough as efficient as possible and that they will, above all things, be particularly careful to select steady, intelligent and active men, for they need scarcely remind the Committee that the peace and good government of the town will equally depend on the character and respectability of the police force.'* The writer, incidentally, was Dr. Heysham, a member of the city's Watch Committee as well as being Chairman of the Magistrates.

There was a further exchange of letters in June. The magistrates felt their powers were being usurped and that the Watch Committee was exceeding its authority regarding prosecutions by operating a system which was open to suggestion that it showed favouritism to certain classes. They further alleged that the Committee was wrongfully approving the practice of police searching prisoners' personal property on arrest, e.g. letters. They insisted, too, that the police force should be augmented by thirty additional officers (it should be noted that at this time, there was considerable excitement in the city caused by the Chartist movement[+]). The Committee objected, claiming that it had no previous knowledge of any magisterial complaints and that it had always co-operated fully with them on matters of policing the city. It suggested that if the magistrates had a complaint, it might have been better addressed by a meeting of the parties rather than resorting to lawyers. The Committee emphasised that they needed no reminding of their obligations to appoint a good and sufficient number of suitable men to the police force and reported that the chief officer was satisfied with the established strength at his disposal.

The justices took the matter further, putting their complaints in writing to the Home Secretary, Lord John Russell, who responded by asking them to impress his instructions on the Committee that *'it should take immediate measures for improving the policing of the Borough of Carlisle.'* He wished to be kept informed of what was being done. The Town Clerk corresponded directly with the Home Office and made clear that the city police force was adequate and efficient but he invited any suggestions the Home Secretary might have for its improvement. He probably did not expect a reply to the effect that *'a temporary addition of not less than twenty men ought to be made to the paid police constabulary.'* In fact, reluctantly, just six appointments were made.[++]

---

* *Authorised by the municipal Corporation Act, 1835.*   ** *TheMagistrates were probably correct in that respect.*

[+] *A popular movement for electoral reform 1837-1848.*   [++] *The Home Secretary had no authority over police forces at this time. However, any advice offered would usually be construed as an order.*

The Home Secretary may well have been influenced by events elsewhere in the land. There were many instances of serious disorder at the public meetings of the Chartist movement, causing much apprehension in towns where they planned to assemble. July 1839 saw serious rioting during a meeting in Birmingham. There was considerable excitement in Cumberland. In Carlisle, the movement was active gathering financial support by door-to-door collections and holding meetings at the Market Cross. The Watch Committee, clearly with a change of heart following their recent clash with the magistrates, directed that the police force be considerably augmented and, in consequence, the Mayor issued a proclamation and the magistrates summoned all householders to the Town Hall. Nine hundred citizens were sworn as special constables and placed on duty around the city. A detachment of the 77th Regiment mounted guard in Green Market and the 95th Regiment from the Castle patrolled the streets. There were rumours in Lancashire that a great part of Carlisle had been burned down whilst the national press were labelled as *'mischievous'* for spreading exaggerated tales of destruction and rebellion in the city. The *'Carlisle Journal'* stated that nothing could be further from the truth, *'The dagger and torch men are, we sincerely believe, few in number.'* It appears that Cumberland, in fact, avoided the serious rioting and violence that other parts of the country had experienced, but the potential was never far away. A Cockermouth blacksmith, Thomas Bell, aged 30, and 22 year old Thomas Wallas were charged with *'conspiring to subvert the government and laws of the country'* in a trial at the County Quarter Sessions. They were alleged to have manufactured 300 pikes and other weapons *'of the most formidable description'* for use by local Chartist supporters. They were advised by the Chairman of the Bench to plead guilty if they were to expect leniency for *'they have been misled by wiser and wickeder heads than their own, by men who travelled about the country inculcating sedition.'*

Meanwhile, in Caldewgate, life continued as normal. The *'wild'* western district of the city was still a problem area for the city police. At 4.30am, on 11 May, 1839, three men involved in a disturbance in Queen Street were confronted by a patrolling constable. The men, armed with a blunderbuss and daggers, threatened the officer. Sergeant John Bird and PCs Kent and Ruddick, who were sent to assist, arrested the offenders. Later in court, their defence lawyer told the bench *'It was just drunken bravado, a mere common assault on the policeman.'* That's alright, then? It is what some claim to this day; drink is frequently offered as an excuse, except in motoring cases. At 1am on 28 September, 1839, PC Robinson, working Caldewgate beat came across a group quarrelling in Bridge Street. He told them to clear off, whereupon they set their differences aside and turned on him (it was ever thus!). The constable managed to arrest one offender, but the others rescued him before pelting the officer with stones. He swung his rattle to call for assistance and his colleagues responded. The offenders were all arrested but not before PC Laird had some teeth knocked out by a stone. The Watch Committee suggested that, for their *'good conduct'*, the policemen be paid a reward of 2/6d (12$^{1}/_{2}$p) each, except for PC Laird who should get ten shillings (50p) because he was injured. The Mayor's, and an Alderman's, proposal that the rewards should be doubled was carried. A few days later, at the beginning of October, an altercation between locals and soldiers in a beer shop, again in Bridge Street, caused quite a stir. After some offensive remarks were passed about the military, the soldiers left the premises, but they returned later when one of them struck a blow. The whole congregation rose to the occasion. Chairs, tables, coal tongs and pokers were used as weapons in the melee that ensued and *'blood flowed in all directions. The family living in the house had to flee to safety.'* The fighting spilled into the street, just as Constable Nixson was passing by. He was asked to interfere, but realising that, alone, he would be unable to put a stop to the fighting, he went off to the Castle and called out the guard. The offenders were arrested and the crowd was dispersed. I can categorically state that one hundred and twenty years later, Caldewgate had improved little, but the city police had to manage without the military!

Whilst drunkenness was without doubt a contributory factor in most crimes of the day, drunkenness amongst policemen also remained at an embarrassing level during Mr. Brown's time in charge of the Force. In fact, it was a common problem in all early police forces. A discreditable incident occurred in the city in February, 1839 when two constables, Joseph Dixon and John Conley entered the Victoria Steam Packet public house at Irishgate Brow and called for liquor. After sitting drinking for some time, they demanded bread and cheese from the landlady. At first they were refused, but as they were both drunk and threatening, and to prevent further trouble, they were given the food. Having eaten their fill, they then began to waste the remainder by cutting it into pieces. They then assaulted two soldiers whom the landlady had called to her assistance. Both officers were taken before the Magistrates and discharged from the force.

One could be forgiven for thinking that all police business revolved around drinking, in one form or another, but other matters required attention, too. For example, road accidents, such as that when Bridget McNarney, a 46 years old weaver, was run over in Botchergate by the London to Glasgow mail in July1839. The coachman saw her carrying a sack of coal on her head, and when the coach was almost upon her, she began to cross the road. He called out to her and the guard blew his horn, but she hurried into the path of the horses. The wheels of the coach passed over the unfortunate woman's neck. Her husband, on his way to meet her and to carry the coals, arrived at the scene just as she died. The City Coroner recorded a verdict of *'accidental death'* at an inquest. The passengers presented the husband with some silver and the coachmen promised to set up a fund amongst coachmen and guards which, he said, should realise a *'liberal sum.'*

The Chief resigns

Mr. Brown resigned his appointment and left the Force on 16 October, 1839 to take over as licensee of an inn in Botchergate (where he could probably be his own boss and have much less hassle). He had not, however, heard the last of his Watch Committee.

On 24 October, 1839, the Committee wrote to Wigton Magistrates who, bearing in mind that there was no county police force until several years later, engaged a police establishment of sorts in that town. It appears that Thomas Hodgson, a Wigton officer, arrived in Carlisle in the course of an investigation into a robbery at Kirkbampton, and that instead of going to the police office to conduct his business, he went instead to Mr. Brown's pub (perhaps he thought he might get better service!). He gave certain information to the former city chief, who, of course, no longer had authority to act as a police officer. One would have thought that Mr. Brown would have had the good sense and courtesy to pass on that information to his former colleagues, but he did not. He went out himself, arrested and charged the two suspects with the robbery, then took them to the city police office, the first intimation Carlisle police had of the crime. The Watch Committee was infuriated and arranged to meet with the magistrates to complain of the improper conduct of Mr. Brown in withholding the information and acting upon it himself.

On 23 January, 1840, three months after Mr. Brown quit, the Committee discovered that certain items from the police establishment's inventory together with articles that officers had brought into the station had gone missing. Mr. Brown was asked for an explanation and must have admitted responsibility. He was probably fortunate to be required simply to make good the deficiencies.

INEXPLICABLE

'AND *although* THE POLICE HAVE BEEN MOST ACTIVE IN THEIR SEARCH, THE MISCREANT IS STILL AT LARGE' (*Daily Paper*).

[*Judy,* JUNE 17 1868].

On 7 January 1913, The 'Carlisle Journal's' *'50 years ago today '* column described life in the town in 1863 in the following terms -

'The streets of Carlisle were no credit to the city as a certain class of woman swaggered along them bare-headed and bare-armed in mid-afternoon, nodding and winking to all and sundry.
The policemen were fat and lazy [unkind and untrue!] and the Standing Order of the Force was a pint.

A few odds and ends from Chief Brown's days

1831

Apr 14 – Watch Committee instructed that the lock-ups be white-washed and the ringbolts therein be altered so as to remove the danger of any prisoner hurting himself by falling upon them. (Could this be the 'turnkey's – the new chief's previous occupation -influence?).

May 5 – Special constables to be paid 2 shillings (10p) a day for duty at elections.

Jun 2 – A Committee of five Commissioners would be chosen annually in June to superintend all affairs relating to the fire engines, and the Superintendent would have the custody and control of them when taken out to fires. The Day-men would look after the *Director*, pipes and 8 Watchmen would be placed at the Superintendent's disposal for fire-fighting purposes – any further assistance to be obtained from active bystanders, who would be given a ticket by the Superintendent to enable them to receive the like remuneration as the regular Force. Any day-time fires to be attended by the whole of the police establishment. Off-duty officers to be called out to assist, and as an encouragement to promptness, the first to arrive will receive 2/6d (12fip). Each man to be paid 6d (2 fip) an hour whilst engaged on fire duties. Each man shall have marked over his dwelling the word 'FIREMAN'.

Jul 7 – 2 new staves, cost 2/6d (12fip) to be obtained for the Day-men and the two old ones painted.

Oct 13 – Insane persons apprehended not to be taken into the police office but instead handed over to the Overseer of the Poor of the township wherein apprehended.

Oct 27 – Bishop of Carlisle planned to consecrate the new church in Caldewgate but Commissioners of Police 'unanimously of the opinion that they cannot guarantee the preservation of the public peace in the event of his Lordship proceeding to do so.'

Nov 24 – County Rates of 1/8d (9p) on the Police Office paid.

1832

Mar 22 – Day-man James Armstrong allowed £1 as a reward for his good conduct and as remuneration for the loss of his hat when taking a woman into custody on Sunday last.

Apr 26 – County Rates of 2/6d (12fip) together with 33/- (£1.65p) house and window duty for the Police Office paid.

Jun 7 – Half-year rent of the Police Office £19.17s.7d. (£19.88p) less the landlord's share of the county rate, approved for payment.

1833

Oct 10 – Dr. Heysham requested to dispose of all cases requiring a single Magistrate, and Mayor Mounsey to act with him in cases requiring two. Mr. Willoughby (Watch Committee Clerk) to be Clerk to Dr. Heysham for all business done as a Magistrate at the police office. (All 3 were members of the Police Committee – therefore a City Police Court).

Oct 31 – William Hetherington of Barwise Court, Tailor, contracted to make the Watchmen's coats at 31 shillings (£1.55p) each and 3 Day-men's coats at 40/- (£2).

Dec 19 – Every 3 years, watchmen may retain their old coats, provided they have had them for at least 3 months.

1834

Feb 20 – Watchman Richard Hornsby discharged for suffering a prisoner to escape from the police office, and for taking some laths from Mr. Gates' yard when on duty.

Mar 6 – Hornsby re-instated whilst James Nicholson demoted to supernumerary, he having given prevaricating evidence against Hornsby before the Commissioners.

May 8 – Hornsby sacked for not calling out the time at 3.30am, and being absent from his beat at 4am this date.

May 15 – Officers not to serve summonses beyond the city limits without the Inspector's permission.

Aug 28 – Watchman John Rigg discharged for not calling out the time at 3am on the 24th, and for losing his lamp, wick and leaden ticket.

1835

Jan 29 – George Rowell contracted for lettering the streets and numbering the houses that still remain undone.

Mar 5 – Watch Committee instructed the Superintendent to call upon the Magistrates to demand one half of the penalty awarded against Isaac Brough, the information having come from the police. All informations supported by the evidence of a police officer to be laid by the Clerk to the Police Commissioners in future. One week later Mr. Brown reported back that the Magistrates had replied that if the Commissioners wanted any explanations as to disposal of penalties, they should apply themselves. (Still, it seems, 8 years after the formation of the city police, animosity existed between the Magistrates and the Commissioners).

1836

Jan 1 – Municipal Corporations Act, 1835 came into force.

Jan 5 – County Sessions, (1) Isaac Thompson 'transported' for 7 years for theft of a watch (2) Thomas Mitchell of Whitehaven, suffered a similar fate for stealing a blanket valued at one shilling (3) William Millar, James Millar and Thomas Hartley, 3 children aged not more than 12 or 14 years, sentenced to 3 months imprisonment with hard labour for theft of potatoes in Caldewgate.

Feb 11 – (1) 4 woodrakes, 2 iron gripes, 1 spade, coal rakes and besoms to be obtained by Supt. Brown for the scavengers.

Feb 15 – (1) Watch Committee employed Thomas Mulcaster of Stanwix to remove the street manure for the ensuing month and to be paid 4 shillings each day (more than policemen!).

Mar 10 – Approval given to Mr. Brown's recommendation that the lock-ups be better ventilated by tunnels.

Mar 24 – Joseph Nixson, giving evidence in a murder trial at Carlisle Assizes, "I am a constable and overseer of the poor of Caldewgate Quarter." 'Overseer of the Poor' was an office established under the Poor Law Act, 1572 – it lasted until 1929.
A churchwarden and the constable had to collect a compulsory rate for the relief of poverty and distribute it as necessary. Each parish was responsible for its own paupers.

Apr 14 – Day-man Thomas Russell died suddenly, aged 34 years – first reported death of a serving officer of the city police force.

Apr 21 – One day-man ordered to reside in Caldewgate (who drew the short straw?).

Apr 28 – Day-officers to carry long painted staves when on duty patrolling (origin of the city sergeants' night-sticks?).

May 12 – Supt. Brown instructed by the Watch Committee to obtain some broom for making besoms for the scavengers.

Jul 13 – 100 men to be appointed special constables to attend the opening of the railway.

Jul 21 – Thomas Scott, a scavenger, suspended (without pay) till next Wednesday for taking Mr. Sewell into custody without sufficient cause.

Aug 18 – Two supernumeraries appointed constables on the railway.

Aug 31 – Supt. authorised to buy waterproof (oilcloth) capes.

Oct 13 – Inspectors to ensure that the racecourse is policed. – PC John Bird rewarded £3 and PC William Slee £1 for their general police activity.

Dec 22 - Messrs Black and Briggs to fit a closet in the office, having offered to do it for 12 shillings.

1837
Feb 20 – Four constables reprimanded for failing to summons Isaac Tweddle of Haltwhistle for leaving his cart in Crosby Street during the last two days and nights.

Apr 13 – Governor of Carlisle Gaol to be allowed such number of constables as necessary to assist him in guarding prisoners, he paying coach hire or travelling expenses if he sends them away from the city.

Jun 15 – 'Whenever any night-patrol shall be asked for his number, he shall immediately give it' – Watch Committee.

Nov 23 – No officer to communicate with any attorney relative to persons in custody, unless directed by the examining magistrates or at the request of the prisoner, on pain of dismissal.

1838
Mar 15 – Day Officer William Slee suspended for one month for allowing a prisoner to escape, unless he shall sooner retake the prisoner when in such case his suspension will expire.

Mar 22 – Instruction from Watch Committee – The day-patrol are to wash out the office alternately, once a week, and each day patrol must wash out his night-soil pail every morning.

May 3 – Three officers, Hetherington, Hayton and Foster allowed three shillings for their drinking expenses whilst at Cockermouth.

May 24 – a new watch-coat to be obtained in place of one accidentally burned by Robert Harper. Harper to be charged ten shillings for the damage, to be deducted from his wages at sixpence a week.

Aug 30 – Supt. Brown to be allowed to have a gas-light in his parlour.

Nov 17 – Newspaper report on inquest into the death of John Graham, a scavenger, who fell down dead in Blackfriars Street – natural causes. The bill of 3/11d for expenses at his funeral to be paid by the Watch Committee.

Nov 29 – from Watch Committee – (1) When it can be proved that any officer hath observed another officer neglect any part of his duty or make any breach of his orders or instructions, and does not report same to the Night-constable or Superintendent, he shall be liable to be punished as well as the man who makes such neglect. (2) 500 copies of a Bye-law providing a penalty to persons who shall offer or give any treat to an officer when on duty, to be printed and distributed in the city.

1839
May 11 –Night-constable John Bird permitted to resign to enable him to take up the post of Chief Constable of Barnard Castle, County Durham.

West Walls Police Headquarters, the city's first purpose-built station was opened early in 1841.
There is no official record of the precise date nor any press announcements.
The building served the Force for one hundred years. One city Councillor said, in the planning stages of the building, "Police lock-ups are not any credit to a town" - perhaps his words were taken to heart.

Top: The police headquarters taken circa 1965 when they were occupied by the Justices Clerk's department.

Left: taken in January 2001. The buildings have now been demolished and the site is part of Town Dyke Orchard municipal car park. The former Dean and Chapter School, used by the Force to supplement its cramped accommodation, is on the right.

John Graham, Superintendant (Chief Officer)
17 October 1839 to 26 September 1844.

John Graham (a good Cumbrian name) was appointed Superintendent and Chief Officer on 17 October 1839, just three months after joining the Force, thus becoming the first officer, and only one of two in its history, to reach the top post from within. He had moved to Carlisle from Liverpool City Police on 5 July 1839, taking up the position of Night Constable and Deputy to Chief Officer Robert Brown. He had previously served in the Metropolitan Police. Though it is purely conjecture, it may be that he had also served and was well known to the Watch Committee in Carlisle. One John Graham was one of the first constables appointed to the city force upon its formation in 1827.

Within five months of his appointment, in a move that was surely popular with his Watch Committee, Mr. Graham recommended a reduction in the size of the Force from 23 to 15, plus three supernumerary officers to be employed as scavengers who would be readily available to step into vacancies that might occur. He told the Committee about new policing methods he had put into effect. No officers, night or day, remained in static positions – a simple remedy to overcome the problem of crimes being committed outwith the sight of the static constables. All were constantly in motion except when at their stands, or, in other words, 'making their points'. He advised the Watch Committee that he was in favour of amalgamating the day and night patrols in line with a system he was accustomed to in Liverpool. Fixed beats would ensure that every part of the city was examined and supervisors *'could tell at any time where to fall in with the men, and if they were not where they should be they would have to give proper account.'* The Committee asked the Chief to report if any officer currently on the establishment was qualified to succeed him as Night Constable. His written, somewhat flowery, response stated, *'Relative to a man being appointed Constable of the Night, I humbly suggest that if promotion should be from among the members of the Force it might be attended with good effects, insomuch as it holds out a prospect for the men that, by a continuance in a proper line of* *conduct, promotion sooner or later will follow, and by exciting a degree of emulation amongst them it would stimulate those who were anxious for promotion to further effects in order to obtain when the opportunity offered.'* He strongly recommended that John Glaister and Joseph Haugh be promoted when a vacancy arose.*

On 24 December 1839, *(as a Christmas present?)*, the Watch Committee imposed on the Force, a scale of punishments for disciplinary offences, to be enforced by the Superintendent:

* *   For a first offence, a fine of 2/6d (12fip);
* *   6 second offence, a fine of 2/6d if the character of the constable is good - if not, to be referred to the Watch Committee;
* *   third offence, a fine of five shillings (25p) and cautioned if character good, but, if not, to be referred to the Watch Committee;
* *   Whatever the character, for a fourth offence, the matter to be put before the Watch Committee;
* *   Late for duty, dirty on parade or at Court, loitering when on duty, gossiping or quarrelling with one another would attract a fine of one shilling for a first offence, two shillings for a second and two shillings and a referral to the Watch Committee for a third.

An officer could be fined half a crown(12fip) if found asleep on duty or absent from his beat for any time and unable to account for it or for being in a public house during working hours except when called upon to perform a duty. Any subsequent similar offence had to be referred to Watch Committee for punishment.

oooOooo

A parliamentary election took place on Tuesday, 29 June 1841 and, as the day approached, the military had to be called out from the Castle several times to suppress instances of public disorder. The windows of the Town Hall and of several houses in the city centre had been broken and, recorded a local newspaper, *'some of our worthy lieges, in addition to being well-bespattered by mud and other filth, have been stoned.'* Sergeant Edward Goulborn, a lawyer and a national figure of the day, was in town as a candidate for one of the city's seats. With a number of other politicians he was attacked whilst canvassing in Caldewgate. His group had to seek refuge in the Minerva public house and had to be rescued by the military. Shades of the 1826 outrage must have occupied the minds of the civic authority and the police.

The Chartists**, a working class movement campaigning for parliamentary changes, were in town canvassing support. In many parts of the country, their activities had caused outbreaks of serious disorder. Millions, sympathising with their aims, had signed their petitions. Many of their number favoured a campaign of civil disobedience, even violence. In Newport, South Wales, a brutal confrontation with the authorities, including an exchange of gunfire, resulted in seventy casualties including twenty dead. In Carlisle, on the afternoon of Thursday, 24 June, large numbers gathered at the Market Cross to listen to the Chartists canvassing speeches and *'mischievous and riotous feelings were displayed.'* So much so that the Magistrates, being fearful of serious disorder, issued a proclamation:

"In consequence of various acts of violence and outrage, both upon persons and property, having taken place yesterday evening, 24 June 1841, by an assemblage of persons in the Market Place, notice is hereby given that no persons will be allowed to assemble together in the Market Place or streets of the Borough, and all persons persisting in so assembling and obstructing the free passage of the streets will be apprehended by the police. And it is particularly recommended to all persons to prevent their children and apprentices from being out at a late hour in the evening."

Dated this 25th day of June, 1841
Joseph Atkinson, Clerk.

---

* *Both were subsequently promoted to sergeant.*
** *A popular movement for electoral reform 1837 -1848, whose manifesto was named 'The Peoples' Charter'.*

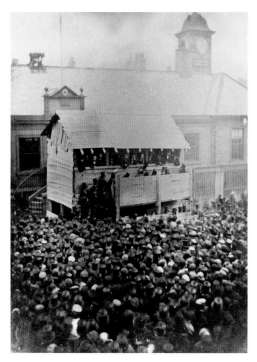

A typical Town Hall hustings scene 1857.

Many citizens defied the order and, given their numbers and the *'thin blue line'* available to oppose them, it was unenforceable. On the eve of the election, excitement and tension in the population were at fever-pitch and in all parts of the town there were scenes of *'disgraceful intoxication.'* Such was the apprehension of the Mayor, magistrates and the police that the playing of music and displaying of banners were banned to prevent further inciting the citizens. A large meeting of the working classes, who were excluded from the vote, took place on the Sands. The speakers pleaded that, throughout the election proceedings, everyone should have strict regard to peace, law and order. Such timely warnings were sadly to be in vain. Chief Officer Graham, reporting for duty on 29 June 1841, surely had every reason to anticipate disturbances during the poll having regard not just to the recent turmoil but also to the reputation of the population at election times, but he could never have imagined the horrific occurrence he was about to witness – every policeman's worst night-mare, the killing of a fellow officer.

Glovers Row and the Market Cross 1897.

Murder of Constable Thomas Jardine

On that fateful day, the Superintendent took seven of his officers to the front of the Town Hall. Shortly before ten o'clock the candidates and local officials took up their places in the hustings. Over 4,000 people had gathered to hear them and, as was to be expected, the crowd cheered and heckled during the speeches. Afterwards, sometime between half past one and two o'clock, the candidates made their ways to their various hotels.

As the city's two sitting members, Messrs. Howard and Marshall, pushed their way through the crowds towards the Coffee House, (the Crown and Mitre Hotel), the mood of the people turned nasty. Several were struck with bludgeons, including Mr. Howard himself. Mr. Graham, and his men took up positions in front of the hotel to prevent unauthorised access. After the Members had entered the building, the crowd, groaning and hissing, turned on the police and began hurling missiles at them. The Carlisle Patriot reported, *'As has been the case in Carlisle throughout this election, the police very speedily became the objects of popular sport.'* Chief Graham, anticipating even more violence, ordered his officers to draw their staves and to clear the mob from Green Market. There was a rush backwards and blows were exchanged as the unruly elements were dispersed leaving Green Market almost cleared. Subsequently, the press and several witnesses were to claim that the police actions were fully justified, they being

A busy Greenmarket c1870.

obliged to strike out in self defence. The task to clear the immediate area was quickly accomplished but the crowds still hung around the area. One of the policeman, 40-year old Constable Thomas Jardine, was standing quietly, off-guard in the cleared Green Market when a man emerged from the crowd and made to cross the square. As he passed the unsuspecting officer, he struck him a tremendous blow on the head with what was later described by witnesses as a *'life-preserver'*. It was quite the opposite when used in these circumstances. The assailant ran into the crowd and escaped. Constable Jardine immediately dropped to the ground, pole-axed. As he began to recover and slowly raise himself to his knees, a second man ran over struck him a severe blow across the front of his head with a stick. He too ran off into the crowd and quit the scene. Though the two men were out of reach of the police officers present, all of them witnessed the attacks. No attempt was made by anyone in the crowd to stop or apprehend the two men. The injured officer was carried into the Coffee House where he was seen by a doctor before being taken to his home in Union Street*, off Botchergate. (No hospital intensive care facilities in those days!!). PC Jardine died at two o'clock next morning, Wednesday, 30 June 1841.

On Thursday, 1 July, an inquest was held before Mr. Carrick, HM Coroner for the city. The jury returned a verdict of *'wilful murder'*. The Patriot recorded, *'What is most extraordinary, the ruffians were suffered to escape by the crowd of onlookers – the crowd connived at the escape.'* It went on, *'The event has occasioned a great sensation in the town and it was a matter of universal surprise that so many Englishmen should have tamely witnessed so brutal an assault, ending in a homicide, in the middle of the day without either attempting to prevent even the second blow or to secure the murderers.'*

The police force comprised just twenty-one officers in 1841, and on the day of the election only seven were on duty in the city centre. Notwithstanding all the indications of the likelihood of disorder, no supplementary force, eg special constables or military, had been deployed to support them. It had previously been customary for the magistrates to swear-in sufficient numbers of Specials to keep the Peace on such occasions but, by 1841, the magistrates had no jurisdiction over operational policing matters. On the day of Constable Jardine's killing, the police contingent at the Town Hall found itself simply overwhelmed by the size of the crowd. If they had wished to do so, and supposing that the whole force of twenty-one had been available, the officers were powerless to enforce the magistrates' edict to prevent assembly. It would have been foolhardy to try.

Following the poll, during the Tuesday afternoon and evening, whilst Constable Jardine was fighting for his life, it was said that *'the beer barrel and spirit tap flowed more freely than ever and people in the most beastly state of intoxication were all over the town.'* A member of the Watch Committee ordered the police to take action against some rowdy youths in English Street whereupon twelve or fourteen officers did so and *'flourished their batons with great emphasis over the heads of some half dozen little boys,'* reported the Patriot. Witnessing this, an agitated crowd of some three hundred men, women and children reacted by throwing missiles at the police and then smashing every single ground floor window along the front of the Coffee House. Riotous mobs forced the police to flee the streets and take refuge in the police station. The Mayor and a number of Magistrates re-assembled and called upon the military to put down the disorder. The soldiers marched into Castle Street and the city centre where they were joined by police officers. Speaking from the front of the Coffee House, the Mayor read the Riot Act, ordering the crowds to immediately disperse, but by then, the excitement had subsided and the troubles were all but over.

Constable Jardine's attackers were quickly identified and two men were arrested on Wednesday, 30 June. They were John Kirkpatrick, 21 years old, the person who struck the first, and what proved to be the fatal, blow and James Jackson aged twenty. Kirkpatrick was charged with the wilful murder of PC Jardine, Jackson with aiding and abetting the murder. Several others were arrested and charged with offences connected to the rioting. All were committed to stand trial at Cumberland Assizes.

The funeral of Constable Jardine took place on 4 July 1841 and was attended by Superintendent Graham and other officers. Funds collected for the widow and children of the officer amounted to £40.9s.4d (£40.47p) from which Mrs. Jardine was able to start a small business as a milliner.

The trial of the accused was set for first week of August 1841. The Lord Chief Justice of England, Lord Justice Denham, presided over the Assizes in the Crown Court. Before the trial commenced, he addressed the Grand Jury, during the course of which he said:

---

* *Since re-named Rydal Street.*

"Half of the crimes in the calendar were committed during the recent General Election, an occasion when all persons ought to act with great forebearance and exert themselves to prevent the committal of crimes. It was painful to find that when a large body of men assembled for the purpose of exercising one of the most important privileges granted by our constitution, instead of proceeding with decency and calmness and respect for the public peace, they banded together for disturbance, for acts of intimidation and violence. It was necessary that the law should be declared distinctly on the subject. It was but right that those engaged in the affairs of the law, the humblest man in the exercise of his duty in the protection of his fellow subjects, had as much right to its protection as he who came in all the pomp and circumstance which attached to high office. It was not to be endured that those who had exerted themselves for the preservation of the lives of their fellow subjects should be exposed to the attacks of anyone without receiving the full amount of the protection that the law allowed."

From the depositions before him, the Lord Chief Justice said he had strong reason to suspect that the life of a police officer, who was employed in preserving the peace of this city, had been sacrificed by an attack of the description to which he had alluded. It was for the jury to inquire whether the attack had been made by an individual with malicious intention ….

"for if a man inflicted a wound which was likely to be followed by death, and which did produce death, that man was clearly guilty of murder. Nothing could be more proper or necessary than for the police to be endeavouring to protect individuals from violence. This, however, was certain; that if such proceedings were tolerated on such occasions, every day of an election would be a day of civil war and, instead of peace and quietness, we might look for nothing but massacres and disturbances."

With these few remarks, he said, he would leave the cases entirely in the jury's hands. As one would expect from the Lord Chief Justice of England, this was a clear and unambiguous statement of the law that should have left little doubt in the minds of the jurymen. All that remained was for the witnesses to come up to proof.

Superintendent Graham, the Chief Officer of the Force, was called. He said:
"There was a riot and I ordered the Square to be cleared, which it was. One of the officers was killed. I saw him on the ground, and while he was there I saw Jackson strike him on the head with a stick which he appeared to have hold of with both hands. The officers were in uniform. Jardine was in uniform. I saw him struck on the head. He had his hat on when Jackson struck him."

Cross-examined, Mr. Graham replied,
"I had no orders from the Magistrates but a general order to keep the Peace. I don't think it would have been better if the police had not been there. The Coffee House might have been destroyed. I told the men not to strike unnecessarily, and I gave no order expressly to strike. As soon as the mob saw the staves drawn they fell back in about two minutes. Jardine was a strong, able man. He was no further ahead than the other constables at first. The last time I saw him he was about thirty yards from the Coffee House door. I think that when we were assaulted we had a right to strike to defend ourselves. As the Square was being cleared blows were struck on both sides. Our staves are made for the protection of the police. They are handy but not dangerous weapons. I saw Jackson strike Jardine, who was on his hands and knees. He struck him with considerable force. Jardine might have been recovering himself when he received the second blow. I do not believe the people struck us for the purpose of warding off blows or defending themselves. Whilst we were going to the Coffee House a stone was thrown which struck Jardine on the head."

John Hamilton, a clerk, of West Tower Street, saw sticks and stones being thrown at the police. He knew Kirkpatrick. They had worked for the same employer. He saw him advance on PC Jardine and strike a blow to his head with an instrument about sixteen inches long. The officer dropped to the ground. As he attempted to get up another man came and struck out at him. He missed his aim but came back and struck him on the head Mr. Hamilton said he saw the policeman striking about but he did not see anyone in the crowd hit.

PC Jardine did not hit anyone, he said. Cross-examined, he did not agree with the suggestion that the police should not have been there. *"I do not think they excited the people. The conduct of the police was necessary for their protection."* Questioned by the Judge, Mr. Hamilton said, *"They (the police) defended the hotel. If they had not it would have been a wreck. Sticks and stones were thrown and it appeared to me that the police were quite right to draw up and defend themselves."*

Next witness was a Joseph Little who said that he knew both the policeman, Jardine, and Kirkpatrick. He said that he saw Kirkpatrick come from the direction of Castle Street and saw PC Jardine *"striking right and left as no man in his sense would. He struck with his constable's cudgel and with all the strength he could."* There was no corroboration of Little's testimony and his account was somewhat discredited when he admitted that he, himself, had been arrested at the scene for misconduct. There was, in fact, no complaint and no evidence from any source of any injury caused by the police action.

A number of witnesses described Kirkpatrick's weapon. It was said that such weapons were available in local shops as *'life preservers'* or *'night protectors'*, being some 12 to 14 inches long, made of whalebone with a ball of lead at each end and a string or strap to fasten around the wrist for a secure grip. These same witnesses testified that they had seen the accused strike the policemen. They had each seen the police with drawn staves, but none had witnessed the police strike anyone.

Thomas Elliott, a surgeon, said that he was called to the Coffee House where he saw Constable Jardine, pale, faint and bleeding from a wound on the back of his head. He had a second wound above his ear. Neither appeared to be life threatening. Just before 10pm, he had visited Jardine's home, when he saw that his condition had substantially deteriorated. He performed an operation on the injured man, but he died. He later carried out a post-mortem examination and found evidence of extensive internal bleeding around the brain. He died from an injury above his ear. A *'life preserver'*, a stone or a stick, or a fall against a convex surface would, in his opinion, have produced such an injury. The deceased, he said, was a big, strong, muscular man. It would need great force to produce such a wound from a fall. This one single wound, however, had caused death. The Court was told that that wound was inflicted by Kirkpatrick. At that point, defence counsel, suggested, having regard to the surgeon's evidence, that perhaps Jackson should not be included in the indictment, Kirkpatrick alone having caused the officer's death. The Judge thought otherwise.

The defence barrister, in what appears to have been a rather distorted version of the events, told the jury that he considered that the placing of policemen in front of the hotel was ill-advised and provocative. *"Instead of arriving with a body of police in battle array, the commandant should have taken his men into the crowd and reasoned with them."* In his opinion, the police had exceeded their duty, and *"they must have known that that their presence on such an occasion had the tendency to excite the multitude."* This, of course, disregarded the fact that it was the duty of the police to preserve the peace and that there was clear evidence that the officers, far from over-reacting, had merely been escorting two Members of Parliament through a hostile crowd to the safety of a nearby hotel, afterwards providing protection to the building, when they were set upon by the mob. If the police had abrogated their peace-keeping responsibilities in such circumstances there would, quite rightly, have been condemnation. Imagine the headlines if, instead of a policeman being killed, the two MPs had been killed or harmed, if several of the crowd had died or if the hotel had been destroyed. Here were police officers doing their job and being blamed for the outrage. That's defence counsel for you!!! The barrister then urged the jury to believe that *"Kirkpatrick and Jackson had not the least malice towards PC Jardine."* Really, was the blow to the officer's head just a token of their friendship? Where do these barristers come from?

The Lord Chief Justice, in his summing up, told the jury, *"Law officers must be protected in the execution of their duty, for if everyone against whom they may be called upon to act is allowed to be judge of the propriety or impropriety of their conduct so acting, and to resist the law accordingly, if this were allowed no law officer would be safe for a moment."* He pointed out that the police had no more authority than they, the jury, but that *"they were bound to respond to breaches of the peace. Of course, any violence by them would be lawful."* He said that it may have been advisable for the police chief to have warned the crowd before advancing on them, and that if the jury considered that the crowd had been taken by surprise and had reacted as they did, so negating intent, it would be manslaughter. If they thought that Kirkpatrick had deliberate intent to cause injury, then that was murder. Jackson would only share his guilt in a case of murder.

The Jury found Kirkpatrick guilty of manslaughter and acquitted Jackson. The prosecution had produced no evidence to show that the two accused had been acting in concert and none to show that they were acting on behalf of a riotous mob. To those ends it would be proper to treat each case separately. But there was ample evidence, surely, to show that each had criminal intent to do injury to PC Jardine, and they had done so. How else could their actions be interpreted? No reasonable person could strike another *'a tremendous blow over the head'* with a weapon made specifically to harm, even if in self defence, without realising that some serious injury would result. Neither accused could, with any justification, claim provocation by the police, as seems to have been implied by the defence counsel, since there had been a *'cooling off'* period, however short a time, between the police charge and the attack on PC Jardine. The police, whilst still maintaining a presence, had stood down and there was much daylight between the police and the mob. Neither of the two accused claimed to have been provoked by the police. Each was in possession of offensive weapons, hardly appropriate to the event taking place in the city centre. It beggars belief that the jury thought there was no intent to cause serious physical injury, even if death was not the aim of the attackers. However, proof of intent to injure would have been sufficient to convict of murder and that would have meant death sentences on the accused. Did that influence the jury? On the clearest of evidence, Kirkpatrick ought to have been so convicted, especially as the medical evidence attributed the blow he struck as the cause of death. For Jackson to walk free is beyond comprehension. At the very least he should have been found guilty of assault, committed in circumstances that merited severe punishment. It is difficult to think of a more perverse verdict. The Coldbath Fields killing of Constable Culley in Clerkenwell, London, in 1833, just a few years before PC Jardine's killing, springs to mind. PC Culley, one of a group of heavily outnumbered police officers, was stabbed to death policing mob violence. The jury, at the subsequent inquest, outrageously returned a verdict of *'justifiable homicide'*. Such was public opposition to an organised police at that time. That verdict was later set aside by a higher court.

Back to the Carlisle case; there was feeling throughout the city that the jury had reached the verdict they did so as to preserve the life of the co-accused Jackson. Each of the accused men could consider themselves extremely lucky they met such a lenient jury. The Lord Chief Justice would appear to have had views very different from those of the jury. As if his initial address to the them was not an indication as to how he felt about the case, in passing sentence on Kirkpatrick, he said:

> *"The jury have taken the most charitable view of the case. They have saved me from the painful necessity of passing judgement of death upon you which would, most undoubtedly, have been carried into effect. It is absolutely necessary that examples should be set to lawless and savage men, and they should not be able to take advantage of any accidental excitement of a canvass or an election. I think it right that an example should be made effective in your person. I have suspicion that something more than what has been found by the jury has been working in your mind, because I find at the time when Jardine was standing and doing nothing to you, or to anybody in whom you took an interest, you came up behind him and struck the fatal blow, and I am quite justified in saying that if the jury had taken the darker view of the case, your life must be forfeited. The punishment must be severe. You will be transported across the seas to such of Her Majesty's colonies as Her Majesty, with the advice of her Privy Council, may think fit, for the term of fifteen years."*

In his final address, his Lordship said:

"It is quite clear an election is merely the pretext, the name, the opportunity and not the cause of the proceedings for, at elections, all the rabble of the town come forward and wreak their vengeance on those who have given, or are supposed to have given, offence. The police are generally the first to be attacked. They are exposed to danger in the execution of their duty and have, in all probability, incurred the hatred of all the bad characters of the town by performing their duties strictly and lawfully. I sincerely hope that this

warning will have an effect on future occasions, and that those who have been most excited, most violent and who have shown the most ill-feeling towards individuals at a time of riots, will feel hurt and distressed by the sad event which has taken place at this election, hardly paralleled in any other contests throughout our country – the death of a poor man in the course of the violence of that occasion."

oooOooo

Chief Graham tendered his resignation in March, 1843, but such was the regard in which he was held that the Watch Committee unanimously pleaded in the following terms that he withdraw: *'The Watch Committee approve of his conduct during the time he has been in the situation of Superintendent of Police and that he be requested to continue his services.'*
The Committee, at the same time, instructed the clerk to write to a Mr. R. Brown informing him that Mr. Graham remained in office. How did this person know that the Chief intended to resign and was this the same R. [Robert] Brown who had previously commanded the Force attempting to make a come-back?

Early in 1843, the Watch Committee suggested that a constable should remain constantly in the police office overnight and sought Mr. Graham's observations. The proposal got short shrift – *'though in some instances it might be a service, still the advantages that might be derived from the adoption of such a measure would not counterbalance the additional expenses which would be entailed, more particularly as I am always to be found in the office till 12 o'clock at night and the night constable (deputy chief) visits it occasionally from that time till the men come in the morning.'* (Who said 'best value' policies in the police service were an idea of the 1990s?) I, at one time, worked with a chief constable – not in Carlisle - who used such flowery language as Mr. Graham, prompting a comparison with many politicians who *'speak a lot and say nowt.'*

On 23 May 1844, a complaint was received regarding the conduct of Thomas Hetherington, the Night Constable and Deputy Chief, and another officer Constable John Kent, (Britain's first black policeman), whilst they were in attendance at a fire at Naworth Castle* on Saturday, 18th May. A Sub-committee appointed by the Watch Committee to investigate the allegation reported that there was no evidence of misconduct though Hetherington was slightly under the influence of drink when he left Carlisle. They also discovered that earlier in the day he had been drinking in the company of a Sheriff's officer. The Committee were *'anxious to avoid any course calculated to impair his authority as Superintendent [+] of the Night Force'* and recommended that the matter be concluded by the officer being cautioned by the Mayor. The Force was still plagued by the problems of drink!

On 8 August, 1844, Mr. Graham again resigned his appointment, requesting that it take effect from 17 October. He wrote to the Watch Committee, *'I beg to say that I shall ever retain a most grateful recollection of the kindness I experienced whilst acting under your orders, and wishing you, collectively and individually, every happiness, I remain, John Graham.'* The Committee this time acceded to his wish.

Considering that John Graham held a senior position in the city it is surprising that so very little is known today about him. Police records relating to him are scant and there is barely a mention of him in local newspapers. No reason for his resignation is recorded and it is not known if he left to pursue his police career elsewhere. He may simply have retired but since records give no indication as to his age this cannot be confirmed. It is however doubtful. In the early days of the Force, the Watch Committee rarely considered an applicant over 40 years of age for the position of chief officer. That being the case, Mr. Graham would be no more than 45 years old when he left.

---

* *Naworth, of course, is situated several miles from the city, but note that until 1856 the Watch Committee had an agreement with the County Magistrates for the City Police to cover the Cumberland Ward area, of which Naworth was part.*

[+] *Note, the Committee were now using the title 'Night Superintendent' rather than 'Night Constable'.*

A few odds and ends from Chief Graham's days

1840

Jan 7 – 6.30am, serious fire at a shop in English Street. Most of the Force called out to assist. Helped by 31 men of the 7th Dragoon Guards from the castle. PC12 Ruddick and PC19 Smith disciplined for asking the shop owner for payment for helping him to rescue goods from the premises.

Jun 25 – Jane Cantwell, a single woman, summonsed for emptying her night-pot in the Market Place. How nice of her!

1841

Jul 24 – Carlisle Journal reports on the marriage of Sir Robert Peel's daughter - ceremony performed by the Bishop of Oxford assisted by the Dean of Carlisle, Dr. Hodgson.

Oct 7 – Resolved that the sovereign, received by Chief Graham and the day officers for attending meetings at the Athenium, be given to the subscription for the widow and children of PC Jardine.

Nov 8 – Funds collected for PC Jardine's widow and children amounted to £40.9s.4d.

Nov 11 – Watch Committee paid rent of Mrs. Jardine and gave her £3 for her own use from the fund.

1842

Jan 6 – Mrs. Jardine given £10.4s.0d. from the fund to enable her to start a small business as a milliner.

Feb 10 – Free medical assistance now available in the event of any officer being taken ill or injured on duty.

1844

Mar 21 – The windows at the north end of the police station secured with ironbars to prevent prisoner escapes.

Apr 4 – PC James Harrison reported for being drunk and fighting in Rickergate on Sunday morning.

Jul 4 – PC 16 Robert Kirkpatrick suspended for a fortnight having been caught twice in one day drunk and unfit for duty, at 3.30am [end of one tour of duty] and 10.30pm [start of the next tour].

Fraudsman

In January 1856 an incorrigible rogue with a cork leg, posing as a clergyman, Reverend Chapman, had fraudently obtained cash at various establishments in the city. Trying the trick again in the Coffee House (Crown and Mitre) the waiter became suspicious of him and called Mr Sabbage to the hotel. *"How do you do, Mr Thompson,"* said the Chief Constable upon meeting him. *"Thompson? Thompson? My name is Chapman"* said the man, indignantly. "Well" said Mr Sabbage, *"you must have changed it recently then. You were Thompson when you were locked up at the city police office a few weeks ago."* Thompson then admitted deceiving several victims with his trick, but strangely the police looked upon his misconduct as a civil debt and took no further action.

After Hours

18 January 1856 - James Stubbs, an innkeeper of Upperby, appeared before the City Magistrates charged with having his house open at 12 midnight on Saturday last. The police found several men inside drinking. The defendant told the court that: *"The frost had stopped the clock".*
"It didn't stop your taps." said the chairman, *"Fined five shillings."*

John Sabbage, Superintendent (Chief Officer)
27 September 1844 to 21 January 1857.

In common with many other provincial towns, Carlisle's Watch Committee looked to London to find their next chief officer. A letter to the Metropolitan Police Commissioners requested, *"We are in want of a Superintendent of Police…the Watch Committee would be obliged if you could recommend a person out of your Force competent to discharge the duties of such a situation. Salary is £78 [per annum], free house, coals and candles. A coat, trousers and a hat are supplied once a year. The Force consists of three day-officers, one night-constable, 15 night-watchmen and three supernumeraries."*

The Commissioners replied that they had chosen 27 year-old Sergeant Sabbage, 'A' Division, who was ready to leave for Carlisle as soon as the Committee desired. Mr. Sabbage arrived in the city early on 27 September, and immediately took up office upon presentation of papers, dated one day earlier, which stated:
'The Commissioners of Police of the Metropolis beg to acquaint you that the bearer, Sergeant Sabbage, is the person they have selected, at your request, to fill the situation of Superintendent of Police at Carlisle. He will leave town tomorrow, present this letter and report himself to you on arrival.'
C. Rowan.

P.S. It is usual for the parties applying for the officer to pay his travelling expenses.

If contemporary reports as to dates are to be believed, he arrived in Carlisle, having travelled 300 miles, on the same day that he left London. Surely impossible in 1844, maybe just possible in 2009!

Mr. Sabbage's travelling expenses amounted to £5.15s.0d for a one-way ticket to what was surely quite a culture shock to him. The city was a dreadful place. Even six years after his arrival, Carlisle Sanitary Authority felt *'bound to express their extreme regret that Carlisle should present so much filth and so many nuisances of the worst kind. Fever [cholera] has found numerous victims in Rickergate, and in Moffat's Yard there was only one privvy for twenty-eight families. Some had none at all. There are more than twenty to a room in some lodging houses, some adjacent to the filthiest privvies and dunghills.'* Dr. Murray, Professor of Chemistry at Edinburgh, reported that *'the common well water in Carlisle was scarcely fit to be used by the lowest class of animals. No water from the pumps is fit for drinking.'* However, Mr. Sabbage clearly was not deterred by what he found, for he remained Chief of the city police for twelve years.

A more pressing concern for the new Chief must have been his Deputy, Thomas Hetherington, the Night Constable, whose past conduct had set a poor example to his subordinates. He was in trouble again a fortnight after Mr. Sabbage's arrival. On this occasion he was admonished for making a ring for a fight to take place on the racecourse. A further two weeks on and he was found drinking in a public house at 1am, in response to which he was ordered either to leave the Force or change his lodgings. He opted for the latter, taking up residence in Annetwell Street. In a small city, how a change of lodgings would address the problem is a matter for conjecture. Hetherington's career as a policeman came to an end when, in March 1845, he was called upon to answer the allegations of a Mary Renwick and others, made in the Magistrates Court. He left the Force on 10 April following.

Other acts of indiscipline, particularly drunkenness, were commonplace and, clearly, could not be allowed to continue. Collaborating with a sub-group of the Watch Committee, Chief Sabbage lost no time in drawing up new rules and regulations for efficiency and good discipline They were approved by the full Committee on 21 November 1844 and adopted by the Force. At the same time, a scale of punishments for disciplinary offences was introduced and the Watch Committee added other instructions for the good governance of the Force (see Appendix 'H'). (One of the first to fall foul of the new rules was John Kent, the black policeman. Chief Sabbage dispensed with his services for offences of drunkenness). From the serious business of running a police force to the ridiculous - a sub-committee was then appointed to confer with the Superintendent as to the efficiency of the street sweepers! They were, after all, first in line for appointment to the constabulary!

oooOooo

One week after this meeting, on 27 November 1844, Mrs Peggy Graham, a farmer's wife, died at her home at Kirkandrews, a few miles beyond the city boundary. Her husband John was also violently sick. It seems no suspicions were aroused, for the poor woman was duly interred with no more ado. Six months later, in May 1845, John's father also died suddenly. Other family members had suffered sickness over a period of time, each time after taking food in the family home. Tongues began to wag in the village, poisoning was suspected and John's odd behaviour came under scrutiny. Though Kirkandrews lay outside of the city, Chief Sabbage was called upon to investigate the occurrences under an arrangement agreed between the county magistrates and the Watch Committee. Note that there was no county police force at this time and that Carlisle officers were sworn in as constables for the county of Cumberland in addition to their city jurisdiction. Poisoning was confirmed after a post mortem examination when traces of arsenic were found in the organs of the old man and in cakes in his home. The Coroner ordered the exhumation and examination of Peggy's body and once again traces of arsenic were found. John Graham was arrested, and though he denied any wrongdoing, he was charged the murders of his wife and father. Just before the trial began at the Assizes in Carlisle, Chief Sabbage seized the accused's clothing from the farmhouse and had it forensically examined. Traces of arsenic were found in the pockets. Despite much suspicion and some circumstantial evidence the accused was cleared of the charges by the jury. Was the investigation thoroughly and competently prosecuted by the police? Perhaps not, but more than six months had passed before Peggy's murder had been reported, ample time for the killer to cover his tracks. Had John's clothing containing the traces of arsenic been seized earlier and had he then been asked to explain it, positive evidence may have been forthcoming. But, before Mr. Sabbage took possession of the clothing, others had had access to it over a period of weeks, a point fastened upon by John's defence counsel. Sufficient doubt as to who had put the poison in the pockets was created. The trial judge agreed and John Graham was acquitted on both charges. The Chief had not long arrived from London with a sound background of policing in the capital, but did he have experience of murder investigations?

In November 1849, Mr. Sabbage was again called to a murder scene in the wilds of Cumberland, this time to Bewcastle, some 25 miles from the city. Here the body of a local gamekeeper had been found two days after he had been reported missing. The body bore marks of violence and the scene showed signs of a scuffle and a number of footprints in the soft earth. Three suspects came to the fore, including 24 years old Andrew Turnbull, a local man. Questioned by the Chief, Turnbull confessed to being present at the killing but denied participation. He named two brothers, Nicol and Joseph Hogg as the killers. The three men were arrested and charged with murder, though the Hoggs vehemently denied the allegation. They were detained in Carlisle Gaol to await trial. All three, however, cheated the hangman. Turnbull hanged himself in his cell before trial, and since his evidence against the other two men (really all that the prosecution had) was neither corroborated nor admitted, the case against them collapsed and they were found not guilty. Two murder investigations, neither successfully concluded. Not the best of records.

oooOooo

The year 1856 was a watershed in police history with the enactment of the County and Borough Police Act. It not only provided, for the first time, for the establishment of police forces in every county of England and Wales but it included a clause (Clause 2) that existing borough forces could be combined with the new county constabularies. That brought the first *'threat'* to the independence of Carlisle's police force. It was a clause that rang alarm bells in Town Halls up and down the country. Municipal bodies were up in arms since it was felt that *'there has been a desire to smuggle it (the Act) through its various stages (through Parliament) with as little discussion as possible.'* (Now haven't we heard that statement repeated many times in recent years?).

See the table of clauses on the next page.

One year before the passing of the Act, Carlisle Town Council had entered into an agreement with the Cumberland Magistrates to consolidate the policing of the city with the surrounding county area known as *'Cumberland Ward'* and had put the arrangement into effect. However, when the new Bill was debated at a meeting in May 1856, fearing amalgamation with a proposed Cumberland County Police and the consequent loss of the city's independence, the Town Council resolved, *'in order to keep themselves clear of any clauses of the Bill, they ought to give notice to the county to terminate the agreement.'* Any previous co-operation between the city and county authorities (the magistrates) then went by the board. Whilst the city's council was determined to resist all attempts to amalgamate its police force, the magistrates were equally resolute in their efforts to take control, petitioning the Home Secretary for his approval of their plans. The city, through its two MPs, resolved to petition against what they considered to be *'an unconstitutional interference with the ancient privileges and due independence of cities and boroughs. Such interference was totally uncalled for in that it was an unnecessary inroad into their independence, which they value, and upon those privileges which they will never willingly surrender.'* The Corporation claimed that the only reason for the Government's intervention was the failure of two or three towns in Lancashire, (Blackburn, Wigan and Stockport), to maintain the manpower of their police forces at an acceptable level. *"Because of this, every town in the Kingdom is threatened with interference,"* said the Mayor. *"Cumberland Police* is lowest in the scale"* said one member. *"Yes, but not in the City of Carlisle,"* responded another, *"there is no reason to connect the city with Cumberland."* The city force, at one constable to every thousand population, was up to optimum strength and was operating efficiently. The Carlisle Journal prophetically commented, *"The public feeling with regard to police has, within the last five and twenty years, undergone a marked change. The importance of an efficient police is now universally recognised and, except for evil-doers, an officer,*

---

* *there was still no County Police force, but constables were operating in a number of areas under the control of the magistrates.*

February 1856. A Bill for Regulating County and Borough Police Summary of clauses	
Clause 1	In every county where a constabulary is not already established for the whole county, the justices in Quarter Sessions are to cause the same to be established.
Clause 2	The Queen may require separate police districts to be constituted into counties.
Clause 3	Her Majesty, on representation from boroughs may arrange consolidation with counties.
Clause 4	County constables to have in boroughs the same powers that borough constables have in counties.
Clause 5	As well as constables having to perform police duties as directed by justices and watch committees, they are also to perform, by regulation of the Secretary of State duties declared by the Secretary of State to be police duties – conferring on the Government the powers of superceding local authorities.
Clause 6	Secretary of State may make rules for the pay and clothing of borough police – merely leaving the watch committees the right of representing special circumstances which may call for amendment or addition.
Clause 7	Disqualifies borough constables from voting at borough or county elections.
Clause 8	Chief constables are to make such reports as the Secretary of State may require.
Clause 9	Justices may grant superannuations to chief constables of counties.
Clause 10	Three Inspectors of Constabulary to be appointed to enquire into the state and efficiency of the police appointed for every county and borough.
Clause 11	Upon the Secretary of State's certificate of efficiency for the year, one fourth of the charge for pay and clothing will be met by the Treasury.
Clause 12	No such payments will be made to boroughs of less than 5000 population not consolidated with the county police.

trimly clad in a tight-buttoned coat and trained in his duties is not an object of derision or aversion like the helpless old fogey whom he superceded in the duty of protecting our persons and property. But the main reason why there is universal confidence in our police is that they are thoroughly under our own control, organised and appointed by local representatives, restricted to the performance of specified and well known duties, and promptly amenable for any misconduct. If the project (The new Police Bill) is passed in its present form, the management of police in towns will be transferred substantially from the Corporations of England to the Home Secretary, and an institution which is confined to the legitimate objects of maintaining the police and furthering the ends of justice will be converted into a state engine which may be prostituted for the vilest purposes of political oppression. The measure, it is true, nominally recognises the present authorities, for to have thrown them overboard entirely would have been an experiment too dangerous to be ventured upon. By this scheme, the police would become, not the servants of the ratepayers, but the puppets and tools of the Minister of State, bound to do his bidding. The clause which requires chief constables to furnish to the Secretary of State all such information as he may from time to time require, opens the door to a system new and odious to Englishmen. It is only necessary to imagine a time of great political excitement to estimate the oppressive uses to which a Secretary of State might, under such a system, apply the enormous arbitrary power with which this Bill professes to invest in him. As if the measure were felt to be unpalatable, the vulgar expedient is resorted to of offering a sop to local authorities. One fourth of the expense of the police is to be given from the consolidated fund, whenever the inspectors certify efficiency."

The newspaper had the wisdom in 1856 to predict that the independence of the police could, and probably would, be compromised by Government interference. It could be argued that, today, we have gone down that road. In the event, despite 150 petitions presented against the Police Bill and only ten in support, it did become law, but only after clauses 5 and 6 had been withdrawn.

A combined force for the counties of Cumberland and Westmorland was duly established, without any further consideration of combining with the city police, and thus the city's worries passed for the time being. I believe there was good reason why the new police authority for the twin counties wanted Carlisle to be included. It had decided from the outset that the county police headquarters would be established in the city and that their new Chief Constable, John Dunne, moving from Newcastle upon Tyne City Police, would reside in Carlisle but it had no premises in mind for the new Force or for its Chief. Or had it? Carlisle City had a relatively new police headquarters that included a chief officer's residence. Amalgamation at that stage would have solved those accommodation problems as well as placing additional revenue at the county's disposal and providing a ready source of professional officers to get the Force off the ground. As it happened, the new Cumberland and Westmorland Constabulary began life with headquarters in rented accommodation in Lowther Street in Carlisle, and several city officers transferred to it.

The new legislation was still much opposed by the towns, but the Home Secretary, Sir George Grey said, *"Interference was necessary because there is no evidence to show that the borough police is perfect."* *"Now"* said the Carlisle Journal, *"perfection is a thing with which Englishmen are not overburdened even in the higher organisations of state. They do not often enjoy the satisfaction of possessing an immaculate government and they are obliged occasionally to endure, with what patience they may, even Home Secretaries of a very inferior calibre. But they have never grumbled about ministers so long as they exhibited a reasonable amount of efficiency; and, surely, it is too bad to come down upon them with a Bill like that before us because they have not secured 'perfection' in the minor matter of police. The test applied by the Home Secretary to ascertain how near any town approaches his celestial standard is fallacious and absurd. The requirements of towns vary according to the nature of their population, and an apparently low proportion of police to inhabitants may not be proof of an inefficient police but the happy consequence of a community comparatively free from crime. "* The new Police Act was not all bad news locally. One of the newly appointed Inspectors of Constabulary, Colonel Woodford, formerly Chief Constable of Lancashire, visited and reviewed the city force within days of the Act taking effect.The Force establishment was increased by one sergeant and four constables on 13 January 1857. The HMI believed that only one night sergeant, as then employed, was insufficient. The increase was at no additional cost to the city since a government grant was available to cover the expense.[+] (See bottom of the opposite page).

One member of the Town Council queried the need, saying: *"to add five men to the police was to increase the establishment beyond that of any town of similar size in the kingdom. In Carlisle we already have one man to every thousand population. Without wishing to oppose the resolution, would the council agree that one of the extra men should look after the town nuisances, for example, the privvies, gullies and other things – in other words, to attend to the sanitary conditions of the town under the directions of the superintendent (chief constable)."* The Town Clerk pointed out that as the Chief was already the Inspector of Nuisances, the proposal could easily be adopted. And so it came to pass, one constable being placed at the disposal of the Health Committee.

oooOooo

City policeman charged with the manslaughter of a prisoner

"We do not wish to have any dictation. We are quite competent to form our own opinion of the case." Thus the jury foreman brusquely addressed HM Coroner for the city on 2 January 1857, at an inquest being held in the West Walls Police Office into the death of a prisoner in custody there. *"Of course you are"* said the Coroner, *"but it is my duty to draw your attention to the legal construction of the evidence given. I shall, however, leave the case entirely in your hands, to deal with as you think right, but if you wish, I shall read over the evidence."* *"We require the room to be cleared,"* said the foreman, dismissing the Coroner's offer. After a ten-minute consideration of the evidence, the foreman announced *"Our verdict is that the deceased's death was caused by exposure to the cold, but hastened by the culpable neglect of William Carson, the officer in charge, after the deceased was brought into the police office."* *"That is manslaughter,"* said the Coroner. *"You have it as it is,"* said the foreman, *"police officers ought to be taught their duty."* The Coroner adjourned the inquest until 5 January to prepare the required Bill of Indictment. When the court reconvened, 27 year-old Constable William Carson of the City Police was committed in custody to stand trial for manslaughter at the next Assizes.

Briefly the circumstances of the case were as follows:

On Wednesday, 31 December 1856, George Atkinson, a 43 year old tailor, of Milbourne Street, Caldewgate, Carlisle, left his home at 8.30pm to go drinking, as usual, in the local pubs. He had very recently moved home from nearby John Street. By midnight, he was much the worse for drink and fell asleep in the Globe Inn on Bridge Street. He was roused and given a snack of bread and beef before a friend, being unaware of his recent house move, helped him across the road to his former home. Atkinson told him that he could find his own way from there. At 5.30am, next morning, he was seen by a witness lying on the stairs of a house in John Street. Constable Joseph Birney Cockburn found him in the same position at 7am. Atkinson, who was known to the officer, was still drunk. PC Cockburn tried to discover his new address, but being unsuccessful, he arrested Atkinson who had to be carried to the police station in West Walls on a stretcher. At 8am, he was searched by PC William Carson, the station officer, and *'tuppence ha'penny and a few buttons'* were taken from him before he was placed in a cell with another prisoner, John Pendley of Botchergate. It was the Chief Constable's policy to have drunks, for their safety, placed with sober prisoners. Pendley said that Atkinson *"was dead drunk but breathing freely"* when he was placed in the cell, but by 9am, was *'gurgling.'* Shortly afterwards, Pendley thought that Atkinson was dead. He tried for fully ten minutes to summon aid, but no officer came near. He then began knocking and eventually PC Carson came to the cell. Twenty minutes had passed since Pendley had first tried to raise the alarm. Carson said that before placing Atkinson in the cell he'd found no signs that he was ill or injured. He'd not heard Pendley calling for him. PC John Cowing was in the station between 8.35am and 9.10am. He said he'd not heard any knocking from the cells. Dr. John Hendrie arrived at 10am and certified death. There were no marks of violence on the body. As the night had been very cold, he believed that death had resulted from exposure, the deceased being under the influence of drink. Although he had lain outside for several hours, *"there would be nothing to indicate anything more serious than a common case of intoxication."* He said that he saw nothing wrong with the prisoner having been

---

the County and Borough Police Act 1856, for the first time, provided for inspection of Forces by a HM Inspector of Constabulary. If forces were certified as being efficient they attracted a Home Office grant of 50% of approved expenditure. This would be the first inspection of Carlisle Police.

placed in the cells. Summing up after hearing the doctor's evidence, the Coroner said that the police had treated the case no differently from others of a similar kind and concluded that, *"It was quite possible that the officer might commit an error of judgement in not ascertaining that the deceased was worse than he really appeared to be, but that would not justify the jury attaching any criminality to the officer in charge."*

The jury had other views and PC Carson was remanded in custody to the city's gaol. However, following an application to a Judge in Chambers in London, PC Carson was released on bail on Sunday, 11 January, he having been in custody for six days.

At Cumberland Spring Assizes on 24 February 1857, HM. Judge, Mr. Baron Martin said, addressing the Grand Jury, *"Out of twenty-one prisoners to take their trial at these Assizes, nine are committed for homicide and one for an offence connected with it. Certainly it does look as though human life were not regarded with so much respect in this county as, happily, in other counties."*

That might have sounded ominous for PC Carson, but when he appeared before the court he learned that the Grand Jury had thrown out the Bill of Indictment, Prosecuting Counsel saying that he would offer no evidence. His Lordship agreed that there were no grounds for charging the policeman with manslaughter, saying,

"It was supposed that some act or conduct on his part had led to the death of a drunken man in a cell. It is very clear that he did not do that, and equally clear that he had followed his Chief Constable's instructions regarding drunken prisoners and that he had no reason to suppose he should act differently with the deceased. It was right that I should say this, and that the prisoner should leave the dock without any imputation. At the same time, however, it was right that he should take care of people whether drunk or sober, but especially drunken people who might be brought into the police office."

oooOooo

The case against Constable Carson was formally dismissed and he was free to resume his police career. However, he did nothing of the sort. Two days after the hearing he resigned his appointment. One could hardly criticise him for so doing. He had served in the Force since 28 August 1851, almost six years.

oooOooo

On 8 January 1857, Carlisle Watch Committee regretfully accepted Mr. Sabbage's resignation in consequence of his being appointed Superintendent [Chief Officer] of Newcastle-upon-Tyne City Police. The post had become vacant following the appointment of Mr. John Dunne, the incumbent, to the position of Chief Constable of the newly formed Cumberland and Westmorland Constabulary, a position Mr. Sabbage himself had sought. Mr. Sabbage, who had applied unsuccessfully to be Chief of Newcastle three years earlier, was one of three applicants to be shortlisted for the Newcastle post. The board appointed to select the new chief had some difficulty with Mr. Sabbage's declared age. Candidates had to be no more than 40 years old. Mr. Sabbage said he was 39. His earlier application was accompanied by a letter from the Commissioner of the Metropolitan Police giving his age as 37. In response to the query, it was stated that Mr. Sabbage did not know his true age. He had obtained his baptismal certificate dated May 1818, showing that he was born in December, but no year was mentioned. It was assumed to be 1817. Sir John Fife of Newcastle Town Council was not at all happy with the situation. He had made no secret that he supported another candidate, a military man. He suggested that Mr. Sabbage should be brought before the board to be interrogated as to his age. The board rejected this proposal and pressed ahead. Voting was 23, 14, 5, in Mr. Sabbage's favour, and, though he expressed some unease at the requirement for him to find and keep a horse, he was immediately confirmed as the new Chief Officer of Police for Newcastle. The Carlisle Journal heartily congratulated Mr. Sabbage on: *"his preferment to so onerous and lucrative a post. During his twelve years in Carlisle we have had many opportunities to notice the humane and judicious moderation with which he has tempered the vigilance and energy essential to his often trying duties."*

The paper reported that the city's MPs, Mayor and Aldermen had *'contributed handsomely'* towards a testimonial in appreciation of his services to the city. There is clear evidence that Mr. Sabbage was not a chief constable to sit back and let his men do all the work. He was personally involved a great deal in the day-to-day policing of the city.

Mr. Sabbage, a much-liked and respected chief officer in Newcastle, died, in office, some ten years later.

oooOooo

A few odds and ends from Chief Sabbage's days

1849
Mar 15 – Canal Company to hire PC for watching canal at night at cost of 16 shillings per week. Force increased by one constable to cater for arrangement.

1850
Apr 25 – Superintendent, one Sergeant and one Constable to travel to London with convicts from the Gaol.

1851
Aug 21 – PC !9 McLean dismissed for falsely accusing Sgt. Barnfatherof being drunk and disorderly on duty.

1852
Apr 22 – Mr. Rome requested a regular police patrol Milbourne Street, Denton Holme road to Holme Head Works, Murrell Hill and the road past Dixon's factory. Agreed by the Watch Committee on payment by Mr. Rome of 12 shillings per week.

1855
May 31 – Copies of rules and regulations of the police forces of Manchester, Glasgow, Newcastle upon Tyne and Preston obtained during review of city's rules.

1856
Aug 7 – At Cumberland Adjourned Sessions in Carlisle the Clerk of the Police recommended that two police forces should be established to cover the county of Cumberland – one East, one West. The Chairman commented "If the county is divided, you'd have the hen and the chickens in each district1"

Nov 27 – PC Anderson resigned upon his appointment as Superintendent at Hexham.

Nov/Dec – A number of constables resign to join new Cumberland and Westmorland Constabulary.

Part Three - Home Office Police Forces

George Edward Bent, Superintendent (Chief Constable)
22 January, 1857 to 17 July, 1873.

Following the resignation of Mr. Sabbage, the Watch Committee once again turned to the Metropolitan Police for a replacement. The person selected was not to exceed 35 years of age, and the emoluments he could expect were £104 from the Watch Committee, £10 from the Inspector of Nuisances, £5 from the Board of Guardians, together with a free house, coal, gas and uniform clothing. Commissioner Mayne proffered four names of suitable Metropolitan sergeants. George Edward Bent was selected and he duly appeared before the Watch Committee on 22 January 1857 when he was appointed and immediately began his duties as, head of the Force in the rank of Superintendent. The County and Borough Police Act, 1856 had taken effect just three weeks before Mr Bent's appointment and for the first time, the Home Secretary had a voice in the running of all police forces in exchange for an Exchequer grant of 50% of Home Office-approved costs.

The Great Chartist Demonstration on Kennington Common, 10 April 1848.

The 33 year-old Sergeant Bent had spent eleven years in the Royal 'A' Division' of the Metropolitan Police, so called because its territory included the royal palaces and parks together with the original Scotland Yard. Mr. Bent, his recommendation stated, had been noted for his attention, intelligence and general good conduct. For many years he had performed royalty protection duties at Buckingham Palace, Windsor Castle, Osborne, Balmoral, and wheresoever Her Majesty, Queen Victoria, happened to be. He proudly recounted that he was the messenger despatched from Buckingham Palace to inform the Duke of Wellington of the birth of Prince Arthur. In 1848, he was one of the constables armed with cutlasses sent to police the Chartist procession from Camberwell Green to Kennington Common. Other officers were armed with guns. Some 70,000 special constables had been sworn to supplement the regular police. They were supported by a considerable military force, backed by heavy guns. Not surprisingly, the demonstration passed without incident. Later Mr. Bent had to attend a Chartist Meeting in Faringdon Hall to protect government reporters. In 1854, he was promoted to the rank of sergeant by Sir Richard Mayne. Can you imagine anyone leaving that sort of life-style and work to be a policeman in Carlisle in Victorian times? Moreover, why would the Commissioner want to lose such a man? Well-versed in the policing of mass demonstrations, he would be prepared for any such upheavals in Caldewgate.

One of the new chief's first actions, just two weeks after his arrival, was to have printed and posted up in the police office a number of placards stating unequivocally that any officer found drunk while on duty would be summarily dismissed from the service.

The Police Officers Superannuation Act was adopted by the Town Council in April 1857. Councillor Howe said that due to low pay, officers did not stay for too long preferring instead to transfer themselves to county forces or to Newcastle. *"Carlisle"* he said, was treated *"merely as a sort of training school"* for other forces. The adoption of this Act was seen as a means of retaining men. It provided that officers who had served for fifteen years in the force would be entitled to retire on half pay, but, if they continued to serve after fifteen years they would receive full pay plus one-third of their last superannuation allowance. There were no offers in my day like that! No constable was to be superannuated below the age of fifty unless he was unfit for further duty. If the fund was at that time insufficient, the council would make it up or payments to the officer would be reduced until such times as it became viable. Officers' contributions would amount to sixpence per week for those on eighteen shillings wages. Fines for disciplinary offences would be paid into the fund. One parsimonious councillor suggested that the entire Force should be dismissed, then promptly re-engaged so that all would start the qualifying period together (and be fifteen years further away from pension!). That way, he argued, sufficient monies would be accumulated before the first officers qualified for benefit. His proposal, mercifully, received no support. Only one constable was eligible to receive the benefit. No other officer then serving in the city force would have qualified for the pension in the ensuing five years. A councillor commented *"The Force has been established for twenty-seven years (thirty actually) and here we find ourselves with only one man who has served us for fifteen years."* Enough said!

In February 1859, a proposal by the Town Council of Exeter that police authorities should refuse to accept the Exchequer grant towards the costs of the police, was debated by Carlisle Watch Committee. Whilst being of the opinion that police forces ought to be entirely locally funded, it concluded that it could not recommend the City Council to refuse such grant.

The title *'Chief Constable'* was established on the operative date of the County and Borough Police Act in January 1857. The heads of city and borough forces, many of which had existed for twenty or more years (thirty years in the case of the Carlisle Force) were appointed in the rank of Superintendent. Mr. Bent was re-titled Chief Constable on 22 October 1857. In December 1859 letters were exchanged between the City Watch Committee and the Home Office regarding the title of chief officers in cities and boroughs. The Home Office' view was that the title *'chief constable'*, should apply only to the chief officers of the newly formed county constabularies and that borough chiefs should be titled *'chief superintendent'* in order to differentiate between the two. Members of the City Watch Committee were infuriated and instructed the Town Clerk to prepare a suitable response objecting to the proposal. The following letter was duly despatched to the Home Secretary:

> *In reply to your circular dated 19 December, 1859, suggesting the title of 'Chief Superintendent' for the head officer of police in towns and cities in lieu of 'Chief Constable' as heretofore. I am directed by the Watch Committee of the City of Carlisle to state that they are of the opinion that no more difficulty can arise in distinguishing between city and county chief constables than between chief constables of various counties, and that alteration would only tend, as far as titles go, to place the city chief of police in an inferior position to the county chief of police, especially where the title suggested is borne by an inferior officer of the county police, as in Carlisle. In addition to all the other reasons, the title 'chief constable' is the one used in the bye-laws now in force in the City of Carlisle. After giving the circular a mature consideration, the Watch Committee have therefore unanimously resolved that it is not expedient that any difference be made in the title of the chief of police, whether they belong to city, borough or county.*

> *Signed Isaac Cartmell:*
> *Town Hall, Carlisle, 30 December 1859.*

In its reply, the Home Office stated that the Minister proposed no change to the chief constable's title.

In August 1872, members of the Force appealed to the Watch Committee, in the following terms, for a reduction in their working hours, for one day per month leave and for an across-the-board increase in pay of two shillings [10p] a week, a laughable amount by today's standards:
'

> *To the Chairman and Gentlemen of the Watch Committee of the Borough of Carlisle.*

> *The respectful memorial of the undersigned Police Constables of the Borough of Carlisle humbly sheweth that your memorialists would draw your attention to the fact that the police force in several boroughs and counties have recently received an augmentation in their weekly wages. They would also respectfully lay before you the fact that in other boroughs, the constables receive considerably greater wages than your memorialists with no more, if so many, hours of duty, your memorialists having on an average with the excess of extra duty, court, etc., over 70 hours per week. As members of the police force they may be allowed to suggest an approaching difficulty in maintaining their efficiency. It is that the recently advanced wages in almost every department of labour may prove sufficiently attractive to induce some of them to leave the*

Force unless a corresponding inducement be held out to them to remain. This, they particularly request, may not be understood as any threat but simply as a fact which might tend to impair their efficiency and embarrass you in supplying the vacancies. Your memorialists cannot think that the ratepayers of Carlisle would object to a small additional charge made upon them if it insured and maintained the efficiency of their police force. They would also respectfully remind you, although it is scarcely necessary, of the extremely high price of butchers' meat, fuel and house rents at present, which, in reality, operates as a reduction of their wages. Your memorialists hope that you will not think it is excessive when they ask for an advance of two shillings per week on their wages, a reduction of extra duty, and one day leave of absence in each month, or twelve days leave in the year.

All of the above facts your memorialists would respectfully press on your earnest consideration in the hope that you may be hereby induced to make the above mentioned concessions and which may be compatible with their onerous duties'.

Wouldn't those pioneers of the police service just relish today's pay and conditions? They were actually awarded their pay increase in the following November, and, at the same time, the Committee introduced a *'Good Service'* award, providing the men with the opportunity of earning, at the top rate, 25 shillings per week (the normal top rate was 24 shillings) – 25 bob for a 70 hour week! The good old days?

On 23 November 1872, the newspaper *'Lancaster Examiner'* made serious allegations against Carlisle Police to the effect that they had failed to respond to requests made by the Superintendent at Lancaster for enquiries to be made in Carlisle to trace a murder suspect. Further, it said, Lancaster's senior officer had himself travelled to Carlisle, made the necessary investigations and arrested the murderess. Carlisle Watch Committee looked into the matter. The murder was of a female child at Aldcliffe, Lancashire. Her mother Mary Davidson had been circulated as *'wanted'* in connection with the crime. Lancaster Police traced the suspect's movements after the killing to Lancaster Railway Station where she boarded a train for Carlisle. Superintendent Jervis at Lancaster sent a telegraph to Mr. Bent asking him to arrange for enquiries to be made at lodging houses and other likely places to trace and apprehend her. Superintendent Jervis said that despite repeated requests Mr. Bent took no action. Carlisle's Chief was having none of that. *" I have felt it my duty, not only in justice to myself but also to the officers under me, to lay before you a true statement of what has taken place in contradiction to the mis-statements which Superintendent Jervis or those under him have been the means of promulgating through the Lancaster Press",* he said. He reported that he had indeed received a letter from Lancaster that said the suspect might have gone to Carlisle. Investigations to trace her were most promptly made, he said, *"without any tidings of her."* He had instructed his detective to carry out enquiries, had placed the *'Wanted'* circulation in the Charge Room for all officers to see, and had read out the details to the men when they paraded for duty. A second letter accompanied by a photograph of the murder victim asked that enquiries be made to see if the child was missing from Carlisle. On the day of its receipt Superintendent Jervis arrived in the city stating that he had himself discovered the suspect's whereabouts. *"A statement more at variance with the truth could not possibly have been made,"* said Mr. Bent, *"for he did not discover any trace of the woman."* Jervis and Carlisle's Constable Stordy had made enquiries but it was Stordy alone who discovered where the suspect was staying. He also found the victim's scarf and hood. The Constable had then gone to the Victoria Hotel where Superintendent Jervis was staying and told him what he had found. Of Superintendent Jervis's account, Mr. Bent said, *"I now give it a most emphatic and distinct denial. The most active measures were taken in Carlisle and to Carlisle Police alone is due the credit of obtaining the information that led to the woman's apprehension. Throughout this case I gave the Lancaster Police every assistance possible and I am only sorry that the goodwill I showed them has met with no return."* The Watch Committee interviewed several local officers. All denied that the Lancaster circulation had been read to them or that they had been instructed to carry out any enquiries. They admitted seeing the notice *'above the mantlepiece on paynight'* but did not know there were enquiries to be made in the city. Sgt. Roscoe said he lived in Swifts Row and that his wife worked in Fisher's pub in Rickergate. The suspect had applied to her for lodgings and if he had known she was wanted he could have arrested her. Another officer, a detective, was living in Solway Terrace only a couple of doors away from where the suspect was lodging. It was clear to the Committee that until the Lancaster Chief came to Carlisle, the men were unaware of the full circumstances of the circulation and that it was Superintendent Bent, not Jervis, who was not telling the truth about the matter.

On 6 December 1872, the Watch Committee considered a motion that *'on account of Mr. Bent's gross negligence of duty in reference to the murderess Mary Davidson and other matters, he be called upon to resign his office as Chief Constable of Carlisle.'* An amendment that *'the Chairman be requested to severely reprimand Mr. Bent and state to him that a repetition of similar negligence would necessitate his dismissal'* was proposed, seconded and carried. The Committee clearly also felt that so specialist an officer as a detective ought to have performed better in the investigation of such a serious crime. They immediately abolished the position and ordered that all future messages of a similar nature to those from Lancaster should be handled by the sergeants to ensure that proper enquiries were diligently carried out. On 20 March 1873, Mr. Bent was cautioned by the Chairman of the Watch Committee and requested to attend more closely to his duties in future.

Whilst not trying to excuse the Chief's conduct, for it was indefensible, the reason for his lack of proper attention to duty may have been much more than simply negligence. Mr. Bent, whose long and unsocial duty hours, like those of all the Chiefs before him, demanded a man of strong constitution, was not a well man. Early in 1873, within weeks of the Lancaster incident, he was suffering ill-health, necessitating absences from duty. In March, then again in July, the Watch Committee instructed their clerk to liaise with Dr. Page, the Medical Officer, as to the Chief's condition and fitness for continued service. On 1 May, Mr. Bent was granted fourteen days leave of absence, extended by a further month at the expiry of that period, and then indefinitely. The Watch Committee meeting of 17 July was informed by the doctor that he had *"no hopes of the Chief Constable recovering and he would never again be fit for police duties, though I would not be surprised if he lingered on for three or four months."* The Committee made clear that in the interests of the efficiency of the Force it was anxious to have a Chief Constable at the helm. Mr. Bent therefore tendered his resignation - did he walk or was he pushed? The poor man died on 3 August at 48 years of age, just seventeen days after quitting, leaving a widow and a daughter. A civic funeral took place on Thursday, 7 August. Many people assembled in West Walls to witness the departure of the cortege. City policeman, together with a detachment from the county force led by their Superintendent and the Carlisle Volunteer Fire Brigade in full uniform marched two abreast. The Mayor and the Chairman of the Watch Committee, Councillors and Corporation officials followed. At the rear, several cabs of citizens accompanied the cortege. The Reverend Tasker of Holy Trinity officiated at Carlisle Cemetery, where the city constables, in turns, carried the coffin into the Chapel and then to the graveside.

It would seem that despite his thirty-two years service and/or his ill-health, the Chief was not entitled to a pension from the superannuation fund. On the day of her husband's funeral, the Watch Committee recommended that a gratuity of £120 be paid to Mrs. Bent. According to contemporary press reports her husband's resignation had deprived her of the pension to which she would have been entitled had he remained in post for a further seventeen days. Good sense must have prevailed, for in the event, in addition to the gratuity, a pension of £75 p.a. (half-pay) was awarded for subsequent years.

So ended another chapter in the history of the Force. Mr. Bent arrived with an excellent reputation, and if his career came to sad end following the Lancaster murder enquiry and his tragic illness, he was nevertheless praised highly by the local press in the following valediction:

"He held that police officers should at all times conduct themselves in such a way as to conciliate the favourable opinion of the public by being good natured rather than irritating them by harsh and domineering conduct. These views animated his whole course of action as Chief Constable. If he erred, it was by being a little too good natured, but on the other hand he succeeded in making the citizens look upon the police as their friends and not their enemies."

oooOooo

A few odds and ends from Chief Bent's days

Judging from some of the entries below, it seems that Chief Bent was keen to improve the appearance of the Force – new style uniforms, head-dress, drilling, etc.

1857
May 1 – Thomas Hetherington, Carlisle, contracted to supply 25 uniforms for constables at 50/6d [£2.52] each and 3 for sergeants at 63/- [£3.15] each, the cloth to be damped and shrunk before being made up.

May 7 – William Burne Nanson to supply 28 hats at 10/- [50p] each and 3 silk hats at 10/- each for the sergeants.

Jun 11 – 28 capes to be procured for the officers.

Oct 1 – Mr. Bent and 1 PC to attend Dumfries Cattle Show at request of Supt. Jones of Dumfries – mutual aid to a Scottish Force was not uncommon for the city police around this time.

Oct 22 – The title 'Chief Constable' introduced into Carlisle City Force.

Oct 22 – PC Parker appointed 'Clerk of the Pork Market' and PC Watson appointed 'Weigher', pay increased by 1/6d [7p] per week for the extra duties.

Nov 12 – Martindale and Storey to supply 28 greatcoats at 32/4d [£1.62] each.

1858
Jan 21 – Chief Constable allowed £4 to provide a frock coat and trousers and 16 shillings [80p] for a hat.

Feb 18 – 25 lamps provided for the night watch at 4/6d [22p] each.

May 20 – Chief Constable to obtain 28 armlets [brassards] to be worn by officers on duty [as in the Metropolitan Police].

Jun 3 – Contract awarded for supply of new uniforms, those for the sergeants to have embossed silver collars.

1859
Jan 13 – Sergeants issued with drill books.

Feb 3 – First mention in Watch Committee Minutes Book of the 'Pinfold' – records of property coming into police possession. [Pinfold Register was still in existence in the 1960s]. Watch Committee allowed to dispose of items as deemed fit [in the final years of the Force, by auction].

Feb 4 – 40 gallons of pale seal oil obtained for the officers' lanterns.

Jul 28 – Chief to allow six city policemen to attend the opening of Silloth Docks on Wednesday, 3 August, 1859.

Sep 29 – Chief Constable to apply to the Magistrates for the monies imposed as fines for assaults on police, as provided by the 22/23 Vic Act, to go towards the augmentation of the Police Superannuation Fund.

1860
Sep 6 – Force allowed to purchase photographic equipment.

Sep 13 – Chief Constable and as many men as are available to attend the Citadel Railway Station on Monday 17 September when HM Queen Victoria passes through.

Sep 20 – Handbills to be distributed in the city re appointment of new constables 'next Thursday' 27th September.

1861
Feb 14 – Chief Constable to arrange for an officer to be at Scotch Street, another at Fisher Street, ends of the butchers' market to collect a penny on each basket of butter and eggs brought for sale.

1870
Apr – Capes issued to patrol officers.

1871
Jun 8 – PC21 Corrie dismissed for taking money from a prisoner's wife.

Jul 6 – Sgt. Stordy severely reprimanded for his conduct towards PC18 Norman, in seizing him in the police office and attempting to lock him up, whilst he, PS Stordy, was drunk.

1872
Feb 15 – Watch Committee announced its pleasure in permitting those members of the police force who rendered their services at the fire at Holme Head to receive the handsome donation of £10 donated by Messrs. Ferguson Brothers.

Feb 15 – Chief Constable Bent to wear uniform at all state occasions when he attends the Mayor.

Mar 21 – Tender of James Robertson for helmets (first mention of helmets being issued to the Force) at 6/5d each [32p] accepted, 'provided they are bound in leather'.

Mar 28 – The detective officer to be supplied by the uniform contractor with such plain clothes as he may himself select, *'provided he pays the difference between the contract price of uniforms and the clothes he takes'*.

Apr 4 – City Council to be informed that a 'Muniment Room' has been provided at the Police Office.

Apr 25 – 'If a PC leaves the Force before completing six months service, he will forfeit one week's pay, before twelve months, half a week's pay.

Jun 20 – PS Cowen reprimanded for using improper language to the Chief Constable while on drill. Required that he fall in regularly for drill each week for six weeks. [That'll teach him!].

oooOooo

Carlisle City policemen of the 1950s and 60s could confidently class themselves as 'experts' in traffic control duties. They had every reason. Added to the considerable local traffic, and with no motorway or city by-pass, all cross border traffic passed along the A6 and A7 highways through the city centre, usually nose-to-tail during the daylight hours. Even night-time levels would surpass those of most towns in the day-time. Each of the principal junctions in the city centre was police-controlled from 8am until at least 7pm, Mondays to Saturdays. Sunday brought the only respite for the Force. The patrol strength was divided for shift-working purposes into five groups. Each of the group working 10am to 6pm, without exception, was engaged on some sort of traffic management duties. In the winter of 1960/61, in some appalling weather conditions, during reconstruction work carried out simultaneously on the A6 London Road and the A7 Scotland Road, point-duties were performed throughout the 24 hour period, under floodlights during the hours of darkness. It became the practice for many residents near the night-time points, before retiring to bed, to bring flasks of hot coffee, tea and soup to the policemen, and very welcome these gifts were, too, in the dead of night. It was generally believed by those serving at the time that such working conditions were responsible for the loss of a number of promising officers who resigned rather than perform such duties. But point-duty was unavoidable. Without it the city would have ground to a halt.

Above: *from left, a 1930's constable on point duty at the English Street/ Victoria Viaduct/Devonshire Street junction. Seems an awful waste of his time – there's hardly a motor vehicle in sight – and he must have been bored stupid; Sergeant Jim Ballantyne steps into the road in Lowther Street to give traffic a helping hand. The two old ladies crossing the road seem oblivious of his presence; TrafficDept. Constable Norman Jackson at top of Botchergate.*

Above: *A constable (Bill Kennedy?) on the English Street/ Bank Street point, outside Marks and Spencer store.*

Above right: *Martin MacAlindon, 'top of Warwick Road' point (Lowther Street/Warwick Road junction) and a second PC on the Lowther Arcade pedestrian crossing to ensure traffic flows without constant interruption by pedestrians.*

My first traffic point duty was performed here, 10am to 6pm. 'Sir', I said, apprehensively, to the duty inspector, 'I've never done traffic control before.' 'Don't worry,' he replied, 'You'll be an expert by six o'clock.

Right: *Martin, again, being 'visited' by Sergeant Eddie Mason, on the same point.*

77

Walter Hemingway, Superintendent (Chief Constable)
21 August 1873 to 3 August 1876.

"He met in the early part of his career (in Carlisle), and at the end, with some troubled scenes," so said Alderman J Bendle, Mayor of Carlisle, speaking as Mr. Hemingway left for Cardiff in 1876. Troubled indeed; only three years in post but probably the most controversial three years of any chief officer's tenure.

oooOooo

As Mr. Bent quit, the Watch Committee's advertisement for a new Chief Constable, in each of the local papers as well as in the Manchester Examiner, London Daily Telegraph and Standard, Edinburgh Scotsman, Leeds Mercury and Newcastle Chronicle, brought a response from more than sixty applicants. A shortlist of five was selected and interviewed. They were:

> Detective Superintendent George Mackay, Edinburgh [Midlothian] Police,
> Superintendent Watson, Kirkudbright,
> Thomas Gibson, Leeds City Police,
> John Jervis, Buckingham and the successful applicant
> Walter Hemingway, Head of Detectives, Birkenhead Borough Police.

Prior to Mr. Hemingway taking up his duties, the Committee introduced a number of new procedures. The Chief Constable would be required to attend all meetings of the Watch Committee, to wear uniform on all official occasions and to select all new police officers himself before presenting them to the Watch Committee for approval.

The new chief had hardly warmed his chair in Carlisle before he began to seek pastures new. He unsuccessfully, sought appointment as Chief Constable of Bradford City Police in October 1874. Perhaps he had a premonition. Success would have spared him the choppy ride he was to experience during the ensuing years. In fact, his troubles had already begun. During his first year in office, from an establishment of just 34 men, fourteen constables resigned, eleven were dismissed and one absconded. Was that a reflection of his man-management skills? Records do not provide an answer. *"Such frequent changes, and the large proportion of inexperienced men consequent upon them, materially affect the efficiency of the establishment,"* understated HM Inspector of Constabulary as he called for special attention, *"to produce a more settled feeling among the constables."* The appalling situation probably accounted, too, for a very high incidence of assaults on the men. The Force was, nevertheless, certified as *'efficient.'* The Annual costs of *'Watching'* amounted to £2,754 against which the Government granted £511.   In July 1874, the Watch Committee debated a motion that *'this Committee have perfect confidence in the Chief Constable and the police force generally and disapprove altogether of the remarks made by the Chairman and referred to in the letter sent by the Chief Constable to the Mayor, and further request the Chairman to withdraw those charges,'* a clear indication that all was not well in Mr. Hemingway's relationship with his chairman whose remarks were not specified in contemporary reports. He would be relieved that the motion was carried.

In April 1874 an outbreak of typhus, typhoid and scarlet fever, inflamed by poor sanitation, struck the city, rapidly becoming an epidemic that raged throughout the remainder of the year. Over five hundred cases, including numerous deaths, were reported. In November, perhaps as a consequence of the epidemic, the Watch Committee ordered a deduction of one penny per week from each officer's pay to fund the appointment of a *'medical man'* to examine and certify officers' sicknesses, thus relieving the chief constable of the need to visit them. The fever claimed the life of 43-year old Sergeant Jeremiah Huntingdon, who died in Crozier Lodge, the Fever Hospital, on 21 December, leaving a wife and seven children. He had served in the Force for seventeen years. His funeral cortege was followed from the city centre to Murrell Hill by the chief constable and thirty uniformed officers and many citizens. The sergeant *'had been struck down in the discharge of his duties,"* said a councillor to the Watch Committee, "and we ought to treat those thrown onto the world by his decease as liberally as possible." The Committee granted widow Huntingdon a gratuity of £75.8s for his dependants.* Another officer, Constable Hetherington, was commended for his

---

* *One year's salary. The maximum allowed by law.*

work during the epidemic. The City Health Committee granted him a gratuity of five pounds for his services as sub-Inspector of Nuisances. The citation included, *'He discharged his onerous duties with zeal, intelligence and a great amount of courage - the discharge of a duty which many might shrink from as repulsive and disagreeable. In a number of instances he had exceeded the strict line of duty, from which he might have been excused altogether. He had incurred severe risk in removing persons suffering from fever, he having taken patients upon his back and carried them into the vehicles and shown a determination to carry out his duty to the very best of his ability. Nothing was too hard or too dangerous for him to encounter.'* No Health and Safety Regulations to worry about in those far off days!! The weather was, I should think, a greater worry to the locals. Little and Ballantyne's Nurseries in Stanwix recorded temperatures on Sunday 27 December of 26° below freezing point and on 29 December, 28° below. The rivers Eden and Caldew were frozen over and snow had lain for a week.

The Chief found in his early days that disposal of cases in the Police Court was a matter of concern. County Magistrates had been replaced in the city by the establishment of a separate Commission of the Peace but those incumbent county justices resident within the city boundaries continued in office, thus occupying a number of the permitted posts. A report from March 1875 shows that there were just eleven magistrates in the city, seven of whom were unable to sit due to ill health while two were medical men in active practice who could not spare the time to sit in court. Administration of justice was thus left to the city Mayor and a former Mayor creating for them a very heavy workload. Representations were made to the Home Secretary by the Town Council and met with success, eight additional magistrates being appointed for the city.

Local government in crisis – the Watch Committee resigns

Two prosecutions that Chief Constable Hemingway instigated in 1875 for offences contrary to the Betting Act, that today would pass almost unnoticed, caused outrage in the city and not only alienated the police from the public but lit the touch-paper for unprecedented rifts between the Mayor, the Watch Committee and the Magistracy. In the context of the city's government, if it was believed that old wounds had healed since the early days of the city's police force they were to be ripped open exposing the fractious relationship that still existed between the various parties in an acrimonious argument over who controlled the police.

The Shakespeare Tavern in St. Cuthbert's Lane

Sporting events involving foot racing, wrestling and pole leaping were customary in the city during holiday weekends and two such meetings were held on Good Friday and Easter Saturday in 1875, one at the City Gardens in Botchergate and the other at Botcherby. Each attracted about one thousand spectators. The first prosecution arose from these meetings. At Botchergate the licensed liquor tents were kept very busy and there were a number of disorderly incidents. Gambling on the outcome of the events was taking place despite the presence of notices drawing attention to the prohibition of betting. Although permitted at horse-racing tracks the practice was outlawed elsewhere. A uniformed police sergeant was on duty, whilst two plain clothed detectives mingled with the crowd, there specifically at the Chief Constable's behest to detect betting offences. There were no professional bookies or punters, simply a few locals enjoying the day and having a harmless flutter. It seems that a similar situation prevailed at Botcherby. Afterwards, the Chief alleged that several spectators had made complaints. He began proceedings against the two organisers of the events, James Fisher, licensee of the Barley Stack Inn in Rickergate and J. Edgar, licensee of the Shakespeare Tavern in St. Cuthbert's Lane. William Irwin and R. Carr were summonsed for permitting premises to be used for the purposes of betting. The case was duly brought before the city magistrates.

From the outset Defence Solicitors gave notice that they would appeal in the event of a conviction and insisted that the evidence should be committed to paper.* The Town Clerk, prosecuting, told the justices that the defence would have a right of appeal to Quarter Sessions. *"I shall go a little further up than the Court of Quarter Sessions,"* intervened Mr. Wannop defending. The Town Clerk continued, *"Betting and drinking were the buttresses of these sports and but for them the sports would not exist. They would otherwise be excellent entertainment but the Betting Act is very stringent – no house, office, room or other place was to be used for betting purposes."* Therein laid the argument. In the interpretation of statutes, a rule, known as the *'ejusdem generis'* rule, must apply. Its effect is that when a list of specific items is followed by general words, the meaning of the general words is to be confined to the same class of items contained in the list. Thus, in the Betting Act, the prohibition of betting was confined to *'a house, office, room or other place,'* in other words to buildings and not to open spaces such as sports grounds or gardens. The defence solicitors so argued, quoting from the preamble to the Act, *'a kind of gaming which had lately sprung up tending to the injury or demoralisation of improvident persons by the operation of places called betting houses or offices.'* The stated case, Bows -v- Fenwick 1874, just one year earlier, was referred to, at which point the Chief Constable interrupted, to the annoyance of defence counsel, to inform the court that he had actually given evidence in that particular case. Defence continued, stating that far from the defendants having something to hide, they had actually applied to the Chief Constable for officers to be present at the games and he had refused. *"Quite rightly,"* said the Mayor, Chairman of the Bench, *"Mr Hemingway was right to refuse public officers being hired as servants for private purposes."* After considering the evidence the magistrates concluded that there was no case to answer and they dismissed all of the charges. Chief Hemingway gave notice of his intention to appeal to a higher court. It is worth noting that contemporary newspapers carried accounts of successful prosecutions in various other parts of the country where the circumstances were identical to those in the Carlisle cases. However, the local Carlisle Journal was scathing in its condemnation of the Chief Constable. *'Though he could not send policemen to preserve order, he did send them in plain clothes to try and get up a case under the Betting Act. The Town Clerk said the object of the prosecution was the prevention of disorder. It would have been more creditable if the policemen had endeavoured to attain that object by direct rather than indirect action. Prevention is always better than cure.'* There is no evidence that the police did appeal the magistrates' decision.

The second controversial prosecution followed in July. Shortly after 8pm on Monday 5 July, the evening before the main race meeting of the year, Chief Hemingway led three sergeants and ten constables in raids on two public houses in the city, the Shakespeare Tavern and the Quarter of Mutton Inn in Brown's Lane, off Castle Street. The raids were in response to evidence of illegal betting gleaned by covert surveillance inside the two premises. Though a practice not unheard of and quite acceptable today, it was, by all accounts, considered extremely odious in 1875. Fifty-six persons were arrested and marched off to the police station, while betting books, slips and other evidence were seized. Only seven were eventually charged and bailed to the next morning's court. Evidence of betting was given by a private detective from Liverpool and a plain clothes city police officer. The landlords of the two pubs were each found guilty and fined £50, an exceptionally heavy sum for the time, with the alternative of four months imprisonment. Although the offences were brought under the Betting Act, the landlords' conduct was considered sufficiently serious to attract disqualification from holding a liquor licence granted under the Licensing Act 1872. Half of the monetary penalty was paid over to the private detective who was also awarded his costs. It was the employment of this man that proved to be the catalyst for an amazing sequence of events. The two licensees successfully appealed to Quarter Sessions against the disqualifications and their licences were re-instated. They were granted costs against the police. Several of the forty-nine persons released by the police without charge threatened to sue for false arrest and much was made of the indignity suffered by being marched like criminals through the streets to the lock-up. A fund was commenced to raise monies to finance a civil action but there is no evidence that such a course was taken. An interesting fact, raised in the court under cross-examination of the Chief Constable, was that there were forty-seven public houses within a radius of 250 yards of the Town Hall.

—————————————

* *Written depositions, recorded in a magistrates court, were an essential preliminary to a trial in a higher court.*

The Watch Committee met on 12 July, one week after the police raids, to consider the chief constable's actions. The local press were permitted access to its proceedings. It transpired that the Committee had given Mr. Hemingway express instructions that he was not to take any such proceedings without prior consultation, a situation that would be intolerable to today's chief officers who have autonomy over operational police matters. Notwithstanding the order, Mr. Hemingway *'had planned espionage of the houses and the raids upon them without telling them (the committee) and they, naturally, felt indignant that they had thus been ignored,"* reported the Carlisle Journal. The Chief Constable said he had the authority of the Mayor, who was the Chief Magistrate of the city, to act as he had and that the Watch Committee had no right to interfere. On that latter point the Chief Constable was undoubtedly correct. The Watch Committee demanded an explanation from the Mayor. He rejected an invitation to meet with them to discuss his part in the affair. Consequently, after giving vent to their outrage at the police action, all but two members of the Committee resigned. One member, Councillor Hair, said that the Mayor had taken the Chief Constable into his confidence but the Chief had not taken the Committee into his. *"He has brought into this town a common spy, which is loathsome to society,"* he said. He proposed a motion, *'that in the opinion of this Committee, the Mayor, by his recent secret instructions given to the Chief Constable to bring into town a spy or common informer, has been guilty of unwarrantable interference with the duties of the Watch Committee, therefore the said Committee consider themselves in honour-bound to tender their resignations and await the appointment of successors by the Council.'*

One member told the meeting that Mr. Hemingway had *"applied to both Liverpool and Birkenhead for a detective but neither Force would tolerate a man coming up here to do such shabby work."* The Chief categorically denied the allegation. *"He then applied to travel to Liverpool on his own to recruit some fellow to come to town to break the law himself to get others punished. He might well be secret over the matter. If he had come before ten honest men, would one of them have sanctioned such a proceeding? I know of no person in the world who would have."* Another member said, *"Mr. Hemingway is highly to blame. Whatever authority he received from the Mayor he should have brought before this Committee. He sits at this Bench. He understands everything connected with this Committee, every tittle of information, even of a private character, mentioned here. Mr. Hemingway knows all, yet he can deceive this Committee."* At a meeting with Watch Committee members on the evening before the raids the Chief had told them that he was only interested in the activities of the roulette table keepers and that he had not planned any police action against betting on the racecourse. Mr. Hemingway did not, indeed, plan any activity *'on the racecourse'.* Instead he was targeting the two public houses. Councillor Hair said, *"At this time, this contemptible spy from Liverpool was in the town and Mr. Hemingway said nothing to us about it."* Councillor Telford, who said that he recognised there was a good deal of vice and evil in the city that required great energy to check it, spoke. *"I am surprised that Mr. Hemingway should have gone from his home to try to engage a man for making mischief and making himself more unnecessarily unpopular than he ought to have been. Mr. Hemingway says he dares do anything in doing his duty, but there is wise discretion to be exercised in every public duty and it is only right that Mr. Hemingway keeps within the bounds of his duty without overstepping them. I have no sympathy with the individuals who were punished, but our chief officer ought not to have brought a man of this kind. It is out of place to have brought him. I certainly think that the magistrates of this town, or the gentlemen who are to blame, have treated this Watch Committee with the most superlative contempt. I see no need for us to sit here. Our Superintendent (actually Chief Constable) tells us we cannot interfere between him and the magistrates and that he has full power and control over the town. What are we for?"* Councillor Maxwell said that he would not resign, adding the peculiar statement, *"Ducks may go with ducks, hens may go with hens!"*

At a meeting of the Town Council, Alderman John Hargreaves, the Mayor, disclaimed all responsibility for importing a *'spy'* and told the meeting that, having discussed the problem with him some three months earlier, he had left the Chief Constable, in whom he had every confidence, to his own discretion. He said that the Watch Committee had for years brought in spies, called *'detectives,'* who go about the racecourse and the city looking for suspicious characters. It was undignified, he claimed, for him to have to explain his actions and make excuses for his conduct as a magistrate. *"I have no excuse to make. Everything I have done is right."* Mayor Hargreaves' constituents in Caldewgate Ward said he had forfeited their confidence in him over the betting issue and they called for his resignation. He refused to go, but he lost his seat on the council in the elections a few months later. Councillor Creighton proposed a vote of confidence in the Watch Committee which was carried, whereupon all resignations were withdrawn. But they did not live happily ever after! Before the Council meeting ended, Alderman Hardy, a city magistrate, said that he thought a good deal of harsh language unworthy of a council of gentlemen had been used in what was a personal quarrel between the Watch Committee and the police. He said that Mr. Hemingway's efficiency was not in question, but he did criticise the solicitor defending the accused in the betting cases. *"If a burglar got into Mr. Bendle's house and was helping himself to plunder, he would hardly have sent word to the man that he was coming to catch him. Anyone who took a prominent part in the work of the Bench and the police would learn what they never knew before."* How true that remark still holds today. In my time in the Force, city policemen often would say that one half of the city had no idea how the other half lived. *"As to the law,"* he continued, *"the Municipal Corporations Act gave magistrates powers to take what steps they liked to put a stop to crime. The Watch Committee need not be consulted. Their functions are clearly defined by the Act. Therefore it was jealousy. It showed that they were touchy."* The Mayor added that the Committee's duties were, *"to provide police officers, clothe them, pay them, see that their duties were properly discharged and then their (the Committee's) duties were at an end."*

A report in the Carlisle Journal suggested that the antagonism between the various parties was simply the renewal of the old struggle for independent control of the city police. A curious claim by the paper, that cannot be verified, was that there existed a condition under which a pension was granted from the superannuation fund to a retired constable that he should not act as a detective when he left the Force. That was clearly a reference to the under-cover agent employed by the chief constable, but it was not divulged during the trials that he was, or was not, a former police officer. The paper commented that whereas, normally, the citizens would have been satisfied that the police had attacked the betting evil, in this particular instance it was considered that they had chosen the wrong targets. Instead of the professional gamblers, *'the colonels, magistrates and the gentry,'* the police had hit two little back street pubs and arrested all of their occupants, guilty or innocent, and had marched them *'in detachments to the police office where they were each searched'* and relieved of their possessions. *'The tritons have escaped Scot-free while the full force of the police has been brought to bear upon a few minnows.'* But the most odious imputation arising from the Chief Constable's action was that there was little trust between the chief and his Watch Committee. The paper was later to say, *'High offices in our ancient city have unfortunately devolved upon men who seem to have no sense of dignity.'*

The Magistrates took space in the Journal to issue a public notice stating the law on betting, adding that it would henceforth be rigidly enforced by the police. The newspaper claimed that such a notice would have served its purpose better if it had been published before race week. How true, but, of course, hindsight is an exact science!

Mr. Hemingway may have made many enemies over the betting case but he appeared to have at least one ally. An anonymous correspondent wrote to the Carlisle Journal:

'Do we want a Chief Constable made of such feminine stuff as to be always trembling in his boots when he sees duty staring him in the face? If human nature were all good, no bad, all sunshine, one would do without policemen and the thousand unpleasant and disturbing elements inherent in their calling. The duties of a chief constable, apart from the meaningless petty cavellings of Watch Committees and Town Councillors, is to see that everyone lives not in violation of the criminal law, whether that law be good or bad, perfect or loose and confused in its drafting, embodying the wisdom of the wisest philosophers and legislators or the converse, or passed by the legislators when in a virtuous mood or in any other mood not in unison with virtue, are questions with which he has nothing to do. His duty is simply to see that the law is carried out. The moral or immoral tendency of gambling is to him in his official capacity a matter of perfect indifference. If a law is passed, the duty of a Chief Constable, whatever his individual opinions may be, admits of no doubt, without any special instructions of either justices or Watch Committee. Although the Town Clerk laid it down that the chief constable is bound to obey the lawful instructions of magistrates, this does not mean he is never to act without this instruction. The framing of the Municipal Corporations Act had intended '

to put magistrates in the position of master/servant over their chief constable with an eye to dereliction of duty. The Act says 'lawful commands.' Neither the Watch Committee nor the magistrates can instruct a chief constable not to meddle. Criticism of Chief Constable Hemingway was not over an 'omission' but a 'commission of duty, which is another thing. It seems ridiculous that a chief constable should take into his confidence a committee of some dozen persons in all matters connected with the operations of the Force under his command. Such a course would no doubt please their vanity. As regards the chief magistrate, the matter stands differently. The constables would not have searched the houses without his warrant. But there was no more necessity of giving the Watch Committee any prior knowledge of the thing than shouting it from the housetops. The latter course would have been just as wise as the former. If the Watch Committee had acted with less vanity and more wisdom, they would first have ascertained if they had any powers in the matter. Somehow, of late, it seems the inevitable fate of provincial municipalities to become in a great measure a kind of public receptacle for feeble capacities. It's one of the evils we must endure for the advantages which are supposed to accrue from local self government. To speak in contemptuous terms of a common spy may sound strong and catching, but all detecting is spying. It is in the nature of all crime to walk in dark and dubious paths and if you intend to pursue it you must sometime step out of the sun's glare, leaving the high roads, and follow obscure and tortuous ways. Was Mr. Hemingway to go in the high polite kid-glove style, hat in hand, to say to those persons, "Will you oblige me by giving as much information about these betting transactions of yours as will enable me to convict you?" If the detective had so acted to create a crime that did not before exist, then we should indeed have loathed him. But his action was merely to collect such evidence as would make convictions clear of all doubt. A general stands before an enemy at a disadvantage when that enemy has reason to think he holds a divided, therefore weak, command."

This was very clearly no ordinary correspondent, but he opted to remain anonymous. Perhaps, of course, the writer was the Chief Constable himself!

On 22 July, the Watch Committee resolved to rescind the decision, passed two years earlier, to admit Mr. Hemingway to its meetings. He would henceforth attend only if he was specifically invited to do so. The Chief Constable was reprimanded for employing a spy and for the partisan spirit displayed by him during the recent libel prosecution.* It was resolved that the Committee's decisions were not to be communicated to anyone outside the meeting room. But they were! And they were announced for all to see in the next morning's Carlisle Journal. Now, could anyone blame the Chief Constable for any lack of trust he may have had?

Unbeknown to the Town Council or the Watch Committee, on 3 September the Mayor wrote on behalf of the magistracy to the Home Secretary. He complained bitterly about the conduct of the Watch Committee which, he claimed, was interfering with the Chief Constable in the discharge of his duties thereby undermining his authority and compromising the efficiency of the Force. The Home Secretary ordered a special inspection by one of the Inspectors of Constabulary but he did not communicate his decision to the Committee believing that the Mayor, as leader of the Corporation, would do so. However, the Mayor kept it up his sleeve, simply sending an instruction to the Watch Committee Clerk *"Please have the members of the Watch Committee and the Chief Constable summoned to a special meeting on Wednesday next, 29th inst., at 2 o'clock pm. Signed, J. Hargreaves, Town Hall."*

Prior to the commencement of business at a Town Council meeting on the morning of the appointed day, the Mayor was asked what was the purpose of the afternoon's meeting. He gave no details, stating only that HM Inspector of Constabulary would be present. That left those councillors who were also members of the Watch Committee wondering what it was all about – just two hours before the meeting. Captain Elgee was the HMI sent to investigate the Mayor's complaints. The Mayor began by outlining the magistrates' concerns, alleging that the Watch Committee's actions amounted to intentional degradation of a most efficient and useful servant. It had excluded the Chief Constable from its meetings and had read out to him a pre-prepared reprimand in response to which Mr. Hemingway had not been allowed to say a single word in his defence. He had been told that, but for his previous good record, the Committee would have taken much severer measures against him. The Chief had been told that details of that meeting's proceedings would remain within the walls of their meeting room, but a group, facetiously known as the 'ducks' (remember the saying,

---

*A reference to an action by the Mayor and other magistrates against the Carlisle Journal newspaper.

'Ducks may go with ducks, etc?) had afterwards retired to a local public house where they had met up with a reporter from the Carlisle Journal to whom they had imparted confidential details. This was subsequently vigorously denied by the newspaper which claimed to have acquired the information from another, unnamed, source but no-one other than the committee members could have known such detail. The magistrates concluded that the efficiency and prestige of the city police force had been so seriously undermined as to adversely affect both the discipline and authority of the Chief Constable and the preservation of law and order in the city, and that steps needed to be taken to restore public confidence. The Watch Committee, which had received a *'pat on the back'* from the Town Council, needed to be made aware of what their responsibilities entailed and what was outside their remit. Councillor Creighton addressed the Mayor. *"Pat on the back? Rather a slap in the face!"* Councillor Walker told the HMI that the Home Secretary was being made a tool for the purposes of carrying out the Mayor's vindictive feelings towards the committee. He further alleged that the Chief Constable was being used to do the Mayor's dirty work. The Chief responded by saying that he had always had a good relationship with the Watch Committee until the betting affair. He denied that he had applied to bring officers from Liverpool or Birkenhead to carry out covert observations in the city's pubs. His reason for going to Merseyside, he said, was to attend Chester Races where he had proceeded against men on the racecourse. He denied that he had anything to do with a raid and betting prosecution in Chester that had attracted much publicity.

Captain Elgee, who had carried out previous routine inspections of the Force, said Carlisle was the only Borough where the Chief Constable was excluded from meetings of the Watch Committee. After the meeting he inspected the Force, examining books, etc., at the police office. There, a Watch Committee member drew his attention to the cases of three constables who had been charged with drinking outside of permitted hours in a local public house. Nice fellow! The men had been off duty at the time and in plain clothes. All had been fined by the magistrates, two had been suspended for one month and the third dismissed the Force. *"Should not the case have been remitted to the Committee?"* he asked. The HMI's singular response was, *"Dear me! How are the men to live during the month?"* Captain Elgee certified the Force as being efficient. Afterwards Chief Hemingway incurred the wrath of the Town Clerk when he claimed his rail fare from Liverpool from where he had been summoned to attend the meeting. *"The Mayor and the Magistrates should pay. They called him,"* he said. Despite the Clerk's views, Mr. Hemingway was reimbursed his expenses by the Town Council.

oooOooo

Chief Constable Hemingway, no stranger to controversy, seems to have had a propensity for upsetting the local establishment. Not long after the betting affair he got under the skin of a local solicitor, Mr. Errington. In a case before the magistrates, Elizabeth Carruthers, a prostitute from Willow Holme, was charged with stealing seven pounds from a client. She was defended by Mr. Errington. The Chief told the Court, *"Her companions have been drinking ever since!"* *"That is a most unfair observation,"* said the solicitor. *"I may also further observe,"* said our intrepid Chief, *"that Mr. Errington has been fee'd with part of the stolen money."* *"That is the first time that I have ever been accused of receiving stolen property,"* claimed the affronted Mr. Errington. The Court Clerk asked, *"Knowing it to have been stolen?"* As the solicitor was about to respond, he was prevented from doing so by the Chairman who could see the matter was getting out of hand. *"Well, Your Worship,"* said the Chief, *"He brought it on himself."* The next edition of the Carlisle Journal contained a letter from the Chief Constable, which said, inter alia, *"The Bench did not believe that Mr. Errington or any other solicitor in Carlisle would knowingly accept as a retaining fee the proceeds of a robbery. Would you kindly insert the above. By doing so you will oblige Mr. Errington and myself."* He would also, no doubt, thereby, escape any further redress from the solicitor.

On 14 January 1876 at Cumberland Assizes, Judge Baron Huddlestone expressed his disapproval of Mr. Hemingway's practice of occupying a seat in the courtroom immediately below the sitting magistrates and alongside their clerk and legal adviser. *"It is not advisable in a court of justice that the minds of the administrators of justice should appear to be prejudiced,"* said his Lordship.

In 1876, the rights of cities and county boroughs to assume the title of *'Chief Constable'* for their chief officers of police was challenged for the second time since 1859. The Home Secretary wrote to Town Clerks stating that there had been some confusion caused by the various titles used by the boroughs and the counties.

'Chief Constable is a title under the Constabulary Act, 2/3 Victoria, cap 93, appropriated to chief officers of county police forces and in all cases used by them and cannot be altered without legislation. No such title had been fixed by the Municipal Act for chief officers of cities and boroughs,' he stated. He considered it desirable that in the latter's case a uniform title should be applied and that it should be 'chief superintendent.' Carlisle City Council was having none of that. They had rejected the suggestion in 1859, saying in a written response to the Home Secretary, "There can be no more difficulty in distinguishing between city and county chief constables than between chief constables of the various counties. Alteration would only tend to place the city chief of police in an inferior position to a county chief, especially where the title is borne by an inferior officer of the county police as here in Carlisle". * The Corporation's position had not changed and Mr. Hemingway's title remained 'Chief Constable.'

Mr. Hemingway's resignation was placed before the Watch Committee on 6 July 1876 and accepted upon his appointment as Chief Constable of Cardiff City Police Force. This was his third attempt to escape Carlisle – fourteen months after arriving, he had applied for a move to Bradford and in January 1876, he had applied to return to his former Force, Birkenhead.

On 31 July Mr. Hemingway made his last scheduled appearance in the Police Court when each of the sitting justices paid their individual respects. Dr. Elliott said, "It has been objected by some that Mr. Hemingway has been here so short a time. All that he has done is, therefore, all the more remarkable and conspicuous." The Town Clerk added, "He has been a first-rate, active Chief Constable." Mr. Hemingway responded, "Mr. Mayor, it is very gratifying to me to hear those kind expressions from the Bench. When I came here I was obliged to lay down some hard and fast lines and to pursue a strict line of action. The remarks that have fallen from the Bench convince me that that was the right course to pursue." He thanked those present for the testimonials they had provided. "They were the means of getting me a more lucrative position. It will be my endeavour never to allow them to be sullied in the least. Thank you, not as a matter of form, but sincerely." Mr. Hemingway was to make one further, unexpected, appearance before the Court. His troubled times in Carlisle were far from over.

oooOooo

The Mounsey Affair

This issue began in May 1874 with compulsory purchases by Carlisle Corporation of properties belonging to the trustees of the late George Gill Mounsey, solicitor, former Mayor of the city and Chairman of the first Corporation Watch Committee. Situated at Bush Brow, Backhouse Walk and English Damside, the land was required for the building of a new viaduct (Victoria Viaduct). There were strong objections and considerable acrimony when the Corporation sought more land than they had originally required for the project, even though the legal opinion appeared to be on the side of the Corporation under the provisions of an Improvement Act. John Giles Mounsey, also a solicitor, acted on behalf of the trustees and demanded compensation. The two parties could not agree a valuation and the matter was placed before a Sheriff's jury for arbitration. It was alleged that there was an unwillingness on the part of the Corporation to admit the true values of the properties and the rights of the owner and that it was being somewhat underhand with the aim of driving down the values. Mounsey moved to invoke further legal process in the High Court which would incur considerable costs upon both parties. Settlement out of court was eventually reached, but the Council was left with a substantial bill from Mounsey over which it 'dragged its feet.' In 1876 John Giles Mounsey obtained a distress warrant against the Corporation for non-payment of the bill.

Thursday, 3 August 1876 was Chief Constable Hemingway's last day of duty before taking up his appointment as Chief Constable of Cardiff City Police. Far from simply clearing his desk and keeping a low profile, he became deeply embroiled in what became known as the 'Mounsey affair.' At 11am, Johnston, a Sheriff's officer, in possession of a warrant, called upon the Chief Constable in his office at West Walls. After confirming that the Chief had possession of the keys to the safe containing the Corporation's mace, gold mayoral chain and other civic insignia and treasures, he demanded that they be handed over in execution of the warrant. Mr. Hemingway refused and told Johnston in no uncertain terms that if he persisted in his efforts he would lock

---

*A Superintendent commanded a division of Cumberland and Westmorland Constabulary based in the city.

85

him up. Johnston, understandably, went away to report to Mr. Mounsey. At two o' clock that afternoon, Chief Hemingway, wearing a smart new white hat, was talking to Mr. Storey, the draper, outside his shop in English Street when he was accosted by Mr. Mounsey who was accompanied by Johnston. Mr. Mousey asked the Chief Constable to assist him in the execution of the distress warrant against the Corporation for the unpaid bill. Mr. Hemingway refused and made it clear that if anyone so much as attempted to take possession of the Corporation's property, he would make certain that they would be arrested. *"You are the Chief Constable and you must do it,"* said Mounsey. Mr. Hemingway adamantly refused before going on to say words that would come back to haunt him. *"You have obtained the Magistrate's signature to the warrant under false pretences."* An outraged Mr. Mounsey demanded him to repeat those words whereupon the Chief Constable duly obliged. Mounsey lost his self-control and *'crashed his umbrella down so hard over the Chief's head that it smashed his new hat and rendered it useless.'* The Chief later said, *"It was a very severe blow which almost drew the tears into my eyes."* The Chief Constable grabbed hold of Mr. Mounsey who, he said, *"was very, very violent and very much excited"* as he tried desperately to escape. Mounsey's coat was torn in the fracas. Not surprisingly,

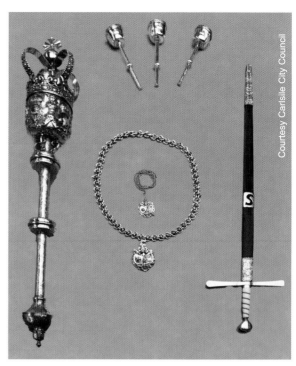

The Great Mace presented to the city by James II, the Sword, Sergeant's Maces and official chains of the Mayor and Mayoress. Mounsey obtained a distress warrant to enable him to seize these city treasures in default of payment of a disputed £530 debt owed to him by the City Corporation.

being in the city's main shopping street, the spectacle attracted a large crowd. Hemingway shouted out that he would give a shilling to anyone who would call a constable, but his pleas were ignored. He dragged Mounsey into Mr. Storey's shop. Shortly afterwards, Sergeant Bone arrived on the scene. He was reluctant to arrest the well-known city solicitor, intimidated, alleged the Chief Constable, by Mounsey's threats of the consequences he could expect if he became involved. The Chief very firmly told the sergeant to do his duty and together they took Mounsey between them, *'each with hold of one side of his collar and marched him up English Street'* amid cheers from the watching bystanders reported the Carlisle Journal. *'Mr. Mounsey's collar and neck-tie had come to grief and he was in the iron grip of Sergeant Bone'.* The prisoner, admitting that he'd made a terrible mistake, pleaded, *"You can proceed by summons, can you not?"* Chief Hemingway, responding that he made no difference between rich and poor, said, *"I pay no respect to persons. You must go to the police office."* The two policemen *'dragged Mounsey off by physical force'* along English Street to the station in West Walls.

In the Police Court next morning, Chief Constable Hemingway conducted the prosecution himself. City Chief Constables always did prosecute, but in a case such as this, in which Mr. Hemingway was personally involved, one might have expected an independent prosecutor. Furthermore, on that particular morning he was no longer Chief Constable of Carlisle and at that time a police officer's jurisdiction did not extend much beyond his own Force area.[*] Mr. Mounsey was represented by a barrister from the North-East. He took up a position alongside the barrister at the *'solicitor's table'* in the courtroom. The Chief Constable's request to the Magistrates to *"have him put in the dock like any other prisoner"* was refused. Mr. Hemingway gave his evidence and was then cross-examined. Despite Counsel's attempts to elicit details of the quarrel between his client and the City Corporation, the Chief insisted, *"I shall refuse any questions except in regard to the assault."* The examination continued and included the following:

Q. What pretence, Mr. Hemingway, do you undertake to lock up people acting under a magistrate's warrant?
R. Under the Police Act if they commit an assault.
Q That is not my question.

---

[*]A city officer had jurisdiction in the city and surrounding county only. Not until the Police Act 1964 did a constable's authority extend to cover the whole of England and Wales.

R	I have a right to lock up anyone in the execution of my duty as a police officer.
Q	How many times did you accuse him of getting the warrant by false pretences?
R	Once, and he asked me to repeat it and I did so. The second time I got a blow on my head.
Q	Do you think you were justified in saying that?
R	I am not here to say what I think. I am here to say what occurred.
Q	Was it not likely to cause a breach of the peace?
R	It was provoked.
Q	You were not in the execution of your duty?
R	I am always on duty.
Q	Do you say that a statement so insulting was part of the duty of a Chief Constable?
	[The Mayor, Chairman of the Bench, intervened and prevented an answer].
Q	Did you threaten to handcuff him?
R	Yes, and I should have done so if he had not calmed down.
Q	On the way to the station, did he say anything to you?
R	Yes, he said he was sorry.

Summing up, the barrister made light of the whole incident saying that the *'insult'* was sufficient justification for any gentleman to act as his client had, and he said that the Chief Constable himself had used unnecessary violence. The Bench found Mounsey guilty as charged and imposed a fine of five pounds, ordering the accused to pay the costs of the prosecution and of the damage to the chief's hat.

At the next session of the Court, the Mayor, Mr. J Bendle, himself a solicitor in the city, said he had received a letter from Mr. Mounsey which he would read to the Court. He said, of the Mounsey case, that he was sure that every magistrate had come prepared to deal out even-handed justice, independently and dispassionately. The letter he had received referring to the previous day's prosecution seemed to be a kind of intimidation directed against him, he said, *"but it shall have no effect upon me in any way. I make no remarks on the temper and character of the letter itself, but, I think, coming as it does from a gentleman of the same profession as myself, and who occupies the position of Under-Sheriff of the County of Cumberland, it is of much graver importance and very much more regretted than if such a letter had emanated from an ordinary person."*

Mounsey's bill was eventually passed for payment, despite an allegation that it contained a *"£300 charge more than it was proper should have been charged."* Councillor Hargreaves said, *"It would be scarcely right to pass the bill without remarking on the extraordinary nature of the proceedings taken to recover payment. The rateable value of the property owned by the Corporation is over one-hundred thousand pounds and there is only one gentleman in Carlisle who would be guilty of the very nasty conduct of which he has been found guilty. I am sure it is not for the want of money, and he could have waited the seven or fourteen days when he was told the bill would be paid. But that he should have attempted to put on the city to which he belongs the indignity of putting the bailiffs in possession of our furniture, and the further indignity of trying to seize the chain which you, Sir, have worn is not conduct which ought to be passed over when we come to the transaction of paying the taxed costs of determining the value of his miserable property. He has put on us an indignity which every citizen must feel. I shall not go into the proceedings the other day when he was dragged through the streets by the constables of Carlisle when his unforgivable temper led him to commit a breach of the peace."*

oooOooo

Mr. Hemingway duly left for Cardiff but before doing so, rather surprisingly considering all that had gone before, several tributes were paid to him by the Town Council, one Councillor going so far as to say, *"I have no hesitation in saying that Mr. Hemingway is the best officer we have had in Carlisle for many years."* Was he talking about the same man who had caused so much antagonism during his three years in the city, the same man whose actions had brought about the resignations of almost the entire Watch Committee?

The Chief Constable received gifts of *'a very handsome and massive gold locket'* from the men and a silver tea and coffee service from the Mayor on behalf of the citizens. The Mayor said, *"During the too short time he has enjoyed the position of chief constable here he won golden opinions from every class of society by the admirable way in which he discharged his duties. That esteem is stronger because his official life was* not *altogether perfectly smooth. He met in the early part of his career, and at the end, with some troubled scenes."* How true.

An action for slander

At the Watch Committee meeting held on 7 September 1876, the Town Clerk read two letters from former Chief Constable Hemingway informing the Town Council that Messrs. Mounsey, Solicitors, had commenced an action against him alleging slander and asking that the Town Clerk defend the case. In the first letter, Mr. Hemingway wrote, *"He has no doubt issued the writ in his hot moments, but I must put in an appearance,"* and in the second letter, addressed to the Mayor, *"he has, no doubt, issued the writ to annoy me and it certainly shows a vindictive feeling."* The Committee resolved to take no action. However, the Town Council meeting on 12 December heard the Town Clerk report that Mr. Hemingway had had served upon him a document alleging:

'slander, assaulting and beating and seizing him (Mounsey) by the neck, and with great violence tore his shirt and coat and they dragged him across the pavement into a shop and pinned him down with a violent grip to the counter of the shop, and although he said he would appear to any charge and to any summons and requested you not to use such extreme violence and to release your grip, you refused to do so and then with another constable, notwithstanding appeals made to you by Mr. Mounsey and bystanders not to use extreme violence, you became more violent and although Mr. Mounsey said that if you would only release your grip he would go with you, you then and there refused and with the said other constable, in a most violent manner and with much greater force and violence than were necessary for that purpose, dragged him out of the shop through the public streets to a police station and there imprisoned the said John Giles Mounsey. And that having arrested and charged him and detained him in a prison in the police station, you wrongfully and maliciously refused to, and would not, take or receive reasonable and proper bail to answer the charges. You then acted as such high constable, and it was your duty as such constable, to liberate the said John Giles Mounsey upon his giving reasonable and proper bail, and that you refused to accept anyone other than the brother of John Giles Mounsey in order to obtain his release from imprisonment by you, and he was forced to send for his brother and procure him to become such bail and thereby John Giles Mounsey was imprisoned for a much longer time than was necessary or proper.'

The Council, at least superficially, appearing to be indifferent and uncaring, resolved to take no action. Unlike today, when damages and costs awarded against police officers may be paid from police funds at the discretion of a police authority, in 1876 no such arrangements were in place. It would have been a malversation of public funds to have applied them to the defence of Mr. Hemingway. Consequently, he was left alone to face the action.

The case came up for hearing in the Nisi Prius Court in Carlisle before Mr. Justice Manesty on 19 February 1877. The trial lasted three days. Outlining the case, Mounsey's barrister told the Court that:

"The Corporation had, for the purposes of building a new road [Victoria Viaduct], compulsorily purchased at a cost of £2,150 land left to Mr. Mounsey by his father. The monies were left at Mr. Mounsey's office by the City Corporation which then took forcible possession of the land. However, additional, disputed costs amounting to a further £537.19s.6d were not paid over. Mr Mounsey, after requesting payment of these further costs without good result, took out a distress warrant at the County Police Court in Carlisle on 29 July 1876. The city's Town Clerk refused to recognise the warrant since, he said, the county magistrates had no jurisdiction over the city. Mounsey therefore applied for a warrant separately to two city magistrates but was refused. After two rebuffs one has to question the propriety of pursuing this course. Imagine the outrage if a police officer applying to a justice for a warrant was refused but persisted until he found one amenable to his request. But Mr. Mounsey was a determined man and he went with a sheriff's officer, Johnston, to the home of a third city magistrate, Mr. Thomas Nanson, in Victoria Place. Mr. Nanson did grant a warrant, whereupon Johnston went to the Town Hall to take possession of Corporation properties which, he said, he intended to sell to realise the amount of the outstanding costs. The Town Clerk refused to allow the warrant to be executed and called in the Chief Constable, Mr. Hemingway, to protect the city's properties. Therefore we found that those who ought to be the protectors of the law against those who resisted it were being employed by the Corporation of the City of Carlisle, with the Town Clerk at the head of them, to prevent execution of that which, if a private person endeavoured to prevent, would bring him severe and condign punishment. At the time of the trial, the warrant by the acts of the police under Mr. Hemingway, had still not been executed. When the sheriff's officer went to the police station to take possession of the city's properties held in the safe there, Mr. Hemingway, with the safe keys in his pocket, threatened to lock him up. Now, Chief Constables are very important personages, and very likely there was not the slightest doubt in Mr. Hemingway's mind that the Chief Constable of Carlisle was only one remove below the Queen and anyone daring to interfere with him was committing, if not treason, at least petty treason against that high functionary. Mr. Mounsey set off to see the Chief Constable and they met in English Street. Mr. Mounsey occupied the important position of Under-Sheriff of the County of Cumberland, and here, in the most important street of Carlisle, he was told by the Chief Constable that he had obtained the warrant under false pretences. Mr. Hemingway repeated it three times and Mr. Mounsey lost all patience. Some may be more cold-blooded and able to bear any amount of provocation; some might be meek enough if they had their faces slapped to turn the other side and receive a second blow, but that was not the general course of human nature. Mr. Mounsey could bear it no longer, and with an umbrella that he had in his hand, he struck at the hat of Mr. Hemingway and knocked it off. What a chance here for the Chief Constable of Carlisle. He had provoked a man into assaulting him. *"Now the chance is mine,"* he said, *"You have assaulted the Chief Constable of Carlisle."* That was what Mr. Hemingway told him and like most persons who are quick at speech, Mr. Hemingway was rapid in action, and being strong and powerful and Mr. Mounsey not being so and not being the Chief Constable of Carlisle, Mr. Hemingway rushed at him, caught him by the coat, tore his collar open and ran him into a shop and pinned him against the counter. Mr. Hemingway said, *"I shall lock you up,"* and he did lock him up. Mr. Mounsey asked, *"What for?"* and the Chief thundered, *"You have assaulted the Chief Constable of Carlisle,"* and he called out, *"I'll give anyone a shilling to go and fetch a policeman."* A policeman is not generally to be found when anybody else wants him, but when a Chief Constable wants a policeman, casually, a sergeant under his control walks past and he is ordered to seize upon Mr. Mounsey and take him and lock him up. Mr. Hemingway showed, first to last, determined hostility towards Mr. Mounsey. Mr. Mounsey came (to Court) for the purpose of vindicating his character, of far greater importance to him than any money compensation, and even now, at this eleventh hour, if ample apology were given for those words he uttered, Mr. Mounsey would not press the case against Mr. Hemingway."

The Judge intervened, and saying that he did not wish to apply any pressure, asked, *"Was this a case which must be fought out?"* The offer to withdraw was refused by Mr. Hemingway's counsel. *"Mr. Hemingway, having done what he believes he was justified in doing, would be mulcted in heavy costs and would really have to pay a very heavy pecuniary fine for doing that which he did not feel he was doing wrong. What was said was said in circumstances that protected him, it was a privileged communication. There was no ill-feeling on the part of Mr. Hemingway towards the plaintiff. What he did was in the course of his duty and he proposes to show the jury that he was justified."*

Details were then revealed as to why the Chief Constable had concluded that the warrant was *'falsely'* obtained. It appears that the magistrate, Nanson, a local hatter, who signed the warrant was a very old man with a less than agile mind and a very short memory. A short time after signing the warrant, and after an attempt had been made to execute it, he was visited by the Town Clerk and City Treasurer. In their presence he wrote a letter to Mounsey claiming that he thought he (Mounsey) had applied for a private summons, not against the Corporation but against a person. The letter stated, *"I find you have misled me as to the nature of the paper you got me to sign this afternoon, and which, if I had understood, I should certainly not have signed. I require you not to act upon it and request you will return it to me."* The letter was promptly delivered to Mr. Mounsey. To Johnston, the Bailiff, he wrote a similar letter giving him notice not to execute the warrant, *"the same having been signed by me under a misapprehension,"* and requiring him to deliver it up to the bearer or to the Magistrates' Clerk. Mounsey replied to the letter stating that he had already executed the warrant, which was manifestly untrue since several days later, on 3 August, the Bailiff was still attempting to execute it with the help of the Chief Constable.

There was some doubt about the Town Council's version of events – a suspicion, not surprisingly, of a conspiracy, though not one expressly stated in Court. Magistrate Nanson's letters, it transpired, had been written by him at the dictation of the Town Clerk in the presence of the City Treasurer, albeit, the Court was told, they comprised precisely Nanson's interpretation of events. At the time of signing the warrant Mr Nanson should have been aware that the city magistrates had a strict policy of issuing warrants only upon application to the Bench in the courthouse. It is surprising that, as a prominent local solicitor practising in the court, Mounsey himself was not also aware of that policy, giving rise to a suspicion that he wished to circumvent the prescribed procedure, though that, too, was never suggested during the trial.

In cross-examination Mounsey admitted that he was very angry at Hemingway's accusation and that when he asked the Chief to repeat his words, he, Mounsey, used the phrase, *"If you do I'll ..."* At that point Hemingway interrupted him. Mounsey claimed that he was about to say, *"I'll issue a writ."* It was put to him that what he was really about to say was, *"I'll punch your head."* He admitted that the payment of the costs had been tendered by the Corporation but, he said, *"I refused it because they had impugned the warrant and I thought I would not accept it until the validity of the warrant had been established."* Mr. Mounsey denied that he had brought the action against Mr. Hemingway as a means of attacking the Corporation.

Johnston, the sheriff's officer, told the Court that the Chief Constable had, indeed, told him that he would be locked up, but *"I think he was only joking."* Who would dare to take the risk that he was only joking?

Mr. Hemingway's counsel, addressing the jury, asked, inter alia, *"Having heard Mr. Nanson's letter read in Court, was it not the natural conclusion to arrive at that the warrant was not good? Whatever the words used by Mr. Hemingway, there was no doubting what he meant, for all Carlisle knew that Mr. Nanson had written saying he had been misled. Mr. Mounsey got angry and said that he would have said, "I'll issue a writ." What Mr. Mounsey meant was, "I'll strike you," and there followed a pretty good scuffle. Mr. Hemingway, having the dexterity of practice, ran him into the shop and used no more violence than was necessary. Mr. Mounsey was taken to the station and because the police would not accept the bail of a bum bailiff, he was detained for ten minutes. What was the conduct of Mr. Mounsey? Was he a person entitled to put himself before the jury as a person who had behaved throughout with moderation? What do you think of his letter to the Mayor after he had been fined? Its meaning was, 'You are not a person to be trusted for a moment because you have, in the course of your duty, fined me five pounds.' As gross an insult could not be put upon any man. The jury must not interpret the words 'false pretences' in its criminal law significance, but as the words used by Mr. Thomas Nanson in his letter which said he had been misled. The squabble in the street should have ended there with summons, and cross-summons if necessary, in which case the matter now before the Court could have been avoided."*

The Judge said that the Chief Constable should have known better than to have used the term *'false pretences'* and that, coming from a person of his standing in the presence of others, its criminal law meaning might well have been accepted by those persons. He told the jury that the warrant signed by magistrate Nanson was a perfectly lawful warrant and that magistrates did not have the power to withdraw a warrant issued in such circumstances. He agreed that the Chief Constable, and the police, had a duty to act upon it.

The jury took just fifty-five minutes to return a verdict for the plaintiff, Mounsey, on the question of slander, awarding damages of twenty shillings (£1). On the question of excessive violence they found in favour of the Chief Constable. Mr. Hemingway was ordered to pay the costs of the action.

The Corporation's monies covering the outstanding costs of the compulsory purchase order were accepted by Mr. Mounsey's solicitors and the warrant was withdrawn. The Carlisle Journal commented, *'We trust that the policeman who has been on daily duty at the Town Hall for several months will now be withdrawn.'* An officer had clearly been placed in a position to safeguard the city's treasures. An exchange of particularly acrimonious letters between Mounsey's solicitors and the Town Clerk followed before the matter was finally put to bed. Thus ended Mr. Hemingway's brief, but eventful, association with the Carlisle City Police Force.

A few odds and ends from Chief Hemingway's days

1873

Oct 16 – Chief Constable ordered to make Court Square a day beat for one man. [2] Sergeants to wear helmets instead of caps.

Oct 30 – Chief Constable to look into the nuisance caused by street preachers in the Market Place.

1874

April 23 – Police wages increased across the board by one shilling (5p) per week.

May 21 – PC Roddick fined 2/6d. [12p.] for being found asleep on his beat. [2] Police Armoury [what weapons, one wonders] to be fitted out as a storeroom.

Nov 26 - PC Johnston fined 40 shillings [£2] for accepting money from a prostitute.

1875

Jan 12 – Watch Committee [1] granted a gratuity of 40 shillings to PC18 Norman for arresting two offenders for robbery with violence. Said "it would stimulate young officers to perform their duties."

Mar 19 – Mr Hemingway reported on the arrest of a 'wandering lunatic' found in the River Caldew and his removal to Fusehill Asylum. Said it was not the duty of police to take care of 'lunatics' [Nobody heard him – it's still going on!].

Apr 27 – Vagrant George Wood fined one shilling for applying to the police office for a ticket to the Vagrant's Ward when he had sixpence ha'penny in his possession.

May 4 – Rough justice? At Frome, in Somerset, Sarah Beachim, 66 years. school charwoman for past 26 years, imprisoned for 14 days with hard labour for stealing a ha'porth (half a pennyworth) of coal from the school. Told arresting constable that she had found it in the yard (Couldn't he have looked the other way?}.

May 10 – Elizabeth McNeilly, Bridge Street, Caldewgate, applied to the police for a whitewash brush [brushes were held at Police Station at disposal of poor persons]. Said she was moving from Drovers Lane to Willow Holme and wanted to clean and decorate. Given brush No. 5, which, later that day, was found in a pawn shop. Fined five shillings or 14 days imprisonment with hard labour in default.

1876

Feb 3 – Watch Committee appoint member John Kirkbride to be 'Swan Warden' for the ensuing year.

Feb 10– Mr Hemingway to be supplied with a new suit of plain clothes.

Feb 17– PC18 Norman to be supplied with a suit of plain clothes and paid 2 shillings [10p.] per week plain clothes duty. He was given an overcoat, too, in October!

Feb 17– House of David Laing in Paternoster Row was on fire [Chairman of Watch Committee and brother of John Laing, builder]. Chief Constable and Sgt. Phillips ran round to see its extent before calling out the fire engine.

Jun 7– From the Carlisle Journal.

'CITY OF CARLISLE - POLICE NOTICE.
HOUSEHOLDERS are earnestly requested
NOT to LEAVE their **HOUSES UNPROTECTED**
during **RACE WEEK**, also on **SUNDAYS**
the 2nd, 9th and 16th JULY.

W. HEMINGWAY
CHIEF CONSTABLE

Jun 15 – Sgt Thompson reduced to the rank of PC for neglect of duty.

Jun 22 – Chief Constable provided with a horse for duty at the races.

Jun 29 - PC4 Thompson, see Jun 15, dismissed for borrowing money from publicans.

In 1845 Punch published an article on the introduction of plain-clothed policeman to the detective branch of the Metropolitan Police. Such officers provoked much ill-feeling, as Mr. Hemingway discovered in his handling of the Carlisle betting cases recorded in this section:

'Its members, disguised in plain clothes, are now known to mix in all societies, to whose manners and peculiarities they are instructed to adapt themselves. They mingle, as exquisites, in the salons of fashion; they creep, as cads, into the 'crib' of the costermonger. They frequent every species of tavern, from the first rate hotel to the Jerry-shop; and neither the freedom of the tap nor the sanctity of the parlour is safe from their intrusion....How much longer are free-born Englishmen to submit to the espionage?

George MacKay, (Chief Constable)
19 August, 1876 to 11 August, 1904.

"The Corporation would get applications of all descriptions, just as the Watch Committee did when it advertised for a Chief Constable. One applied because he was the cousin of the Queen, another had been a Lieutenant Colonel and another a Commander in the Navy. All sorts would apply!" So said a city councillor when consideration was being given to advertising the vacant position of city surveyor some four months after the appointment of the new Chief Constable. There were, indeed, *'all sorts'* amongst the sixty-four applicants for the vacant chief constable's seat following the departure of Mr. Hemingway. They included two Major-Generals, two Lieutenant Colonels and a further twenty-eight army or navy officers, all rejected without consideration. George MacKay, the Deputy Chief Constable of Edinburgh (Midlothian) County Constabulary was appointed. Short-listed with him were Chief Constable Walter Jones (Newcastle under Lyme), Chief Constable John Garden (Berwick on Tweed), Inspector William Bennet (Birkenhead Borough) and Inspector David A. Drysdale (Manchester).

Mr. MacKay, who began his police career as a constable in the Metropolitan Police in 1857 before moving to Edinburgh as Deputy Chief Constable, took up his duties in the city on Friday, 19 August, 1876, at a starting salary of £200 per annum; he had to wait five years for his first increase - to £250. It was Mr. MacKay's second application to become Carlisle's chief, having been unsuccessful three years earlier when Mr. Hemingway was appointed. Thus began the longest term in office of any Carlisle City Chief Constable – twenty-eight years, a relatively uneventful time that passed without any noteworthy innovations in the Force. In my experience it is far too long for a person to hold such high rank, certainly in the same organisation. Such a term may stifle new ideas and changes for the better leading to stagnation and discontent amongst the men, made worse if the incumbent possesses authoritarian and Draconian tendencies (although there is no suggestion that Mr. MacKay was so inclined).

In 1877, the Chief was subjected to a private prosecution alleging assault. Thomas Brown, a farmer from Low Cummersdale, applied successfully for a summons alleging that the Chief Constable assaulted him in Lowther Street on Saturday, 11 November, the day of the Martinmas hirings in the city. It appears that the Watch Committee and city traders had complained to the police that the huge crowds congregating for the hirings hindered public access to shops and thus affected business. In response, Chief MacKay went to Lowther Street to take stock of the situation. He saw Brown on the footpath. He asked him several times to move away but he adamantly refused. The Chief arrested and charged him with loitering and refusing to move when asked to do so by a police officer. Brown cross-summonsed via the county magistrates who decided that they would hear the allegations[*]. Carlisle's Town Clerk, on behalf of Mr. MacKay, protested that they had no jurisdiction to try offences committed in the city. *"As soon as a Borough gets a Court of Quarter Sessions,"* he argued, *"the county court is ousted."* Not so, responded the Court Clerk, *"At the time that the Act [charged] was passed, the city had no Quarter Sessions."* *"The city has had a Recorder for two to three hundred years[**] and has had the right to commit prisoners to gaol since time immemorial,"* said the Town Clerk. The Court Clerk rejected the argument and said that the county magistrates would press ahead and hear the case against the Chief Constable. The Town Clerk again intervened, *"I have a second objection,"* he said. *"If you assume that the county magistrates have jurisdiction to decide cases in the city, I maintain that it is only a concurrent jurisdiction that can only be exercised when sitting with the city justices at the proper petty sessions in Carlisle at the Town Hall."* The Chairman of the Bench said that his court *"deal all the time with city cases."* The Town Clerk declared that their actions in such matters would be *"totally void and invalid. It would be illegal, and if not, very improper. If it was brought to the notice of the Home Secretary I think he would prevent it."* The Chairman said, *"We will take the case at once."* The Town Clerk responded, *"I am instructed by the Mayor of Carlisle to say that if you go ahead with this case he (the mayor) claims to attend here as Chairman of the Bench under this Act."* [+] The Town Clerk then quoted from an Act of Parliament, *"The Mayor has precedence over all Justices acting in and for a Borough and may act in the*

---

[*]Summary offences committed within the city would normally be tried by the city magistrates.

[**]In 1561 an ordinance made menton of the City Recorder.

[+]By reason of their office, city Mayors are entitled to sit and, at least on one occasion during their tenure, do sit as Chairman of the City Bench of Justice.

county in relation to business of the Borough. For the sake of justice," he continued, *"there has been a summons taken out against Mr. Brown for an offence against city bye-laws returnable next Monday and it is desirable that both cases should be heard together."* "We will take this case," insisted the Chairman. *"You will understand that you do so under protest and if there is any illegality it will fall upon the heads of the magistrates,"* warned the Town Clerk. The case went ahead, the court being told that on Martinmas Saturday many people attended the hiring market and were jostled in a most unjustifiable manner by officers of the Corporation (city police) although no previous notice had been given to them as to where they should stand. Mr. Brown was violently pushed by the Chief Constable. Being a responsible man, the oldest member of the Board of Guardians, he did not feel disposed to sit quietly down under the indignity which had so unjustifiably been committed upon him. He said the police were pushing innocent country people about in a most disgraceful way. He remonstrated with Mr. MacKay and told him not to push him about, whereupon the Chief said, *"I will treat you all alike,"* and proceeded to take him by the shoulders and push him into the street *'with a bang.'* He would have fallen over had it not been for the density of the crowd. He told the Chief that he would summons him. He told the Court *"there were a great many policemen about, but they are people I do not like to keep company with."* The Town Clerk said that there were eight policemen there to keep the footpaths clear. Brown was given two chances to move away but refused, whereupon the Chief Constable led him away. *"City bye-laws state that if a person refuses to move when requested by a constable, he commits an offence and renders himself liable to be arrested summarily."* PC English corroborated the Chief Constable's version of events and the Magistrates dismissed the case against Mr. MacKay.

On 23 June 1878, PC 21 Robertson was on duty in Milton Street, Caldewgate, when he was assaulted by Wilfred Dunn, a private in the Royal Cumberland Militia. Dunn was arrested and taken before the Police Court. Chief Constable MacKay told the Justices that he was unable to proceed with the prosecution. *"The constable lies in a precarious condition, stabbed in the right eye which penetrated his eyeball and the doctor's opinion is that he will lose eyesight. He also has a two-inch wound over his right wrist, cutting an artery and other wounds on his head and body. The prisoner also had some minor head wounds."* Dunn appeared at Quarter Sessions before Mr. Farrer Herschell, QC, [*] Recorder of Carlisle. Evidence was given that the officer responded to a call from a man alleging an assault had been committed upon him. Conflicting evidence then followed as to what happened next when the officer confronted the defendant. PC Robertson claimed that he was subjected to a violent knife attack. The defendant claimed the wounds were self-inflicted when the officer tried to push him through a shop window. A local resident said that, upon hearing the commotion, he looked from his window and saw the constable strike Dunn fifteen or sixteen times in the face. After a lengthy hearing, the charges were dismissed. The jury clearly was swayed by the independent evidence.

A novel form of crime prevention was witnessed at the City Quarter Sessions on 5 July 1878, when a man appeared charged with indecent assault on two little children. The Deputy Recorder ordered the jury to throw out the case due to a lack of evidence. *"By throwing out this Bill you will prevent the filthy evidence from becoming public and so prevent it having an evil tendency on the public mind."* In another case in the same court two prostitutes from South George Street in the city were charged with theft of a leather purse containing £4.00 in gold, some banknotes and silver coins from a man named Ashworth from Nottingham whom they had met outside the railway station. One was sentenced to three months imprisonment, the other two months with hard labour. Afterwards the Deputy Recorder recalled Ashworth before him. *"If it had not been for your disgraceful conduct, a married man, the two prisoners would never have attempted to rob you. It was therefore through your misconduct and the temptation you offered them that the offence was committed."* He refused Ashworth's application for costs. Ashworth began to reply, *"It was not through my misconduct, I ..."* The Recorder cut him short. *"I am the Judge here and that is my opinion. The public have no right to pay for the misconduct of other people."*

In September 1878, Chief MacKay applied to the Watch Committee for an increase in his establishment of one sergeant and two constables. Five hundred new houses had been built in the city and the increased size had presented him with difficulty in providing the police cover it merited. A Councillor asked, *"Why don't you apply for even more? In London an increase of 200 police had been demanded in consequence of an increase of 14,000 houses. In Carlisle, each PC was doing duty for 200 houses whereas in London each had not more*

---

[*]Later Lord Herschell, Solicitor General in Gladstone's Government.

than 65." The Mayor, no doubt with an eye to his budgets, said, *"There is a great deal more wickedness in London than in Carlisle."* The Committee approved an increase of one sergeant and three constables. I am only too well aware of how much policemen object to, and grow frustrated at, the imposition of *'extraneous'* duties that seem to have little or no bearing on police work. Imagine then, how chief constables today would re-act to being told, as Mr. MacKay was in 1878, to undertake the duties of Inspector of Lodging Houses in the city. On 28 January, he brought a Thomas Burnett before the Magistrates charged with keeping an unlicensed common lodging house. He had visited the house at 10pm and found three beds in one room and a number of lodgers in another. He told the Court that in his opinion the house was unfit for the purpose. The defendant was fined ten shillings. The Mayor told the Chief Constable that he hoped he would look sharply at such places and let the Magistrates deal with them for he believed that there was a great deal of disease caused by people being huddled together in such a manner.

In January, 1879, Mr. MacKay found a foreign national in the Market Place behaving in a disorderly manner and causing an obstruction by setting up a stall to sell pictures. *"He was shouting and bawling and I thought the man was mad. I arrested him,"* the Chief Constable told the Court. The man was fined five shillings or seven days imprisonment in default. *"I have no money,"* said the man, *"I will write to the Home Secretary and tell him I have ten questions to ask the Chief Constable and you won't allow me to do it!"* Nice to know that chief officers had a hands-on role in those days. I know of only one, (Frank Williamson) , in my police service of over thirty years that was prepared to get so involved.

The state of Carlisle, 1878/79

A contributor writing in the magazine *'The Builder'* commenting on Carlisle, said, *'It spins and dyes, bakes and brews, casts and moulds, and by the variety of the processes it carries out, proves that all is fish that comes into the net. The railways and sea-port contribute.'* To him, all appeared well. However, the New Year 1879 began with over five thousand citizens receiving relief. On 3 January, the Carlisle Journal recorded that there had been *'no diminution in the amount of distress that has existed for the past month. Many are prevented from working due to the severe frosts, mill-hands are on half-pay though they work all the time the mill is open, and many are out of work. They are forced to seek help to feed their families to stave off starvation. One woman in Caldewgate is reported to be living in an unfurnished house and sleeping on a bed of shavings. Most people are poorly clad and in desperate need of additional clothing to keep warm. Outdoor workers had not worked for six weeks.'* An appeal was made to the better-off public for cast-off clothing and monies. Weavers in a number of factories came out on strike in protest at the reduction in wages. They were told that they would receive no relief. The Relief Committee distributed, daily, 125 gallons of soup in Botchergate, 85 gallons in Fisher Street and 200 gallons in Caldewgate. Coal and grocery tickets were distributed. Publicans, spirit merchants and brewers organized collections. Relief Funds were sufficient only for food and coal. On 24 January the Mayor made a further appeal for contributions to the fund. *"Frost that had been continuous since December 1st,"* he said, *"had increased intensity and pressure of privation and has become terribly severe."* Since the beginning of October there had been 66 days of severe frost. By the time the thaw set in, the city had been at a virtual standstill for seven weeks.

Significantly, despite the wretched conditions, there was no increase in crimes, (perhaps because few had anything to steal?). Maybe the police and the courts were also performing well. Another reason may be found in the Carlisle Prison statistics. The total number of prisoners for the year was 1252 males and 419 females. The highest daily number was 182 and the lowest 101. In all probability, given the hard times, these numbers included some who had committed minor peccadilloes in order to secure a place in the gaol, thus ensuring food and warmth. It was not unknown for that to happen in my time in the Force. The annual gross cost of running the prison amounted to £2681. Whatever, in July 1879, the Mayor presented the Deputy Recorder with a pair of white gloves, the emblem of *"the purity of the city."* The Judge responded by congratulating the Grand Jury on the absence of serious crime. But, out there there's always the opportunist who will *'volunteer'* for a spell in prison. William Armstrong, a labourer of Denton Hill, appealed for help telling the Relief Officer that he and his family were on the point of starvation, but the police received information to the contrary. Detective Constable Norman obtained a search warrant and went to Armstrong's abode. Inside he found seventeen loaves of bread, thirteen hundred-weight of coal, half a ton of potatoes, two fine shot pigs, teens of poultry, Indian corn and meal, much of it hidden under a bed. He was arrested and taken to the police station. *"Will I be sent to prison?"* Armstrong asked. *"Oh, yes,"* said the Chief Constable.

Murderous attack on Constable 16 Fortune
Rudge, Martin and Baker gang.

At Netherby, at 8.15pm, on Wednesday, 28 October 1885, a housemaid passing Lady Graham's bedroom door noticed that it was closed and on checking she found it to be locked. She was aware that Lady Graham had left it unlocked before sitting down for dinner some fifteen minutes earlier. The maid immediately brought this to attention of Sir Frederick and he and members of his staff went to investigate. Sir Frederick discovered that his home had been burgled, entry having been gained by the bedroom's open window and its door secured from the inside. Valuable jewellery had been stolen from the room. Early discovery of the crime had, without doubt, prevented a much greater haul and it was most likely that the offenders had been disturbed by the housemaid. Obviously, they still had to be very close to Netherby having had little time to flee the scene. The police at Longtown were informed and details of the offence were telegraphed to nearby police stations including the city station in Carlisle. Police enquiries revealed that earlier in the day four suspicious men, strangers to the area, had been seen in and around Longtown and had been asking questions about Sir Frederick's movements.

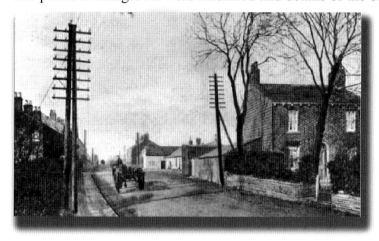

Looking North along Kingstown Road, Moorville, shortly after the Netherby robbery.

The perpetrators of the crime were eventually traced, arrested and identified as London criminals Anthony Benjamin Rudge, 45 years old, John Martin, 36 and James Baker, 29. However, more heinous crimes were to be committed in Carlisle and district before their capture and an abrupt end to their criminal careers. The fourth man, who was last seen in Carlisle, was never identified.

At about 11pm, some three hours after the burglary, Sergeant John Roche and Constable Jacob Johnstone of the Cumberland and Westmorland Constabulary, posted to keep observations for the gang, intercepted four men on the main A7 (Scotland) road at Kingstown, a district that did not at that time form part of the city of Carlisle. Both officers were shot by the men, Johnstone sustaining serious injuries. The assailants made off towards the city. Sergeant Handley, of the County Police was at Stanwix when he heard the gunshots. He called on the assistance of two local men before setting off towards Kingstown. At Moorville, less than a mile from the scene of the shootings, they came across the gunmen who threatened them with firearms before making good their escape towards Kingmoor.

PC16 Christopher Fortune, who had the reputation of being a determined and fearless officer, joined the Carlisle City force on 25 February 1875. A young Irishman from Wicklow, he drew the short straw on that particular night when he was posted to work the Denton Holme beat (a popular beat in my time on the force) for it was to him that fell the duty of confronting the villains. At about 2.30am, next morning. Sergeant Norman instructed PC Fortune to go to Dalston Road level-crossing. By then, of course, the city force would be fully aware of the drama that had unfolded a short distance away to the north and that the villains had been making their way into the city. Their local knowledge would tell them that from Kingmoor the railways would provide an ideal escape route for the fleeing felons, in particular the *'goods'* line of the North British Railway Company which circled the western side of the city bypassing the centre of Carlisle. It is pure conjecture, but I suspect that is why PC Fortune was sent to Dalston Road – to make enquiries of the gatekeeper and/or to keep a look-out for any suspicious movements on the railway property. In the event, when he reached the crossing, Mr. John Strong, the gate-keeper met him and told him that just a few minutes earlier he had heard footsteps as someone passed his cabin. He looked out and, in the bright moonlight, he

CONSTABLE JOHNSTONE
(Severely Wounded)

BYRNES, THE MURDERED CONSTABLE

CONSTABLE FORTUNE
(Severely Beaten)

INSPECTOR ROCHE
(Wounded)

Above: *Geddes the Goods Guard, captured two of the robbers at Tebay.*

Top: *Netherby Hall, (the home of the Graham family), lies about ten miles north of Carlisle. In the 19th Century it was occupied by Sir James Graham, twice Member of Parliament for Carlisle, (1826-1829 and 1852-1861)) twice First Lord of the Admiralty (1830-1834 and 1852-1855) and one time Home Secretary (1841-1846) in Sir Robert Peel's Government. Sir James died in 1861 and was succeeded by his son, Sir Frederick.*

Above: *aerial photograph of Netherby Hall ©copyright Simon Ledingham and licensed for re-use under Creative Commons Licence.*

had seen three men in the shadows moving along the railway tracks towards Denton Holme and Wapping. He did not see a fourth man. He was sure, though, that the men had seen him watching them. Very bravely PC Fortune, with no means of raising the alarm or summoning assistance, went alone after the men. Sergeant Norman would not have known that the suspects were in or near Dalston Road at the time, there had been no reported sightings of them in the area, otherwise he would surely never have sent the lone constable into the path of an armed and, by now, desperate gang. The constable first saw two of them as he crossed the railway bridge over the River Caldew. As he passed the signal box at Rome Street, behind Iredale's Brewery (the brewery was in a yard behind what was, until recent times, the *'Cumberland Wrestlers'* public house), he saw three men. He caught up with them at the point where the railway lines fork, just before the Bog Road road-bridge. He called out *"Hello chaps, what's up here at this time of the morning?"* The men turned towards him and he got a good look at their faces. PC Fortune then saw a fourth man who struck him over

Below: Dalston Road Crossing, showing the gate-keeper's cabin (arrowed) from which Constable Fortune took up the trail of the gang.

Above: *Canal Yard and signal box, looking towards the city - the route followed by the criminals following the shootings at Kingstown.*

Peter W. Robinson

John Packham

John Packham

Carlisle Library

D. F. Tee

Above: *a closer view of Rome Street signal box.*

Centre right: *They continued along the track to where it runs parallel to Currock Street, Wapping, passing Scott's Leather factory(on the left of the picture) and Iredale's Brewery (on the right) in Wapping. Rome Street Viaduct can be seen in the course of construction.*
It was in this vicinity that Constable Fortune challenged the gang and where he was savagely beaten senseless and left on the tracks.

Baker claimed that he returned to the unconscious officer and threw him down the embankment to save him from being run over by a train.

Bottom Right: *the same area pictured in September 1960. The railway signal box, (Rome Street Junction), into which PC Fortune climbed after regaining consciousness, is in the upper centre of the picture.*

the head with a heavy instrument that knocked him to the ground. He was given a savage kicking and left, insensible, for dead. The prisoner Baker, under interview after his arrest, told police that Rudge and Martin had laid the constable across the railway track, so that a train passing over him would so badly damage and disfigure his body as to conceal the wounds which they had inflicted. Baker initially made off with the others, he claimed, but quickly returned to the scene and removed the officer from the track by pushing him down a low embankment, thus probably sparing his life. As PC Fortune regained consciousness he recognised where he was and became aware that he had been thrown down the embankment. He crawled his way to the nearby signal box at Rome Street, where the signalman Thomas Evans first heard and then saw the officer, on hands and knees, climbing the steps up into the box. The time was then 2.50am. Mr. Evans thought that PC Fortune had been struck by a train, so badly was he injured. *"I saw it was Police Constable Fortune. He was in a dreadful state. His face looked as if he had a mask over it. There was blood all over it. He asked to sit down for a moment, and I allowed him to do so. He then asked for a drink and I gave him two lidfuls of warm tea."* Later Mr. Evans told investigating officers that the policeman was *'drinking tea and blood together.'* *"I took my handkerchief and tied up his head. After that I helped him through the window of the cabin onto the street (the signal box windows were at street level onto Rome Street). The last I saw of him was when he was going down the road."* PC Fortune made his way back to the police station in West Walls. No ambulances in those days – policemen were clearly made of stronger stuff than they are today! Witnesses were traced who saw the gang in the streets of Wapping making off in the direction of Currock then, later, there were reports of suspicious characters at Blackwell and on the Brisco to Wreay road. They were last seen as a group of four by PC Fortune in Carlisle. Chief Constable MacKay, Sergeant Shiach and several city constables went in pursuit and found traces of the attackers in the St. Nicholas railway goods yard. Travelling by pony and trap they thoroughly searched as far as Wreay without success.

Robert Walker, the City Police Surgeon examined Constable Fortune just over an hour after the attack upon him. He found nineteen scalp wounds. Three at the front of his head were clean cuts, which may have been caused by an instrument or kicks. He later reported, *"I had him removed to his own house, where he lay in a dangerous state for a week from shock. I think he will eventually recover, but it is quite possible he may suffer permanently from some nervous complaint. He is not in a fit state to attend (court) as he is unable to stand without support."* Constable Fortune had not returned to duty by the time of the trial, some three months later, in January 1886.

Constable Arthur Baker, a detective in the city force, examined the scene of the attack on PC Fortune, at daylight on the Thursday morning. He found evidence of a struggle and a large area covered in blood. He also found Constable Fortune's lamp which had been damaged and which was spotted with blood. He saw signs that someone had been dragged and then rolled down the embankment. A short distance away, in a pool of blood, he found PC Fortune's helmet, cut and with blood, hair and skin sticking to it. PC Baker walked the estimated 210 yards from the scene of the attack to Rome Street signal box and found traces of blood all the way.

It is believed that, during the daylight hours the criminals laid low until darkness fell, for they were not seen again until 7pm, (29 October) when they surfaced at Calthwaite railway station, just 11 miles south of Carlisle.

Murder of Constable Byrnes at Plumpton.

At that time, three men were seen on the railway at Calthwaite. An hour later they enquired at Plumpton railway station about trains to London. Told there were none till next morning, they made their way into the village which lies on the main A6, Penrith to Carlisle, road. The village policeman, Constable Byrnes, a 34-year old Irishman with twelve years service in the Cumberland and Westmorland Force, was tipped off by a messenger sent by the station-master that three suspicious looking characters, whom he thought might be the fugitives, were at the railway station. By the time the officer arrived at the station, the men had left. He set off back towards the village. Meanwhile, the suspects had been seen by a number of locals going into the Pack Horse Inn. As they left the Inn at about half past eight, Constable Byrnes challenged them. The policeman was callously shot through the head and thrown over a roadside wall into a field. He was found about an hour later and taken into the Inn. A doctor was called but PC Byrnes, beyond hope of recovery, died at

1am next morning. Earlier in the day, during a visit to Plumpton by Superintendent Fowler, Constable Byrnes had been fully appraised of the incidents at Kingstown and Carlisle. The two of them visited Plumpton railway station where they gave details of the gangsters to the station-master telling him to contact the police, quickly and by whatever means possible, should he see anything suspicious. The superintendent later said

that he firmly impressed upon the constable that, should he encounter the suspects, on no account should he tackle them alone but that he should follow at a discreet distance until he could summon sufficient aid to arrest them. Sound advice given that the officer would be able to remain concealed from the suspects but not much good in the event of him coming face-to-face, as he did, with such desperate characters. Perhaps he could have delayed confronting them until he'd obtained help; he was well aware of the danger involved but perhaps that was not an option open to him. We will never know. Shortly before he was shot, PC Byrnes had spoken of *"the imprudence of the Kingstown policemen, unarmed, assailing an armed band of four."* PC Byrnes left a widow and four children, the youngest being only one month old.

Christopher Geddes, of Grey Street in Carlisle, was the brakeman (guard) on a freight train that travelled south from the city on Friday morning, 30 October. As his train was about to leave Penrith, he saw three men climb into a wagon and conceal themselves under a sheet. He shone his lamp on them and though the men knew that they had been spotted they stayed put. Geddes guessed they were the wanted felons. He kept them under close observation, at the same time dropping a number of messages from his moving train that he hoped other railworkers would pick up and, thereafter, alert the police. When his train stopped at Tebay, a telegraph signal had just, at that very time, been received in response to his messages, giving no time to arrange a 'welcoming party.' Geddes quickly mustered a force of several railway workers and they began a search for the suspects. Geddes himself jumped into a wagon and was surprised to find it occupied by the wanted men. All three were startled and scrambled out. One of them drew a revolver but railwaymen, armed with makeshift weapons, struck down two of the gang and captured them, lashing them to posts until the police arrived. The third man (it was Baker) escaped. Guard Geddes accompanied the two prisoners back to Carlisle with the police. As the train resumed its journey south, Baker somehow managed to clamber back on board but he was seen and arrested when it reached Lancaster. He, too, was returned under escort to Carlisle. There were unparalleled scenes upon Baker's arrival at Carlisle railway station, pictured, left, in the 1890s.

The station was packed with a large excited crowd. As the police, including the County Chief Constable, Mr. Dunne, dragged Baker along the platform, the crowd surged forward in an attempt to seize him with the intentions of lynching him. Police officers present had to draw their batons and beat off the crowd. The Chief Constable, standing on a station barrow, appealed for calm. The prisoner had to be secured in a waiting room until most of the crowd had dispersed before being smuggled away via the underground exits.

Rudge, Martin and Baker were detained in the county police cells in Earl Street, Carlisle, and were visited there by H.M. Inspector of Prisons, Captain Wilson. A man named William Baker (there is no evidence that he was related to James Baker) was arrested in Manchester on the Saturday morning following the crimes.

Baker was brought to Carlisle where he admitted that he had been in Longtown and Carlisle on the day of the Netherby burglary. He had at least one previous conviction for a jewel 'robbery' at a country mansion, the home of the Duke of Montrose at Newcastle-upon-Tyne, and had served a term of imprisonment. However, he could not be identified by any of the witnesses to the Cumbrian crimes and, consequently, he was released without charge. Was Lady Luck on his side, or did he really have nothing to do with the crime? We'll never know. A Mr. Hayes of St. Ann's Hill, Carlisle, had been interviewed by the police in the course of their enquiries into the crimes. He had told them that about a week before the 'burglary', four men had been in the area and had questioned him about rail routes in the city. He had directed the men across the main West Coast lines at Kingmoor. It seems Mr. Hayes had come across the gang doing a recce for their escape south from the scene of the planned burglary at Netherby. They would, of course, have anticipated police patrols in Carlisle and a serious obstacle to their progress would have been a possible police presence on Eden Bridge, the only way across the river into the city apart from the railway bridges. In the event that is precisely what the villains did encounter on the night of the shootings. Interviews with them revealed that as they approached the bridge they found a police road-block. To avoid capture they turned to their contingency planning. They diverted by way of the Scaur and Etterby onto the railway tracks where they had been directed, innocently, by Mr. Hayes a week earlier. As they made their way through the city they hurried over the level-crossing on Dalston Road, near to where the Cumberland News' offices now stand. Mr. Hayes, giving evidence in Court at the gang's trial, positively identified one of them as one of the four who had questioned him about the railways.

At Cumberland Assizes in Carlisle, before Judge The Hon. Sir John Charles Day, the three prisoners were each formally charged with the murder of Constable Byrnes at Plumpton and with three charges of attempting to murder Sgt. Roche and Constable Johnstone at Kingstown and Constable Fortune in Carlisle. They pleaded 'not guilty' to each charge. Constable Fortune positively identified all three as the men who had attacked him. Outlining the circumstances of PC Fortune's case, counsel said, *"He was fearfully beaten by an iron instrument and thrown down an embankment ... a pistol shot would have roused the neighbourhood."* Each of the accused was found guilty as charged and sentenced to death. Judge Day told them, *"You have no hope of a pardon ... not at the hands of man."* The Judge commended Inspector Roche, Sergeant Johnstone (they had both been promoted for their bravery) and Constable Fortune and granted each a reward of twenty pounds. He also commended and rewarded the railway guard, Mr. Geddes, who was instrumental in the arrests of the felons.

The prisoner Martin had earlier been identified as a man wanted for the murder of Inspector Simmonds at Romford, Essex, on 20 January 1885, twelve months to the day before his convictions in Carlisle for the crimes herein described. His accomplice on that occasion, a man named Lee, had already been hanged. In that case, the Inspector and another officer had been giving chase to three suspected robbers who were making their way across fields, carrying stolen goods, to a railway line. When the policemen caught up with the suspects, Inspector Simmonds was shot and the gang escaped – an almost identical M.O. to that used in Cumberland. The Inspector later died. Two of the men were arrested. Lee was found guilty and hanged, the second man was acquitted. A Detective Sergeant Rolfe attempted to arrest the third man near London but was fired at and warned, *"If you step an inch further I'll send a bullet through your eye."* The man escaped but, in the Magistrates Court at Carlisle, Rolfe identified Martin as that man. Martin was not charged with the Essex murder, probably on the basis that, such was the strength of the evidence against him in Cumberland, there was little liklihood of his acquittal and the ultimate penalty was almost certain to be paid.

On Monday, 8 February, 1886, Rudge, Martin and Baker were hanged simultaneously in Carlisle Gaol and buried in the Gaol Yard on Bush Brow. A crowd of about 4,000 people was gathered outside the gaol at the time of the executions. With the closure and demolition of the prison, the three bodies were exhumed and re-interred in unmarked graves in Carlisle Cemetery. Locally, it is frequently stated that these were the last executions in Carlisle Gaol. Not so. That dubious distinction applies to Joseph Wilson, a 24-year old quarryman from Haverigg, Millom who murdered his landlady and was executed at Carlisle on Tuesday, 22 March 1892.

In preparation of the sentences of death being carried out, it was necessary for the city police to organise a Coroner's jury. Shown opposite is the police list of jurors, prepared five days before the event. After the executions, H.M. Coroner for the City of Carlisle held inquests into the three deaths. The jury brought in verdicts of 'Death by judicial hanging'.

H M Prison, Carlisle, photographed from Victoria Viaduct.

CITY POLICE OFFICE,

BE JUST AND FEAR NOT

Carlisle, 3rd Feby 1886

Coroners' Jury Summoned for 8th inst

1	John Strong	English Street	Grocer
2	Joseph Gibson	do	Draper
3	William Taylor	Church Street	do
4	John Wilson	English Street	Grocer
5	Thomas Herring	Randal Street	do
6	William Routledge	English Street	Tailor
7	Joe Todd	do	Chemist
8	George Pawson	do	Shoemaker
9	John Robinson Wilkinson	do	Tailor
10	James Smith	Botchergate	Tobacconist
11	John Little	Paternoster Row	Spirit Merchant
12	William Urman	St Alban's Row	Game Dealer
13	Thomas Dugdale	English Street	Draper
14	Tom Scott	Peter Street	Joiner

Tributes to the bravery of all the police officers, and the railwayman, Geddes, poured in from all quarters. Her Majesty Queen Victoria wrote commending the bravery of the men and inquiring about those injured. The Mayor of Carlisle opened a fund for the benefit of PC Byrne's widow and family and for the injured officers. He promoted it in the national press and a total of £1081 in public subscriptions was collected. A donation of five hundred pounds was given anonymously for the education of PC Byrne's children in the London Police Orphanage. Fifty pounds went to each of the three injured police officers. Shortly after the shootings, Sir Frederick Graham rewarded the injured police officers and the railwaymen.

On 2 December 1886, the Watch Committee promoted PC Fortune to merit class permitting him to wear the appropriate badge on his left arm. The award meant a salary increase of one shilling per week. He never fully recovered from the attack and continued ill-health forced him to leave the Force in 1891 after completing just sixteen years service. Though, normally, he would not have qualified for a pension, the Watch Committee granted him a 'special' pension. Despite his sufferings, Christopher Fortune lived to the ripe old age of 79 years. On 20 January 1925, he passed away at his home at 54 Broad Street, Carlisle. A funeral service was held at Our Lady and St. Joseph's Church. Six uniformed officers of the City Police acted as pall-bearers and a uniformed contingent led by Superintendent Johnston marched ahead of the cortege from the church to Carlisle Cemetery.

Christopher Geddes, the railway guard, subsequently joined Cumberland and Westmorland Constabulary as a constable. Appointed on 30 April 1887, his praiseworthy actions leading to the arrests of Rudge, Martin and Baker placed him in a somewhat favoured position from the outset of his career in the force. Unfortunately for him, it seems his senior officers considered that perhaps he took advantage of, and failed to properly handle, his 'celebrity' status and he was required to resign on 25 March, 1892.

oooOooo

Inspector Cowen retired on 14 November 1879. He joined the Force in August 1846, was promoted to sergeant in 1847 and Inspector in 1874. He had deputized for Chief Officer Bent during his illness, but when the Chief retired, Mr. Cowen was beyond the age limit for appointment to the top position. At a function to mark his departure from the Force, he recalled the time when officers wore glazed hats. He remembered working with Chief Bent, and talked of how the Chief had instituted a system of having a detective look after the felony cases. Such was the efficiency of the Force that for eight years after the arrival of the Chief there were no cases of housebreaking or burglary in the city. The most serious troubles occurred at election times. He described how, in 1847, not a single pane of glass remained in the Bush Hotel and Coffee House (Crown and Mitre). Chief Constable Sabbage took a detachment of men to the Market Place but was unwilling to involve them since a constable had been murdered at the previous year's election. Many stones were thrown at the police and he (Inspector Cowen) had insisted they did something about it. Sabbage said, *"Very well then. Go in and have a brush with them."* The police charged and the mob quickly dispersed without a fight. Chief Constable MacKay, on behalf of the men, presented Mr. Cowen with a suitably inscribed silver watch.

'Don't advertise to criminals' is sound crime prevention advice. It went unheeded by one local trader in April 1880. A jeweller's shop in English Street was entered through the roof from Devonshire Street and gems to the value of £4,500 were stolen. Earlier in the day a notice had appeared in the Carlisle Journal:

> *Jas. N Routledge [Est 1800] Watchmaker, Jeweller and Silversmith, begs to call attention to his magnificent stock of silver and gold gem jewellery, gold jewellery set with diamonds, rubies, sapphires, emeralds and other precious stones at prices much lower than usual having recently bought for cash at a great discount the stock of a London manufacturing jeweller retiring from the business.*

At 10.30pm a neighbour saw a man on the roof and assumed it 'was someone going to court a servant girl'. (Really, did that sort of thing go on in 1880?). It was thought that the crime was completed by midnight so that the offender(s) could escape the city on one of the midnight trains. Drinkall, bootmaker in English Street, told the police that a man had bought a pair of tennis shoes from him, the sole pattern of which exactly matched some found at the crime scene. It appears that several witnesses saw suspicious characters taking note of the jeweller's premises in the weeks leading to the attack. None thought it necessary to tell the police. A ladder used to access the roof had been taken from a building site in Lonsdale Street. At 9pm, same evening, a constable had seen a man hanging around the site and had chased him away. It was believed that a small boy had been used to enter the jeweller's shop since the access space was too small to admit an adult. The offenders were never traced.

On 1 April 1881 (All Fools Day) the Carlisle Journal reported an amusing incident, though not for the policeman involved. A prisoner, Pitchford, arrested for stealing poultry, complained of a bad smell from the WC in his cell at West Walls police station and asked the gaoler to turn on the water. The constable unlocked the cell door and stepped inside. He was immediately overpowered by the prisoner who escaped, locking the officer inside the cell. A warrant was obtained for Pitchford's recapture. It is not known if he was ever traced. Today, such an event would have the bobby taunted mercilessly by his colleagues. Policeman, amongst themselves, are a cruel lot!

At a Town Council Meeting in November 1881, the Town Clerk raised the issue of City Bailiffs. *"From the earliest times,"* he said, *"Carlisle was independent of the Sheriff of the County, the city's own sheriffs, or bailiffs, exercising within the city the jurisdiction of the sheriff. The Charter of King Edward III re-iterated this position – Carlisle was, in all but name, a county in itself. The Charter of Charles I said that there should be two men called bailiffs of the city and four other officers, one a bearer of the sword before the Mayor and three sergeants at Mace for the execution of process. The Sergeants at Mace are to carry or bear maces of gold or silver engraved with the Arms of the Kingdom of England everywhere within the city before the Mayor."* The Clerk recommended that the Chief Constable and his Deputy should be appointed City Bailiffs, that the Corporation should revert to the ancient practice of appointments, that two senior police sergeants be appointed Sword Bearer and Mace Bearer and three others Sergeants at Mace, the senior of the three being appointed Mayor's Sergeant. All were to carry small silver maces when performing their duties. His recommendations were agreed and put into effect.

On 19 December 1882, in what must have been a 'first' for the City Police, the Home Office informed Mr. MacKay that the German Government had granted his application for the extradition of the man 'Gray', wanted for theft of £300 from a cattle dealer at the Red Lion Hotel in Botchergate. Gray, he was told, was then on his way from Germany.

In June 1899, the Chief asked for a pay increase, adding that *"the last was in 1891 since when the population has considerably enlarged and my duties and appointments increased."* Other Chief Constables had had considerable pay improvements and he asked that his salary be compared with theirs. *"I could have claimed my pension in 1891, but so long as I am fit to carry out my duties I do not intend to resign."* He was given another pound a week, his new salary being £350 a year.

City Police Group, November 1893

A group of 41 officers pictured outside the Bowling Green Hotel in Lowther Street. Chief Constable George MacKay, centre,(standing), Inspector Peter Eckford seated to his left, Inspector William Shiach to his right, four sergeants and Mr. Hill, the city's sanitary inspector (wearing the bowler hat). The Constables include, standing, Tiffin, ?,?, Mattock, ?, Fox, ?,?,?, Barnett, Baker, ?, M.Armstrong, Taylor, ?,?,?,?,?,? Seated, Shiach, SgtsTurnbull and McKen, Constables Campbell, ?, Baker, ?, Dixon, Hayton, Pattinson, Hind, Sgt?, and Sgt William Clark (next to Mr. Hill). Individuals have been identified by Cumberland News readers, relatives of PC Armstrong and PS Clark,and from names on copies of the picture in their possession. One reader recognised the location – she was brought up in the hotel where her father was landlord – and recalled other police groups being photographed there.

On 27 May, 1904, Mr. MacKay resigned, asking for a pension from the superannuation fund in accordance with the Police Act of 1899. He said that he felt he'd had enough active service after 46fi years (who could possibly disagree?) and that *"with the city boundaries being extended it would be wise to hand over to a new man."* The Watch Committee placed on record its appreciation of his *'able, courteous and zealous manner during the long period of 28 years as Chief Constable of the city'* and wished him well in his retirement. David Laing, the Chairman, (brother of John Laing, the building contractor) said Mr. MacKay would continue to live in Carlisle after his retirement. Advertisements were placed for his successor at a salary of £300 per annum, plus free house, coals and electric lighting. A man of between 30 and 40 years old was sought, medically fit and qualified in Weights and Measures legislation and procedures. He had to be prepared to take on the role of Director of the city's Fire Brigade and preference would be given to an applicant with relevant experience.

A few odds and ends from Chief MacKay's days

1877
Jan 4 – [1] Capes at 9/6d [47p] each to be procured for the patrolmen.
[2] Clerk of the Peace announced that the Treasury would in future only allow one guinea for prosecution briefs instead of 2 guineas as hitherto. Barristers walked out of court. The Deputy Recorder agreed on this occasion to pay the higher amount before the barristers returned and City Quarter Sessions business began.

Jan 12 – Police being too few to prevent nuisance of 'dissolute characters' resorting to the backlanes in the east end of the city, Chief Constable recommended the erection of 9 lamps. Council agreed.

Jan 26 – A 'churchgoer' wrote to the local newspaper re his annoyance caused by the impertinence and damage done by 'gatherings of uncultivated lads' at and within the gates of his church. *"The oft repeated question is 'Where are the police?'* Answer *'Not to be found!'* Is it asking too much of the guardians of the peace to keep a strict eye when people are going to and fro?"* [Now where have I heard that before?']

Jan 29 – PC McTaggart charged Edward Muirhead, a 'potter' of Broadguards with keeping a donkey in his house. Evidence showed it had been there for several days. The Mayor asked *'It slept with you? We'll let you off this time and advise you to keep better company in future'*.

May 18 – James Haig, aged 12 and David Stanton, 10, charged with stealing four bottles of lemonade from a railway wagon. As each had been in court previously, City Magistrates ordered each to receive ten strokes of the birch rod.

Jun 26 – Robert Doran, aged 10, charged with office-breaking and theft of a pair of clogs. Sentenced to 6 strokes of the birch rod.

Jun 28 – Hugh Donoghue, 14, charged with theft of two stones [28lbs] of old iron. Sentenced at Cumberland Assizes to 12 strokes of the birch rod.

Jul 12 – PS Stordy [previous discipline for drinking on duty] fined £1 for allowing two prisoners to escape from the cells.

Jul 26 – PCs McTaggart and Boon each fined £1 for fighting on West Walls when coming off duty.

Aug 30 – Detective officers to be employed, 4 horses provided and refreshments to be supplied to the men, during the visit of Princess Louise on 20 September [opening of the new Viaduct].

Nov 15 – PC33 Kirkpatrick fined five shillings for gossiping on duty.

1878
Jan 3 – William James Morgan, 12, at City Quarter Sessions charged with wounding – slashed face of 15 year-old boy at a Temperance Meeting in Mary Street. Sentenced to 3 months imprisonment with hard labour.

Jan 4 – [1] Mr. Redin, Governor of Carlisle Gaol for past 27 years retired on pension of 2/3rds his salary - £400pa. [a lot of money in 1878!]. 110 prisoners lodged in the Gaol.
[2] 453 lunatics were being held in the Asylum, chargeable to the counties of Cumberland and Westmorland at 9s/11d [50p] per week [the cost of their keep].

Jan 10 – Waterproof overalls to be provided for wet weather – 5/9d [29p] pair also gloves at 13d [6p].

Feb 28 – new uniforms at £2.11.5d [£2.57] each and helmets at 8/9d [44p] each to be issued.

Mar 14 – Chief MacKay applies to return to his former force, Midlothian and Linlithgow, as Chief Constable – unsuccessful.

Apr 9 – Town Council approved plans to construct a mortuary in the garden of West Walls police office.

Jun 7 – Detective Norman appeared before magistrates for having a chimney fire. [Much laughter in the court]. *'As this is the first offence of this kind, we will let you off by paying the mitigated penalty of one shilling [5p]'*. [More laughs].

Aug 22 – Force increased by 1PS and 2PCs – 'during the year 11 new streets, 487 dwellings, 17 shops and 1 manufactory have been built, so extending beats as to make it extremely difficult to give the necessary attention to the preservation of property.

1879

Jan 2 – PC19 Threlkeld dismissed – found in a brothel whilst on duty.

Feb 13 – New uniforms at £1.19.9d [£1.99] supplied by Smith's of Derby. Smiths were still supplying the Force with uniforms up to the time of integration in 1963.

Apr 10 – The Caledonian Railway Company to maintain the telegraph communication system between the police office and the gas works for £3p.a. [This was to maintain a buzzer at the gas works which summoned men to the fire brigade].

May 15 – PC Keep to be paid one shilling a week extra for drilling the men.

Oct 2 – PS Stordy [see 1877] reduced in rank to Constable for being drunk on duty and making false entries in his pocket book.

Oct 30 – new capes, extra stout duck regulation pattern, whatever they may be, issued at a cost of 8/3d [41p] each.

Dec 11 – PS Shiach, as the Mayor's Sgt. to be supplied with a new hat.

Dec 18 – Waterworks Committee asked to supply turncocks with a loose scarlet flannel jacket and cap with a red band to be worn at fires so as to make them distinguishable.

1880

Jan 9 – John Corrie, English Street, charged with being drunk in charge of a horse attached to a hearse. PC English said Corrie had fallen from the vehicle and was unable to stand. Fined 2/6d.

Jan 23 – 2 x 12 year old and 1 x 9 year old boys before the police court charged with theft of pigeons. All sorts of keys in their possession. Each ordered to receive 5 strokes of the birch rod.

Jan 27 – CC Mackay traveled to Glasgow to help escort 3 prisoners back to Carlisle for theft of £300 from a Botchergate Hotel – a major crime in those days.

Jan 27 – Case of Manslaughter at Dalston – furious driving of a horse drawn 'gig' that collided with another horse and cart killing the driver.

Feb 26 – new punt at a cost of £14 to replace worn out police boat, after proposal to alter the old punt into a rowing boat was overruled.

Apr 29 – Watch Committee set aside £140 for provision of detectives during the Royal Show in the city.

Jun 24 – PCs on special duty at the Royal Show to be charged for at five shillings a day.

Jul 8 – Chief Constable MacKay to be provided with a horse during the Royal Show.

Jul 22 – Watch Committee thanked the Chief and the men on duty at the Royal Show and paid the men, except PC13 Mooney, ten shillings each [Was it just his unlucky number, or what, one wonders, did he do to justify such treatment?].

Nov 11 – Murder [domestic] in Broadguards. John O'Neil a basket maker arrested by patrolling constable.

1881

Mar 10 – Chief Constable to ensure that all houses within the municipal borough are numbered before the census.

May 6 – Robert Nixon, a former inmate of Carlisle Gaol, convicted of throwing tobacco from the Viaduct into the prison yard. Fined 5 shillings or 7days imprisonment.

Jun 9 – PCs to be allowed an extra 3 days annual leave provided they are six months clear of charge in the defaulters book.

Jun 16 – Chief Constable authorised to obtain ornaments for the helmets at a total cost of £4.10s. [£4.50].

Sep 1 – Carr and Company allowed to fix a telephone wire to the police office [to save the cost of an unsightly telegraph pole].

Nov 10 – New uniforms of hats, frock coats and trousers, complete with gold lace trimmings, to be supplied to the three Sergeants at Mace – the Mayor's Sergeant, the Sword Bearer and the Mace Bearer.

1888

Jan 19 – City policemen present retiring Dr.Lediard with a gold Maltese Cross as a testimonial of thanks for his First Aid and Ambulance lectures to the Force.

1889

May 30 – Inspector Eckford provided with a character reference to enable him to apply for the position of Chief Constable, Wakefield City Police.

Aug 1 – 4 dozen whistles procured from J.Hindson and Co., Birmingham, numbered and engraved 'Police Force, Carlisle', at cost of 19/-[95p] p.doz.

Sep 26 – Officers directed to acquire 'silent' boots, and boot allowance increased from 9d. to 10d.p.week to meet the additional expense.

Nov 7 – Due to numerous accidents, police to have posters printed and distributed warning public against putting up clothes lines in thoroughfares and back streets.

1890
Feb 6 – PC37 Sewell awarded £1 for conspicuous bravery in stopping a runaway horse in Botchergate.

Mar 13 – St.John Ambulance badges to be worn on left sleeve of uniforms.

1898
Feb 18 – Chief Constable reported that he had caused an identifying mark to be placed on the left foot of each of the Corporation's swans.

Apr 15 – White gloves to be worn by the force.

Nov 11 – City Surveyor to arrange for electric lighting in the police station and Chief's house.

Dec 9 – Death reported of ex-PC Thomas Linton, who, for 38 years, had received a pension of nine shillings a week for injuries received on police duty.

1899
Sep 15 – Laying of the foundation stone of St. Aidan's Church, Warwick Road – police Guard of Honour for the Duchess of Devonshire and the Primate of All England, The Archbishop of Canterbury. The Bishop of Carlisle gave a donation to Police Funds in appreciation.

1900
Jan 19 - PC9 Davidson resigned to join the Imperial Yeomanry for service in South Africa [Boer War].

May 25 – 16 City Constables sent to Newcastle on Tyne for the visit of HRH The Prince of Wales.

1904
Jun 16 – Alexander Henry, LLB, Recorder of Carlisle appeared in London Bankruptcy Court upon examination. Said his income was £600 but his expenditure was £750. Made a proposal to pay his creditors 7s/6d in the £1.

Sep 2 – Thomas Turner of Crown and Anchor Lane appeared before the city magistrates for 130th time, charged under the Inebriates Act with being disorderly in English Street, He was fined 5 shillings [25p], "Why wasn't I locked up?," he asked.

Nov 18 - Alexander Henry, LLB, the Recorder of Carlisle since 1891 collapsed and died during the hearing of a case in the King's Bench Division. He was the third Recorder of the city. In a remarkable coincidence, his younger brother, a magistrate and civil engineer, died suddenly at Lisburn on the same day.

George Hill, (Chief Constable)
12 August, 1904 to 7 January, 1913.

To select the new chief constable, the nine members of the Watch Committee who formed the selection panel on 6 July 1904 decided upon an exhaustive voting system, one candidate dropping out of consideration at each vote. A short-list of six applicants was interviewed for the position, George Hill (Chief Constable of Kilmarnock), Arthur M. Berry (Chief Constable and Captain of the Fire Brigade, Kendal), William Frost (Superintendent and Chief Officer, Sheffield City Fire Brigade), Henry Galloway (Chief Inspector and Deputy Chief Constable, Cambridge), L.W. J. Jagger (Inspector and Chief Clerk, South Shields) and Henry Woolnough (Superintendent and Deputy Chief Constable, York). When only three candidates remained Mr. Berry received five votes, the others two each. At this stage, Mr. Berry, being the overall winner, had by any standards, secured the appointment. Right? Wrong! For whatever reason one of the applicants who attracted two votes was dropped and a further round took place producing an amazing result. Mr. Hill polled

George Hill.

five votes, Mr. Berry four. Mr. Hill was declared the winner and was appointed Chief Constable. The panel then dispersed. Quickly, rumour spread around the city that there had been a mistake in the voting. There was embarrassment because many telegrams had been sent announcing Mr. Hill's appointment. The Town Clerk stated the obvious, that Mr. Berry had dropped a mark in the final round, but he offered no explanation. One member said he thought he may have written the name 'Hill' rather than 'Berry' which he had intended. Members of the Committee approached the Chairman and asked that he reconvene the meeting arguing that there should be a *"fair and square vote."* The Chairman refused, saying that he had verified the papers which showed that Mr. Hill received five votes. Reports state that Mr. Berry was 'much chagrined' at the outcome. Who, in the same position, would not have been? A little information about Mr. Berry's background – he is reported to have been *"Thirty years old, had served in all grades of the Constabulary and had been in six police forces."* Surely, he wasn't long enough in any of them to gain the experience demanded of a chief constable!

George Hill, a native of Lanarkshire, was educated at Airdrie Academy. He received legal training in the Procurator Fiscal's Office in Airdrie before joining Edinburgh City Police as a constable in 1890. With just over three years service he was appointed Detective Inspector and six months later he was promoted to Lieutenant in charge of the forty detectives that comprised Edinburgh's CID. In 1898 he was appointed Chief Constable of Kilmarnock Burgh Police. He had previously been short-listed for the vacant positions of Chief Constable of Edinburgh and Assistant Chief Constable of Liverpool. Mr. Hill, a 35-year old married man, was an impressive figure, over 6 feet tall. In Kilmarnock where he had charge of thirty-three men to police a population of 36,000, the Convenor of the Burgh's Watch Committee described his departure to Carlisle as *"a calamity for the town of Kilmarnock."* He continued, *"At the time of his appointment the Force was in an antiquated and primitive condition. Under Hill, the men were rapidly strung up to 'concert pitch.' Gymnasium and drill were established and the old-timers who had outlived their usefulness were quietly shelved on small pensions. The new men were carefully selected. Only those of sound physique and character were chosen. The men, generally, soon realized that promotion was only to be had by attention to duty, and the esprit-de-corps has been something altogether unusual. Now the Force in Kilmarnock is recognized as one of the finest in Scotland."* One old constable said, *"Carlisle's gain is Kilmarnock's loss. We will not look upon his like again. Had I been twenty years younger my ambition would have been to get a post in the Carlisle Force."* A local newspaper reported that it was perhaps in his 'outside' work of a philanthropic nature that Mr. Hill was seen at his best. He organized concerts that brought in considerable monies for the Force's widows' and orphans' fund. For three years prior to his move to Carlisle he had put together a fund to provide boots and stockings for poor waifs, and *'the stigma of the poor little souls walking the streets of Kilmarnock in frost and snow with bare feet has been removed.'* In his early days in the town he thought it would be a good idea if every poor child in Kilmarnock could have a substantial Christmas dinner and *'Hey Presto, a magnanimous and anonymous donor came forth and the scheme was a huge success. The Baillies, Town Councillors with their wives and daughters are to be seen on these occasions acting as waiters and waitresses to the poor 'flotsam and jetsam' at their annual feast. The hungry guest, as they ravenously devour the roast beef, mince pies, oranges and sweets provide a spectacle worth seeing and remembering.'*

As Mr. Hill left Kilmarnock he was presented by the townsfolk with a rosebowl and a purse of gold; Mrs. Hill received a diamond ring. A superintendent speaking for the policemen and lamplighters as he presented gifts on their behalf to Mr. Hill said, *"Kilmarnock never had a better, abler or more approved chief constable. When he came here from Edinburgh he had a big name. He leaves for Carlisle with a bigger name still. In Kilmarnock he has been the policemen's chief friend. It is due to him that we have bigger pay and shorter hours. Kilmarnock is losing a splendid chief constable and the police Force the best friend it ever had."* Mr. Hill responded, *"I have a very strong feeling that in leaving Kilmarnock I would like to take the Burgh Police Force with me to Carlisle."* The men sang, *'Will ye no come back again?'* A Glasgow newspaper commenting on his appointment to Carlisle, and in particular to his relentless attack on the nuisance of betting in the Scottish town, said *'Mr. Hill, it may be safely assumed, will not tolerate in Carlisle what he has practically crushed out of existence in Kilmarnock.'*

A few days after Mr. Hill's arrival in the city, a Carlisle newspaper carried a humorous tale. A local gentleman went to the police station in West Walls seeking an interview with the new chief. He was taken to his office by a constable who knocked at the door. *"Come in,"* was the response and the constable obeyed, but there was no-one in the office. With a look of complete amazement the officer turned to the visitor and told him that *"It was only the parrot speaking."* The bobby had not been made aware that his new boss was the owner of a bird that was a very clever talker.

Policing the city was not the Chief's only task. Soon after his arrival he was in action at the scene of the fire, discovered by a patrolling constable, which destroyed Her Majesty's Theatre in Lowther Street on 16 September, 1904. The brigade, with the assistance of military firefighters, were playing water on the blaze within five minutes but were unable to save the building. The Chief was to find that he was also responsible for licensing the city's luggage-porters, whom he supplied with old police caps for identification.

In November 1904, the Chief Constable reported to the Watch Committee that he had met with his men and together they had resolved to hold annual police concerts to raise monies for a recreation room for the Force and also to establish a city police band. Thirty officers, musicians, had already volunteered their services. The news met with hearty approval and the proposals were put into effect (but, several years later, one month after Mr. Hill left the Force, the band was discontinued and its instruments put up for sale).

On 23 October 1908, Chief Hill asked his Watch Committee to impose a speed limit of 10mph on vehicles using the city's streets. Checks had shown that speeds were averaging 15 to 17mph and the police were finding much difficulty proving to the satisfaction of the courts the offence of driving to the common danger of the public, contrary to Section 1 of the Motor Car Act of 1903. In the previous twelve months, the Chief said, there had been three reported cases of personal injury arising from reckless driving of motor cars and three motorists had been prosecuted and fined. A cow and several sheep had also been killed by cars in the streets!

Chief Hill, together with his deputy Superintendent Eckford, Detective Inspector Pattinson and Sergeant Burnett were awarded the Police Coronation Medal in July 1912.

Her Majesty's Theatre on Lowther Street (photo – Tullie House Museum).

Above: *the city police/fire brigade at a demonstration at the Turf Hotel. The man in the light coloured suit is recorded elsewhere as Chief Constable Hill, but he does not resemble Mr. Hill, positively identified in other photographs included here.*

Above: *a city luggage porter*
(photo – Carlisle Public Library).

Above: c1905. Fifty-seven officers pictured with new Chief Constable George Hill. Here the chief is seated centre, with his deputy, Superintendent Peter Eckford, on his right. The picture includes two much younger inspectors than the one in the earlier group picture, six sergeants and two plain-clothed detectives.

Left: City Police Band 1905. Chief Constable George Hill, centre, front row, Superintendent Peter Eckford to his right. Sergeant W J Sinton, the Bandmaster, to his left, Sergeant Burnett, Secretary, front row to his right.

Enforced retirement

In September 1912, following the prosecution of Carlisle Motor Company, Limited, for leaving a motor vehicle on the road longer than was necessary in contravention of City Bye-laws, local newspapers printed details of serious allegations made in court against the Chief Constable. They recorded that in evidence a Mr. Couch, acting for the company, said it had been victimised by the Chief Constable because it declined to provide him with the free use of a motor car. He alleged that when the company had been threatened with prosecution the Chief Constable had called suggesting that he should have the use of a car, free of charge. *"He gets it,"* said Mr. Couch, *"and we hear nothing further about it (the prosecution)."* Mr. Hill promptly denied the allegation and declared it an absolute fabrication.

The Watch Committee called for a report from Mr. Hill, to be presented to them through the Town Clerk, the Corporation's chief law officer. It demanded that the Chief Constable clear himself of the serious charges made against him on oath. Mr. Hill subsequently told the Committee that he had consulted his solicitor who advised him either to lay a statement before the Home Secretary and invite an inquiry or alternatively begin an action for slander against Mr. Couch. The Town Clerk expressed his opinion that the Home Office would not intervene in such a case. Mr. Hill, however, opted for this course, providing a statement of the facts of the case together with the official depositions of the evidence taken at the hearing in the Police Court, the newspaper reports and other documents. The Home Office responded as the Town Clerk had predicted by saying, *'it was not desirable for the Home Secretary to direct the holding of an inquiry…the matter was one to be dealt with by the local police authority.'* On receipt of this news at the end of October, the Watch Committee, surprisingly, did not think any action on its part was necessary. It took none and neither did the Chief Constable.

It is common knowledge that it is so easy, maliciously, to make false accusations in court against a police officer, well knowing that he has little hope of redress. Often an accused person, or his lawyer, takes the view that the only hope of defence is to attack and discredit a prosecution witness. Police officers grow accustomed to it and simply shrug off these attacks, accepting them as a hazard of the job. If that is what Mr. Hill and his Watch Committee thought, and if they considered that this matter had been put to bed, they were soon to discover they were mistaken. A Councillor pursued the issue at the next Town Council Meeting, listing a motion that the Chief Constable should take immediate steps to clear himself of the allegations made against him. The Council, by twenty-two votes to five (four of whom were from members of the Watch Committee that had decided on no further action) agreed. Alderman H.K.Campbell said that *"nobody will venture to deny that if the charges, which were most deliberately made on oath in open court, were true, he is unfit to remain as Head of the Police Force. On the other hand, if the charges were trumped up against him, no damages would be too heavy to compensate him for so gross an aspersion upon his personal honour and professional reputation. This is a most serious allegation to make against a chief constable."* The press commented that even those who had no hesitation in accepting the denial must have felt that the matter could not be allowed to rest there. The Watch Committee had failed to recognise the duty it owed not only to the Council and the citizens but to the Chief Constable himself. *"It is astonishing that the Watch Committee or the Chief should choose to leave the matter there."* If the response from the Home Secretary had been understood by the Committee to mean vindication and that there was no need for an inquiry, then by its decision it had done the Chief no favour. *'Seldom,'* commented one paper, *'has a man had stronger reason to wish to be saved from his friends.'* A Councillor suggested that it was rather un-English to make charges against a man and invite him to prove them untrue. *"The Watch Committee had contended that the charges were so flimsy and malicious that nobody could possibly credit them but the more they argued this point the more they strengthened the argument of those who held that the Chief Constable should take the most simple, obvious and conclusive method of rebutting the allegations and vindicating his character. A man conscious of his integrity may naturally be disposed to treat allegations of this kind with contempt but in the case of a public official something more is required and nothing but a judicial inquiry can satisfy public opinion. Mr. Hill has only to disprove the charges in open court to secure sympathy and in the event that damages awarded him are insufficient to recompense the expense of legal proceedings the people of Carlisle have a sufficiently strong sense of justice to see that he was no loser when in compliance of a Council requirement."* It appears that the strain of this particular case was the catalyst of what was to follow at the next Watch Committee meeting on 26 November. A letter from solicitors acting for the Chief Constable was submitted by the Town Clerk for the Committee's consideration. It intimated that Mr. Hill was unwell and unfit for duty and had been ordered complete rest. He requested, and was granted, leave of absence. Upon receipt of the letter the Town Clerk had put in train arrangements for a medical examination by the Police Surgeon. On 31 December, a further letter from the solicitor stated that the Chief Constable had been advised to see a consultant in Edinburgh. The Town Clerk, acknowledging the correspondence, replied that the Council would need some early indication of the state of Mr. Hill's health, *"as the matter could not be allowed to stand over indefinitely."* Superintendent Eckford was appointed Acting Chief Constable to command the Force in the Mr. Hill's absence.

On 6 January 1913, Mr. Hill wrote to the Town Clerk stating that due to his continued ill-health he was incapacitated from performing his duties as Chief Constable and he suggested two options that might be available to him. Firstly, that the Committee could grant him six months leave of absence in the hope that he might fully recover or, alternatively, if the Committee considered that it would be in the best interests of the Force, it could retire him. The Committee chose the latter course and resolved that, *"In accordance with the terms of his agreement, the appointment of Mr. Hill as Chief Constable be terminated by the payment of three months salary in lieu of notice."* He was 43 years old and had completed just 23 years service, insufficient for him to qualify for a pension. The City Council endorsed the proposal without comment. Mr. Hill had failed to comply with the Council's instruction to clear his name of the allegations and the Watch Committee felt there was no alternative but to dispense with his services. The Council calculated his contributions to the superannuation fund in the three forces in which he had served to total £120.6s.6d. This amount they agreed to refund him. He was still a comparatively young man who had been a Chief Constable for some fifteen years but was now without a job. Hard times indeed, and so thought some, but by no means all, members of the Council.

At a Council Meeting in March, Alderman Gibbings suggested that the refund of pension contributions to Mr. Hill be supplemented by the Council to provide him with the sum of £500. Without going into the history of the case he thought that the Watch Committee did what they considered proper but, he said, *"After all, when justice has been done, there was still a handmaid to justice to be considered. As Shakespeare said; 'Though justice be thy plea, consider this – that in the cause of justice none of us should see salvation. We do pray for mercy and that same prayer doth teach us all to render the deeds of mercy."* He said he held no brief for Mr. Hill and he had nothing to fear or expect from him but he did feel that whatever his indiscretions might have been the punishment was really out of proportion. *"Consider what the punishment was – it meant ruin, absolute and complete, for himself and his family. Mr. Hill was a policeman, pure and simple, and that avenue of employment was now closed to him. All these things should have been taken into consideration before. He quite admitted it, but that was poor consolation for his family. In less than two years he would have retired on a pension of £270 a year of which the actuarial value was something like £5,000 and the contemplation of the loss of that, and of the loss of a life's work, was punishment enough. There is no doubt that Mr. Hill is labouring under a deep sense of injustice and it is within the power of the Council to remove that feeling and close a very unpleasant chapter in the municipal history of Carlisle by the grant of what could be little more than a year's pension."* The Alderman said he did not know if he would get a seconder. He hoped that he would. He hoped the Council would support his proposal. He *"didn't think they would sleep any less soundly if they did."* A Councillor, seconding the motion said, *"The punishment meted out to the Chief Constable was severe and the amount proposed was small and would not be felt by the Council."* Councillor Rutherford was opposed and supported the decision of the Watch Committee. *"Mr. Hill failed to play the man. He played the coward,"* he said. *"If he had played the man, he would not be in the position he is today."* The Mayor said he would not support the motion as the Watch Committee had done all they legally could. Another Councillor said there was the possibility of poverty staring the ex-Chief in the face if all he was to get was £120. The cost of him moving from Carlisle was considerable. He believed that *"the Council were so large-hearted and sympathetic, although they might not feel justified, that they might not vote against the proposal."* The Watch Committee refrained from voting. The proposal was carried. The Town Clerk said Mr. Hill would get another cheque for £243 which, together with his salary paid in advance, would amount to £500.

oooOooo

Mr. Hill appears to have made a remarkable recovery for he 'popped up' again, in Canada, in June 1915 when he was then reported to be the Chief Constable of Edmonton, Alberta* On that occasion, newspapers stated that he had appeared in the local Police Court together with a number of his officers charged with permitting a prisoner to escape and with falsely charging a man with being a frequenter of a disorderly house. The case against Mr. Hill never got off the ground, the Magistrate at once dismissing the charges as *'frivolous'*.

'Carlisle Journal' on 3 June 1938 commented that the Winnipeg correspondent of the 'Daily Mail' had reported that *'Mr. Hill, the former Chief Constable of the City of Carlisle, was presently the Chief of Assimiboia Municipality, a suburb of Winnipeg.'* He would then be 69 years old!

oooOooo

April 1911 – the funeral of Alderman William Phillips, Mayor of the City and Chairman of the Watch Committee, who died on 31 March.

Mourners are greeted into the Town Hall by the Mayor, who is watched over by two city police officers in the uniforms of Sergeants at Arms.

Superintendent Peter Eckford, who was shortly afterwards to be appointed Acting Chief Constable, accompanies the police contingent from the Cathedral.

City policemen, as Mayor's Sergeants, carrying the city's mace and sword ahead of the Mayor (centre) and Corporation, while other officers carry ceremonial halberds as they lead the civic procession towards the Town Hall. Chief Constable Hill can be seen on the right behind the Halberdmen.

Inspector Greg Alcorn, currently serving in the Corporate Planning/Corporate Communications Section of Edmonton Police Service confirms that George Hill was Chief Constable of Edmonton from 1914 to 1920.

Left: *Chief Constable Spence , front row centre, with his Deputy, Superintendent Johnston to his left. An Inspector, to his right, and nine Sergeants complete the picture. Given the officers uniform style, the picture probably dates to c1920.*

Above: *HRH The Princess Mary is greeted by the City Mayor and the Earl of Lonsdale on 11 August 1928. Chief Constable Spence is on the right of the picture.*

DIAS & CO.
MOTOR
ENGINEERS.

Above: *Two city policemen lead the procession of the Lonsdale Battalion on a march through the city sometime between September 1914 and June 1915.*

A few odds and ends from Chief Hill's days

1904

Dec 20 – Appointment of permanent police firemen upon the formation of the City Police Fire Brigade. Ernest Wakeford appointed Sergeant and Albert Dugdale appointed Constable, both on transfer from Oldham Borough Police Fire Brigade. Each asked for help towards costs of keeping their families in lodgings for 8 weeks – the generous Watch Committee granted them £1 each.

Dec 27 – New Recorder of Carlisle appointed [the fourth] – Ernest Page, QC who was a native of the city.

1905

Jan 6 – Prison Commissioners agreed to pay a contribution of £20 towards costs of conveying prisoners to HM Prison [Carlisle?] on the understanding that the monies included the costs of painting, repairing and depreciation of the prison van.

Feb 3 – [1] Practice of police officers issuing tramps with tickets to the Workhouse discontinued. [2] Chevrons to be worn on uniforms, over the left wrist –2 years service, 1 stripe; 5 years, 2stripes; 9 years, 3 stripes; 15 years, 3 stripes plus a star.
Two constables who frequently act as sergeants to wear sergeant's stripes, but on one arm only.

May 26 – The National Telephone Company agreed to fix a line into the Cabmen's shelter in Court Square – for the use also of city police officers for passing messages to the police office.

Jun 23 – Dand's, Saddlers, to supply a new harness, cost £6.10s.0d., for the prison van.

Jul 7 – Chief Constable applied for, and awarded, a pay increase – from £300 to £400 per annum.

Jul 21 – PC45 Murdock required to resign for frequenting a brothel in Chapel Street.

Oct 13 – Rooms let from Messrs. Little and Ballantyne on the viaduct for use as a 'Police Institute' at a cost of £12.10s.0d per half year [first half year free]. Newspapers and periodicals provided for officers.

1906

Feb 16 – Watch Committee approved a new style summer cap for the Force.

Apr 27 – I Sergeant and 10 Constables supplied on mutual aid to Cumberland Police for duty at disturbances at Maryport.

Jun 8 – 20 officers to be supplied on mutual aid to Newcastle City Police for the visit of the King to Newcastle on 11 July.

Oct 26 – HMI demands to know what Watch Committee intends to do to improve West Walls Police Office.

Nov 16 – Superintendent Eckford, 52 years old, requested a pay increase of 7/6d [37p] a week to stay in office rather than retire on pension.

Nov 28 – PC33 Richard Farish dies – 7 years service. [33, same as George Russell, was an unlucky number?].

1907

Apr 26 –Det.Sgt. Pattinson promoted to Det. Inspector [the first DI] after asking the Chief for promotion.

Jul 26 – Chief Constable reports that the prison van is worn out and unfit for further use. A new one, costing £68, ordered from local company.

1908

Feb 28 – Chief Constable instructed to have a hat rack and stove fixed in the mortuary – (had the occupants complained about the cold?).

Jun 26 – Thomas Wilson of 128 Warwick Road applied to the Chief Constable for use of a fire hose to water Carlisle United's new football ground – refused.

Jul 24 – Chief Constable and family moved out of the residential part of West Walls Police Office to house at 13 Chatsworth Square.

Sep 7 – 10 Constables and one detective borrowed from Cumberland County Police for the visit of Princess Louise to the city. Horses borrowed locally for mounted police use. 7/6d [37p] paid to Sgt. May of the Westmorland and Cumberland Yeomanry for the loan of saddles for the mounted men.

Oct 23 – Chief Constable requests imposition of a 10mph speed limit in city's streets.

Dec 18 – A horse-ambulance, fitted with rubber tyres, to be purchased for £90 and kept at Spring Gardens Lane Fire Station. Chief Constable arranged for a Richard Crosby to provide a horse to pull it and a driver at 2/6d [30p] per call, plus a shilling [5p] a mile outside the city. Use subject to conditions [1] no-one with infectious disease to be carried. [2] serious injury or invalids to be certified by a doctor to be fit for removal by ambulance.[3] city residents to be charged 5 shillings for each removal, extra for those outside the city boundary, and 50% extra for all use between 9pm and 7am.

Dec 18 – Letter received from Mrs. Catherine Gurney, Hon. Secretary of the Northern Police Convalescent Home at Harrogate – a donation of £1000 had been received from Dr.Lightfoot of Newcastle-upon-Tyne for provision of a bed for use by officers from Cumberland Constabulary and the City of Carlisle Police.

1909

Feb 11 – PC52 Davidson asked for reimbursement of cost [£2] of transferring his telephone from Portland Place to Grasmere Street. £1 granted, but as there were already plenty of telephones in Currock, PC Davidson would be moved to another area as soon as possible. Man-management 1909 style!

Mar 6 – Sergeant Wakeford appointed Fire Inspector for the Borough of Northampton. PC17 Dugdale appointed sergeant in his stead.

May 14 – Chief Constable's Order prohibiting officers from discussing police business with the Watch Committee – *'breaches will be visited with serious consequences to any offender'*.

Jul 23 – Acting PS McLeod appointed Coroner's officer - probably the first?

Sep 24 – One shilling per day to be docked from pay of officers off duty sick.

1910

Jan 28 – Juveniles in custody under Children's Act 1908 to be detained, on remand, in Fusehill [Workhouse] at a cost of 1/6d [7p] per head per day.

Apr 29 – Force petitioned Watch Committee for a weekly rest day [Police WRD Bill before Parliament]. Town Clerk instructed to write to the Home Secretary stating that the city would not implement the Act until financial provisions were in place.

1911

Mar 31 – The death of the Mayor and Chairman of the Watch Committee, Alderman William Phillips was reported to the Committee.

Apr 28 – Watch Committee, having asked the Chief Constable *'when his time was up'*, required Inspector Campbell to retire. Town Clerk said *'ultra vires'* –Superannuation Act permitted an officer of Inspector rank and above to retire as of right after 25 years service, having given written notice, and to continue until compulsory retirement age of 65 years. The Inspector had not given notice. The Town Clerk added that the office of constable was a public office with no master/servant relationship. An officer could only be removed as directed by statute. The Watch Committee had no authority over the situation.

Jul 28 – Inspector Campbell voluntarily retires from the Force – he obviously knew when he wasn't wanted!

Jul 28 – Officers granted one rest day in every 14 days. Three additional constables to be appointed to provide cover.

Sep 29 – Letter to the Chief Constable from the Secretary of the Amalgamated Society of Railway Servants following a rail strike, thanking him for the police handling of the dispute *'We are unanimously of the opinion that the police of Carlisle have shown a splendid example to all Britain in this Great Industrial Upheaval'*. The Watch Committee resolved to pay the men an additional two days wages for the *'arduous and difficult duties imposed on them during the strike'*.

Sep 29 – Watch Committee expressed its thanks to the Chief Constable of Cumberland and Westmorland for the loan of twenty constables 'on the occasion of H.M. The King's journey through the city on 21st ultimo'.

1912

Jul 26 – All officers entitled to full pay for six months if off duty sick.

Jul 26 – Police Coronation medals awarded to Superintendent Peter Eckford, Detective Inspector Thomas Patterson and Sergeant James Burnett.

Oct 25 – City boundaries extended. 1PS and 1PC stationed at Stanwix. PCs posted to Harraby and Belle Vue, Upperby added to Currock beat. Police houses at Stanwix and Harraby connected to the central police station by telephone, and rent rebate of 50% allowed since they were now used as police stations.

1913

Jan 28 – Supt. Eckford reports receipt of £55.18s.7d from late Chief for the Police Aided Scheme for Clothing for Poor Children.

Feb 25 – [1] City Police Band to be discontinued and the instruments sold [2] Approval given for 1 sergeant and 16 constables to police a rugby match at Brunton Park on 1 March..

Mar 14 – The Journal reported the extraordinary case of a constable [not in Carlisle] who had shot himself dead because his sergeant had died. Inquest verdict [quite rightly] 'Suicide whilst insane'.

Mar 26 – Watch Committee gave notice to terminate tenancy of premises used as a Police Institute.

oooOooo

From the Chief's annual report 1912

Carlisle Extension Order, 1912, took effect - Stanwix, Harraby and Belle Vue, with a total population of 6000, was added to the city. The Force was augmented by one sergeant and three constables.

Two bicycles, which were purchased some months ago for the police. have been of much service, especially to the detectives and warrant officers – almost 1800 warrants were served during the year.

Foot and Mouth Disease broke out in a herd of Irish cattle at Harraby.

Ninety crimes were recorded, including one of manslaughter – a man knocked down and killed by a pedal cyclist riding recklessly in Warwick Road. The case was subsequently withdrawn.

Above left: *Chief Constable Hill, arrowed, at the unveiling of the Creighton Monument which now stands in the gardens at Hardwicke Circus.*

Right: *Sergeant William Oliver, a native of Matlock, Derbyshire, who joined the City Police on 2 October 1897(pictured c1910).*

Eric Herbert deSchmid (later Spence) Chief Constable
2 May, 1913 to 30 November, 1928.

Mr deSchmid.

Despite his Germanic sounding surname, Mr. deSchmid was a Devonian through and through, the son of Captain V.H.F. deSchmid, late of the Devonshire Regiment, who since leaving the army had served for 29 years reaching the rank of superintendent in the Devon County Constabulary. Mr deSchmid was, himself, a superintendent in the same Force before his appointment as chief constable of Exeter City Police two years before moving to Carlisle. He came very highly recommended by Exeter Justices who said, 'he had showed ample proof of his professionalism, a good organiser and administrator who was strict in discipline but one who inspired confidence in his subordinates and who had raised, considerably, the morale of the Exeter Force. He had a thorough knowledge of the law and procedure making him a valuable officer. He had a high sense of honour and fully appreciated his responsibilities. He was totally fearless in the discharge of his duties.' They don't come much better than that.

Mr. deSchmid began his career in 1900 in Nottingham City Police spending much of his time in the Detective Branch in the rank of sergeant. He transferred in 1908 to the Devon Force on promotion to Superintendent, (missed out a few ranks there!). As Chief Constable of Exeter City Police he commanded a Force of sixty-five men. He was still only 32 years old when he took up his duties in Carlisle. Four others were interviewed by the Watch Committee, Superintendent R. Hodges, Deputy Chief Constable of Norwich City Police, Superintendent Barrow, Cumberland and Westmorland Constabulary, Inspector E.G. Mylne of the Royal Irish Constabulary in Dublin and Major A. Goring of Lancaster, late of the 20th Hussars.

On being informed of the new appointment, Councillor Hutchinson commented, *"I hope it will not be a test as to whether a man was drunk or sober if he failed to pronounce the new Chief's name correctly."* The Town Clerk responded, *"You may say he is sober if he does!"*

It didn't take Mr. deSchmid long to upset 'the troops' in Carlisle. Very soon after his arrival they rose up against enforced changes he had made to their working conditions. On Saturday night, 15 June 1913, a public meeting was held at Carlisle Cross to protest against the action of the Watch Committee in refusing to entertain a petition by the Force against certain changes made in their hours of duty. The Chairman, Mr. W. Egglestone the President of Carlisle Trades Council, explained that the men had been required to work 'split' shifts – that is two shifts of four hours each instead of eight hours continuous duty (NB. Detectives were still working this shift system in the 1960s and 70s, 9am to 1pm followed by a 6pm to 10pm tour). *"The day has long gone for employers, especially municipal employers, to refuse to hear grievances of their own workpeople. The Committee must not be allowed to act in this manner. It is difficult to find a town where the police force is better regulated than at Carlisle, but the new Chief Constable has made changes that are unjust and irksome, and it is incomprehensible that he has the support of the Committee,"* he said. There was considerable public condemnation of the Chief's order. The policemen, themselves, claimed that this work pattern, by greatly extending their working day, was detrimental to their health. The meeting resolved to condemn the Watch Committee's action in refusing to meet a deputation of policemen and to protest at the Mayor's decision to disallow the use of the Town Hall for a meeting, which they considered to be a matter of public importance. A further grievance aired at the Market Cross meeting concerned the new Chief's decision to appoint a drill instructor on promotion to sergeant from Liverpool City Police to take over from a local officer whose work had hitherto been entirely satisfactory, and who had consequently had his pay reduced upon the new appointment. Mr. Lowthian, of the Trades Council, said he did not know why this new Chief Constable from Exeter should go to Liverpool for men when it was common knowledge that Cumberland men were in demand all over the country for police forces. The Trades Council considered these matters to be of significant public importance.

The issues were raised at the meeting of the City Council on 9 September 1913, when Councillor Hutchinson asked what steps had been taken to revert to the working hours prevailing before the advent of Mr. deSchmid. In reply, the Mayor said that the Watch Committee had no intention of so reverting, as the hours being worked were very satisfactory. *"Not so far as the men are concerned,"* interrupted Councillor Hutchinson. *"This discussion is out of order,"* ruled the Town Clerk, but the argument continued. The Mayor eventually decreed that the question was not one to be answered by the City Council, but by the Watch Committee and the Home Secretary. Councillor Hutchinson concluded, *"If the Watch Committee does not look after it, somebody else will!"* The Councillor did not enlarge on his statement and there is no evidence that the matter was resolved to the men's satisfaction. Little over a year into Mr. deSchmid's tenure, he and the men had more serious matters to contend with – the effects of the Great War, 1914-18.

oooOooo

World War 1.

On the evening of Tuesday, 4th August, 1914, Britain declared war on Germany bringing fresh duties to the police. Officers began to guard, by day and by night, the main entrances into the city together with all railway bridges and other vulnerable points. All 'strange' cars crossing Eden Bridge were stopped and the occupants were not allowed to proceed until they had given police officers a satisfactory account of themselves and the reason for their journey. (What is a strange car and was there reason to suspect the Hun had arrived in Carlisle immediately upon the declaration?). The assistance of the Boy Scouts Association was acquired, for which the police authority paid the Association £5 per week. The scouts remained 'in service' until the end of November, 1914 (many would argue, facetiously, that a Boy Scout element has never left the police service since!). They were engaged, alongside regular officers, on guarding vulnerable railway locations, and after a short while, they practically took over the duties entirely from the police. Several foreign persons, including hotel staff and their spouses, resident and employed in Carlisle were arrested as being *'alien enemy'* and at least two were interned in concentration camps. The keeping of carrier and homing pigeons without a permit issued by the Chief Constable was prohibited on penalty of a fine not exceeding £100 or six months imprisonment, with or without hard labour, and public notices to this effect were published in local newspapers. Lighting had to be extinguished by 11pm for fear of attack by hostile aircraft and a steam buzzer was installed at the gasworks to be sounded on the approach of enemy planes (Surely not much chance of that in 1914?).

As the war began, two serving constables were recalled to the colours. Soon afterwards one of them, serving with the Border Regiment, was wounded and hospitalised for a month before rejoining his regiment at the front. The other rejoined the Grenadier Guards and by the end of 1914, after fighting continuously since August, he had been promoted to the rank of sergeant. The Chief Constable reported to the Watch Committee on 29th September, that two officers, PC 47 George Henderson and PC 56 John Potts had volunteered for military service for the duration of the war. The committee granted them permission to join the army, and decreed that their military pay should be supplemented with an allowance so that they would receive the full salary of their police rank. They would be permitted to rejoin the city police upon their discharge from the military, subject to their being medically fit for further duties. A number of officers followed them into the armed forces, and on 25 April 1915, the Watch Committee directed that the chief constable should post a notice in the police station advising all officers that they would receive full police pay upon enlistment. The chief was authorised to fill the consequential vacancies, by appointing police pensioners or others, at a rate of thirty shillings per six-day working week.

Neither the passage of time since the Force was formed, nor the effects of war, had removed from the Force the unremitting problem of drink. It seemed always to be the root cause of police indiscipline and misbehaviour. On 16 November 1914, PC 43 Robert Brown was disciplined for being drunk on duty, assaulting a soldier and for punching his sergeant, PS Bone, in the face. He was reduced from First to Third Class Constable (reduction in pay) and cautioned by the Chief as to his future conduct – a very lucky man indeed to hold on to his job. In December, Constable 31 Charles Cranston was fined five shillings and cautioned by the Chief Constable for drinking on duty. He had been seen by his sergeant leaving the Three Crowns Hotel in English Street at 6.55am.

The unfortunate barman who gave him the drink found himself charged with supplying a duty policeman with liquor. He came off worse than the bobby, being fined one guinea plus costs. The barman said the policeman had entered the hotel covered in snow, and said *"Give me a claret, hot, I'm perishing!"* *"Claret seemed a half-way house between a temperance drink and a stimulant,"* said the barman, *"I wouldn't have given the constable a whisky."* It was said that *"the barman had listened to the constable's plaintiff cry as it was about Christmas."* The Chief Constable said he had circularised local licensees warning them against harbouring his officers. Several years later, in 1928, Cranston was in more serious trouble when he was convicted at the City Police Court of receiving stolen hams. He was dismissed the service and his pension deductions were ordered to be paid to his wife at the rate of five pounds a month. In 1921, PC43, George Thompson, and a colleague PC 19 John Bryson had come to attention for *'keeping the company of two prostitutes.'* They were ordered to resign. In December 1922, PC 50 Davidson was ordered to resign forthwith for using insulting and abusive language to a member of the public and for being under the influence of drink, while PC 64 Alexander Jardine was fined forty shillings for soliciting drink in the Turf Hotel whilst on plain clothes duty.

1915.

At the May Watch Committee meeting, Mr. deSchmid reported that twenty-six constables were then serving with the colours and that he had taken on fourteen replacements, including four police pensioners. Members of the Force at home voluntarily subscribed monies to a local relief fund and began a fund for supplying clothing and comforts for their brother officers in the army. By the end of June, 1915, forty city policemen had enlisted, exactly 50% of the Force establishment. In his annual report, the Chief Constable reported that three constables had been wounded in action, including PC Keefe who had been awarded the Distinguished Service Medal for conspicuous bravery in Gallipoli. The Watch Committee asked for the names of those men of military age still serving in the Force (nudge, nudge!). In fact, only fifteen remained, of whom ten had been attested and four had been rejected on medical grounds. At the end of the year, from an approved establishment of eighty officers the Force was carrying fifteen vacancies and employing twenty-one temporary constables. In July, one of the temporary officers, Andrew Johnston, a retired policeman, collapsed and died whilst on duty. Chief Constable deSchmid reported that *"owing to the high rates of wages prevailing in the district, it is almost a matter of impossibility to get men over military age to take up appointments as constables. In June, 172 principal citizens were sworn in as special constables, and since then have policed the city every Sunday, thereby permitting a certain amount of leave to be given to the permanent Force.'* When the Force asked for a pay rise owing to the increased costs of living the Watch Committee awarded a war bonus of two shillings a week, for the duration of the war only. Mrs. McTaggart, the cleaner and charwoman also qualified for the bonus - quite rightly! She was no doubt struggling to survive too.

During the year, 114 deserters were arrested in the city and handed over to the military authorities. Seven aliens were ordered to concentration camps and two German nationals were deported. Juvenile crime was rampant, with 273 children being brought before the courts. Fourteen were ordered to be whipped. The Chief Constable compared the city's high figure with those for the City of Leicester. There, with a population of over 227,000, there had been only 160 juvenile offenders over the same period. He suggested that perhaps the reason for Carlisle's disproportionately high figures was due to the fact that so many fathers were away on military service and mothers in full-time employment. (Surely a similar situation existed in Leicester?) Despite the pressures on the Force, it performed remarkably well returning a high detection rate for the more serious crimes. The total value of property stolen during 1915 was £650.10s.8d and all but £66 worth was recovered.

Quintinshill Rail Disaster

By far, the most serious incident in which the Force became involved in 1915 was the Quintinshill rail disaster near Gretna. During its existence, the Force had no major incident, of national significance, to handle within its area. However, the worst rail disaster in British history happened about six miles north of the city boundary on the Scottish border in the Dumfriesshire Constabulary area. Investigations were, of course, the responsibility of, and were conducted by, that Force. Carlisle City Police rendered assistance, particularly the police fire brigade, and dealt with some of the aftermath that spilled over into the city.

At about 6.50am, on Saturday, 22 May, a beautiful summer morning with the sun shining brightly, a southbound troop train carrying 470 men of A and D Companies of the 1/7 Royal Scots from the Falkirk area sped towards Gretna. At the same time, two trains travelling in the opposite direction, an express from London to Glasgow, scheduled to leave Carlisle at 6.05am but running late, and the 6.10am local from Carlisle, due to leave after the express but sent on ahead of it to Gretna by the area controller in Carlisle to prevent further delay to its journey, converged on Quintinshill on the Scottish border where there was a trackside signal-box and loop sidings alongside the main lines. The plan when the local train left Carlisle was to shunt it into the northbound loop to allow the express to pass, a not unusual procedure on the occasions when the express was running late. However, unknown to the controller, a fourth train, laden with coal, was parked in that loop preventing its use by the local. When the latter reached Quintinshill, the duty signalman directed it, instead, over a cross-over onto the southbound line intending to switch it back after the express had passed and before the arrival of the troop train. He took none of the usual precautions to safeguard the train.

Above left: *workmen searching the debris for remains of the victims after the fire had died down.*

Above right: *a fireman tackles the fire in one of the trains.*

George Meakin was the night-shift signalman in the box. He was scheduled to be relieved by James Tinsley at 6am. The two men had agreed to an unauthorised delay to the change-over time by 30 minutes to allow Tinsley extra time in bed. It was Meakin therefore who dealt with the local train. Written records of the changeover times and activities in the box were to be fabricated to show that Tinsley had arrived at work on scheduled time. In the minutes that followed Tinsley's arrival, the two signalmen set about completing their paperwork. This distraction caused Meakin to forget that he had the local train waiting on the southbound track. It was standing directly in the path of the approaching troop train. The troop train ploughed into the local with a tremendous crash and wreckage was thrown over both tracks. The Glasgow-bound express was now converging on the scene at speed. The signalmen made desperate attempts to alert the driver, but the train was travelling too fast and was too close to the crash scene, little more than one minute away, to take evasive action. It ploughed into the wreckage of the other two trains. Fire broke out and the wreckage quickly became a roaring furnace, spreading to the parked coal train. The driver and firemen of the express, both Carlisle men, were killed instantly. The other train crews, also from Carlisle, survived. Of the 470 troops, only eight officers and 67 men could be accounted for after the crash. The remainder were either dead or seriously injured. Survivors fought like heroes to free comrades trapped in the wreckage. At the same time others worked frantically to unload a cargo of ammunition at the rear of the troop train. *'It was no exaggeration,'* reported a Carlisle newspaper, *'to say that many a VC was gallantly earned in the face of fire, smoke and escaping steam.'*

The crashes were witnessed by a local farm-hand who went to Carlisle for the Fire Brigade. By 9.30am, *'the fury of the flames was such as no-one could have conceived.'* Chief Constable Gordon of Dumfries and a force of police officers were in attendance at the scene. Shortly before 10am they were joined by Chief Constable deSchmid from Carlisle and his men who got to work fighting the inferno. Very soon after their arrival there was an enormous explosion in the midst of the debris, followed by several others. The fire eventually burnt itself out leaving an enormous heap of metal and charred wood and a horrific scene of carnage, *'heads and limbs disconnected from bodies.'* Surviving soldiers said there had been no equal in the most dreadful events of war. A story circulated of one soldier, trapped under the wreckage and seeing the approach of the flames with no hope of escape, implored a comrade to shoot him, and he did. Similar accounts of officers shooting doomed comrades circulated. There was no confirmation of such actions.

Doctors and emergency services were taken to the scene from Carlisle in special trains, which carried the injured back to hospitals in the city. At the Cumberland Infirmary there were unparalleled scenes as 150 casualties were admitted. One hundred and fifteen people lost their lives at the scene of the crash and another

Left: *His Majesty, King George V sent a message to the city Mayor.* **Right:** *The engine drivers and firemen who survivied the Gretna crash pictured outside Carlisle Town Hall. They were to give evidence in the City Coroner's Court at the inquests into the deaths in Carlisle of a number of the crash victims [Picture from the Carlisle Journal].*

150 were injured, all but six of the casualties soldiers. Twenty died en-route to Carlisle hospitals, twenty-one died in the city. The death toll reached 227 and 246 were injured. Inspector Johnstone of the city police was detailed to arrange identification of the bodies and inquests into the deaths certified at Carlisle. HM. Coroner for the city opened the inquests at the Police Office on 25 May.

A message from His Majesty King George V was received by the Mayor, *'The King is shocked to hear of the terrible railway disaster near Carlisle which has cost the country so many valuable lives.'* Queen Mary sent word that she wished to send gifts to the surviving soldiers.

Scottish Police arrested the signalmen, James Tinsley and George Meakin, and charged them with manslaughter. They appeared at Dumfries Sheriff Court and were remanded in custody for trial at the High Court in Edinburgh. Tinsley was sentenced to three years penal servitude and Meakin to eighteen months imprisonment.

1916.

By January, all members of the force were working their weekly rest-days for payment, to make up for the shortfall in establishment.

During the year Carlisle came under attack, not from the German army, but from the army of navvies that descended on the area to work on the construction of, and later in, the largest munitions works in the British Empire at Gretna. Stretching nine miles long and two miles wide, some 30,000 people, mainly females, were employed on site and housed in the area and in Carlisle. Earnings there were exceptionally high, about £20 a week, and every evening Carlisle, the nearest town, became a Mecca for several thousands of these workers. The local 'Lakescene' publication, *'A city under the influence'* by John Hunt, carried the tale of a Methodist minister visiting the city at the time who was appalled at the number of demoralised women he found. Finding two such persons lying in the middle of English Street surrounded by a jeering crowd, he called a policeman to move them on, expressing his outrage at the spectacle. *"It's an everyday sight,*

Sir, you soon get used to it", retorted the policeman. Drunkenness and disorder was such that the depleted city police force, already under pressure due to war-related duties, was almost overwhelmed. There were 964 prosecutions for drunkenness during the year, an increase of 663 over the previous year. 788 of those prosecuted worked at Gretna. The citizens were up in arms, whilst the magistrates made vain attempts to abate the nuisance. Total prohibition was considered. However, someone else, no less a person than the Minister of Munitions, David Lloyd George, was also taking notice of the situation since, as a sequel to this hard drinking, production of vital munitions at the Gretna works was being adversely affected. The problem became one for the Government to solve and to that end it 'nationalised' the liquor trade, all breweries and pubs in Carlisle and District including Gretna, taking control of them from the hands of the owners and removing the local licensing magistrates' powers in relation to the trade. The *'Central Control Board'*, the scheme's governing body, immediately began to reduce the number of public houses in the city - there were 119 in June 1916 – fifty-three were closed before the war ended. Other drastic steps were taken to prevent drunkenness, including Sunday closing. Even as recently as the 1950s, the city's pubs, compared to today's, were very austere places without music or other entertainment, no doubt deliberately kept so to lessen their attraction and to serve as a disincentive to excessive drinking. By the end of 1917 offences of drunkenness had been reduced to 329, a drop of 635. Almost two-thirds of the two hundred and seven prosecutions involved Gretna munitions workers. During 1918 there were only eighty-eight prosecutions, a clear indication that the nationalisation experiment had worked. The Carlisle and District State Management Scheme which was established to combat a war-time problem was to last until 1971.

The strength of the Force dropped to just sixty-two officers, including twenty-two temporary constables. Mr. deSchmid reported that the year had been *'one of exceptional difficulty, as, apart from the shortage of regular members of the force, the great increase of drunkenness and the influx of thousands of workmen, an enormous amount of extra work had been thrown on the police. Carrying out the numerous 'Defence of the Realm Regulations', special work in connection with the Central Control Board (liquor traffic), dealing with registration of aliens, often complicated by language difficulties (927 aliens had to be interviewed, frequently through an interpreter), the issuing of Identity Books, regular visiting of enemy aliens, inspection of registers at hotels and lodging-house keepers, reports re local suspects and a very large number of enquiries for other police forces. Several hundred visits have been paid to pigeon lofts and numerous enquiries for other towns as to pigeons sent by rail. The police have been required to billet troops, make a very large number of enquiries as to absentees and deserters, report on the conduct of the wives of soldiers and sailors, and carry out other duties too numerous to record. Long hours have been worked by every member of the force without extra pay, every demand has been cheerfully met.'* One hundred and one special constables were serving with the force, several of whom were promoted to the rank of sergeant. All were issued with a uniform, *'which added to their confidence and efficiency. The city owes a deep debt of gratitude to the men. Their services have been fully appreciated by those in a position to know their value.'*

Carlisle's policing difficulties were exacerbated by its being a garrison city. Following many complaints of undesirable conduct on the part of young girls, which was, incidentally, the norm in towns throughout the country where large numbers of troops were billeted, and being a delicate and sometimes difficult problem for male officers to handle, women patrols were introduced by the National Union of Women Workers of Great Britain and Ireland. Recognised by the Home Office, police and the armed services, each patrol carried an identification card signed by the chief constable which carried an instruction to officers to render any assistance possible. They wore a stamped armlet with the registered number and the initials NUWW. They kept order and offered advice to females as appropriate. Chief deSchmid spoke very highly of their work and despite the many difficult and often unpleasant tasks that they faced they almost eradicated the problem in Carlisle. The city force had no establishment of policewomen, but a number were also sworn in during the year to police the large numbers of female workers from the 'special' works at Gretna who were lodged at various hostels in the city. By the end of 1917 their number had swelled to one sergeant and eight constables. They occupied and worked from premises in Portland Square.

During the year one constable was invalided from India, and three were returned to police duties at the request of the Watch Committee. One constable died from disease while serving in the Westmorland and

Cumberland Yeomanry. Three enlisted constables were rewarded with Military Medals for bravery in the field. The majority of the serving officers were promoted to non-commissioned rank.

On 27 June the chief constable reported that *'consequent on its depletion by enlistment, the force had been totally inadequate to meet requirements of the city, having regard to the large influx of workers at the Gretna munitions works'* and urged *'that immediate steps be taken to obtain release from military service of all married constables who had been permitted to join the colours, but were subsequently found unfit for general service and who were now performing police, canteen and other duties at training establishments in the Kingdom.'* The Committee Clerk was instructed to write to the Home Secretary accordingly, resulting in two officers being returned to the force – hardly an effective measure to address the problems of the city!

1917

King George V and Queen Mary visited Carlisle on 18 May. Following the visit, the Watch Committee expressed their appreciation of the efficient policing arrangements.

1918

On 30 April, PC25 Johnston, who had been wounded in action, was directed to resume police duties. Doctor Beard, the Police Surgeon reported that he was apparently recovering from the effects of gassing. On 10 August, it was reported that Sergeant Harry Wharton of the Border Regiment, a city policeman from Herbert Street, Carlisle, was a prisoner of war in Germany and that he had been shot through both thighs.

In 1962 the Cumberland News carried a tale of an incident in the trenches of Ypres during the war. The correspondent related how one night, at midnight, a Scottish Regiment was passing his unit. *"Is there anyone here from Carlisle?"* called out a voice from the Scots. *"Yes"*, the writer responded. *"Do you remember me?'* shouted the Scot, *"Sergeant McMeakin of the City Police."* 'And a very fine figure of a man he was, too,' added the correspondent.

City Policemen killed in action in the
Great War, 1914 – 1918

Constable 49 Alfred E. PEARSON,
Lance Corporal,
Westmorland and Cumberland Yeomanry
reported, on 28 March, 1916,
to have been killed in action

Constable 74 John SMITH,
Royal Fusiliers,
reported missing since 29 April, 1917, and
presumed killed in action on that day

Constable James DALZELL,
7th Battalion, The Border Regiment,
killed in action in France on 18 June, 1918.

Constable 57 George RITCHIE,
Westmorland and Cumberland Yeomanry,
reported, on 24 September, 1918, to have been
killed in action in France

WARTIME DECORATIONS AND AWARDS, 1914 - 1918

Military:

Constable Joseph ADDISON,
who had been granted a commission in the Black Watch, was awarded the Military Cross. (Reported 27 January, 1917).

Constable 47 George HENDERSON,
a sergeant serving in the 9th Battalion Gordon Highlanders, one of the first two serving officers to enlist, was awarded the Military Medal and granted a commission. (Reported 26 September, 1916).
(On New Year's Eve 1918, PC Henderson resigned his appointment as a constable in Carlisle to take up a commission in the Indian army, but, after a change of heart, he withdrew to continue his police service in the city).

Constable Patrick KEEFE,
2nd Battalion, The Border Regiment, was awarded the Distinguished Conduct Medal (Reported 26 September, 1916)
As Company Quarter Master Sergeant, he was awarded the Military Medal (1916)

Constable Arthur STEVENS,
a sergeant, (his regiment not known) was awarded the Military Medal and was highly commended for an invention in connection with a machine gun

Civil: (New Year Honours, 1918)

Special Sergeant H.E. WINTER
awarded the British Empire Medal for his services in connection with Carlisle City Special Constabulary.

Constable [clerk] Stanley HARPER
specially commended by the Home Secretary on 26 March, 1918, for his good work in assisting Colonel Kell of MI5, War Office, in numerous enquiries as to aliens and other suspects.

Watch Committee's commendation:
Constable 22 Henry GATE
commended and granted a reward of one pound for arresting two German prisoners of war who had escaped from an internment camp at Crawford in Scotland.

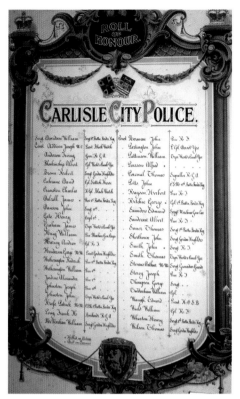

Above: *The Police Roll of Honour is in Cumbria's Military Museum in Carlisle Castle.*

After the War, on Friday, 9 April 1920, the war service of members of the Force was recognised by a Roll of Honour unveiled at the police office by the Chairman of the Watch Committee, Alderman F.P. Dixon. It contained the names of the forty-four (out of the Force total of seventy-six) men who served in the colours during the war and was paid for by those members of the Force who could not be released for military duty and who wished to show their appreciation of their comrades' courage and service. An illuminated parchment bearing the names, it was framed in oak and flanked by panels containing the photographs of the four comrades killed in action. The Chief Constable, expressing regret that it would have to hang in the passageway of the (overcrowded and inadequate) West Walls police station until a suitable new police headquarters could be found, (that was a less than subtle political statement!), described the memorial as a 'lasting tribute to what Carlisle City Police did during the European War.' The Chairman, who had been connected with the Force for forty-five years through the Watch Committee, said he was very proud of the city's police – 57% of the men had enlisted, four had died, three obtained commissions and almost all had attained non-commissioned rank. Decorations had included a Military Cross, three Military Medals and a Distinguished Service Medal. Sergeant Davidson returned the thanks on behalf of the ex-servicemen, saying that many of those left behind would also have enlisted had they been allowed to do so. He said he was 'struck' by the handsome workmanship of the memorial. The Roll of Honour and photographs were put on display in the shop window of Messrs. Wright, Drapers, Highmore House in English Street (now Marks and Spencer store). It is currently displayed in Cumbria's Military Museum in Carlisle Castle.

On 23 July, the Chief Constable volunteered for military service for the duration of the war. However, by the time of the Watch Committee meeting, one week later, it was known that his medical examination had revealed a heart problem, and that his application had been rejected, he being classified as 'Grade Three'. The committee resolved that owing to his low medical grade, and having regard to the importance of his current duties, he should remain in office in the city. The minutes of the same meeting, 30 July, record that Chief Constable SPENCE attended. There is no mention as to why the Chief had changed his Germanic sounding surname since the previous meeting, nor is there any explanation in any other records nor, amazingly, in the local newspapers. Since the war with Germany had raged for almost four years such a change seems to have been long overdue if it was causing him some difficulty or embarrassment. The answer may lie in his application to enlist in the army.

The President of the United States of America, Thomas Woodrow Wilson, visited the city on 29 December. Janet Woodrow, the President's mother, was born in Carlisle in 1826, the daughter of the minister of Annetwell Street Congregational Church. The family, whose home was in Warwick Road, moved first to Glasgow and then to America, where Janet met and married Joseph Ruggles Wilson. Their son, Thomas Woodrow Wilson, became the 28th President of the United States of America. Breaking his journey to the Paris Peace Conference, it was President Wilson's wish to visit his mother's birthplace. At a civic reception he was granted the Freedom of the City of Carlisle. It was one of a number of visits he made to the city. Afterwards, the Watch Committee's appreciation of the work of the Chief Constable, officers and men, including the special constables, and also of the assistance provided by the county police on the occasion of the visit of the President, was recorded at its meeting of 31 December 1918.

On 12 May 1919, the Watch Committee resolved to purchase, for occupation by the Chief Constable, the dwelling house 20, Warwick Square, Carlisle, for £800 [leasehold – unexpired term of 200 years at £4.9s.0d pa. ground rent].

Left: *18/05/17: Chief Constable deSchmid outside the Gretna Hall, Lowther Street on the occasion of the visit of King George V and Queen Mary.*

Right: *29/12/1918: Chief Constable Spence, right of picture, and other city policeman in the Crown and Mitre hotel for the visit of American President Woodrow Wilson.*

Just to illustrate that 'zero-tolerance policing' is not a modern invention, the following examples from Mr. deSchmid's days detail circumstances that would be *'laughed at'* today. On 26 August 1919, Detective Constable Thompson arrested two local men, one in Wigton Road and one in Denton Holme, for acting as bookie's runners and for assault on police. 'John Bull' in the Cumberland News scornfully commented that *'Detective Thompson would make the heroes of Sir Arthur Conan Doyle's fiction weep with anguish. To spare them grief, we will not recount his wonderful work among the bookies.'* On 1 May, 1920, Stanley Rogerson of Blencowe Street, Carlisle, appeared before the city magistrates court to answer summonses for driving recklessly and in a manner dangerous to the public, and for failing to give audible warning of his car's approach to pedestrians. Two detective officers were standing talking to a man between the tram-lines in English Street, when the defendant approached in his car at 12 to 15 mph. One detective pulled the other clear as the car passed. The defendant and his passenger both grinned at the pedestrians. In his defence, Rogerson argued that the policemen should have found a safer place than the middle of English Street to stand and gossip, that they should have got out of his way, (who could argue with that?), that he sounded the car's horn all the way down English Street from the Viaduct, and that when he passed the pedestrians he was only travelling at 3mph. He was found guilty of failing to give warning, and the reckless driving charge was dismissed. In October 1920, John Baxter of Tait Street, Carlisle, was summonsed for selling two-penn'orth (1p) of chocolate after hours (8.30pm) in the Star Picture House, Denton Street. He was fined £1, but the magistrates pointed out that they could have imposed a fine of £100. It's a good job he wasn't selling drugs, they'd have thrown the key away. This case was rather like the fictional tale of the magistrates fining a cyclist fifty pounds for riding without lights. Police said afterwards that if it had been dark at the time he would have got six months in jail.

Superintendent Eckford died suddenly on 7 May 1919. His place in the Force was taken by Staff Sergeant Andrew Johnston, promoted on transfer from Newcastle-upon-Tyne City Police, at a salary of £250 pa x £10 to a maximum of £300 pa, plus a free house. Mr. Johnston was to become the city's chief constable ten years later.

In June 1921, the Branch Board of the Police Federation, drew the Chief's attention to the large number of married officers serving in the Force who were without housing of their own at a time when the Corporation were building new council houses. The Federation asked the Chief to use his good offices to secure an allocation for policemen. The Watch Committee supported the application and the Council instructed that the City Surveyor and the Chief Constable should work together to acquire suitable housing for policemen.

On 27 January 1925, it was reported that Mr. Spence had been awarded the Kings Police Medal for his outstanding contributions to the police service. The award in those days was not automatically given to chief officers.

Death of Superintendent Eckford
'An institution in himself'

Superintendent Peter Eckford, the second-in-command of the Force died suddenly on 7 May 1919 after an illness of several weeks, one month away from his retirement on age limit. He was 64 years old and had completed 44 years and two months service in the Force. He was described as 'an institution in himself, so long did he hold an important post in the police'. Mr. Eckford, a bachelor all his life, was a native of Selkirkshire. He joined Lanarkshire Police but transferred to Carlisle City eleven months later on 18 February 1875. He was promoted to Sergeant in January 1879, Inspector in February 1886, Chief Inspector in January 1890 and Superintendent in January 1903. He was appointed Acting Chief Constable of the Force for five months in 1913. Mr. Eckford had been present on forty-three annual parades before H.M. Inspectors of Constabulary, which might well be an all-time police service record. The superintendent lived in Nelson Street, Denton Holme and West Walls, his sister keeping house for him. His funeral at Stanwix Cemetery was 'characterised by the impressive simplicity of the Scottish Presbyterian Church'. The service was mostly inside his own home, but outside the Chief Constable, 4 Inspectors and 50 Sergeants and Constables followed the cortege to the cemetery.

On 30 May 1928, Mr. Spence intimated to the Watch Committee his intention to retire shortly. His formal notice was accepted on 19 June, with the response *'his tenure of office has been distinguished with exceptional ability, tact, zeal and courtesy.'*

Rarely can a Chief Constable have created such an impression on his civic leaders and townsfolk alike as did Mr. Spence, as witnessed by a ceremony in the Town Hall on Wednesday, 28 November. A testimonial raised by public subscription to mark his leaving was presented to him by the Mayor. It took the form of a half Hunter gold watch, a cheque, an illuminated address and an album containing the names of all subscribers. Regret was expressed at the Chief's retirement as the Mayor said that he had performed his duties with devotion and to the great satisfaction of the citizens. If there were some who had come into conflict with him through their misdeeds, the Mayor said he was *"sure it was against his office and not the man that they had a grudge."* Soon after his appointment the Chief had had enormous responsibilities and difficulties thrust upon him due to the war. A tremendous number of new 'wartime' offences had been created which required a great deal of tact and skill to carry out without upsetting the public who themselves had faced conditions far different and more difficult from those in peacetime. The Mayor commented that with only a few professional and amateur policemen to police the city, crime and other minor offences had significantly decreased during wartime, a quite remarkable achievement since the force had been so considerably depleted and the streets unlit. Post war problems associated with the return of men from military service and later the general strife experienced throughout the land had passed almost unnoticed in Carlisle due in large part to the Chief's professional skills.

The Chief Constable replied, *"No man could give up the command of a Force like Carlisle after nearly sixteen years without realising what an enormous break it would make in his life and how many friends he would be temporarily parted from. The Mayor has spoken with pride of the police force, and quite rightly. Every authority considered its police force to be the best and that is the proper spirit. If communal life is to be anything at all, pride in one's town and county is a matter of the greatest importance. The police are pleased to hear that he (the Mayor) was proud of them, but perhaps what gives still greater pleasure is the nice things said about the appearance of the Carlisle City Police by strangers visiting the city".*

Mr. Spence seized the opportunity to add that he hoped they (the Mayor and Corporation) would show their pride in the Force by providing them at an early date with proper accommodation in a new police station. The current station, he said, was erected 100 years ago when the Force had only twenty men. Now it had eighty. It had been condemned by H.M. Inspectors of Constabulary long before he had become Chief Constable. It had no parade room large enough to accommodate the Force as a whole. Nor did it have a recreation room – instead, his men had had to pay for one themselves in another part of the city. Worse, they had no drying room for wet uniforms thus creating the risk of illness. He added that they must realise that in the average house occupied by policemen soaking overcoats and trousers must be hung in the living room thereby causing great inconvenience to wives and possible risk to young children.

Whilst he recognised the council's priorities after the war in spending on housing, bridges, gas and electricity undertakings, it was hopeless to expect the best from either the police or the fire service (of which he was also the Chief) if their working conditions were not improved. He said he hoped to be able to attend the opening of a new police station in the city. He would have known about the new police station at Rickergate if he had kept in touch with his colleagues, as he died in retirement in Exmouth, aged 80, in 1960. Mr. Spence thanked the gathering for the watch adding, with a turn of phrase that could be misconstrued these days, that in a sense it was a token of his inefficiency since he had been told on joining the service that, *"No detective officer was worth his salt who did not acquire a gold watch within the first three months of his service. It has taken me 28fi years to get one."* The Chief said that as this was his last chance of speaking publicly in the city he wished to place on record his appreciation of the co-operation and friendships of the Mayor and Corporation, Town Clerk, Magistrates and Magistrates Clerk, Solicitors and the two local newspaper editors. He left the Force on 30 November 1928.

oooOooo

Right: *On the occasion of his retirement a presentation was made, at the Town Hall, to Chief Spence.*

Lower Right: *Mr and Mrs Spence on the steps of the Town Hall.*

Below: *1928: the Force's presentations to the retiring Chief Constable Spence at the Silver Grill in English Street.*

Seated from the left: *Chief Constable Spence, Inspector Seaton, Inspector Percival, Constable Marshall and the new chief constable, Mr A. K. Wilson.*

Standing: *Constable Shorthouse, Sergeant Harper, Sergeant Waite, Sergeant Walker (who ten years later, as Chief Inspector, became Acting Chief Constable of the Force upon the sudden retirement of Chief Constable Johnston) and Inspector Dugdale (Police Fire Brigade).*

A few odds and ends from Chief deSchmid's (later Spence) days

1913

May 27 – Watch Committee meeting – [1] Supt. Eckford granted honorarium of £50 for the extra duties of Acting Chief Constable.
[2] House at 42, Thornton Road, Stanwix, leased from Miss Slee for 5 years at £19.10s.0d. per annum, the tenant to pay the rates and subject to payment of half the rent by the sergeant resident therein. [3] PC 11 Edgar W. Johnson, Chief Clerk, promoted to sergeant. [4] PC.56 Rupert Miller accused by a single woman, a cripple, of being the father of her child born on 8th inst. and not paying his debts. Dismissed the Force. [5] All PCs to make themselves proficient in swimming within six months of joining the Force – it is a condition of appointment.

Jun 24 – PC Samuel Finney appointed Sergeant [Drill Instructor] on transfer from Liverpool City Police – pay 35 shillings per week[£1.75] plus1/-[5p] for drilling, and 2/-[10p] as member of fire brigade.

Oct 24 – PS Johnston's residence at Junction Street Fire Station to be altered to allow for the reception of juvenile offenders – Home Office approval sought for certification as a juvenile detention centre.

Dec 30 – [1] Under provisions of the Police Act 1890, PC66 Frank Linton, 16 years service, certified as suffering from general paralysis of the insane and removed to Garlands Hospital – unlikely ever to be fit to resume duties and pensioned off at 11/6d[57p] per week.
[2] Christmas boxes and gratuites amounting to £10/15s/6d [£10.77] given to the police and in possession of the City Treasurer to be handed to the Chief Constable to form the nucleus of a fund for a Police Athletic Club. [3] Speed limit of 12mph to be imposed on city's principal streets.

1914

Jan 9 – Chief Constable requested the Mayor to present the Recorder with a pair of white gloves on the occasion of there being no prisoners for trial at the City Quarter Sessions.

Jan 14 – Fire Station now in Spring Gardens Lane, off Lowther Street. Brigade to be increased to 20 men.

Jan 27 – Electric lamp to be obtained for the horse ambulance.

Mar 31 – Inspectors, Sergeants and Constables petitioned for a pay rise.

Apr 28 –[1] CC sought increase in establishment to take account of new weekly rest day Act – 2 sergeants, 3 constables and 2 cycles. PCs 15 Dickson and 19 Williams promoted wef 1st June. [2]Pay was advanced by one shilling [5p] per week. [3] Insp. Kerr rewarded with 2 guineas [£2.10] for stopping a runaway horse in Scotch Street. [4] Chief Constable said that the young horse at the fire station was unfit for work and he needed another in its place.

May 26 – [1] Female cells reported to be damp and smelly and the WCs were worn out. 7 new WCs at cost of £63 provided.
[2] German silver badges at 7^1/$_2$d each to replace worsted badges for all members of the Force. [3] Members of the Force wrote thanking the Watch Committee for its "magnanimous" gesture in raising their pay to the levels of other forces.

Jun 24 – The Force Band's instruments were sold for £37.14s.0d. which was paid to the City Treasurer.

Jul 1 – Police [Weekly Rest Day] Act, 1910 came into force.

Nov 24 – PC55 David Cochrane awarded a Diploma of Honour from the NSPCC for rescuing two children from a burning house in which they had been left by their parents with the doors locked, The Watch Committee gave him a reward of £1.

1915

Mar 30 – Watch Committee granted £25 to Mrs Chalker's Home for Girls in consideration of her services to the police.

Apr 21 - Prison van to be repaired and repainted at a cost of £13.

Dec 30 – Rev. Canon Rawnsley, on behalf of subscribers, presented the Corporation with a motor ambulance.

1916

Central Control Board, 'to prevent such drinking as renders workers unfit for National Service', introduced by Lloyd George fearing uprisings as in Ireland. There were 4 breweries and 100 pubs in the city.

1918

Mar 26 – Detectives to be paid 5/- [25p] per week plain clothes allowance and 2/- [10p] out-of-pocket expenses, clerks and firemen to get 2/-[10p]

Mar 25 – Miss Mary Faulder appointed policewoman and Assistant Matron wef 1 April.

Apr 30 – [1] Officers promoted to Inspector automatically cease to be members of the Fire Brigade. [2] Special Constables allowed to keep their whistles and truncheons as momentos of their war service. [3] New house, max. cost £1500, to be found for Chief Constable. [20,Warwick Square purchased for £800].

Jul 29 – Watch Committee discussed findings of the Committee on the Police Service of England, Wales and Scotland [Oaksey Committee] re police pay increases wef 1 April 1919 – Immediate payment of £10 to all officers serving on 1st April pending full implementation of the Committee's recommendations. Rent allowances introduced – Seven shillings [35p] per week for married men, four [20p] for single men.

Sep 30 – [1] PW Faulder's pay increased from 30/-[£1.50] to 35/-[£1.75] plus four increments to a max. of 45/-[£2.25].
[2] Supt. Johnston's wife appointed police matron

Nov 25 – Fred Blacklock appointed probationer constable [later to become Superintendent and Deputy Chief Constable].

1920

Jan 27 – PC29 William Haig appointed Sergeant at Mace in place of PS Oliver Fox, retired.

Feb 24 – [1] Messrs. Merryweather and Sons, London, purchased old horse-drawn steam fire engine for £100. [2] 42,Thornton Road, Stanwix bought for £500 –police house and station.

Oct 12 – Chief to report re the obtaining of a motor prison van.

Nov 18 – Chief to get estimates for conversion of horse drawn prison van to the motor ambulance chassis. To obtain cost of supplying new motor ambulance - £600 from County Garage.

1921

Jan 25 – [1] Watch Committee applied to Ministry of Transport for a speed limit of 10mph on Stanwix Bank, Eden Bridge, Botchergate and London Road. [2] Chief Constable to furnish the Place of Detention for Juveniles in Junction Street.

Aug 28 – Police Pensions Act, 1921 took effect – compulsory retirement for sergeants and constables at 55 years old, inspectors and superintendents at 60, Chief Constables at 65.   Policewomen to enjoy same pension conditions as male officers.   The Act applied retrospectively, enabling PWs to calculate pensions from date of appointment.

1922

Oct 10 – PW Faulder granted clerical allowance of 3/6d[17p] per week.

1923

Jan 30 – During 1922, 556 items of found property handed in to police, 318 restored to owners, 238 remaining sold for total of £2.9s.7d [£2.47p] and paid into city funds.

Feb 27 – The pay of policewoman Faulder was increased by 2/6d per week.

Mar 27 – [1] Chief Constable reported that during the winter months a number of officers had been undertaking educational and police duty classes in accordance with Police Regulations. 4 PSs and 12PCs had taken exams.   The PSs and 11 PCs had passed in all subjects.

Apr 24 – [1] Chief Constable authorised to purchase fingerprinting apparatus. [2] David Thompson and Son's application to store 50lbs of dynamite in their workshops in David Street refused.

May 29 – Distemper to be substituted for wallpaper in decorating firemen's houses.

Jun 26 – Chief Constable authorised to buy a typewriter for police use.

Jul 24 – Pay increases: Supt from £415 to £450; Insps £340 to £350, Sgts 2/6d [12p]week, PCs 2/-[10p] week.

Oct 9 – Chief Constable authorised to obtain legal assistance for conduct of prosecutions, where necessary.

Nov 27 – White gauntlets to be worn by officers on point duty.

1924

Apr 29 – [1] Married man's rent allowance p.week [max] Insps 14/6d [72p], Sgts 13/6d [67p], PCs 12/8d[63p], single men 5/3d [26p]. Home Office approval for these new increased rates refused – must be in accordance with H.O. recommendations, ie. Insps 15/6d [77p], sgts.15/-[75p] and PCs 12/6d [62p] [2] Chief Constable granted allowance of 6 gallons petrol p.month for use in his private motor car on police business. [3] All members of Force to be vaccinated by Police Surgeon at cost, to Force, of 5/-[25p] each.

Nov 25 – Guildford Town Council ask Watch Committee to support their proposals for bicycles and motor bicycles to display a red rear light.

Dec 30 – Police Christmas Fund [gratuities in respect of police services] amounting to £14.4s.6d. divided amongst members of the Force.

1925

Jun 23 – Town Clerk complained to the Prison Commissioners of the added costs and inconvenience of conveying prisoners from the city to Preston Prison following the closure of Newcastle Prison. His request to make use of HMP Dumfries was rejected by the Home Office.

Jul 28 – [1] Town Clerk to sign a General Mutual Aid Agreement for the loan of police officers from one force to another.
          [2] Home Office ordered a deduction of an extra 2$\frac{1}{2}$% of police pay of every member to cater for payments to those retiring without a pension or to the wives and children of those officers dismissed the service.

Oct 13 – [1] White lines for traffic regulation to be placed on city streets, including Stanwix Bank, Etterby Street and Scotland Road.
[2] Cocoa to be supplied to night-duty officers during winter months.

Nov 24 – [1] CC instructed to make arrangements for the removal, by motor or other suitable means, of corpses from the streets or public places after accidents, etc. [2] Measures to combat Botchergate's traffic congestion, especially in Tait Street and Crown Street areas, and including trams, discussed.

Dec 29 – Watch Committee agreed a rental of £50 per month for Coledale Hall as a Home for Friendless Girls!

1926

Jan 26 – County Garage win order to supply new motor ambulance at cost of £678.

Nov 30 – Old motor ambulance to be converted into a prison van.   Cost of £17 offset by sale of old prison van for £3.10s.0d.

1927

Jan 25 – New badges and buttons bearing city Coat of Arms approved for police uniforms.

Mar 1 – CC authorised to appoint an Inspector of Hackney Carriages to examine and test motor vehicles at a wage of £4.5s.0d per week.

Apr 26 – [1] Bells installed in police cells at cost of £13. [2] Services of a matron when female prisoners in cells approved at cost of one shilling per hour.

Jul 27 – Superintendent's house, part of Police HQ declared unfit for habitation-converted into additional police office space.   House 155, Warwick Road purchased for £700 for Superintendent's occupation.

Nov 29 – 6 mackintoshes obtained for officers on traffic point duties.

1928

Jan 31 – 1. CC requests replacement of Force boat due to its dilapidated condition.

Jun 19 – Home Office approved the strength of the Force at 72 officers.

Left: a funeral procession for a policeman passing Hardwicke Circus on its way to Stanwix Cemetary.

Cumberland News

Right:1911, a bearded police inspector, bottom left, looks on as Prince Henry of Prussia is greeted into the city during a tour of Britain jointly organised by the RAC and the IAC of Germany. Some 300 participants took lunch in the Crown and Mitre Hotel. The policemen are wearing their summer uniforms???

From the Chief Constable's annual reports

1913

The Force establishment consisted of 1 Chief Constable, 1 Superintendent, 1 Detective Inspector, 3 Inspectors, 10 Sergeants and 57 Constables. One Chief Constable retired, one was appointed in his stead. 3 PCs were dismissed, 2 were ordered to resign, 1 resigned voluntarily and 1 became insane. 366 days were lost through sickness, averaging 5 per man.

"That so many children have to be brought before the Juvenile Courts, and the fact that in many cases the same children appear time after time, forces one to the conclusion that something is radically wrong in their home surroundings. In many cases, parental control appears to be absolutely wanting, and one can only hope that the system now adopted by the Justices in making an Order for the parents to pay the fines inflicted on their children will presently bring them to a sense of their responsibilities, as there is little chance of these children ever becoming useful citizens if they are allowed to continue running about the streets at all hours of the day and night."

287 persons were prosecuted for drunkenness, 13 drunk in charge of horses. 158 were summonsed for chimney fires. There were 85 street accidents involving carts or motor cars. In several cases, police officers *'with great promptitude and at some personal risk, stopped runaway horses'*. 227 motor car licences were taken out in the city, 219 licences for horse drawn carriages and 121 Gun licences. 94 Pedlar's Certificates and 1 Chimney Sweep's certificate were issued by the police.

1914

Noticeable decrease in juvenile crime was down to two factors – *"[1] Orders upon parents to pay the fines, damages and costs and [2] the use of two cycle patrols who have been instrumental in reducing the incidence of petty crimes and the number of complaints by nearly 50%. I hope to extend their scope of action."*

All annual leave and rest days were suspended following the outbreak of war. *"I hope the Watch Committee will see their way to make up the lost days at the end of the war"* [1, What's the betting that it didn't? and 2, How long did he expect the war to last?]

1915

40 members of the Force are now serving with the colours. Force establishment of 80 includes 21 temporary constables and 19 vacancies. 172 Specials have been sworn in.
During the year I have examined 761 [pictorial] posters before they were exhibited on public hoardings – 748 were passed, 13 refused and 10 amended to remove what were, to my mind, objectionable features.

1928

Sixty-six children were prosecuted, 'indicating that some parents fail to exercise control over their children.'
68 chimney fires reported – all of the householders concerned were prosecuted to conviction.
70 prisoners were escorted to HM Prisons [Durham and Preston] at a cost of £107.3s.2d.
Aliens registered in the city – 57 Italians, 17 Americans, 15 French, 8 Germans, 3 Swiss, 1 Russian and 1 Belgian.
232 street accidents, including four fatal – Mondays' and Saturdays' traffic is particularly heavy.
79 sudden deaths were investigated.
344 houses were notified as 'temporarily unoccupied' – police gave day and night attention to them.
380 premises were found insecure by patrols.
114 stray dogs were seized – 70 were returned to their owners.
748 items of lost property were handed to the police.
545 days duties were lost through sickness of officers [74 per man].
One officer was specially detailed to work at the auction marts – 218,000 animal movements – enforcing Ministry of Agriculture Regulations.
260 buses, 14 tramcars, 17 motor taxis and 2 horse-drawn cabs, together with 365 drivers and 193 conductors, were licensed in the city. There were 50 bus services, 17 entirely within the city, 16 radiating from Town

Hall Square.

68 fire calls were received, the highest number since the Brigade was established in 1904.

850 places within the city were liable to inspection by the Weights and Measures Officer – 4000 weights were examined and tested, 700 were found to be of incorrect weight.

CARLISLE HISTORICAL PAGEANT - The Force performed 2,300 hours of duty, 300 of them unpaid, during the week-long pageant, which had included a visit by H.R.H. Princess Mary. Superintendent Stewart of the County Police and 25 R.A.C. guides had been loaned to the Force for traffic duties.

Archibald Kennedy Wilson, Chief Constable
1 December, 1928 to 30 November, 1929.

Mr. Wilson, a native of Galston, Ayrshire, succeeded Mr. Spence. Educated at a large public school in Mid Lothian, he joined Cardiff City Police on 22 December, 1909, and rose to become Assistant Chief Clerk in the rank of Staff Inspector. In that capacity he acted as Deputy Chief Constable in the absences of the post-holder. He had previously been short-listed for the chief constableships of Neath, Coventry and Hereford.

On 11 September, 1928, from thirty-nine applicants for the vacant chief constable's seat , five were selected for interview - Mr. Wilson, Superintendent & Deputy Chief Constable, A.A. Johnston, (Carlisle City), Inspector A.R. Crosbie,(Liverpool City), Inspector J. Scott, (South Shields Borough) and Chief Inspector J. Wells,(Huddersfield Borough). Starting in Carlisle on 1 December, 1928, at a salary of £550.00 per annum, he was to stay in post for precisely twelve months before moving on to become Chief Constable of Plymouth City Police.

Did Alderman Edmondson, JP, a former mayor, who was quite outspoken about his views on Mr. Wilson's appointment, foresee an early departure from the Force? *"There was another good man who was deprived of putting in an application because he was three days too old,"* he said. *"I congratulate you, Mr. Wilson, but I suppose you will only be using us as a stepping stone to something better."* The new Chief replied, *"I am a young man full of ambition. I mean to settle down and stay with you a little time, but you could not blame me if I did not."* *"We could go on appointing young men every twelve months,"* said the Alderman. A Councillor agreed and suggested that the Committee should make the office of Chief Constable tenable for five years. Another commented that, *"an older man of more experience might be of greater value to the city. Lord Byng was well over 60."* (Field Marshal Lord Byng [1862-1935] following an illustrious military career and five years as Governor-General of Canada, was appointed Commissioner of the Metropolitan Police in 1929 at the age of 67. He retired in 1931).

A contributor to the national 'Daily News' said that *'Mr. Wilson, the new Chief Constable of Carlisle, possessed one qualification in which the average police officer is deficient – he is an orator of considerable charm and power.'* Mr. Wilson had been prominently associated with the Caledonian Society of Cardiff and his speech at a recent annual dinner, a brilliant and witty performance, had attracted much attention and had illustrated an intimate knowledge of Latin, mythology and folklore. Now that, no doubt, qualified him well for the office of Chief Constable of Carlisle and swayed the selectors!

Amongst the Chief Constable's multifarious tasks, in January, 1929, was the prosecution of two 'lazy fellows from Fusehill Workhouse' for refusing to carry out work as inmates, one because he wasn't given a smoke, another because he objected to having his clothing searched. Both were sent to prison.

Two hundred and seventy persons, including the Chief Constables of Carlisle and of Cumberland and

Westmorland, the Mayor, Aldermen and Councillors, the Town Clerk, Magistrates, Magistrates Clerk and senior officers of the city's military establishments, attended the Force's Annual Ball, in aid of police and local charities, in the Crown and Mitre in February 1929. Could such a turn-out be achieved today? Very doubtful. The function was organised by a committee under the chairmanship of Inspector Dugdale, the Police Fire Brigade senior officer, who was in attendance. Two evenings later, after the poor fellow was taken ill during a billiards match, he died at his home in Spring Gardens Lane.

'A policeman's lot is not a happy one' – an observation as applicable to the Carlisle Force as many other early constabularies, and well summed up at the retirement party of two retiring officers in March1929. Calling it a day after 34 years service, Inspectors Lynn and Percival were presented with testimonials from the Chief Constable and comrades in the Force. Inspector Seaton, making the presentations, said that when they joined *"there was no such thing as recreation for they had to work almost all the hours that came. There was no such thing as a match with another force, and if such a proposal had been mentioned, it would almost have sent a Chief Constable into hysterics. They started on 24/3d a week [£1.21], compared with a starting wage today of £3.10s [£3.50] plus allowances. A policeman's life was not all beer and skittles in the early days. In fact, he had a pretty hard time in making ends meet."* Inspector Percival responded *"It will be a great wrench to leave fellow colleagues"* whilst Inspector Lynn advised young officers *"Put your shoulder to the wheel and try to make the best of things – conditions in the Force are very much better, in every respect, than when we started."*

In June 1929, Chief Wilson informed the Watch Committee that, concerned at the standard of training undertaken by new recruits to the Force, he had looked at the training centres in Sheffield and Manchester and advised that future recruits to the City Force should undergo initial training at the Manchester City Police Training Centre. The Committee accepted his recommendation. This was undoubtedly his biggest contribution to the City Force.

One of his last duties as Chief Constable of the city was to report to his Watch Committee, on the tragic circumstances of the death of a promising young constable, PC 16 Walter Bell, who was knocked over and killed by a motor car on Kingstown Road whilst off duty and cycling towards his home in the city, on 5th September 1929. Bell, a 29 years old single man, a native of Blackford, where he had attended the village school, lived with his parents in Warwick Road, Carlisle. He had been a city policeman for four years. PC Bell was a keen sportsman who played football for the city police. His father was, at one time, a Border Rural District Councillor; his brother a constable at Bury in Lancashire. On the fateful day, Constable Bell, enjoying a half-day off duty, visited friends at Rockcliffe leaving at 10.30pm to cycle home to Carlisle. He was seen at Moorville by two witnesses, one a bus driver travelling towards Kingstown, as he rode along Kingstown Road, near to where the Aldi store now stands. Each said that he was well over onto his own side of the carriageway and that his bicycle displayed lights. They also saw a motor car travelling at a fast speed towards the city, some considerable distance behind PC Bell. Four lamps on the front of the car were described by the witnesses as 'glaring' and 'dazzling'. The bus stopped at Moorville to allow a passenger to alight. As the car passed alongside the bus, there was a loud crash, *"like a shop window smashing."* The bus driver and one of his passengers alerted by the noise looked out and saw a man lying on the road in front of the whitewashed cottages close to the County Police Station (Moorville was at that time outside the city boundary and was policed by Cumberland and Westmorland Constabulary) on the east side of the road. They rushed to his aid. They could see that he was seriously injured and each assumed that the car, which had not stopped, had collided with him. The bus driver thought that he must be the cyclist whom he had seen riding towards the city but there was no sign of a bicycle. Yet none of the witnesses had seen a pedestrian nearby. PC Oldcorn, the Moorville policeman, was quickly on the scene, and he requisitioned the bus to take the casualty to the Cumberland Infirmary, where he died, shortly after midnight, from very severe head injuries. An examination of the carriageway revealed broken windscreen glass strewn along 400 yards between the scene and Knowefield.

Elizabeth Wilson, a passenger in a lorry travelling along Scotland Road towards Moorville at the time of the incident, unaware of what had occurred ahead of her, saw a car about 100 yards in front of her and moving towards her as she approached Waverley Road. The car was showing three lights to the front. She saw it stop close to where Briar Bank and Morrison's traffic lights are today. There was a bicycle on *"the left hand side of the car between the radiator and the mudguard. The handlebars were against the windscreen."* The driver of the car, a tall, broad shouldered man wearing a suit, got out and walked round his vehicle which the witness thought was either a dark red or dark blue Morris Oxford. She saw that the driver was smoking a cigarette but she did not get a good look at his face. When she arrived at the 'accident' scene, on being told that the injured man had had a bicycle, she concluded that it was probably his cycle that she had seen on the car further along Scotland Road. She told PC Oldcorn but in the short time it took to reach the location the car and its driver had cleared off. Chief Constable Wilson, and Superintendent Stewart of the County Police, appealed to the public for information through the newspapers and on the radio. It was reported that, in the couple of days following the incident, several cars, as far apart as Edinburgh and Preston, had been examined by the police.

Top right: PC Oldcorn.

Above and left:
Kingstown Road, Moorville,
the scene of the collison.

At the inquest into PC Bell's death, Mr. T. Strong, the City Coroner, ruled out any fault on the deceased's part. PC Bell had been hurled a distance of twenty-seven feet. His cycle had been thrown up onto the car and fixed there. In the Coroner's opinion, *"that could not have happened if the car was being driven at a moderate speed."* The bicycle was found 150 yards from the accident scene, propped against a hedge *"round a corner after the driver had got out of sight of anyone who might be on the scene. He was seen by a witness to stop, and presumably remove the cycle from the car. He must have known what had happened. The fact that he disappeared seems pretty equivalent to a plea of guilty of having done something wrong. It makes my blood boil almost to think that a fellow countryman should be so callous and cruel as to leave a fellow creature lying in a dying condition on the road and not make any enquiry or give any assistance."* The jury unanimously brought in a verdict that Constable Bell was killed by the gross negligence of an unknown motorist. *"This"* said the Coroner, *"amounted to manslaughter."* The offending driver, however, was never traced. Large crowds gathered along the route of PC Bell's funeral cortege through the city. Two cars were needed to carry the sixty floral tributes. The mourners included the City's Mayor and Mayoress together with Magistrates' and Court representatives. Fifty city police officers, led by Superintendent Johnston in the absence of the Chief Constable from the city, marched four abreast along Warwick Road ahead of the hearse with three constables, coffin-bearers, each side of the hearse. The bearers were Constables Sloan, Henderson, Little, Smith, McGinley and Percival and were under the direction of Sergeant Turnbull. At Warwick Road/Lowther Street junction, the police officers formed into two ranks to allow the cortege to pass between. They then entered motor vehicles to travel with the procession to Arthuret Church, near Longtown, for the funeral service and burial. Crowds lined the route at the 'accident' scene in Moorville, and in Kingstown. Others thronged the churchyard at Arthuret.

oooOooo

The Town Clerk received Mr. Wilson's resignation notice on 1 October 1929, consequent upon his appointment as Chief Constable of Plymouth, a city of 210, 000 people with a police force of some 300 officers, (one of whom, incidentally, was one, Willie Lakeman, who was destined for greater things, here, in Carlisle). Mr. Wilson left Carlisle on 27 November 1929, with a reputation of being popular with his staff having done much to promote the recreational side of police life, an observation touched upon at the retirement presentations of Inspectors Lynn and Percival. The Watch Committee thanked him for his 'short stay', wished him continued success and wished him, his wife and "little Carlisle daughter" health and happiness.

Mr. Wilson left Plymouth to become Chief Constable of Liverpool City Police, a Force of some 2,500 men, but, it seems, he was not the most popular of chief officers that force had had. Known there as 'Plymouth Bill' he was noted for his strict discipline. One constable who had reported late for duty on three occasions in fifteen years was told that it was getting to be a habit, and that he'd better look for alternative employment. Could it have been this man, whilst Chief Constable of Plymouth, from whom one, William Lakeman, his chief clerk, learned his trade? He, too, was a hard disciplinarian.

Mr. Wilson was hardly in Carlisle long enough to make any impact. Apart from his initiative on recruit training there is little to record about his stewardship of the Force.

A few odds and ends from Chief Wilson's days

1928.
Dec 15 – [1] Two inspectors give notice of their intention to retire. PC John Johnston does likewise, having completed 25 years service, but he indicates a willingness to continue. Whatever he does, his pension is fixed at £3.2s.0d. per week. Councillor J H Minns did not think it fair that the PC be allowed to continue considering the numbers of people out of work. He also protested at police pensioners taking other jobs after retirement when there are many ex-servicemen and others who could be employed. [2] Councillor George Rigg said that in appointing AK Wilson they had got the right man for the job. Councillor JW Smith said he deprecated eulogy of someone who had not yet given the city any service.

1929.
May 28 – Motor ambulance restricted to use within 12 miles of the city, and county cases to be charged at 7/6d [37p] per call out.

Andrew Alexander Johnston, Chief Constable
1 December, 1929 to 31 August, 1938.

It was second time lucky for Superintendent Johnston, the city's Deputy Chief Constable for the previous eleven years, when he applied, for the second time in twelve months, to become the chief officer in succession to Mr. Wilson. Of the fifty-four applicants, six were interviewed by the Watch Committee - Mr. Johnston, Chief Constable E.W. Tinkler, Kidderminster Borough, Deputy Chief Constable D. Warnock, Ayr, Superintendent H. J. Gunston, Swansea Borough, Chief Inspector W. Gate, Manchester City and Staff Inspector W.J. Price, Cardiff City.

Mr. Johnston was educated at Trinity Academy and Moray House College in Edinburgh. He began work in the General Post Office Savings Bank Department in London later transferring to the Accountants Branch in Edinburgh. The 34-year old Scot became a constable in the Newcastle-upon-Tyne City Police Force in 1905 and served there for fourteen years until his appointment as Superintendent in Carlisle. In Newcastle he served in both uniform and detective branches before promotion to sergeant into the Chief Constable's office as assistant chief clerk. In 1917 he was promoted to Staff Sergeant (Divisional Inspector). He was responsible for sixty officers charged with the responsibility of protecting the Armstrong Whitworth munition works during the war. At the time he accepted his appointment in Carlisle, he was on a short-list for the vacant post of Chief Constable of St. Alban's. In Carlisle, he was the Deputy Chief Constable with particular responsibility for the investigation of crimes. Mr. Johnston was welcomed into office by the city magistrates whose spokesman commented that he *"was fortunate in two things. In the first place he knew his men, and in the second place, he was taking over a force which for discipline and efficiency it would be difficult to find the equal of."* So why, one wonders, did he miss out twelve months earlier?

Bravery

On 28 September 1926, Superintendent Johnston was highly commended by the Watch Committee for his conspicuous devotion to duty and his exceptional courage and skill displayed in arresting an armed thief, Victor Carassov, known also by the aliases George Washington Harrison (the name of his victim) and Victor Mortimer. Carassov was wanted by the police in Harrogate, Yorkshire, for the theft of securities valued at £10,658 and a quantity of jewellery, the property of a retired banker. The Chief Constable, Mr. Wilson, was instructed to report the circumstances of the arrest to the *'proper authorities'* with a view to some testimonial being awarded to the Superintendent for his *'meritorious service'*. Whether the Chief did so or not is debatable for, it seems, Mr. Johnston never received the recognition of a bravery award that seemed to be the wishes of the Committee.

Briefly the facts of the incident were as follows. On the 26 August, a man giving the name William Mortimer, aged 26, *'well groomed and stylishly dressed'*, went into the offices of a leading Carlisle stockbroker to negotiate the sale of some share certificates. There was a later meeting with him but in the meantime the stockbroker informed the city police of his doubts. Superintendent Johnston arranged to be present at the meeting masquerading as the stockbroker's chief clerk. The three men met and at an appropriate time during the negotiations Mr. Johnston identified himself as a police officer and told the man he was arresting him. Mortimer sprung from his chair and, pulling a revolver from his pocket, demanded that the Superintendent *'put his hands up'*. Johnston leaped upon him, grabbing his hand and pointing the gun towards the ceiling. The stockbroker moved swiftly and snatched the weapon, whilst the Superintendent overpowered the offender and found a second loaded revolver and £5000 worth of share certificates on his person. Other officers arrived on the scene and took Mortimer to the police station. There he was identified by his true name, Carassov, a 22 year old from Cardiff. Mr. Johnston was subsequently commended by Sir Ernest Bane, the chairman of Harrogate Magistrates.

Motor patrol

In December 1930, the Home Office recommended that a motor car be provided to police road traffic but it was not until two years later, on 8 December, 1932, that the Watch Committee responded by acquiring a Triumph car from the local SMT Garage, the Force's first traffic patrol car.

Retirement, rumours and serious allegations

The unexpected headline news in the Carlisle Journal on 31 May 1938 announced, *'Chief Constable resigns on score of ill-health.'* *'Startling statements regarding rumours concerning the Police Force and Corporation officials,'* reported the Cumberland News. The resignation had been received by the Town Clerk the previous day. The same papers carried details of cases in the City Police Court that the Chief Constable had himself prosecuted only four days earlier on 27 May. It seems that Mr. Johnston reported sick later that same day. He apparently became unwell and the police surgeon, Dr. Alan Semple, advised him to take sick leave at once and to give consideration to resigning. The Chairman of the Watch Committee, Mr. Tassell, talking to the press on 27 May, said, *"The Chief Constable had carried on under difficulty for some time, and in spite of ill-health. He really is a*

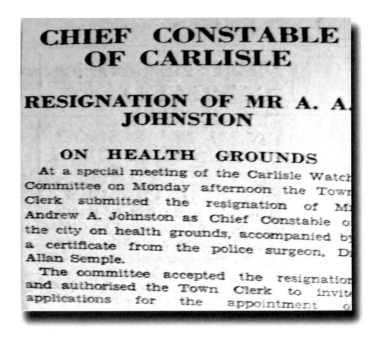

CHIEF CONSTABLE OF CARLISLE

RESIGNATION OF MR A. A. JOHNSTON

ON HEALTH GROUNDS

At a special meeting of the Carlisle Watch Committee on Monday afternoon the Town Clerk submitted the resignation of Mr Andrew A. Johnston as Chief Constable of the city on health grounds, accompanied by a certificate from the police surgeon, Dr Allan Semple.

The committee accepted the resignation and authorised the Town Clerk to invite applications for the appointment o

very sick man. We don't know yet if he'll carry on. All these rumours about the town are without foundation."

On 30th May, the Town Clerk reported that the Chief Constable had intimated his wish to be relieved of his appointment, on the grounds of ill-health, to take effect from 31 August 1938. The police surgeon had certified him medically unfit to continue in office and, as he was already absent from his post on sick leave the Council had little option but to accept the resignation and advertise for a replacement. Come in Willie Lakeman! In the meantime Chief Inspector Walker was appointed to command the Force during Mr. Johnston's absence. Mr. Johnston retired with a pension of £433, having completed 32 years and 360 days pensionable service.

That was the official announcement of Mr. Johnston's retirement which, with hindsight, may have been considered ill-timed. There was no evidence to suggest other than that the poor man was ill but apparently some very different opinions were circulating in the city. From the Carlisle Journal's editorial column: *'Rumour has been busy in the city for several days. Scarcely a citizen can but have heard something affecting one of our main public services. While all apparently have knowledge, none can say with certainty, and the tales are permitted to multiply themselves to the detriment alike of the service concerned and the common good. It is not right that this should be so. A public statement, given with authority, whether of the nature of a disclaimer or otherwise, is clearly called for and should be forthcoming without further delay.'* The speed at which Mr. Johnston departed, it seems, added fuel to the rumours that were already circulating in the town.

"Wicked and malicious innuendos," said the Chairman of the Watch Committee, Mr. F.W. Tassell, a fortnight later when he urged the Council to accept the Chief's resignation. The Town Clerk added that, *"If proof was available of any person making false statements, steps would be taken which would have very unpleasant consequences for them and which would teach them to keep their tongues under control and refrain from making such lying and slanderous statements."* Mr. Tassell said that the honesty and integrity of the Police Department had come under attack. *"May I say,"* he continued, *"that the finances of the Police Department are, and have been, perfectly in order in every way."* The Town Clerk said every effort was being made to

trace the origin of the rumours, some of which were so ludicrous and improbable that they had been received with disbelief and contempt by all right-minded citizens. He went on, *"To make false statements reflecting on the probity and integrity of a public officer is a very serious matter for which the law provides very heavy penalties,"* and he threatened legal action against anyone discovered to be making such allegations. *"I wish that statement had been made a month ago,"* said one Councillor, whilst another commented, *"If the public had been told the facts there wouldn't have been any rumours!"* Councillor Edgar Grierson said he did not feel disposed to sit quiet. He added that the Watch Committee was desirous not to discuss the matter in open council, but he disagreed and felt justified. Rumours were rife and the Watch Committee, to have stopped a *"lot of talk,"* should have made public what had actually taken place.

What were these rumours? It appears the talk, *"by people of substance,"* was of misappropriation of funds by executive officers, not just in the Police Department but across the Council's many departments, and the setting up of a syndicate amongst officials and various members of the Council to purchase property in Rickergate and sell it on to the Corporation at a profit of 200%. Very serious allegations indeed, and easy to understand why the Town Clerk was so furious and threatening. Councillor Edgar Grierson said that he knew everyone was against discussing this topic in open forum, but as the rumours were in circulation at the time that the Chief Constable left Carlisle, the Watch Committee should have made the facts of the case public at that time.

Briefly, the background to all this lay in plans, which did not appear to be within the knowledge of all Councillors, to build a new Town Hall and municipal buildings in Rickergate where the Civic Centre now stands, opposite the site of the proposed new city police headquarters. It had been generally believed that a new Town Hall would be built in Chatsworth Square. Derelict buildings in Rickergate had been bought by the Corporation under the pretext that the land was needed for road widening and for improving the entrances to the city. *"Supposing a private buyer did purchase the land on which to build, could not the Council have insisted on a new building line to allow for a wider road, without having to pay anything at all?"* quite reasonably queried one member. Rickergate was a squalid, slum area, with *"properties one could scarcely walk into the bedrooms of which without falling through the floors."* The allegations being made related to the extravagant expenditure of public monies on such properties, some £18,000 already spent in addition to the costs of procuring the land for the new police station, with proposals to purchase other buildings at a further cost of £5,350. Councillor Vasey, who was the first to raise the issue of inflated prices in Committee on 13th May, said *"Not one member of this Committee would ever consider paying these sort of prices if it was their own money they were spending."* He said that some time earlier he had been engaged by the Corporation to act on their behalf in what turned out to be an unsuccessful attempt to purchase some of the properties. The value of these properties was far below that now under discussion. He knew of one property now valued at £8,000 that was worth only £5,000, another block recently purchased for £1,500 was now supposedly valued at £3,500. He said that no-one could convince him that the values of such properties had appreciated to that extent, quite the reverse. The prices paid for the land for the new police station and those presently being quoted for the remaining Rickergate properties were *"absolutely scandalous."* The properties were slums, he told the meeting. They could not be put into habitable condition and were scheduled for demolition. The Town Clerk agreed with him. Told that the Corporation was forced to pay a high price because of other interest being shown in the land, the question was asked *"Could this other party be a speculator knowing that the Corporation was interested?"* A newspaper correspondent wrote that he knew of a private sale of a piece of the same land going for half the rate that the Corporation had paid. The 'Cumberland News' was critical of the Corporation's proposals for the area and, whilst not commenting on the premium paid, made the point that the Council had until recently an excellent piece of land right in the heart of the city eminently suitable for new municipal buildings and had deliberately sold it, being satisfied that its existing properties would for the time being be adequate. Now they were considering moving *'to the very outskirts of our city'* (Rickergate!).

It would have been very easy in the circumstances for a populace that had been starved of any positive and official explanation of the Council's plans to jump to the wrong conclusions, especially when such corrupt practices as alleged were not ones entirely unheard of, even if none such had come to light before in the city of Carlisle. In the event, it seems that either the belated public airing of the matter satisfactorily answered public concern and/or, more than likely, the Council's unequivocal determination to prosecute anyone repeating the rumour, was sufficient to deter any further gossip.

A few odds and ends from Chief Johnston's days

1930
Nov 4 – City Watch Committee oppose Home Office plans for a Police College.

1931
Jun 22 - Carlisle Divisional Council for Social and Moral Welfare ask to have additional policewoman appointed.

1932
Apr 26 – Govermental Committee letter to Town Clerk suggesting amalgamation of small city and borough police forces with neighbouring counties. Categorically rejected by Carlisle City Council.

1938
May 13 – Cumberland Infirmary had a waiting list of 1415.

May 25 – 1] PC 72 Harold Simons rescued a bullock stranded in the River Eden. [see Jul 26 below].

2] PC Sutcliffe [later Supt. and Deputy Chief Constable] arrested man for begging in Botchergate and English Street – case dismissed on the man's promise to leave the city immediately.

Jul 26 – PC 72 Harold Simons awarded RSPCA Bronze Medal and permitted to wear it on his uniform.

oooOooo

William Henry Lakeman, Chief Constable
1 September, 1938 to 15 November, 1961.

Mr. Lakeman, 42 years old, a native of Plymouth, joined the Plymouth City Police Force in 1919, moving into the administration branch after just two years service. He was promoted to the rank of sergeant in 1931, inspector in 1933 and chief inspector in 1937. Mr. Lakeman was short-listed for the post of Chief Constable of Maidstone, Kent in March, 1937. By the time of his appointment in Carlisle, he had spent some twelve of his nineteen years police service in an administrative capacity. On the morning of 24 January 1932, as a sergeant operating under the command of Mr. A.K. Wilson, his Chief Constable, (formerly Chief Constable of Carlisle), Mr. Lakeman was one of a group of Plymouth officers called to quell the serious mutiny in Dartmoor Prison. Travelling to the scene by motor coach, the officers could see columns of smoke from the fires, started by the convicts, in the prison buildings. Mr. Wilson ordered a baton-charge of the prisoners - *"In you go lads, it's them or us so spare no mercy."* Thirty-one officers entered and though heavily outnumbered, they restored order by mid afternoon. Some sixty prisoners were treated for the injuries inflicted by the police.

Joining Chief Inspector Lakeman, on the short list for vacant post of Chief Constable in Carlisle were Mr. R.C.M. Jenkins, Chief Constable of Penzance, Superintendent Collins, Gateshead Borough Police, Chief Inspector A.E. Rowell, Deputy Chief Constable, Exeter City Police, Detective Inspector F.E. Devey, Nottingham City Police and Inspector William Rawson, Huddersfield Borough Police. William Rawson was born and brought up in Carlisle, an ideal candidate one might have thought. The Police and Constabulary Almanac 1941 shows him still in Huddersfield as Chief Inspector and Chief Clerk, third in seniority in a Force of 152 officers. Whilst he joined Huddersfield Police as a constable in 1919, his brother, Thomas, joined the Carlisle City Force and rose to become Chief Constable of Swansea Borough and later of Bradford City Police.

Mr. Lakeman began his term of office in Carlisle on 1 September 1938. He was to be the city's Chief Constable during the Second World War, which was just twelve months away. His tenure was to prove the second longest of any Chief of the city police, twenty-three years, a term that would be unthinkable today.

'One of the first things he will be called upon to deal with will be our traffic problems,' recorded a local newspaper, *'everyone will hope that he may find a solution satisfactory to motorist and trader alike.'* One is tempted to ask, *"What's changed?"* The City Council had a proposal before them for the imposition of a *'ten minute in any hour'* parking restriction in any of the city centre streets. Shopkeepers were up in arms fearing disastrous effects on their trade. That well-known local solicitor Mr. Lionel Lightfoot, objecting, and expressing his opinion that the plan would be unworkable in English Street, said *"Supposing a lady went into Binns on a Saturday morning. I understand they have a splendid system of giving change by shooting pieces of paper to another part of the building, and sometimes, to buy a yard of silk and get change for six-pence, it takes twelve to fourteen minutes when they are busy."* He stressed that he was not a shareholder of the company. He said that the Council should *"appreciate the position of the motorist even if they regarded a motor car as a capitalist luxury!"* One objector said *"If one car moves away after ten minutes and another immediately takes its place, the whole scheme is useless."* How much less is that true today? The Council decided to defer their decision until the arrival of the new Chief Constable, in order for him to consider the proposals and report. In the event, in the light of considerable opposition, the scheme never came to fruition. See (reproduced on the next page) the front page of the Carlisle Journal, 13 May 1938, for the newspaper's light-hearted look at the proposal.

A procedure said to have originated in America before being introduced into the UK in the 1950s by Liverpool Police, was tried in Carlisle several years earlier than that. *"Boys are not born criminals,"* said Chief Lakeman in April 1939 as he launched an innovative project, his Force believed to be the first in Britain to try it, in an effort to combat the serious problem of juvenile delinquency in the city. *"The problem of the child delinquent has been the concern of many during the past few years. Half the trouble is lack of parental control,"* he continued. *"My slogan is 'Get the parents on the side of the police'. The police are not the enemies but the friends of youth. Boys will be boys, but they are not inherently bad. Police proceedings besmirch the family name. Every juvenile will be made the subject of unobtrusive enquiries as to upbringing and environment. The experiment will run for one year. It will not be extended to louts in their teens."* The local newspapers predicted that if the Carlisle experiment was a success it was sure to be copied throughout the country. Thus began a scheme, commonplace throughout the UK today and with statutory support, that provided for first-time juvenile offenders to be cautioned by a senior police officer rather than prosecuting them in the courts. Mr. Lakeman himself took on the role of cautioning the youngsters. In his Annual Report for the year, returning to the theme, he commented *"Many parents do not accept their normal parental responsibilities and a child is, by circumstances, forced to carry a character stain that could have been avoided if a parent had exercised a reasonable amount of discipline and forethought. It cannot be sound procedure to punish a child (by a court appearance) for sins that are really the fault of the parent."* During the experiment the Chief cautioned forty-nine young offenders in his office at the police station in the presence of their parents. However, a disillusioned Chief Constable saw an increase in crimes committed by juveniles during the experimental period and concluded *"It may well be that black-out conditions (the war-time lighting restrictions during the hours of darkness) have, to some extent, encouraged offences. I can foresee that some corrective punishment of a more severe nature will have to prevail before this problem can be termed satisfactory, as leniency and kindness which has hitherto been used is useless. If parents were (ordered) to bear a part of the punishment they would give the child that disciplinary education it needs. There is another serious aspect to this problem. Many of the crimes committed are so cleverly perpetrated, and so much criminal cunning used, that one must realise that these probationary criminals are bound to be a potential menace to the country in after years."*

1939 –1945, World War 2

All serving officers under the age of 24 years were conscripted shortly after the outbreak of war. The Corporation resolved to pay the salaries/wages less their armed forces' pay, and to preserve the pension rights, of permanent officers and employees of the Corporation serving in H.M. Forces, and their appointments were to be kept open for their return. The Home Secretary authorised an extra sergeant and two constables to take account of additional war duties. Six members of the First Police Reserve were recalled to duty at salaries of £3.10s.0d per week. The Watch Committee authorised enrolment of Special Constables to augment the Force during hostilities, to equip them with uniforms, and to pay them at the rate

"TIME, GENTLEMEN, PLEASE!"

EIGHTY-NINE AND REMEMBERS JOHN PEEL

MR. THOMAS BELL, Bothel, aged 89, is probably the last living link with John Peel.

Mr. Bell was born at Prior Hall Farm, which is in the neighbourhood of Ruthwaite, the famous hunter's home in his latter days, and he clearly remembers, as a boy of five years, Peel's death—

TRAGIC STORY OF ELDERLY WOMAN'S DEATH IN A POOL

THE mysterious actions of an elderly woman, who, apparently, lost her—

of £3 per week, under the terms of the Special Constables Order, 1939. Mr. Lakeman declined an offer to recruit women officers.

Upon the declaration of war, an armed constable was placed on guard outside the city police station. He carried a pistol but had no ammunition. One officer who carried out the duty asked, facetiously, if he could have some bullets so that he could kill the Germans if they came. His request was refused. *"I might as well have been armed with a brush pole,"* he said. Air Raid sirens on the roofs of Carr's biscuit factory in Caldewgate and Woolworth's in English Street were manned by police officers working eight-hour shifts. Officers were required to perform eight-hour duties guarding the entrances to the Corporation's electricity power station in Willowholme, the gas works in Rome Street, at the telephone repeater station in London Road and at Mark's (Hide and Skin) Depot in Tyne Street off London Road. All of these locations were under 24-hour guard. Beat officers had to mask all traffic lights at sunset and unmask them at sunrise. Special duties, for which they could earn an extra shilling per hour, were carried out at Slater's fun-fair in King Street, at H.M. Theatre and at various dance-halls (all usually for two hours on a Saturday evening). The owners of these establishments were charged two shillings per hour for the policemen's time. The Force organised a *'clog and stocking'* fund, looked after by the chief clerk, from which needy parents could receive help in obtaining footwear for their children.

Patrolling officers wore belts over their outer clothing, attached to which they carried *'Wootton'* wet battery lanterns, capable of lighting up objects 100 yards distant during the hours of darkness, and claimed by the manufacturer to be *'The World's Finest'*. These large, heavy lamps were handed in at the end of a tour of duty to be recharged in the fire station for the following night shift.

In 1939 Winston Churchill proposed a *'Home Guard'* of men, aged 40 and above, to protect key points in Britain, such as bridges, rail terminals, and the coastline. On 14th May, Secretary of War, Anthony Eden appealed in a BBC radio broadcast, for men aged 17 to 65 to report to police stations to volunteer for a new citizen defence force to be known as the *'Local Defence Volunteers'* (LDV). Almost immediately, the city police station in West Walls was overwhelmed with volunteers with many more men than the number actually required coming forward. By the end of June, 1940, 14,909 men had volunteered across Cumberland and Westmorland (This and further information can be seen on the Tullie House website).

In August 1941, due to the war conditions, the city police and fire service functions were separated when the government took responsibility for the brigade. It became part of the National Fire Service and was never to return to the control of the Chief Constable. There were suggestions that the government was considering amalgamating a number of small police forces with their larger neighbours, usually county forces. Ostensibly for war reasons the Home Secretary did order the amalgamation of several small southern forces. It was a policy strongly resisted by Carlisle Corporation whose view was that its long association with the ancient city's police force should be preserved for fear that more central government control would lead to interference with the rights and liberties of the citizens. One has to say, given the state of today's police, that those city fathers were wise men.

As compared with records maintained during the First World War, there is a dearth of information about conditions, events, injuries suffered and achievements during the 39/45 war. Several officers attained promotion in the military. A number of them served in the Military Police, PC Roy Harrison as a captain.

Above: *Above, a war-time presentation, Chief Constable William Lakeman looks on as PC 'Cash' Little receives a presentation from the Chairman of the Watch Committee. Inspector 'Happy Jack' Davidson, and another, look on. The Chief is wearing a 'Sam Browne' belt, PC Little carries his gas-mask.*

Above: *war preparations - the Mayor and Corporation try out new gas masks at the ARP testing station in the old gas works. Lurking in the centre of the picture is the city's new Chief Constable, WH Lakeman [arrowed]. The local newspaper took the opportunity to feature the Chief in a "Who is it?" quiz.*

144

No city policemen lost their lives and most returned, battle-hardened, courageous and fearless, to police duties upon the cessation of hostilities. It was an experience to work alongside them. Paying tribute after the war, the Town Clerk said that the citizens owed a debt of gratitude to the special constables, and auxiliary firemen, stating that they had rendered valuable services, voluntarily, in very difficult circumstances.

Left: *Rickergate, looking towards Scotch Street and the Old Town Hall.*

Below: *the view from Scotch Street.*

Right: *Slum dwellings in Drovers Lane viewed from Rickergate.*

Warwick Street, Rickergate - a proper police headquarters

Above: *Warwick Street, Rickergate, before demolition to make way for the new headquarters.*

Above right: *the headquarters, pictured in 2011 after the police had moved to their new headquarters at Durranhill.*

Not before time, on 17 April, 1941, the Force moved into a modern headquarters, a newly built emergency services and courts complex in Rickergate. The Chief Constable, of course, was responsible for providing fire, ambulance and weights and measures services all of which were brought together under one roof. The Fire Brigade actually occupied its part of the new premises eight months ahead of the police in August 1940. However, the Chief was to have command of the fire service for only a further four months before its war-time nationalisation. Although it was returned to the Corporation Watch Committee after the war, it became an independent department with its own command structure.

Built by Carlisle construction company John Laing and Son, Limited, at a cost of some £80,000, including purchase of the land, the new headquarters were officially opened by the Mayor, Alderman Matthew Thompson, JP, on 17 April 1941. At the ceremony, Mr F W Tassell, Chairman of the Watch Committee, commented on the fact that HM Inspectors of Constabulary had complained about the old building for years. *"They had often wondered how the Force had carried on so successfully in such premises,"* he said. (It was his committee that had failed to provide anything better!!!). *"We now have a police station worthy of the city"*, he continued, *"Even the cells are most comfortable and, I am afraid, there will be some aspirants, through minor offences, for comfortable bed and breakfast."* Vice Chairman, Mr J H Minns commented, *"The old police station, opened in 1840, had gloomy cells, locks, bolts, bars and chains, built to hold characters such as Burke and Hare, Jonathon Wilde, Jack Shepherd and Blueskin and has served its day and generation, haunted perhaps by the spirits of Chief Constables and officers from the past who were a credit to Carlisle and to the police force of which they had the honour to belong, confirmed in a government report as long ago as 1858 which said that the police establishment of the city was quite respectable with a very active Chief Constable."* Mr Thomas Wardle, manager of John Laing's said, *"It has not been easy to complete the building during a major war but nothing about the premises is a substitute material."* The Mayor also inaugurated a new street pillar telephone system before officials and guests had tea in the parade room.

Left: *Carlisle Old Town Hall, the home of the City Police Court and Quarter Sessions Court (presided over by the Recorder of the city) as well as being the meeting place of the Watch Committee prior to the opening of the new buildings in Rickergate.*

Later in the day of the headquarters' official opening, during the hours of darkness, German bombers over-flew the city on their way to attack Glasgow. The Town Clerk, Mr. Fred Webster commented, *"How ironic it would have been if the buildings had been destroyed or damaged on the very day of their opening."*

The new complex occupied a plot 250 feet square. The Magistrates Court, which also served as the City Quarter Sessions Court, dominated the plan. It was set in the centre of the main block on the first floor, away from all sounds of traffic and other disturbances. Adjacent to it were a magistrates' room, retiring rooms, conference rooms and rooms for barristers and solicitors. There was direct access to the courts from the charge office and cell corridors, accommodation for warders, baths and washing facilities and an exercise yard. Warm air was circulated. *"Prisoners are really more comfortable than some who are free"*, remarked one official. Separated from the main court was a juvenile court and waiting room. The police benefited from chief officers' and admin accommodation, a large public enquiry office, charge office, telephone exchange, a large parade room, drying facilities, clothing store, mess rooms, three research rooms for the CID (fingerprints, photography and scenes of crime). The CID occupied first floor accommodation adjacent to the courts. Outside, with access from an enclosed yard, was a garage, mortuary and post-mortem room, cycle shed, dog kennels and a gas decontamination station. A Civil Defence control room was built underground, below the police station. All in all, light years away from the premises the force had recently vacated. The Magistrates who had moved from the court-room in the Old Town Hall thought likewise. *"Those who remember Rickergate of old with its teens of public houses, narrow lanes and ramshackle dwellings see with delight the transformation of the area now effected,"* said the Mayor, sitting as Chairman of the Bench for the first time in the new court-house. It is interesting to note that the first local citizen to appear before the magistrates in the new court was charged with a war-time *'black-out'* offence, the second time he had been so prosecuted. He was fined £5, the most anyone in the city had been ordered to pay for such a misdemeanour. The first case disposed of, however, was quite different. It was stated that an Englishman, a Scotsman and an Irishman met in a carriage in Carlisle Railway Station. The Englishman was a policeman and the others defendants then in the court dock charged with travelling on the railway without tickets. They explained that they were seeing off friends in Glasgow when they fell asleep on the train and didn't wake up until it was on its way to Carlisle. The Mayor thought it was a cock and bull story but turned an indulgent ear. Dismissing the charges he ordered the defendants to leave the city without delay.

The Rickergate headquarters served the city police for the rest of its days until amalgamation with the county police in April 1967, twenty-six years, at an initial cost of £80,000, that included fire, ambulance and weights and measures stations as well as the city's courts. Costing little over £3,000 a year, with no further building costs, was pretty good value for money. Following the demise of the old city force, the buildings continued in use, with relatively minor alterations, until 2005, as a county divisional police headquarters. The fire service still occupy their part of the complex. The ambulance service moved to purpose built headquarters next to the Cumberland Infirmary after it fell under the control of the NHS.

When, in 1941, the Town Clerk remarked how easily the police station might have been destroyed by enemy bombers on the very day of its official opening, he could never have guessed that, almost as quickly, nature could, and would, bring about its destruction. During the night of Saturday, 8 January 2005, Carlisle was hit by severe weather and flooding causing the Rickergate area of the city centre to become awash with contaminated water some seven feet deep, swamping the police and fire stations and condemning them to immediate closure. Many existing and retired officers would argue that, even before January 2005, the Rickergate accommodation was beyond its sell-by date and that the flooding presented an opportunity to create a new building for the 21st Century. Now, some four years after the disastrous floods, a new divisional police headquarters is open at Durranhill. The Fire Service remain for the present time in Rickergate, but plans are in hand for a move to two new premises.

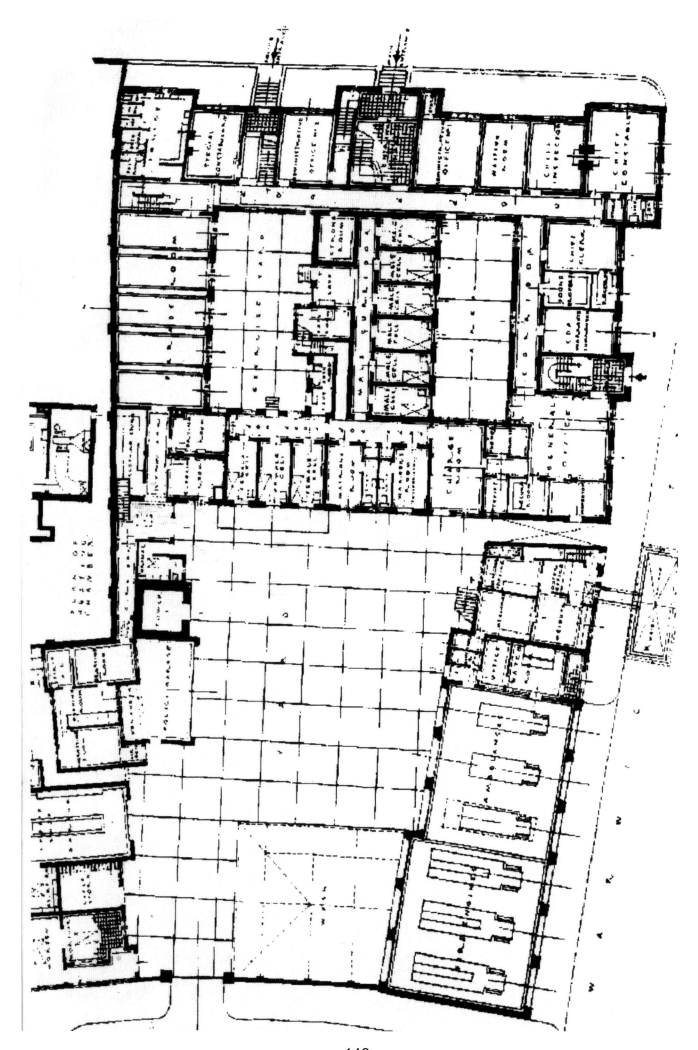

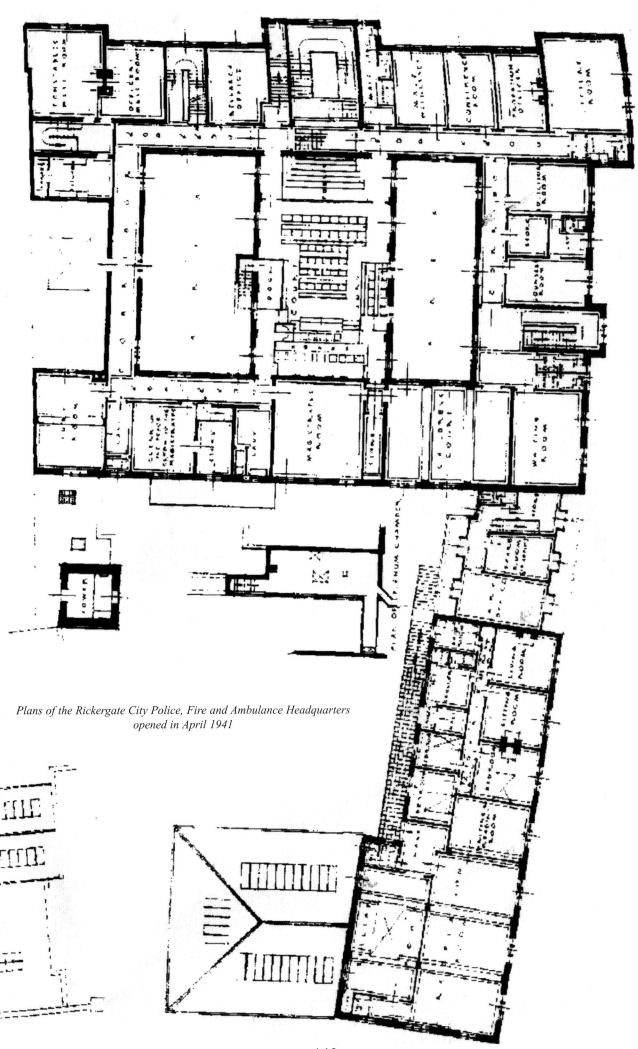

*Plans of the Rickergate City Police, Fire and Ambulance Headquarters
opened in April 1941*

Harraby sub-station

In June 1949, the Home Office approved plans for the construction of a police sub-station to serve the southern and eastern areas of the city subject to a total cost, buildings and land, not to exceed £5,000. The site first chosen, quite close to the centre of the city, was located at the corner of London Road and Brook Street. It was rejected in favour of an alternative at the corner of Mayfield Avenue and London Road, Harraby. The self-contained station included office, kitchen and rest-room toilet and storage facilities. It was used mainly by officers policing the Harraby cycle beat and, occasionally, the Botcherby area but was closed after amalgamation.

Above: *The former Harraby Sub-station on London Road close to the junction with Eastern Way, pictured May 2009. It is now a Benefits Advice Centre.*

Police housing

The recommendations of the Desborough Committee in 1919, which was convened to examine police pay and conditions, led directly to new Police Regulations for the whole country and required police authorities, inter alia, to provide officers with residential accommodation free of rent and rates or an allowance in lieu thereof in default. The consequence of this provision was the removal of an officer's choice of residence and its location in favour of the police authority's direction as to where he should live. Nothing new about that in Carlisle! Residential restrictions were a feature of the city policemen's conditions of service long before Police Regulations were even thought of and were imposed because of the men's refusal to live in Caldewgate. *'Could anyone blame them for that?'* one might ask. On 20 September 1838, just two years after the Corporation took control of the force, the Watch Committee decreed that officers' residences would be dispersed about the city and that future appointees would be required to live where the Watch Committee directed. Furthermore, no officer would be allowed to change his address without the Committee's approval (the Committee retained these rights until it ceased to exist in 1967). Finally, notwithstanding that the houses were neither owned nor subject of any allowance from the police authority, the Committee directed that sign-boards should be placed over the door or lane to the house of each officer so that the public could find one in an emergency. The boards were to display the word 'POLICEMAN' and the officer's name. Imagine that in Caldewgate anytime, let alone in 1838! However, a very understanding committee took into account that *'so many of them have other businesses such as small shops, superintended by themselves and carried on by their families that it would be injustice to remove them from their present residences, and the Committee think it would likewise be impolite to recommend the removal of those men who are not so circumstanced as it would make a distinction which, to say the least of it, would be invidious and cause a feeling of dissatisfaction amongst them.'*

**The Great Flood
8 January, 2005**

A flooded Rickergate -

Above: *the police headquarters seen from the east.*

'A 'blessing in disguise.'

A modern divisional police headquarters was built to replace the old city station.

*The view from the west. The building on the left is the Fire Station, part of the original complex.
Housing, originally for fire brigade members, is in the centre.*

151

There is no record to show who drew the short straw and was made to live in *'Caudagate'* but it's a fair assumption that the next recruit would be the lucky chap. The Watch Committee, over the years, did acquire dedicated police residences and thirty purpose built houses were constructed for married officers and their families after WW2. They were scattered around every part of Carlisle but there was never a sufficient housing stock and many officers received rent allowance in lieu. This was recognised as one of the principal advantages of serving in a city or borough police force - the ability, early in service, to purchase one's own home with the assistance of a rent allowance. An officer's choice of residence, however, still had to be approved by the police authority and in Carlisle, as in most cities, it had to be within the city boundaries so that, in effect, the allowance was returned, as rates, to the city coffers. Carlisle's police houses were instantly recognisable by their architectural style but otherwise there were no other signs or features to identify them for what they were. In 1965, with the strength of the Force standing at 149, forty-one officers occupied tied housing, fifty-five lived in privately owned properties and seventeen had rented accommodation. Unmarried officers received a lodging allowance.

Chief Constables had no more freedom than the men to choose their places of residence. Until 1941, the chief was provided with a house (in King's Arms Lane) leased to the police authority for a period of five years by a Mr. E. W. Thurnam. West Walls police station opened in 1941 and contained residential accommodation for the incumbent chief. By 1908, the Force had outgrown its working space in the station and the Chief's house was converted for operational use. The Chief was re-housed in the dwelling-house 20 Warwick Square, newly purchased by the police authority for that purpose, at a cost of £800, leasehold, for the unexpired residue of 200 years granted by the Duke of Devonshire. It was retained until Chief Constable Spence retired in 1928, when once again the authority reverted to the system of paying an allowance in lieu of tied housing. In July, 1940, the Watch Committee purchased the dwelling known as *'The Grange'* on Wood Street, Botcherby, for £1450. It was occupied by Chief Constable Lakeman until shortly before he retired.

The street pillar system.

Introduced in 1941 to coincide with the opening of the new police headquarters in Rickergate, street pillars in every area of the city not only provided a major improvement in communications between headquarters and patrolling constables, but also gave the public quick and direct access to the emergency services. From the earliest days of the Force, patrolling city constables were required to make *'conference points'* at prescribed locations and times, usually at no more than hourly intervals. The practice maximized the ground covered by patrolmen since the points were widespread across their patrol areas. It provided early warning should harm befall an officer and facilitated the duties of sergeants and inspectors who had to meet up with officers out on their beats to satisfy themselves that the beats were being worked correctly and to advise and assist their subordinates. The established system of *'making points'* continued with the new pillars replacing public call boxes as beat conference points. The orange light at the top of the pillar was flashed to alert the beat officer that he was required to telephone police headquarters to receive an urgent message. The picture shows an officer at a pillar, probably making such a *'point'*, writing notes in his pocket-book on the drop-down desk.

The pillars were numbered and located as follows:

1.	Outside No. 165 Scotland Road, Waverley Road junction.
2	Outside No. 163 Brampton Road.
3	Outside No. 10 Scotland Road, opposite Etterby Street.
4	Kingmoor Road, opposite Etterby Road.
5.	Moorhouse Road, bifurcation Burgh Road.
6.	Newtown Road, corner of Bellgarth Road.
7.	Church Street, Caldewgate, opposite Carr's Biscuit Work.
8.	Castle Street, corner of Annetwell Street.
9.	English Street, on island, by Steel's Monument.
10.	Warwick Road, corner of Howard Place.
11.	Warwick Road, on Petteril Bridge.
12.	Fusehill Street, corner of Rydal Street.
13.	Botchergate, corner of The Crescent.
14.	Botchergate, corner of Charles Street.
15.	London Road at Gallows Hill.
16.	Blackwell Road, corner of Beaconsfield Street.
17.	Blackwell Road, corner of Ridley Road.
18.	Durranhill Road, opposite Merith Avenue.
19.	Upperby Road, corner of Lamb Street.
20.	Currock Street, corner of Rome Street.
21.	Junction Street, corner of Lorne Crescent.
22.	Denton Street, corner of Norfolk Street.
23.	Murrell Hill, corner of Dalston Road and Pugin Street.
24.	Dalston Road, corner of Richardson Street.
25.	Wigton Road, corner of Orton Road.
26.	Thomlinson Avenue, corner of Shadygrove Road.
27.	Lowther Street, opposite Victoria Place.
28.	Outside No. 165 Scotland Road, Waverley Road junction.

City boundary changes and the construction of new housing estates brought about a number of changes and additional pillars:

    1 Removed from outside No.165 Scotland Road and withdrawn from use.
    27 Removed from Thomlinson Avenue and re-sited on Newlaithes Avenue, opposite Westrigg Road.
    29 [new] Kingstown, bifurcation of the A7/A74 roads.
    30 [new] Briar Bank, opposite Fernlea Way.
    31 [new] Edgehill Road, corner of Arnside Road.
    32 [new] Pennine Way, corner of Tindale Drive.

The introduction of unit beat policing to Carlisle in 1966 brought an end to the street telephone system since officers patrolling both on foot and in cars were equipped with personal radios. All of the pillars were duly removed and passed into history.

The street pillar system in Carlisle

Clockwise from left: *Sergeant Walter Biggar at 7 pillar, Caldewgate.*

No. 9 Pillar in Carlisle Centre on a snowy day in the fifties.

No. 9 pillar again in 1953.
The monument is decorated for the coronation.

A member of the public using 2 pillar in Brampton Road.

999' emergency telephone system

There was no other 'emergency' telephone system available in 1941 when the pillar system was taken into use. Calls via the GPO simply had to take their turn in the telephone operator's queue. However, following a major fire in London at a doctor's house in which five people died, the '999' system was introduced in the capital on 1 July 1937. The number was chosen because it had to have three digits to work in the London district. All had to be the same so that they were easy to find in the dark or in smoke. With the equipment in use at the time, the number '9' presented the GPO with the least technical drawbacks. By the end of its first month in use, some 13,000 genuine emergency calls had been handled. The service was extended to Glasgow in 1938, but, due to the war, it was not until 1948 that major towns, served by automatic exchanges, were covered.

oooOooo

The Force establishment totalled 71 officers at the end of 1945. Seven were still serving with the military but others had returned from war duties to a very different police force. In their absences, Chief Lakeman had presided over many major changes and innovations unmatched in the history of the Force. The war-time *'Specials'* were stood down, though 72% of their number volunteered to carry on as a peace-time Special Constabulary. By 1948, the authorised strength of the Force had increased to 102 male and two female officers, but there were thirty-four vacancies that were proving very difficult to fill. Chief Lakeman reported that *'there is little doubt that the existing rates of pay, coupled with the disadvantages of police work when compared with other industries have adversely affected the position with little prospect of the situation being improved.'* The year 1949 brought improvements in pay and conditions of service with the adoption of the recommendations of the Oaksey Committee, a Royal Commission on the Police and the provision of sixteen new police houses in the city. However, the Force was then still twenty-one officers below establishment, which was clearly to the detriment of adequate and efficient policing. Mr. Lakeman therefore introduced a *'team policing'* experiment on 30 October 1949. Mobility was the keynote. The traditional methods of routinely patrolling and working beats on foot were suspended and patrol sergeants were given the authority to deploy officers where they considered the need to be greatest. For example, they were able to 'flood' problem areas at material times with uniformed constables. Having shown an effective presence, they could be collected and transported quickly to another area or incident. This system, pioneered by Aberdeen City Police, simply created an illusion that the police had the city well covered, whereas, in fact, areas of it were not patrolled at all. The Chief recognised this fact, for just six months later, in April 1950, he reported that *'an entirely mechanised method of operation did not work efficiently.'* He re-established foot patrols in the centre and north of the city, but the remainder continued to be policed by the mobile unit until the manpower situation improved such that the whole city could once again be traditionally patrolled, 24 hours per day. O that the service would so act today and respond to the public's concerns!

A radio typical of those fitted in police cars in the 1950's and 60's.

Under Chief Constable Lakeman's stewardship another milestone in the development of the Force was reached on 10th May 1954 with the establishment of an Information (Control) Room at police headquarters and the introduction of a Home Office wireless communications scheme shared with Cumberland and Westmorland Constabulary and with the city Fire and Ambulance services. The city police operated under the Home Office call sign M2BU and the County M2BB. The City Fire Brigade used M2BUF and the ambulance service M2BUA. Police vehicles, fitted with two-way radio, were able to respond immediately to the instructions of a controller in the Information Room and conversely, traffic officers were able to obtain instant response to calls for assistance or crime intelligence.

An urgent call would merit the immediate despatch of a traffic patrol or CID car, others would be passed to a beat constable through the street pillar system to deal with as soon as practicable and certainly within his eight-hour tour of duty. The public in those times would certainly not have been told, *"Sorry, we have no officers to send to your assistance."* Such a response would almost certainly have resulted in the officer being disciplined and possibly dismissed the service. In its first few months of operation, wireless proved to be a valuable asset, twenty-one arrests directly resulting from its use. As in the case of street pillars, the wireless system was to serve the Force well until the introduction of unit beat policing in 1966.

oooOooo

William Henry Lakeman was a hard task-master, a formidable character who did not suffer incompetence, inefficiency, carelessness or fools lightly. Towards the end of his tenure, if not earlier, he was a tough and humourless, autocratic character who ruled with an iron fist. He had a brusque manner towards his subordinates, and did not mince his words. His abrasive, authoritarian style was certainly not from the man-management text books and he had few friends amongst his subordinates. Nevertheless, his style seemed to keep them on their toes and he got results. He certainly stood on ceremony and there was no mistaking who was in charge of the Force. Woe betide the policeman, patrolling or on traffic-point duty, who did not spot him pass by in his car and respond with a smart salute, even though instructions at Training School forbade the practice while directing traffic since a salute might be misinterpreted by motorists and result in an accident. Furthermore, he expected not to be held up by traffic pointsmen as he moved about the city in his car. He would never allow such *'misdemeanours'* to pass. An *'offending'* officer would be recalled to the station from his beat, for an appearance before him for an explanation. Of course, not a single officer would have deliberately held him up or missed saluting, out of respect for his rank if not for the man himself, but no matter what the explanation the officer would be wrong. Being truthful and saying, *"Sorry, Sir, I didn't see you,"* would bring forth an angry response including, *"You're paid to see everybody. I could have been a wanted murderer. Don't let it happen again"* (my personal experience). A former traffic sergeant recalls how he approached the Chief in his office to ask if heaters could be installed in the patrol cars, since, during very cold spells, the vehicles' windows would steam up, thus creating a potential danger. *"Get out,"* he bellowed, *"Heaters!"* *"But,"* the sergeant tried to begin negotiations. *"Get out. I've told you,"* cutting him off. End of conversation. In my thirty years police service in three forces, four if integration with Cumberland and Westmorland Police is counted, none of my other eight Chief Constables dispensed with the services of probationer constables at anything like the rate of Chief Lakeman (those in their first two years of service could have their appointments terminated, without appeal, as being *'not likely to become efficient'* officers'). Many officers would argue that this regulation was misused simply as an excuse to off-load. It was just as well that, apart from the immediate post-war period, there was never a dearth of applicants to join the city force.

The police service generates a wealth of yarns, about occurrences and characters both within and outside of the *'job'*, but of the many told about Mr. Lakeman, few ever relate to his humour, his friendliness or his physical involvement at the sharp end of policing operations. Most of his subordinates, especially the young and inexperienced, were in fear of the man. In spite of all that, the Force he ran had a *'family'* feel about it, the esprit de corps second to none. He has to be credited with being at the helm during times of great change for the better (after all, he had twenty-three years to achieve it) and during the difficult time of war (though Carlisle experienced few enemy attacks. Houghton Road and London Road were bombed). The question often arises today, *"What would Lakeman make of today's force?"* and the usual response, *"He'd turn in his grave if he knew how the service operated."* That's not so much a criticism of today's officers as it is about how much policing methods and management practices have changed since his times. He was truly one of the police service's characters, but if a modern day Chief Constable copied his management style there is little doubt it would very soon be challenged by aggrieved subordinates in the courts or tribunals. Today's police service simply would not stand for it.

What was the Force like towards the end of Mr. Lakeman's tenure? Certainly different from today's. Recruits had to pass an entrance examination in English, Arithmetic, Geography and General Knowledge. The Force did not demand certificated educational/academic qualifications though there were several former grammar school students in the ranks. Medical and eyesight examinations by the Force Surgeon had to satisfy certain standards – for example, Police Regulations disqualified any candidates for appointment if they required spectacles. Once appointed, absences through sickness were rare. I cannot recall any officer suffering from stress, a common problem today. The minimum height was 5'10" for men, though the majority were 6ft and over, 5'4" for women. Society was reflected in that recruits came from a wide variety of backgrounds, administrative, commercial, skilled and unskilled trades and almost all had work experience outside of the police service. Most male officers had served in the armed forces, National Service still being in existence, and they brought the self discipline and experience of a uniformed service with them. Many had served throughout the Second World War in campaigns in Europe, North Africa, the Middle and Far East. Others had served in more recent theatres, Malaya, Korea, Cyprus and Aden. Consequently, the potential dangers of the police service held no fears for them. Several were former military or, like myself, RAF, policemen. All were well able to take care of themselves and their community, as a few local *'hard men'* found to their disadvantage. Uniform meant just that. All officers on duty were identically dressed, the only variation being for traffic officers and Inspectors and above who wore caps instead of helmets – and head-dress was always worn, unlike today. Shirt-sleeve order was not allowed. Sergeants carried *'night-sticks'* and Inspectors and above carried swagger canes. Expectations of promotion could not be entertained before at least twelve years service were completed therefore those with aspirations just got on with the job in hand to the best of their ability without suffering anxiety and frustration at lack of early advancement or apoplexy at the sight of their contemporaries being promoted before them. Apart from having to pass national qualifying examinations, (which could not be taken until four years service had been completed and which were held only twice per annum) the procedures leading to promotions were very *'secretive.'* Those selected had to appear before the Watch Committee for confirmation and promotions took immediate effect thereafter. Colleagues had no intimation until the promotion was promulgated in Force Orders. Many officers were quite happy to soldier on throughout their thirty years service as constables. Lack of ambition certainly did not affect their ability to perform their duties efficiently. There was a good esprit-de-corps, and all could turn to one another for advice and assistance, rather than address all problems to those of senior rank. A great sense of humour prevailed – policemen have that knack of always being able to see a funny side to things, no matter how serious - and thus the tensions from some of the horrific sights they face, the desperation of some of the people they are called to assist and sometimes just the boredom of the job, can be broken. These latter two characteristics, and the generally accepted security of employment (after completing two years service) probably compensated for the relatively low rates of remuneration. Foot and cycle beats were covered 24/7 and officers spent minimal time away from them completing reports, etc. Prosecution reports were written in pocket books while out on the beat and handed in at the completion of tour of duty for typing by admin staff. Routine reports were copied and hand-written onto appropriate forms before submission. Officers were allowed to leave their beats fifteen minutes before completion of their shift to return to the police station to complete handwritten reports. A constable found off his beat without very good reason would face disciplinary action. The only other time beats were vacated was for a 45 minute mid-shift meal break in the station. Those working overlapping shifts then covered the vacated beats as well as their own, thus providing 24 hour cover throughout the city. Officers rarely worked the same beat for more than one week at a time, an arrangement that equipped them with an intimate knowledge of every area of the city. Mistakes were surely made, but the Force liked to consider itself very efficient. A wealth of knowledge of the city and its people, not least its criminals, existed. One hundred and twenty officers with an average service of, say, 15 years, accumulate an awful lot of local intelligence which was, generally, shared with colleagues. Over half of the 120 officers serving when Chief Lakeman retired either then held rank or went on to promotion – two reached Chief Constable rank (Dewsbury Borough and Lincolnshire County), two Deputy Chief Constables (West Yorkshire and Durham), one Assistant Chief Constable (West Yorkshire), five Chief Superintendents, eight Superintendents, thirteen Chief Inspectors, fourteen Inspectors and thirty-one Sergeants – not a bad record for one of the country's smallest forces that had an establishment of just one Superintendent and two Chief Inspectors at senior level.

 oooOooo

William Lakeman retired from the Force on 15 November 1961, having been Chief Constable for just over twenty-three years. He continued to live in Carlisle and often bumped into and, uncharacteristically, exchanged pleasantries with his former men. A sergeant stepped into the carriageway of Lowther Street, the A7 road, and stopped traffic to free congestion in a side road. Afterwards, signalling the main road traffic to proceed, he noticed an approaching car driver winding down his window and intent on speaking to him. He recognised his former Chief, who commented, *"You wouldn't have stopped me a few weeks ago sergeant, would you?"* He may have been joking, but he was not wrong.

oooOooo

Above: *visit of HRH The Princess Margaret, 1957.*

From left: *Chief Constable Lakeman, Inspector Bert Boak, City Mayor, Alderman George Routledge, Lord Lieutenant Sir Robert Chance, HRH Princess Margaret, Edward Wooll QC, Recorder of the City and Mr.HDA Robertson, Town Clerk, seen here on a walkabout in Market Street.*

"The Police Force serves the general public in enforcing laws enacted by elected representatives of the people for the good of the majority of the people. The constant endeavour of the Watch Committee has been to ensure that the Carlisle City Force maintains the high tradition of efficient and loyal service which has at all times been displayed during the 150 years of its existence".

William H Lakeman, Chief Constable
City of Carlisle Octocentenary celebrations, 1958.

A few odds and ends from Chief Lakeman's days

1938
Chief recommended appointment of two junior clerks/shorthand typists, 16/17 years of age, height and build able to meet standards of the Force, so that when they reached qualifying age, they would be appointed constables.

1939
Jan 31 – [1] Chief granted a car allowance of £100 pa.

Apr 25 – Chief's pay increased to scale £600 to £800 pa. Inspectors' rates of pay in Forces with establishment of 60 or more officers standardised at £360pa..

Jul 25 – Home Office now providing training for motor patrol officers – PC 37 Maurice Hendry to attend.

Oct 3 – [1] Dean and Chapter School in West Walls taken over for police use. [2] Chief to hold promotion examinations with the papers being set by and marked at the Birmingham City Police Training School.

1941

Feb 25 – Chief Constable required telephone system to be continually manned when new HQ opened – recommended two junior male clerks, who would be appointed to the Force as constables upon reaching age of 20 years. Further recommended replacing police officers currently engaged on administrative duties with two female shorthand typists.

Oct 7 – Four additional motor cycles to be purchased as recommended by HMI.

1944

May 23 – Major Egan, HMI of Constabulary, recommended the appointment of four female officers, their pay to be reimbursed in full by the Exchequer [Womens Auxillary Police Corps].

1946

Apr 1 – Tender of J. and R. Bell of Carlisle, in sum of £2154.5s.9d. per pair of semi-detached houses, accepted for 20 police houses.

Jul 31 – Old Police Headquarters offered as offices for the new full-time Clerk to the Justices and for the Probation Officers.

1947

May 24 – Establishment increased and now stands at one Chief Constable, one Superintendent, six Inspectors, ten Sergeants and 84 Constables – total 102. Chief Constable authorised to advertise for recruits, but only in local papers.

Jun 17 – Appointment of 2 policewomen, additional to the establishment, confirmed – 8 applications received.

Oct 13 – Chief reported that Constable 58 Maurice Thornthwaite had resigned to further a career in the Military. He joined the City Police in 1941 before being called up for war service, during which he had attained the rank of Captain.

1948

Mar 23 – Force rent allowance appreciably lower than in other forces – Home Secretary approved an increase to 26 shillings per week for constables.

Apr 27 – The Police College established at Ryton on Dunsmore, Warwickshire – courses for potential Inspectors commencing 15 June 1948 – PS 9 Roy Harrison nominated to attend, a good choice – he later became Chief Constable of Dewsbury and retired as Deputy Chief Constable of West Yorkshire Constabulary.

Apr 27 – Two Humber Hawk patrol cars to be purchased from Harrisons Garage at a total cost of £1803.3s.4d., plus £75 per vehicle for wireless equipment.

Jun 22 – Appointment of Constable 45 George Carlton confirmed upon completing his 2 years probation. [George was first officer to be appointed to the City Police after the war].

Sep 28 – Doctor G.M. Jolly appointed City Police Surgeon.

Nov 30 – Home Office approval obtained for the appointment of one additional policewoman – provided she was not employed as a shorthand typist or clerk or on indoor duties.

1949

Jul 26 – John Laing and Son, Ltd., to build ten police houses at a cost of £12,755 -4 at Harraby, 4 at Belah and 2 at Upperby.

Sep 27 – Pay of Chief Constable now £1,050 x £50 to £1200pa., and of Superintendent £700 x £25 to £750 plus £50 Deputy Chief Constable's allowance.

Sep 28 –1949 clothing contract to provide for the first time for open-neck type jackets, shirts, collars and ties.

1950

Apr 18 – Four male telephonists to be appointed at salary of £5.5s.0d per 40-hour week, releasing 4 police officers for outside duties.

Aug 29 – Establishment increased by one chief inspector and one detective sergeant – Home Office recommended that Borough Forces based on a single division should have a deputy to the superintendent to ensure proper continuity of control and supervision, and CID should have a rank between the current constables and inspector.

Sep 26 – Chief Constable recommended erection of 3 section boxes, one on the island at Wigton Road/Orton Road junction, one at London Road/Mayfield Avenue junction and one at Scotland Road/Briar Bank junction, following the city boundary changes under the Carlisle Extension Act, 1950. Approved by the Home Office but only the Harraby box was built.

1951

Apr 1 – City Boundaries extended.

Jul 10 - The Police Long Service and Good Conduct Medal was introduced for officers with over 22 years service. 22 city officers were recommended for the award.

Top left: *Sergeant Arnold Coulthard happily promoted to Inspector.*

Right: *PC 72 George Kerr seen in the Information Room.*

Above left: *Inspector Eric Rice, who served in the armed forces in the rank of Major during World War II.*

Centre: *Sergeant Tommy Bowerbank.*

Right: *Sergeant Thelma Ellis. in charge of the Policewoman's Department. Thelma was brought to Carlisle by Chief Lakeman from his former force, Plymouth City.*

From the Chief Constable's annual Report

1938

Force establishment – 1 chief constable, 1 chief inspector, 3 inspectors, 11 sergeants and 58 constables. One constable dismissed upon conviction of a criminal charge. 810 days lost through sickness, averaging 10.2 per officer, 432 due to the long-term sickness of just six men. Special Constabulary increased to one hundred men.

415 indictable offences recorded, 241 detected [58.08%]. Value of property stolen £1,085.18s.3d, recovered £423.3s.2d. 1152 non-indictable [summary] offences reported, 590 of them motoring offences. Fines totalled £572.

Road Traffic Accident reports numbered 663, including six fatal, all pedestrians running or stepping into the paths of moving vehicles. One person was killed by a pedal cycle, another by a motor cycle. Botchergate, between Tait Street and St. Nicholas was labelled the most dangerous thoroughfare in the city. One motor car patrolled the city covering 12,709 miles, and its crews reported 277 persons for breaches of road traffic laws.

CID – Taking of fingerprints of those charged with indictable offences introduced at the beginning of the year – one copy sent to New Scotland Yard, one to West Riding Constabulary [Regional Criminal Record Office] and one retained in Carlisle.

Four sets of impressions were photographed at scenes of crimes for comparison with records held, and two criminals were identified and arrested as a result. A Photographic Department was set up and 107 prisoners photographed; scenes of crimes and road traffic accidents also photographed. Lack of space in the present police headquarters [West Walls] had limited the development of the department, but its needs were adequately catered for in the new police headquarters under construction in Rickergate.

197 firearms certificate holders in the city, 71 pedlar's certificates issued and 19 hackney carriage licences. 2530 movement licences issued for animals passing through the city's auction marts [a total of 297,373 animals]. 192 stray dogs were seized.

1939

56 publican's licences and 2 off-licences under control of the State Management Scheme. Only 3 licensed premises [Crown and Mitre Hotel, County Hotel and the Silver Grill Restaurant] under the control of the city's Licensing Justices. 84 offences of drunkenness reported.

Establishment – 82 officers [16 newly appointed during the year]. The outbreak of war led to the suspension of the weekly rest-day and an increase in working hours and to the mobilisation of the 100 Special Constables [including a Specials' mobile section] and 20 Police War Reservists. 1202 days were lost through sickness [514 days lost by 5 officers].

Crime – 421 Indictable, 939 non-indictable offences – 63.42% crime detection rate.
Road Traffic –622 accidents, 276 involving personal injury, 8 fatal [7 pedestrians]. The eighth involved a 6 years old child who fell from a toy pedal cycle under the wheels of a horse-drawn cart in a lane at the rear of Eldred Street. 3 of the fatalities during 'black-out' conditions. 16 persons injured whilst using pedestrian crossings.

801 ARP Wardens [Air Raid Precautions] were employed, in 13 groups each under a Head Warden, covering 118 sectors each with a population of about 500 people.

1940

Establishment – 82 officers,[but Force was 9 below strength] plus 4 First Police Reserve officers, 17 Police War Reserves and 120 Special Constables.

422 crimes with a detection rate of 69.9%. Five 'Whipping Orders' were made. Non-indictable offences numbered 2029, [increase of 1090 over the previous year] including 990 offences against the Defence Regulations – lighting restrictions [known commonly as 'black-out' offences].
595 road traffic accidents, 269 involving personal injury. Six of them 'fatals', in one of which, an 11 years old girl ran off the footpath in Blackwell Road into the path of a military ambulance. Two involved buses, and two were in black-out conditions. There were a total of 84 'black-out' accidents.

75 permits issued under the Defence Regulations enabling persons to keep pigeons, 650 Training and Liberation labels issued and lofts in the city periodically inspected by the police.

718 ARP Wardens with a reserve of a further 180 appointed. 782 [595 males and 187 females] were actually engaged on the provision of instructions to the public.

112 offences of drunkenness placed Carlisle high in the table of similar sized towns and cities. Population of Carlisle was, however, some 25% greater than the official census figures due to the wartime circumstances and the employment situation favourably altered during the year making more money available. Against this, the price of drink increased considerably.

1941

Establishment 82 officers, plus 145 auxilliaries. Special Constables allotted periods of duty working the beats, but services of some dispensed with because they could not give the increased demands.

479 crimes recorded of which 67.64% were detected. Increase in the theft of pedal cycles - *"due to the prevailing circumstances consequent upon the war, cycles and cycle accessories are almost impossible to purchase. Another factor is the limited travel facilities available."* There was a corresponding large decrease in thefts from motor vehicles *"which can be solely attributed to an emergency measure whereby it is compulsory, under penalty, for a driver to leave his car with the doors and windows secured"*. 2317 summary offences reported, including a large increase in motoring offences – 952 due to emergency legislation – lighting offences and failing to immobilise vehicles.
550 road accidents recorded including 286 personal injury accidents, 14 fatals. 8 fatalities occurred during the black-out, when war conditions have resulted in lighting restrictions being imposed. The Minister of War Transport has taken all possible steps to bring home to the public the need for special precautions. Five fatalities involved buses.

The Police Pigeon Service was established and birds were trained to fly between vantage points in the North of England. Police Messenger Service employed 78 youths in the city, trained in anti-gas and incendiary bomb control. 342 people were enrolled into Civil Defence duties.

1942

Special constables were engaged every night on beat patrol and picket duties.

446 crimes were reported, with a detection rate of 75.78%. Value of property stolen £3258.15s.1d recovered £2117.4s.0d. 1600 non-indictable offences reported, a decrease of 717 [31%]. 376 road accidents, 11 were fatalities, 6 during black-out, 6 involving buses.

1943

15 officers of the Force now serving with H.M. Forces. 130 'Specials' employed, 25 of them qualified for the Police [Special Constables] Long Service Medal, 9 were awarded Bars to their medals.

511 crimes reported, of which 67.71% were detected. 1062 summary offences reported.
307 road accidents, 8 fatalities', 5 involved buses. 5 children under 7 years old killed on the roads of the city.
20 drunkenness offences, the lowest number ever recorded in the city. *" Reasons were [1] the increased costs of drinks which has precluded 'company drinking' and brought into being a modified form of 'no treating' without the need for any special legislation - though not entirely responsible since wages were higher than for many years, [2] the scarcity of spirits."*

1944

16 officers serving in H.M. Forces. Number of Special Constables engaged has fallen to 85, 'due to the demands of industry'.
Since October, 1944, vitamin capsules have been issued to members of the Force with a view to reducing the incidence of sickness.

Crimes recorded 548, detection rate of 68.08%. 839 non-indictable [summary] offences.
346 road accidents recorded included 8 'fatals' – 4 in the black-out, 3 involving buses, 3 involving military vehicles.

1945

The Police Pigeon Service discontinued on 18 February and 15 birds and a loft were returned to the previous owner. The legislation governing the keeping of homing and racing pigeons was revoked on 10 May.
478 crimes recorded – 65.48% detected.
There were 337 road accidents, including 8 fatalities.

1948

Decrease in absences due to sickness reported. "Carlisle is now more in keeping with what is occasioned in other police forces, absences being reduced by 50% from 1947 and being approximately 66% lower than in 1946, when the figures reached alarming proportions [2543 days lost].

Police Surgeon – on 5 July, the National Insurance Act came into operation and members of police forces, who had hitherto been outside the scope of the National Health and Insurance Scheme, became compulsory contributors. In consequence, police officers are entitled to register with any medical officer they care to select. The retention of Doctor Jolly as Medical Practioner to members of the Force was therefore no longer necessary. He will be retained as Police Surgeon.

879 crimes, including one murder, recorded. Detection rate 48.12%. Value of property stolen £12,211.18s.10d, recovered £5,540.0s.3d.
530 road traffic accidents, 5 fatalities, all pedestrians, four of them aged over 73 years and one child aged 17 months playing in a quiet street when he was run over by a motor lorry. In September, a Road Safety Week was organised. 15,478 persons attended the exhibition. A Road Courtesy Patrol was started, attached to Traffic Department, and was a contributory factor to improved driving conditions.

1952

The one policewoman previously attached to the establishment resigned her appointment at the end of March. The question of recruitment of further women constables received serious consideration during the course of the year, when it was finally decided to appoint two women to the strength of the Force. In this connection, Miss K.M. Hill, Staff Officer to the Assistant HMI of Constabulary, visited police headquarters when candidates were interviewed. Two were offered appointments to commence early in 1953.

866 crimes recorded, 54.73% detected. 682 traffic accidents reported, six fatalities.

Foot and Mouth Disease – in May, the city was declared a 'controlled area' and restrictions were enforced for a period of 11 days. In July, the disease was confirmed on two farms within the city and on 13 in the surrounding area. A 'standstill area' was enforced for nine weeks, when all movements and sales of animals were prohibited.

Right: *A picture taken in the 1920s of Constables 36 Bert Boak and 27 Harold Banks. Bert was later an Inspector [pictured right during the visit of HRH The Princess Margaret].*

After retirement from the Force, Bert owned and ran a number of well known, popular local hostelries.

Note the uniforms and insignia, closed-neck tunics [still worn on night duties until 1959], warrant number on collar, city arms on shoulder and St. John Ambulance First Aid award on left sleeve.

Right: *1958 - Visit of Her Majesty Queen Elizabeth ll.*

Chief Constable William Lakeman, in the centre, ahead of the civic party as it leaves the Cathedral preceded by an escort of city policemen led by Sergeant John Walker.

On the left: *Constables 78 Sid Peel and 92 Eddie Day*

On the right: *Constables 23 Norman Robinson, 40 Harold Armstrong and 20 Stan Brown.*

Photographs taken by the Force after World War 2 and following the return of officers from military service

Top row: *Chief Constable Willie Lakeman and Superintendent/Deputy Chief Constable Fred Blacklock.*
Second row: *Sergeant 8 David Sloan, PCs 36 Bert Boak, Sergeant 11 Jack Davidson, PC 70 Harold Joffre Robinson.*
Middle row: *PCs 23 Cash Little, 38 Walter Biggar, 48 Eddie Mason.*
Fourth row: *PCs 18 Jack Caird, 63 Andy Lowry,43 Jimmy Dunn and 65 Sandy Bremner,MM.*
Bottom row: *PCs 19 Jack Nixon, 44 Jim Black, 37 Maurice Hendry, 22 Dick Curry.*

Part Four - The end of the road

Frank Edgar WILLIAMSON, Chief Constable
16 November, 1961 to 31 March, 1967.

Like Benjamin Batty, the first Chief of the city police, Frank Williamson arrived in Carlisle from Manchester. He was to be the last Chief Constable of the city force. A native of Newcastle-upon-Tyne, where his father had served in the city's police before moving, first on promotion to Huddersfield Borough Police and later, as Chief Constable, to Northampton Borough, Mr. Williamson was a 44 years old married man with one daughter. The Williamson family had strong connections with Cumberland and Westmorland, his father hailing from Kirkby Thore and his mother from Tebay. They had lived for many years in Lazonby. Mr. Williamson, himself, joined Manchester City Police Force as a constable in 1936. In 1939 he was awarded the Watch Committee's medal for bravery for his arrest of an armed man. During the war, between 1942 and 1945, he served in the Military Police with the rank of Captain. Returning to Manchester after hostilities, he was promoted to Detective Sergeant in 1948, Detective Inspector in charge of Manchester Criminal Record Office in 1952 and Detective Chief Inspector in 1953. He had a formidable knowledge of criminals operating in Manchester and the North of England, and a remarkable memory with which to recall them and their methods. In 1958, promoted to Detective Superintendent, he became Second in Command of Manchester's Criminal Investigation Department, deputy to Chief Superintendent Robert Mark, later Sir Robert, Commissioner of the Metropolitan Police. Between his interview for the vacancy in Carlisle and taking up office, he was promoted to the rank of Chief Superintendent and placed in command of Manchester's 'C' Division, covering the Bradford area of the city. Mr. Williamson took up his appointment in Carlisle on Monday 16 November 1961, at a salary of £2,175 per annum, together with a car allowance and a rent allowance of £220 per annum.

Of the fifty-two applicants who chased the vacancy created by Mr. Lakeman's departure, four in addition to Detective Superintendent Williamson, were interviewed by the Watch Committee on Tuesday, 29 June 1961. They were Chief Superintendent John K. Halhead, Commandant, District Police Training School, Bruche, Warrington, Lancashire; Superintendent Arthur Burns, Deputy Chief Constable, Norwich City Police; Superintendent Ronald Joyce, Kingston-upon-Hull City Police and Superintendent Colin O. Makin, Sheffield City Police.

Mr. Williamson proved to be *'a breath of fresh air'* to the force and very popular with his men. Under his command, the city police *'galloped into the 20th Century'* with new equipment, streamlined procedures and new uniforms. *"Give me twelve months"*, he told the local Police Federation representatives, *"and you'll have the dearest dressed and the best dressed Force in the country."* He kept his promise. Very approachable, he put a *'human face'* on the office of Chief Constable, attending not only to the welfare of his men but by giving consideration to their wives and families too. He showed much empathy with his staff and their operational duties. He was a *'hands on'* chief. A very experienced detective, he quickly earned respect for his professionalism. Rarely an evening passed that he was not there in the police station showing interest in occurrences and giving guidance to, and building confidence in, his men as necessary. Unfortunately for the city force, union with the county, not even discussed, at least not by the rank and file, at the time of the Chief's appointment, came much sooner than anyone in the Force could have expected. Many years later, Bob Sutcliffe, the Deputy Chief Constable at the time, told me that he soon became conscious that amalgamation was imminent and held that Mr. Williamson was aware of that fact upon his appointment. Mr. Sutcliffe's opposition to a merger with the county police led to conflict between him and Mr Williamson which was instrumental in him resigning from the service. As a consequence of integration, in 1963 Mr. Williamson moved to the county police headquarters at Carleton Hall, Penrith as Chief Constable of the three forces of Cumberland, Westmorland and Carlisle City. Though a frequent visitor to the Rickergate station, he clearly was not able to concentrate so much of his energies in Carlisle as when the Force was independent.

Royal Commission on the Police 1960 –1964
Small forces consigned to the dustbin.

Home Secretary, Roy Jenkins, speaking in the debate on the Report of the Royal Commission on the Police in the House of Commons on 9 May, 1963, said:

> *"I am not suggesting that small police forces are inefficient; a small force can attain a very high standard of 'esprit de corps', but I agree with the Royal Commission that small forces tend to be handicapped. They lack the flexibility of larger forces; they cannot always make the best of available manpower, and the efficient policing of wider areas is sometimes impaired by the preservation of what are often arbitrary and irksome police boundaries, from the point of view of crime and road traffic. Some areas are better policed by a large force than by a number of small forces however efficient each of the small forces is."*

The only part of that statement upon which I agree is the point that wider areas may not be so efficiently policed. But surely that is not a valid criticism of small forces. For small forces, generally, read borough police. I served in both a small and a large city force and visited many other city and borough forces in the course of my duties. Very few were handicapped as suggested. Quite the opposite. Most were usually operating with a full complement of officers serving in a place of their choice and living in their own homes without the upset of having to move family and home every few years as in county constabularies. If such criteria, as listed by the Home Secretary, applied to *'small'* forces then how much less did it apply after the wholesale amalgamations under the provisions of the Police Act of 1964? The service still comprised numerous autonomous forces, therefore *'irksome boundaries'* still existed. I eventually served in a mid-sized county force of some 1,800 officers and doubt that the best use was always made of available resources. Joe Public, even police officers themselves, would take some convincing that the best use is made, even now, of the large pools of manpower in present-day forces. Many would argue, with ample justification, that some forces are too large and impersonal with the top management too distant from the man on the ground. Several forces now comprise over 6,000 officers, the Met has almost 30,000. The extension of a constable's powers beyond his own backyard to cover the whole of England and Wales, the formation of Regional Crime Squads to work across police force boundaries and the system of *'mutual aid'*, seen working at its best during recent industrial disputes such as the miners' strike in 1984/85, (in which I was heavily involved and witnessed at first-hand) knock on the head all of the objections mentioned by Jenkins.

Integration
The city force first to fall.

The Royal Commission, though it had not finalised its work, had given clear indications that it considered the optimum size for a police force was 500 or over. It opined that the retention of forces of under 350 was justifiable only in very special circumstances and that forces below a strength of 200 were too handicapped to be fully efficient. The Government was in general agreement. What hope was there then for the Carlisle City Police Force? As it turned out, none at all. However, the *'beginning of the end'* was to come not after the passing of the Police Act of 1964, an Act consequential to the Royal Commission's final report that brought about wholesale amalgamations, but much earlier, in April 1963, when Mr. Henry Watson, the Chief Constable of Cumberland and Westmorland, vacated his post for a similar appointment in Cheshire. Integration with the County Police was not imposed upon Carlisle, but the Home Secretary's nod was as good as his wink! Seizing upon the opportunity, he invited the City Watch Committee to submit its views on the policing of Cumberland, Westmorland and Carlisle, having regard to the Royal Commission's criteria.

'Whilst not yet having reached any conclusions on the relevant recommendations' quoted the Home Office letter, *'he (the Home Secretary) is disposed to think that there may be a prima-facie case for establishing, under the Police Act of 1946, a combined police force for the area. Alternatively, a joint Chief Constable might be appointed for the three forces.'* The Watch Committee, with little alternative, and recognising both the hopelessness of retaining an independent city police in the light of the Royal Commission's interim announcements and the need for co-operation and goodwill, met representatives of the Home Office and the two County Standing Joint (Police) Committees at Penrith on 21 June,1963. Three options were discussed, viz. (i) a complete merger under the 1946 Police Act, (ii) a joint Chief Constable for the three forces, the forces being integrated on the same lines as the existing Cumberland and Westmorland Forces and (iii) a single chief constable for the three forces which would themselves remain entirely distinct. Cumberland's Police Authority opted for a complete amalgamation. That was unacceptable to both Carlisle City and Westmorland. Integration, as at option (ii) was therefore agreed and the three separate police authorities, and thus three separate police forces, though integrated and working together, would remain in existence. This was the best outcome to be expected by serving city officers since it avoided the most unpopular option, amalgamation. Frank Williamson, the city Chief Constable, would be recommended to the two county police authorities for appointment as Chief Constable in succession to Mr. Watson, and John Dagg, the twin counties' Assistant Chief Constable, would be designated Deputy Chief Constable. He would be recommended to the Watch Committee, and to Carlisle City Council, for appointment as Deputy Chief Constable of the City Force. Mr. Williamson would be required to occupy the county Chief Constable's residence in Penrith. The Force would be known as the Cumberland, Westmorland and Carlisle Constabulary. Carlisle City Police Headquarters would be moved to Carleton Hall, Penrith, and though still a separate force, the city police would, for all practical purposes, simply become a division of the enlarged force. The county police station in Abbey Street, Carlisle, would be closed and staff merged with the city personnel. Thus what might have happened in 1856 came about almost 110 years later. A common radio network would be operated for city and county. Each force's Criminal Investigation and Traffic Departments would merge and there would be centralised purchasing of uniforms and equipment. The city police force lost its distinctive uniform and separate warrant (collar) numbers.

The Watch Committee, at its meeting on 16 July, 1963, resolved to accept the proposals subject to the agreements of the two Standing Joint Committees and to Home Office approval. A Joint Advisory Committee, containing four members of the Watch Committee, was to be constituted to advise the three police authorities on matters of common concern, including financial arrangements (subject to triennial review), which were to be apportioned pro-rata to the authorised strength of each constituent force. It was agreed that the operative date for the new arrangements to come into effect would be 1 September, 1963. On that date, Donald Roy, newly promoted to the rank of Superintendent, became the senior officer in day-to-day control of the city police upon his appointment as 'Divisional Commander'. No officers were sworn in after that date as city policemen, new recruits joining the newly combined force. However, in 1967, upon full amalgamation of the three forces, those who had served continuously in the city since appointment after 1 September, 1963 were legally adjudged to have the same rights as the established city personnel and were thus protected from enforced transfers from Carlisle to other postings within the new Cumbria Constabulary area.

Re-organization.

'We trained hard, but it seemed that every time we were beginning to form up into teams we would be re-organized. I was to learn later in life that we tend to meet any new situation by re-organizing, and a wonderful method it can be for creating the illusion of progress while producing confusion, inefficiency and demoralization'. (Petronius Arbiter, 210BC).

A quotation used sarcastically, but often aptly, within the police service.

The Chief Constable's Annual Report for the year 1964 recorded that considerable progress had been made in the re-organisation of the Force consequent on its integration with Cumberland and Westmorland Constabulary.

166

For example, the county police station at Abbey Street, Carlisle, had been closed down on 31 March, 1964, and its staff, uniformed and detective, transferred to accommodation in the City Police Headquarters on 1 April. There was no mention that those headquarters, which had become barely adequate for the city Force, were now bursting at the seams. A new Carlisle Division, covering the whole of north Cumbria, under the command of the city's Superintendent Donald Roy, was created on that date with four sub- divisions, Carlisle City (Chief Inspector Stanley Blair in charge), Carlisle County (Inspector Stuart Gibson), Wigton (Inspector Holmes) and Brampton (Inspector Howe). The City's Detective Chief Inspector, Traffic Inspector, Administration Inspector, Crime Prevention Officer, Road Safety Officer, Coroner's Officer, Firearms Officer, Aliens Registration Officer and Civil Defence Officer all extended their areas of responsibility to cover the whole division. The Traffic Departments of the City and County forces merged, for operational purposes, on 4 November, 1963, with all traffic patrols for the Carlisle area operating from the Rickergate station. If the Chief's report was intended to acclaim the changes, the men on the beat were not persuaded that facilities had improved and remained to be convinced that this was the dawn of a new and better era. Far from integration being popular, the general consensus in the city force, perhaps in the county too, was that the change was to be regretted. In particular, the Force had lost its status, and, with that, its sense of pride and belonging. When the Chief conducted a survey of city officers' intentions, very few opted to make themselves available for duty elsewhere in Cumberland and Westmorland, a figure in far in excess of 90% electing to remain in the city, as was their right. Some attitudes softened over the ensuing years, for, as well as time healing the old wounds, there was undoubtedly greater opportunity of achieving senior rank and/or appointment to specialist departments in the new force, and many more former city policeman progressed to the rank of inspector and above than would have been able to do so in the city Force.

The establishment of the City Police in 1964 was increased by 1 sergeant and 9 constables and stood at one chief constable, one superintendent, 2 chief inspectors, 7 inspectors, 20 sergeants including one female, 113 constables including 4 females, a total of 143. There were 4 vacancies. Shortly after integration, the establishment was again increased, Donald Roy becoming Chief Superintendent. Stanley Blair was promoted into the ensuing Superintendent vacancy. Before full amalgamation, in December, 1966 the force was further increased to a total of 149 officers.

Amalgamation

The decision to fully amalgamate the city police with the twin counties of Cumberland and Westmorland was taken at a Watch Committee meeting on 1 November, 1966. The Committee consisted of Aldermen Hayhurst, Chairman (note that chairs in those days were items of furniture), Burrow, Caven and Mrs. Howarth, Councillors Matthews, S. Roberts and Miss Sibson and Magistrates K. Payne, Mrs. W.M. Shepherd and A.C.G. Thomson. Although the issue was 'fait accompli' by that time, the Watch Committee considered recommendations from the Joint Advisory Committee subsequent to a Home Office letter which made clear that *'the Secretary of State was satisfied that an amalgamation scheme would be in the interest of efficiency and wished to know whether the three police authorities of Cumberland, Westmorland and Carlisle would be prepared to join in the making of a voluntary amalgamation scheme.'*

It was resolved (I) to voluntarily establish a new combined police authority as an independent body corporate (ii) to adopt the title 'Cumbria Constabulary' and (iii) that the operative date should be 1 April, 1967. The City Police Station in Warwick Street and other police buildings, including forty-one houses in the city, would continue in their current use, free of rent, so long as they were so required by the new authority, but would revert to the City Council's ownership should they cease to be required. I don't think they ever did, though the housing stock was eventually made redundant to requirements.

The Watch Committee were informed at their meeting on 31 January 1967, that the Secretary of State had signed the Cumbria Police (Amalgamation) Order, 1967, to take effect on 1 April 1967. Thus the city force began life on the usually unlucky Friday 13 and ended on 'All Fools Day'! Aldermen Hayhurst and Burrow together with Councillors Matthews and Sibson were appointed to serve as city members on the new police authority. The Watch Committee, exercising its powers to promote for the final time on 30 March, 1967, advanced Sergeant 11 Richard (Dick) Cowen to Inspector and Constable 479 Kenneth Grainger to Sergeant, the last promotions to take effect during the life-time of the City Force. City PC Arthur Ferry was promoted to sergeant on the first day of the new Cumbria Constabulary.

The last officer to complete the whole of his thirty years service in the Carlisle City Police Force was Inspector Harold Simons. He was appointed constable (PC72) in January, 1937. A popular and able senior officer, he entered the record books by retiring from the Force on the very last day of its existence, 31 March, 1967, having completed 30 years and two months service. Some officers continued to serve for the remainder of their careers within the city but as part of the new combined force. On 26 July, 1938, Harold was awarded the Bronze Medal of the Royal Society for the Prevention of Cruelty to Animals and was permitted to wear it on his uniform (unusually, above the right breast pocket). The citation recorded that on 29 May, that year he battled for over half an hour in the swollen waters of the River Eden to rescue a bullock stranded in the river. Nearly exhausted before he managed to secure a rope around the animal, he was taken home for a hot bath before returning to complete his tour of duty. Getting time off wasn't easy in those days!

A nominal roll of the last city police officers can be found at Appendix 'H'

The final meeting of the city police authority took place on 30 March, 1967. Present were Aldermen Hayhurst, the chairman, Burrow, Caven and Mrs. Howarth, Councillors Matthews, S. Roberts, Smith and Miss Sibson, and the four magistrate members R. Graham, K. Payne, Mrs. W.M. Shepherd and A.C.G. Thomson. The Chief Constable's monthly report included the sad news of two deaths, Sergeant 532 Mike Thomas on 12 March, and recently retired Constable 550 Lenny Hodgson on 22 March. An application from the Joint Branch Board of the City Police Federation for an increase in rent allowances was referred to the new police authority with a recommendation that it adopt a rent allowance for the new combined constabulary in conformity with the city police request. To commemorate the passing of the Committee, it agreed to provide a trophy to be known as *'The Carlisle Watch Committee Cup for First Aid'* to be competed for on a divisional basis within the new force. Thus ended the deliberations of a 131-year old city institution. All that remained was for the Chairman, Town Clerk, Chief Constable and Magistrates to make suitably appropriate speeches in appreciation of the services all had rendered the city in pursuit of law and order. At the invitation of the Mayor, members of the City Police Federation joined those present to partake of refreshments in the Civic Centre. The sorrows of the remainder of the Force were drowned elsewhere in hostelries around the city, where, it was rumoured, the beverages were diluted by many a tear.

The provisions of the Cumbria Police (Amalgamation) Order, 1967 were executed early on the 1 April, 1967, and Carlisle City Police Force passed into oblivion. Some consolation may be taken from the fact that, even if it had survived beyond this date, its fate would have been sealed by the wholesale amalgamations following the Local Government Act of 1974, which left only one city police force in the whole of Britain – the City of London Force, which exists to this day.

In his last Annual Report, the Chief Constable commented on the Home Office's innovative system of policing, 'unit beat policing', that had been introduced into the city, the first in the country to try it (or, more likely, have it imposed upon it). Out had gone the traditional beat patrols – which many considered to be a ludicrous decision when the Force was able to so patrol, efficiently, 24 hours a day. The new system allocated a single constable to a beat, in the manner of 'village' policemen, where they worked their eight-hour tour of duty. During the remaining sixteen hours a day motor patrols covered their beats. Thus the constable patrolling on foot or cycle began to disappear from the streets of Carlisle, and subsequently, as the system spread, of the rest of Britain! The frustration of rural dwellers at the loss of their village policemen and the sight only of an occasional police car speeding through their communities had arrived in the urban areas.

The approved costs for maintaining the city police force in its final year, 1966-1967, amounted to £275,099, a far cry from the £700 of 1827. This figure included pay and allowances of £153,673, pensions of £36,543, rent/lodgings/taxation of £13.365 and expenses for police premises of £5,430. An Exchequer grant of £143,024 left the Corporation to raise the remaining £132,075 through local rates.

STATUTORY INSTRUMENTS

1967 No. 102
POLICE
ENGLAND AND WALES

The Cumbria Police (Amalgamation) Order 1967

Made - - - - 29th January 1967

Whereas the police authorities for the counties of Cumberland and Westmorland and the county borough of Carlisle have, under section 21 of the Police Act 1964(a), submitted to me the Scheme set out in the Appendix to this Order for the amalgamation for police purposes of the areas comprised in the said counties and the said county borough:

Now, therefore, in exercise of the power conferred on me by the said section 21, I, by this Order, approve the Scheme set out as aforesaid.

This Order may be cited as the Cumbria Police (Amalgamation) Order 1967.

Roy Jenkins,
One of Her Majesty's Principal
Secretaries of State.

Home Office,
Whitehall.
29th January 1967.

APPENDIX

THE CUMBRIA POLICE AMALGAMATION SCHEME 1967

Cumbria combined police area

1. On the appointed day, the police areas consisting of the counties of Cumberland and Westmorland and the county borough of Carlisle shall be amalgamated for police purposes and be constituted a combined police area, which shall be known as the Cumbria police area.

Cumbria combined police authority

2.—(1) There shall be established, before the appointed day, a combined police authority for the combined police area, which shall be known as the Cumbria police authority.

(2) The combined police authority shall be constituted in accordance with Schedule 1 hereto and shall be a body corporate.

(a) 1964 c. 48.

What was going on in the city in 1967 at the time of amalgamation? G.P.O. had bought a site in Cecil Street opposite the Telephone Exchange Building for an additional Exchange, the site stretching from Botchergate along Portland Place. The owners of the site, a Yorkshire Company were quoted as saying, *'In about three years time the front portion of the site in Botchergate will be demolished and new shops will probably be built there'* - 37 years on, after years of dereliction, the newly developed Botchergate emerged, and of a vastly different character from that of 1967 it is. A new Bishop of Carlisle, Rt. Rev. S.C. Bulley was about to be enthroned. Preliminary work on the railway bridges which would be in the path of the new M6 Carlisle bypass was due to begin. The first phase of construction of a new factory in the city for Pirelli would commence in June. Carlisle United, on 41 points, were in 5th position in Division Two (The Championship) behind Wolverhampton Wanderers (top), Coventry City, Blackburn Rovers and Ipswich Town and were confident of attaining promotion to Division 1 (now the Premiership). What good company United kept in those halcyon days! The Walker Brothers, Englebert Humperdink, Cat Stevens and Jimi Hendrix were performing on stage at the Lonsdale in Warwick Road. The County Garage had new Ford Anglias at £310, Cortinas at £330 and Zephyrs at £475; Laing's new houses at Lowry Hill cost between £4,000 and £5000, Beck and Leslie had semis at Belle Vue for £2995; Redmayne's the tailors had suits at £15.12s.6d. It isn't just the old City Police Force we oldies hanker after!

oooOooo

Constable 24 [524] Lyall Law Milton – died 29.10.1964

Lyall Milton, a Scot, joined the City Police in 1959 and after service as a beat constable transferred to the Traffic department as a motor-cycle patrolman in May 1964. Lyall was found lying dead by the side of the A7 highway at Blackford, just north of the city in the early hours of 30 October, 1964.

Whilst the attacks upon Constables Jardine and Fortune in the early days of the Force were clearly the handiwork of vicious criminals who were made to face the consequences of their evil actions, the death of Constable 24 Lyall Law Milton, an on-duty traffic patrol officer was never satisfactorily resolved. The circumstances were not officially recorded as a criminal offence but there was nevertheless considerable suspicion that the death may not have been entirely accidental.

The M6 had not reached Carlisle at that time and a constant flow of traffic along the main A6 (London Road) and A7 (Scotland Road and Kingstown Road) throughout both day and night, was the norm. Motor cyclists were employed during the daylight hours mainly on the task of escorting abnormal loads through the congested streets. It was also a well recognised fact that high profile motor cycle patrols had a steadying effect on the behaviour of motorists. Following many complaints of vehicles speeding through the city, and in the wake of several accidents during the hours of darkness, Chief Constable Williamson was persuaded to provide a night-time main road motor-cycle patrol in an effort to abate the problem. PC Milton was posted to carry out the first of such patrols on the night of 29/30 October 1964, coming on duty at 10pm. His last radio contact with the Force Control Room was at 11.15pm when he gave his location as Brampton Road. He was last seen alive at 11.35pm by a member of the public on the A7 Kingstown Road. He was heading towards the city boundary, apparently in pursuit of a red E-type Jaguar motor car. Both the car and the

motor-cyclist were travelling at fast speeds. The witness was unable to provide the red car's registration number. In the early hours of the following morning, two Traffic Department colleagues, Constable 33 George Russell, who, a little over three months later was himself killed on duty, and Constable Joe Trim, patrolling north of the city, found PC Milton lying dead at the side of the A7 road at Blackford in the county police area, about three miles from where he was last seen at Kingstown. His damaged motor-cycle, its engine still warm, was a short distance away leaning against the wall of a roadside cottage. There was evidence that the nearside of the machine had been in

Over 130 colleagues lined the route as the cortege approached St. Michael's Church, Stanwix, on Tuesday, 3 November 1964, for the funeral service for Constable Milton.

contact with another, red coloured, motor vehicle, indicating that the officer had drawn alongside of it. It was reasonable to assume that that vehicle was the one he was following along Kingstown Road. Despite extensive enquiries, including thorough examinations of the police motor-cycle and suspect vehicles by the expert staff of the North West Forensic Science Laboratory at Preston, neither the driver of the red Jaguar, nor the vehicle itself, were identified. The Chief Constable immediately discontinued night-time motor-cycle patrols.

An inquest was held at Blackford School on 19 November 1964 when an *'open'* verdict was recorded. County Police Inspector Stuart Gibson, told the Court that PC Milton was probably travelling at speed but *"knowing the officer, he would not have been speeding for anything other than in the course of his duty."* Mr. Lionel Lightfoot, solicitor, attended on behalf of the Police Federation representing the deceased officer. He commented that PC Milton was a long way off his patrol area. Inspector Gibson replied that *"something must have taken him outside the city limits."* Lyall, his colleagues would all agree, was an extremely conscientious and well-disciplined officer who would neither have strayed off his beat without just cause nor taken unnecessary risks. The last moments of his life remain a mystery but there is good reason to suspect that he drew alongside the speeding car he had followed out of the city and was nudged, whether or not wilfully, causing him to fall from his machine and sustain injuries from which he died.

In 1964, Mr. Williamson was appointed by the Home Secretary to carry out an investigation into the alleged mismanagement of certain police funds by the Chief Constable of Southend-on-Sea, Essex. He took with him from Carlisle Detective Inspector George Beck, who joined up with a team of experienced detectives, known personally to the Chief, from Manchester and Birmingham. The Southend Chief was subsequently convicted of a number of criminal offences. It was while Mr. Williamson was in Southend that the tragic Oxenholme shooting incident occurred resulting in the death of city Constable George Russell.

Murder at Oxenholme

A city policeman with 12 years service, George was shot dead in the early hours of Wednesday, 10 February 1965, when he and three unarmed colleagues were confronted by a gunman, John Middleton, in the railway station at Oxenholme in Westmorland.

George Russell was a local man, five days short of his 36th birthday when he lost his life. He joined Carlisle City Police, as Constable No.33, in 1953 after service as a sergeant in the Scots Guards in Malaya and had served in the city as a beat and motor patrol officer. He was a married man with two children, a daughter aged 11 years and a son aged just seven months. The Russells were no strangers to tragedy. Two years earlier, a third child, a boy aged seven years, had drowned whilst on a family holiday in Scotland.

Alec Archibald, a native of Musselburgh, was 28 years old, and he, too, was a former Scots Guardsman. A married man with one child and another expected, he joined the City Police in 1958, PC 57, after his military service. He was a beat patrol constable in Carlisle. Alec had had a previous confrontation with a gunman during a siege at a house in Raffles in the city during which the criminal threatened, *"If you try to get in here I'll put one through the door and the next will be through you."* Despite his disablement following the Oxenholme incident, with the support of Chief Constable Frank Williamson, he continued to serve in the Force though clearly he was not able to undertake the full range of police duties. He left in 1967 being declared unfit for further police service. He now lives in his home town near Edinburgh and still maintains close contact with a number of his former city police colleagues.

Constable 57 (557) Alexander Archibald *was shot sustaining serious leg and spinal injuries that unfortuntely ended his police career.*

Right: *the letter from Her Majesty the Queen congratulating PC Archibald on his award of the British Empire Medal for gallantry and wishing him well for the future.*

Lower Centre: *PC Archibald BEM wearing his medal.*

Below: *PC Archibald being taken to hospital after the shooting.*

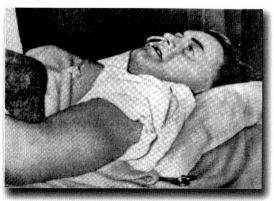

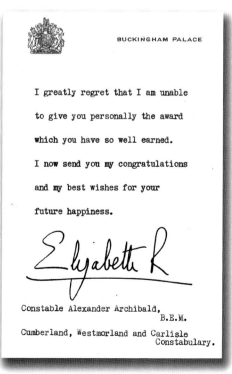

Alf Harrison, aged 43 years, joined the Kendal Borough Police in 1946, before it amalgamated a year later with Cumberland and Westmorland Constabulary. He later served as a sergeant at Wigton, Workington and Low Hesket. Seven months before the Oxenholme incident he was transferred to the City Police on promotion to the rank of Inspector. Mr. Harrison was married with two children. He was the brother of the former city Chief Inspector Roy Harrison who, at the time of the Oxenholme incident, was Chief Constable of Dewsbury Borough Police in the West Riding of Yorkshire, and who was later to become Deputy Chief Constable of the much enlarged West Yorkshire Constabulary. Alf ended his police career as Superintendent back in Kendal where he began. Unfortunately, he met his death in tragic circumstances whilst still serving in the Force.

Inspector Alfred Harrison
was shot sustaining shoulder injuries.

George Russell was a member of the Road Traffic Department in Carlisle. His duties on Tuesday 9 March, 1965 entailed working from 8pm to 4am as driver of the city's night-time crime patrol car accompanied by a plain clothes detective officer, DC Andy Rutherford. (I had completed my week's turn as crime car detective the previous morning). It was a covert patrol of the city and surrounding areas in a plain, unmarked police car, in search of active criminals and persons wanted or suspected of crimes. When performing this particular duty, the traffic department driver dressed in a 'civvy' jacket over his uniform shirt and trousers, but had with him his uniform cap and tunic to wear should the need arise (It is a legal requirement to be in uniform when carrying out certain duties, for example, when stopping vehicles). The crime car crews spent time operating within the city and along the A6 and A7 trunk roads between the south city boundary and the Scottish border at Gretna. They had considerable success in arresting not only many local criminals but others for police forces throughout England and, particularly, throughout Scotland. Alf Harrison was the city's duty inspector, and Alec Archibald was on beat patrol in Carlisle, each working a 2pm -10pm shift.

Shortly before 6.30pm, on that Tuesday evening, the driver of a Morris 1100 motor car drove off without paying after obtaining petrol from a filling station at Firbank, near Kendal in Westmorland. The police were informed, but were given only part of the car's registration number. It was sufficient, however, for them to suspect that it was a car stolen earlier in the day from a car park in Kendal. Details were circulated to patrolling officers, and a sergeant and a number of constables set off from Kendal towards the crime scene at Firbank. En route, on the Sedbergh road, the officers passed the suspect vehicle travelling in the opposite direction to them. They turned, gave chase and stopped it. They were unable to arrest the suspect driver, a male, who locked himself inside the car before reversing it at speed. He lost control of the vehicle and it rolled over into a ditch. The officers again made to arrest him but at this point, they saw that he had a gun and ammunition. Believing that he was trapped inside the car, the unarmed policemen stood back, keeping observation from a safe distance whilst summoning assistance. The driver, however, managed to clamber out of the car into the ditch, concealed from the officers' view until he surfaced further along the hedgerow. He made good his escape in the darkness.

A huge police operation to trace and arrest the suspect was launched, including the checking of all vehicles on main roads. Shortly before midnight, a sergeant and three constables manning a road block in Kendal came face-to-face with the wanted man when he jumped from a lorry in a queue waiting to be examined by the officers. Pointing a revolver at them, he threatened to shoot. The man fled, pursued by two of the constables, Bob Fell and Tom Wood. He fired several shots at the policemen before eluding them. The search for the gunmen was now concentrated on the town of Kendal. Deputy Chief Constable John Dagg gave instructions for firearms to be issued to police officers, a rare occurrence in those days and especially so in a rural area like Kendal. Police Forces had neither the tactically trained officers nor the weaponry that is available to today's police. Most officers, fortunately, had previous military experience, as a consequence of which they had experience in the use of firearms. Assistance was called in from across the Force area, and the Carlisle crime car and several officers were despatched to Kendal, some 45 miles south of the city. At about 3am, the Carlisle CID car driven by George Russell and now containing Alf Harrison, Alex Archibald and Constable Dennis Graham (also from the City Force) patrolling and searching the Oxenholme area, some two miles from Kendal, called at Oxenholme Railway Station, on the main west coast London to Glasgow line. The station, as usual, was closed for the night and in total darkness. The officers began a check of the public rooms, and Inspector Harrison and Constable Archibald shone their torches into the waiting room on the southbound platform. They saw a man, apparently sleeping, on a bench inside. He matched the description of the one wanted in Kendal. Constable Graham returned to the police car, raised the alarm and called for assistance. Meanwhile, a decision was made to take the suspect by surprise whilst he slept. However, he either was not asleep at all and had heard the officers' movements or had been disturbed by the noise of a passing train, for when the policemen returned to the waiting room the man had moved. George Russell, because he was partly in plain clothes hiding his uniform, volunteered to go inside first. He was confronted by the man who was pointing a gun at him. He told him to put it down, but the man advanced towards the officers and fired a shot into PC Russell's chest. Inspector Harrison went to his aid, but he too was shot, in his shoulder. PC Archibald drew his baton, and using the cover of darkness in the station, crept towards the gunman who was now outside on the platform. PC Archibald remembers the man crouching down, looking all around him, the gun pointed forward ready to fire, but the gunman did not see the officer. PC Archibald ran towards him and was almost at arms length, ready to strike out at the man, but an approaching train caused the gunman to look up. He saw PC Archibald and fired a number of shots into his body. He collapsed to the ground. One bullet had lodged in his spine. Paralysed from his injuries and unable to move, PC Archibald was conscious of his assailant leaning across him, examining him. He is convinced that had he moved, he would have been shot dead. The man, he feels, must have considered him already dead or no longer a threat, for he did not shoot, but instead ran off along the platform. He was spotted by the railway signalman in the nearby signalbox fleeing along the railway tracks. He escaped yet again. The injured officers were removed by ambulance to Kendal Hospital, where George Russell died from his injuries shortly before 6am.

Above: *newspaper photographs of officers on duty at roadblocks on the A6 road in the Kendal area following the shootings. One paper captioned the picture of the armed policewoman from Lancashire Constabulary, 'A sight never before seen on British roads'.*

Top: *County Sergeant Stan Nixon, later Inspector in Carlisle City,*

Above left: *Sergeant Bob Foster of the City Police.*

Oxenholme Station shortly after the shootings.

Alex Archibald, suffering from serious internal injuries, was transferred to Preston Royal Infirmary for specialized treatment. Alf Harrison was allowed home after treatment for a superficial shoulder wound.

Chief Constable Frank Williamson returned by air from his investigations in Southend to take charge of the urgent business in his own Force area.

Police dogs were used to scour the area surrounding Oxenholme station, but no trace of the gunman was found. Arrangements were made for a thorough search during daylight hours, and some two hundred officers (including yours truly!) from throughout the Force area and from the neighbouring counties of Lancashire and the West Riding of Yorkshire converged on Kendal for deployment. Many were armed. Probably for the first time ever in Cumberland and Westmorland a helicopter was used by the police in the search. Although the wanted man had not been positively identified at this stage, enquiries had caused investigating officers to suspect that he was John Middleton, a 23-year old married man from Warrington in Lancashire. Middleton was a known persistent criminal offender with strong links to the Sedbergh area, some ten miles from Kendal. He was suspected of, and wanted by the police in Warrington, in connection with a burglary and theft of firearms and ammunition from a gunsmith's shop in that town. Investigations revealed that Middleton had indeed been in Sedbergh during the material times of the crimes in Kendal and that he had been in possession of ammunition. At 8.45am, an unarmed, patrolling constable saw and positively identified Middleton making his way towards Sedbergh. Middleton pointed his gun at the officer and ran off into a field.

At 11.30am, a farmworker at Underhelm Farm, a mile from Oxenholme, saw the gunman and alerted the police. Officers were then positioned so as to contain Middleton in the area and prevent any further escape. He was next seen by policemen near Bleasehall Wood and was challenged by the officers to stop. He replied by firing several shots in their direction. One armed constable fired shots into the air. Middleton ignored his warning and ran off firing further shots. He was clearly now desperate. He broke his cover, still shooting, but as he did so an armed constable, PC Derrick Thompson of the Cumberland and Westmorland Force, returned his fire bringing him to the ground. Middleton was disarmed of his revolver and ammunition by Constable Geoff Harrington, also of the County Constabulary, before being taken to Kendal Hospital. Like PC Archibald, he was later transferred to Preston Infirmary suffering from leg and head injuries.

Left: *Middleton breaks cover after firing a volley of shots at the pursuing police officers. Seconds later he was shot by the police.*

Right: *Cumberland and Westmorland Constables Geoff Harrington, who arrested Middleton, and Derrick Thompson, who fired the shot that grounded him.*

Ballistics experts at the Nottingham Forensic Science Laboratory established that Middleton's head injuries were inflicted by a bullet from his own gun. Further, they were able to prove that the same weapon had been used in the shooting of the police officers at Oxenholme. However, there was to be no court appearance for Middleton. His injuries were so serious as to render him unfit ever to stand trial on the charges of murder and attempted murder that he would undoubtedly otherwise have faced. During his time in Preston Royal Infirmary, he was kept under close police scrutiny twenty-four hours a day for several weeks, a considerable strain on the Force's resources. He was in no physical condition to escape, but it was necessary to take note of his every uttering should it later be of evidential value. The guard was maintained until Middleton was stretchered into Kendal Court, with no little difficulty, for the Magistrates to be formally notified that he would be unfit to plead. Under those circumstances, the court was obliged to order the prisoner's detention in a hospital specified by the Secretary of State, and, accordingly, Middleton was committed. He died in a hospital in the Liverpool area round about 1990.

Local and national newspapers thoroughly reported the incident, publishing many photographs which were exceptional at the time, for example, the armed policewoman manning a roadblock. Border Television cameramen scooped the nation by capturing on film the shooting of Middleton by the police, securing for themselves some prestigious awards from within their industry. This was the first police murder for four years, the thirteenth in England, Wales and Scotland since 1948. The shootings caused outrage. Newspapers contained much criticism of the government's recent decision to suspend capital punishment, which was academic in this particular case as the accused was unfit to stand trial.

The Lords Lieutenant of Cumberland and Westmorland, together with the Mayor of Carlisle, launched a fund, that realised some £18,500, for the dependents of the dead and injured police officers. The House of Commons, which was then debating the abolition of capital punishment, expressed sympathy for the relatives of the victims. Tory MPs pressed for its retention for the killing of on-duty police officers.

Mrs. Russell became the first beneficiary of a new Police Regulation, introduced just six months earlier, which provided widows of officers who lost their lives on duty with an award equivalent to two years salary. The Police Federation had negotiated the deal to cater, especially, for those widows and families who had to vacate police-owned accommodation upon the deaths of their husbands. Mrs. Russell was such a person.

George Russell's funeral service was held in Carlisle Cathedral on Monday, 15 February, 1965, the Bishop of Carlisle, Dr. Thomas Bloomer, and the Dean, the Very Reverend L.M.S. du Toit, officiating. The city came to a standstill as the cortege of over twenty vehicles made its way to the Cathedral. City taxi owners, with whom George had had dealings as a traffic officer (police had the legal responsibility for licensing and roadworthiness of hackney carriages) gave their services to carry the many floral tributes. Led by City Police motorcyclists Peter Ullyart and Bill Little, the cortege was met at the Cathedral entrance by a lone piper of the Scots Guards, George Russell's former regiment, who played the lament *'Flowers of the Forest'* as they moved towards the Cathedral's main doors. There they were met by Chief Constable Frank Williamson, and the coffin was borne into the Cathedral by Sergeant John Walker and Constables John Lennox, Brian Henderson and Harold Armstrong of the City Police and Sergeant John Sarginson and Constable Joe Trim of the Cumberland and Westmorland Force, all colleagues of George in Carlisle Traffic Office. Four chief constables, three assistant chief constables, eleven superintendents, thirty-four chief inspectors and inspectors and over four hundred policemen from across Britain attended what was said to be the city's biggest funeral of the century. The procession of uniformed police officers who had lined Castle Street, took fifteen minutes to enter the Cathedral. Members of the public filled the few remaining spaces. Chief Constable Frank Williamson, the President of the Christian Police Association, gave a very moving address as tributes were paid to the courage of the officers, and prayers were said for PC Archibald's speedy recovery. Of George Russell, the Chief said, *"He was a policeman in the truest sense of the word. He was not protected by armour or shield. He drew his confidence from his courage and determination which he had borne upon so often before. We must never forget his shining example."*

For their parts in the Oxenholme incident, George Russell was, posthumously, awarded the Queen's Police Medal for Gallantry, whilst Alec Archibald and Alf Harrison, together with Bob Fell and Tom Wood, were each awarded the British Empire Medal.

Above Right: *Led by six sergeants of the city police, from front right, Tommy Bowerbank, Joe Richardson, Jim Kerr, from left, Eddie Mason, George Kerr and George Carlton are George Townsend, Brian Firth, Dennis Mattinson, Brian Watson, Roy Wadeson, Bob Taylor, Val Clark, Bobby Robinson, Sid Monk and several officers representing other Forces (note different helmet plates).*

Centre: *The cortege makes its way along Botchergate, English Street [Sergeant Tommy Dawes salutes as it passes through the Viaduct traffic lights] and Castle Street where over 400 policemen from across Britain lined the route.*

Above left: *It was met and led into the Cathedral by a lone piper of the Scots Guards, the regiment in which both PCs Russell and Archibald each served.*

Topright: *Traffic Department colleagues carry the coffin into Carlisle Cathedral Sergeant John Sergison, Constables Brian Henderson and Joe Trim together with [not in view] Sergeant John Walker and Constables John Lennox and Harold Armstrong.*

Right: *Motor cyclists Peter Ullyart and Bill Little escort the cortege from the Cathedral.*

Officers from all over Britain attended the Cathedral service. I am not able to recognise any officer nor the Forces they represent in the picture above.

Left: *Local stonemasons, working on a Cathedral restoration project for local contractor John Laing and Son, Ltd., carved a stone sculpture of a policeman, wearing the city's distinctive 'cock's comb' helmet. It was included in the restoration works and dedicated in a ceremony led by the Dean and attended by Chief Constable. It remains, in perpetuity, high on the Cathedral's south wall, looking out over the entrance roadway, a fitting tribute to a brave officer and a proud little police force.*

What the papers said ……

From the Daily Mail, 16 February 1965.
The Chief Constable, speaking quietly in the solemn stillness of the Cathedral, said, *"Most of all I will remember the manner of his passing."* Tracing his past, he told of PC Russell's six years in the Scots Guards in Malaya. *"He was no stranger to danger and action. My personal knowledge of him is over the past three and a half years. He was a policeman in the truest sense of the word. During that time he has overcome a tremendous physical handicap."* He recalled sitting at his hospital bedside, and said, *"His determination was unbounded. Then last year his seven year old son was drowned while the family were on holiday. But he never lost his courage and determination. Those of us near to him could not help but be inspired by his example."*

From the Daily Mirror, 16 February, 1965.
Half a million people in a city and two counties mourned yesterday as one of their policemen, shot dead doing his duty, was laid to rest. Women wept unashamedly as the funeral procession of Constable George Russell slowly motored through the streets of Carlisle. And four hundred policemen from all over Britain stood grim-faced and bare-headed in silent sympathy along the route.

And Russell's Chief Constable, Frank Williamson, brought complete stillness into the packed Carlisle Cathedral when he said this of the hero officer, *"He stood on a cold and desolate railway station platform faced with a decision. In simple words, he indicated that he had made up his mind to do his duty and that he would go first into known danger, unprotected by armour or shield. We, his comrades all over the country, must never forget the shining example he showed. And, if in the future the call comes for any of us to face such a decision, our answer must be, like that of George Russell, "I will go first."*

Mrs. Russell cried a little as the *'Chief'*, as his men called him, went into the pulpit to say that he was proud to be a friend and a comrade of her husband. He told of PC Russell's fight for life after a kidney operation, of his gallant service with the Scots Guards in Malaya and of the tragic drowning of his seven-year old son, Stephen, while on holiday last year. He showed the marks of his burden, the Chief said, but never at any time did he lose his courage and determination.

The Dean of Carlisle asked the congregation to pay tribute to a *"very brave man."*

Two hundred wreaths were delivered yesterday to the semi-detached home in Springfield Road, Harraby, Carlisle, and hundreds of letters of sympathy arrived.

From the Cumberland News, 19 February, 1965.
It was the biggest funeral the city has seen this century. At the Russell's home in Springfield Road, neighbours lined the pavements, women weeping openly and men grim faced. For streets around blinds had been drawn and the whole area was still. The quiet was shattered only when the police outriders kicked the starters of their motor cycles and the motorcade carrying family, relatives and flowers moved slowly forward. Crowds lined the route. Shopkeepers came out to pay their last respects. As the cortege passed Carlisle City Police Headquarters and the Fire Station, a guard of honour was formed along Rickergate. Policemen lining the route turned and fell into step in two's behind the procession. Following the hearse there were seven cars bearing family mourners, followed by eight taxis bearing wreaths. Five more taxis completed the cortege. At the Cathedral entrance, the cortege was met by a piper of the Scots Guards, who marched slowly in front of the hearse to the lament of *'Flowers of the Forest'*. At the Cathedral doors, the cortege was met by the figure of Frank Williamson, the Chief Constable. The long procession of police officers took fifteen minutes to file into the Cathedral. The service began with the Dean saying, *"We are here to pay tribute to a very brave man, and also to the whole of the police service. This event has revealed to us the underlying meaning of the police service – to serve the public and to make decent and civilised life possible."* He added, *"It is fitting that such an exceptional act of service should be marked, as it is this morning, by the exceptional event of a civic funeral."* Mr. Williamson said that George Russell was a policeman in the truest sense of the word.

The civic procession was headed by Chief Superintendent Donald Roy, followed by Mace and Sword

Bearers, the Mayor and Mayoress, the Mayor of Kendal, the Town Clerks of Carlisle and Kendal, the Governor of Carlisle Castle, Lords Lieutenant, Sheriffs and Members of Parliament, City Aldermen, Councillors, Heads of Corporation Departments, Members of the Police Authority, City and County Magistrates, the City Coroner, members of the legal profession, HM Inspector of Constabulary Sir Charles Martin, Roy Harrison, Chief Constable of Dewsbury Borough (a local man who began his career and rose to Chief Inspector in the Carlisle City Police Force and whose brother Alf was also shot in the incident at Oxenholme), the Chief Constables of Dumfries and Galloway and of Hamilton representing the Scottish Chief Officers Association, and numerous other chief officers, many former city policemen. As well as Home Office police forces, British Transport Police and the War Department Constabulary were represented. A Colonel of the Scots Guards represented PC Russell's regiment.

A poignant story from the Daily Express, 16 February, 1965.
A policeman yesterday passed along his regular beat for the last time. At a steady pace Constable George Russell, a shooting victim, was carried in his coffin through the streets he knew so well to Carlisle Cemetery.

Down the roads where small children regularly waited for him to guide them safely across. Along the bustling A6 where he often threaded a patrol car through teeming traffic. Past the police station which was his *'second home'* for almost fifteen years. Over the cobbled pavements where he had worn out at least a dozen pairs of boots.

Appropriately, the Scottish border soldier who became an English bobby, travelled down English Street and Scotch Street on his final tour of the sorrowing border city.

And with Police Constable 533 went the thoughts of Britain's policemen. For Chief Constable Frank Williamson, head of the 594-strong Cumberland, Westmorland and Carlisle Force, spoke for them all at the civic funeral service in Carlisle's 12th Century Cathedral. Mr. Williamson recalled that when faced with known danger, Constable Russell said to his fellow policemen, *"I will go first."* Added the grieving Chief, *"If in future the call comes for any of us to face the same decision, our answer should be the same as that of George Russell – "I will go first."*

The Dean of Carlisle, the Very Reverend Lionel du Toit, told the congregation, *"Let us hope the result of this awful tragedy will be not only in Cumberland and Westmorland but also throughout the entire country – a new spirit of understanding between the police and the public. This man died in the execution of his duties making life safe for you and me."*

The 1,400-strong over-flow congregation at the Border Cathedral – both Mary, Queen of Scots and Edward I of England once worshipped there – were headed by Constable Russell's widow, 37-year old Mrs. Joan Russell, and daughter Vanessa, who is twelve today, her father's 36th birthday.

Before joining the police at Carlisle, George Russell was a sergeant in the Scots Guards, 2nd Battalion, fighting terrorists in Malaya. Yesterday, the Guards remembered him with a piper, bugler and a wreath of Scottish flowers in the regimental colours.

More than 500 policemen formed a guard of honour round the Cathedral. Almost every police force was represented or sent a wreath, from Scotland Yard and the Flying Squad to village bobbies in England, Wales, Scotland and Northern Ireland. There were twenty chief constables and a host of other police VIPs. There were tiny children who brought posies to honour the big policeman who always helped them across dangerous roads. There were local taxi drivers who charged no fee to the mourners they drove to the funeral.

Inside the red sandstone Cathedral, tough policemen, overcome with emotion, wept as they joined in Constable Russell's favourite hymns, *Psalm 23, The Battle Hymn of the Republic, He who would valiant be* and *Abide with Me.*

Muffled bells rang. The Civic Sword and Mace were draped in black. Flags throughout the city were half-masted. Finally, the Scot, in his casket of English oak, was borne along an avenue of 100-year old yew and holly, over the Fairy Beck to a grassy plot ringed by lime trees and roses.

Six of his police comrades tenderly carried him there, two sergeants and four constables, all wearing the crest of Carlisle with the motto that meant so much to Dundee-born George, *'Be just and fear not.'*

And, as the coffin was lowered into the ground, two miles away at Carlisle Police Station this final entry was marked on Police Constable 533 George Russell's record card,

'Died, February 10th
Shot in the execution of his duty'

OXENHOLME RAILWAY STATION
21 June 2007

Thursday, 21 June 2007: *Chief Constable Michael Baxter, pictured above, unveiled a plaque commemorating the tragic events at Oxenholme in February 1965. Funded jointly by Cumbria Constabulary and Cumbria Police Federation the plaque was dedicated by the Force Chaplain, The Reverend Graham Betteridge.*

Pictured, left: *former Sergeant Brian Firth whose suggestion it was that led to the placing of the memorial that most would say "was forty years overdue." Despite the passing of so many years, many former comrades attended the ceremony.*

In September, 1966, the Carlisle Force was selected by the Home Office to be the first in the country to adopt an experimental style of policing known as '*Unit Beat Policing*'. The city was looked upon as an ideal location, since the new pocket radios, a significant part of the scheme, could operate only within a radius of four miles of its base station (with a central headquarters, sufficient to cover every part of the city). Lancashire Police had pioneered a similar system of beat patrolling in Accrington and Kirby, near Liverpool, before the revolutionary project was developed further by the Home Office Research and Development Branch and launched in Carlisle amid much national publicity. The scheme brought an end to traditional policing and was the forerunner of national change. Instead of officers alternating between all beats and gaining knowledge of all areas of the city, a single officer only was dedicated to a specific beat. He patrolled the area on foot for his daily eight hour tour of duty, in the manner of '*village*' policing in county areas. The remaining sixteen hours, and his rest days, were covered by a '*panda*' car. Thus the patrolling policeman disappeared from the city's streets. There are many who would argue, with some justification, that the system destroyed the police service and that the consequences of it alienated and lost the respect and confidence of the public. There is little doubt that public dissatisfaction with the service can be traced back to this development.

oooOooo

In 1967 Mr. Williamson was appointed one of Her Majesty's Inspector of Constabulary with special responsibility for Crime. He remained in post until 1972.

As HMI (Crime), Mr.Williamson was called upon to investigate corruption in the Metropolitan Police by the then Commissioner, and his former Manchester City Police colleague, Sir Robert Mark. As an Inspector of Constabulary he had no police powers to rely upon, was unable to give orders to anyone of whatever rank and was able to act only in an inspectorial and advisory capacity. He was faced with the added problem of a similar in-house investigation being carried out contemporaneously by Metropolitan detectives, the very department that was under investigation. Though the enquiry was not entirely conducted in the way that he would have wished, it resulted in two senior detectives being jailed. Mr. Williamson, however, had become increasingly frustrated and disillusioned when faced with deliberate obstruction, especially by senior officers. He had found also that corruption in the London Force was so endemic and so repugnant to him, that he resigned his position rather than continue in a service which was so alien to all his expectations of what should constitute acceptable personal and professional police behaviour. Mr. Williamson, President of the Christian Police Association like his father before him, was noted for his very high standard of personal integrity and for his outspoken views on police malpractices. After leaving the service, he was frequently in demand by the media to respond to reports of such incidents. His departure was a sad and premature ending to a very successful career and his experience was a huge loss to the police service. I, and many other Carlisle City police officers, considered it a privilege to have worked under his command. His management style certainly brought out the best in his men and he gave total support to those who worked for him.
Frank Williamson died on Christmas Day, 1999.

A few odds and ends from Chief Williamson's days

1962

Oct 12 – Radar Speedmeter taken into use – Carlisle City was one of only 3 forces with such advanced equipment. Notices erected on approaches into the city warned motorists of its presence.

Oct 30 – New helmets issued – cost 46s/6d each plus 5s/1d for chrome badges [Like City of London and Metropolitan Police Carlisle's officers had worn black badges until this time].

1963

Apr 1 – calendar monthly pay introduced

Sep 1 - Integration of the City with Cumberland and Westmorland County Forces under the command of City Chief Constable Williamson. Uniquely he became chief constable of 3 separate police forces.

1964

Mar 13 – Chief reports only 2 vacancies in the City Force with no shortage of new applicants and recruits.
May – City Police Wireless system[M2BU] removed and Force began to operate on County Police frequency. A wireless station at Hazelshawhill in Dumfriesshire covered the North Cumbria area.

Jun 10 – The Police Act, 1964 received Royal Assent.

1967

Feb 17 – Chief Constable Williamson recommended to the Police Authority the appointment of 16 Traffic Wardens for the city.

Apr 1 – Cumbria Constabulary came into being.

Marching into the history books.

1962: *shortly before integration with the County Police - City policemen march off from Carlisle Castle parade ground after an inspection, the last of the autonomous city force, by HM Inspector of Constabulary.*

Nearest column, from left: *PCs Spencer Stockdale, Bill Mitchell, Bob Lowther, Irving Lyon, Mike Coleman and George Townsend. Also in picture Martin McAlindon, Laurie Inglis, Jim Crawford and John Bardgett.*

Part Five - H. M. Inspectors of Constabulary

The County and Borough Police Act 1856 provided for the first appointments of Inspectors of Constabulary (HMIs). Their role was redefined by the Police Act 1964. The first HMIs (3) were military men, though two had been Chief constables, Lt.Colonel Woodford of Lancashire and Capt. Wills of Manchester City, together with Major General Cartwright. In the 1960s, the Inspectorate consisted of a Chief HMI and eight Inspectors, one for each of the police districts. They were selected from serving Chief Constables, who had to retire from the service, on the recommendation of the Home Secretary. Two female Assistant HMIs were appointed after 1964.

The Inspectors were not serving police officers and therefore had no police powers. Their main duties in relation to forces in their district were to make one formal annual visit to each force and to report to the Home Secretary on their efficiency and adequacy as well as on their co-operation with neighbouring forces. They were available to advise and assist Chief Constables on the administration of their forces and offer recommendations for improvements. They could make other special visits to forces as considered necessary, eg. to advise on building projects referred to the Home Office for approval, to advise on applications for increases in establishment. HMIs had to be satisfied that forces dealt properly with public complaints against individual officers and with welfare issues. To assist them, staff officers were appointed, selected from experienced senior police officers seconded to the Home Office for that purpose. HMI's annual reports on forces provided the Home Office with a picture of the state of policing in the country, with crime and other statistics and with information to assist future planning. Satisfactory reports as to a force's efficiency qualified it for a Government grant of 50% of approved costs of running the force. HMI recommendations almost had the force of orders that a chief constable or police authority would have been unwise to ignore. HMIs had numerous other duties within the Home Office.

Top. HMI, Sir Charles Martin speaks with PC Sandy Bremner,MM, [about their war-time experiences?] during the ceremonial parade at Carlisle castle, 1963.

Also in picture from left,: *PC Mike Coleman, Inspector Tom Farmer, [later Deputy Chief Constable of Durham] Mayor of Carlisle, Alderman Hamilton, Chief Constable Frank Williamson, [himself, later HMI for Crime] and PC Lyall Milton who was killed a year later whilst on motor cycle patrol duty.*

Above, from left: *Sergeant Tommy Bowerbank, PC Spencer Stockdale, PC Bill Mitchell and the author, PC Bob Lowther.*

Though the Municipal Corporations Act 1835 empowered municipal boroughs to create police forces for their particular areas, under the watchful eyes of a Corporation Watch Committee, it made no provision for central government involvement, neither in financial, supervisory or any other capacity. However, when the Act took effect in January, 1836, there was a requirement for the Watch Committees to furnish the Home Secretary with quarterly reports on the state of their police. That situation prevailed until the implementation of the 1856 Act and the involvement of the Home Office, the introduction of HMI annual inspections and efficiency certificates, the issue of which paved the way for the Government grant of 50% of authorised costs. Thus, whilst all forces remained independent of central political control, the Home Secretary was able to exert considerable influence under the threat of withdrawal of the government grant. A recent example of the

Front row: *Sgts. John Walker and George Lawson, PCs Bob Dewsnap, Brian Firth, Eddie Day, Val Clarke, Jimmy Dunn, Howard Nixon, Charlie Stevens, Ron Harden, Joe Richardson, Eddie Mason, [?], Brian Watson Tommy Bowerbank, Jim Kerr, (later Chief Constable of Lincolnshire), Shaw Milligan, Dick Cowen and PW Eileen Robinson.*

Second row: *PC Gordon Coupe (between sergeants), Harold Armstrong and Dennis Mattinson.*

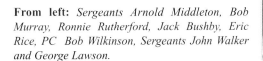

From left: *Sergeants Arnold Middleton, Bob Murray, Ronnie Rutherford, Jack Bushby, Eric Rice, PC Bob Wilkinson, Sergeants John Walker and George Lawson.*

Left: *Chief Inspector Clarence 'Bob' Sutcliffe, [later Superintendent and Deputy Chief Constable] and Inspector Roy Harrison [later Chief Constable of Dewsbury Borough and Deputy Chief Constable of West Yorkshire Constabulary] lead the march-past along Warwick Street in front of police headquarters.*

Home Office exercising this power was in the 1990s when Derbyshire Constabulary was found wanting and the local HMI refused to issue an efficiency certificate until it fell into line. It was actually the inefficiency of the police authority rather than a failing of the force. Similarly, a couple of years earlier the Home Secretary refused to approve that authority's selection and appointment of a new Chief Constable and insisted it appoint from a Home Office approved list. Given present day force budgets amounting to, in many cases, hundreds of millions of pounds, withdrawal of a 50% grant exercises minds. Today, staffing levels and appointment of chief officer ranks, uniforms, equipment, vehicle fleets and buildings all have to meet with Home Office approval. However, theoretically at least, chief constables enjoy operational autonomy, much more so than in the earliest days of the police service. Annual inspections in Carlisle usually comprised a formal ceremonial drill parade and inspection in the presence of civic dignitaries and the press. For many years, the Covered Market was the venue, then the Rickergate Headquarters yard (until it became congested with police, fire and ambulance vehicles) and finally the military parade ground at Carlisle Castle.

The uniformed contingent afterwards marched back through the streets to police headquarters, where the inspection continued in the Magistrates main courtroom. Officers were selected at random and questioned as to their duties and workloads since the previous inspection. Incidents that the selected officers had handled were then thoroughly scrutinised by the HMI, including the roles played by officers called upon to assist, eg. CID, Scenes of Crime, Traffic patrols, to ensure that all cases had been properly handled. Typically, such meetings would last approximately one hour, after which the Inspector would turn his attention to the administration and management of the Force, examining departmental records, etc..

Parade and kit inspection in Carlisle Covered Market: *Two Inspectors on the left with two detectives in the background. The men's turnout is immaculate. It is doubtful if Carlisle City Police, or any other Force, ever had a smarter uniform than this. Photograph obviously pre-1914 [absence of war medals in spite of 60% of the Force serving in the military during hostilities 1914-1918]. The right marker sergeant is wearing a medal and is almost certainly Sergeant Burnett who was awarded the Coronation Medal in July 1912.*

HMI Inspection, Covered Market, c 1919: *Superintendent Andrew Johnston who was appointed on promotion from Newcastle City Police in 1919, is the senior officer on the left of the picture. Chief Constable deSchmid/Spence leads the parade. The parade sergeant is Sergeant Samuel Finney, appointed drill sergeant on promotion from Liverpool City Police in 1913. Many of the men are wearing Medals awarded for service in the Great War, 1914/1918. Col. Tomasson, MVO. CBE, HMI [not in picture] was the inspecting officer.*

1938: *Chief Constable Andrew Johnston in uniform, Colonel Brooks, HMI [with cane] and members of the City Corporation make their way to a formal inspection of the Force.*

185

Top: *HM Inspector of Constabulary, Lt.Col. Brooks [with cane] inspects the Force in Carlisle Covered Market Hall, 16 March, 1939. Chief Constable W.H. Lakeman, in ceremonial uniform, appointed the previous year, is accompanied by the Mayor, Alderman T. Robinson and the Chairman of the Watch Committee, Alderman F.W. Tassell.*

Above and right, 1924, Covered Market:
HMI talks to the men, many of whom are war veterans wearing their campaign medals, as Chief Constable Spence and civic leaders look on.

Left, 1962: *Carlisle Castle. Sir Charles Martin, HMI admires 'Buckshot' Firth's tie watched by the City Mayor, Frank Derry, Chairman of the Watch Committee Jack Hayhurst and Superintendent. [Deputy Chief Constable] Bob Sutcliffe.*

Front row: *from left, Bill Mitchell, Brian Firth, Ian Scott, Bill Davidson, Val Clark and Sid Peel. Middle row, John Brown, Bob Lowther, Andy Lowrie, John Lennox and Charlie Stevens.*

Back row: *?, Ken Darling.*

1963, Carlisle Castle

Right: *HMI Sir Charles Martin, one-time Chief Constable of Liverpool, inspects the 'troops', followed by the Mayor, Alderman David Hamilton, Chief Constable Frank Williamson, Superintendent Bob Sutcliffe and Watch Committee Chairman Alderman J Hayhurst.*

Front row: *from left, Billy Orr, Charlie Stevens, Jim Crawford, John Bardgett, Gordon Coupe, Jim Johnstone and Frank McCormick. Back row, ? ,Bob Taylor, Brian Dunn and Laurie Ingles.*

Below: *general view of the parade.*

1963 - A detachment of Traffic Department officers: *Officer in Charge Inspector Arnold Coulthard, Sergeant John Walker, Constables John Singleton-Brown, Norman Robinson and John Lennox, with Morris Oxford saloon patrol cars, Austin patrol van and Triumph 650 motor cycle.*

Top: 1960, Police Station yard. *HMI Sir Charles Martin inspects the parade, watched by Chief Constable Lakeman, Supt. And Deputy Chief Constable Bob Sutcliffe, the city's Mayor William John Hunter and Councillor Irving Burrows, Chairman of the Watch Committee. Inspectors Jack Bushby and Eric Rice lead the parade.*

Front row: *PCs 91 Peter Firth, 65 Sandy Bremner, 56 Irving Lyon, 25 Gordon Sowerby, 77 Bob Lowther, 14 Gerry 'Slim' Congreve, 78 John Singleton Brown, 61 Jimmy Hetherington and PWC4 Yvonne Harvey.*

Second row: *PCs 82 Bobby Robinson, 24 Lyall Milton, 96 Billy Orr, 91 George Abbott, 79 Ken Grainger.*

Back row*: 38 Sid Monk..*

Following the ceremonial parade, inspections moved indoors. Here, in the late 1960s, in the Magistrates Court, officers are examined on their operational duties.

Front row: *Inspector Dick Cowan, Det.Sgt Bill Wilkie and Det.Chief Inspector Stanley Armstrong. Behind them, DCs Brian Dunn, Frank McCormick, Jeff Woodburn and Det.Sgt Norman Robinson.*

Third row: *Sgts. Peter Firth and Tommy Dawes, DC John Howarth, PC Gordon Coupe (?), (?) Fourth Row, PWCs (?) and Jennifer Watson. Road Safety Sergeant John Walker is on the left of the fifth row.*

Examples of Force insignia:

Top row, helmet plates:
silver c1885-1940; black pre-1952; silver helmet plate 1961-63 (an identical plate, but, coloured black, was used on night duty helmets).

Second row:
cap badges, constable's and sergeant's pre - 1930's.

Third row:
stud to fasten helmet strap to helmet, silver helmet crown (1890's), brass belt buckle (pre 1893).

Fourth row:
Carlisle City Police Motor Club badge.

Right, Epaulette rank insignia from left:
constable, sergeant, inspector, chief inspector, superintendent and chief constable.

A collection of pocket books carried by all uniformed patrol officers in the 1950s and 60s for reporting incidents occurring on their beats.:

The books had to be produced for inspection at muster parades, together with baton, handcuffs, whistle, pillar key and, appropriate to the time of day, torch. Incident reports were entered into the appropriate book/booklet at the time of the occurrence, so far as was practicable, completed whilst on patrol, and submitted at the end of the tour of duty for further action as deemed necessary, eg. processing by Admin. Departments for court. Thus officers were able to concentrate on their principal function of street patrols and very little of their time was spent away from their beats on tedious or unnecessary paperwork..

Part Six - Departments
Traffic and Road Safety

Constables Dick Cowen and Shaw Milligan with Austin Westminster, KHH 484 – c1959. The former ambulance, by this time in use by the Force Coroner's Officer, stands alongside.

The advent of the motor car and increasing numbers of motor vehicles on the roads spawned new duties and new problems for the police. The Road Traffic Act 1930 created scores of new offences requiring enforcement, road traffic accidents had to be investigated and reported, whilst increased traffic flows called for officers to perform point duties at busy junctions – all time consuming duties, many of which brought officers into conflict with the public. On 30 December 1930, the Town Clerk submitted to the Watch Committee for consideration a letter he had received from the Home Office proposing that a motor car be provided for policing purposes to supervise traffic on the roads and to detect traffic offences. After discussions with the Chief Constable the matter was deferred until the next visit of H.M. Inspector of Constabulary in order to obtain his views. The Committee surely could not have expected the Inspector to argue against his own Ministry's recommendations but the fudging of the proposal postponed any early decision and the expense of establishing motor patrols and preserved the Corporation's reputation for hesitancy and parsimony on policing matters. However, on 22 July 1931, the Committee did approve the purchase of two bicycles at a cost of thirteen pounds.

Records show that the Force's first patrol vehicles were a MG Magnette, acquired at a cost of £345.00 in November, 1935 and a Triumph 16, bought for £313.00 in December 1937. It appears that they were garaged at the West Walls Fire Station, for when two new trailer pumps for the Brigade were delivered in October 1938, it became necessary to garage the police cars elsewhere. The headquarters across the road had no such facility. The Viaduct Hotel, with a garage for their guests further along West Walls (where the Tesco store now stands), came to the rescue and the two cars were garaged there at a cost of five shillings a week each.

On 28 March, 1939, Chief Constable Lakeman reported to his Watch Committee on *'the dilapidated condition of the M.G.'* He claimed that it would cost a lot of money, fifty pounds, especially when considered against the cost of a new car, to put it in good order and make it roadworthy. Note, it wasn't even four years old. Now, these days patrol cars can clock up vast mileages in a very short time, but in the 1930s, given that the use of the cars was confined within the city boundaries, and a much smaller city than it is today, they really cannot have covered many miles. What a disgraceful state of affairs for a police force to allow them to become *'dilapidated'* but, with comparatively few vehicles on the road and with war looming, probably monies were needed for more pressing matters. In the event, the Committee authorised the Chief Constable to invite tenders for a replacement car of 8 to 10 horse-power, the old vehicle to be taken in part exchange by the successful bidder.

In the entire existence of the Force, it never had more than two liveried patrol vehicles at any one time, but since every beat was patrolled on foot, that was probably a sufficient number. The chart at Appendix 'J' lists the vehicles I have been able to trace. There may have been others, but none that surviving records show. Except for the two Triumphs, the motor cycles were used as beat patrol transport. The GP (general purpose) vans were available for use by all departments, including the Coroner's Officer for the transportation of cadavers to the city mortuary - the ambulance service, generally, and especially after its independence from the police, did not carry dead bodies, e.g. from scenes of crime or accidents. For this specific purpose, in 1963 the Force acquired a Morris Commercial ambulance which had become surplus to Ambulance Service' requirements. After integration in 1963, vehicles were allocated to the city from the county police fleet. The chart shows that, exclusive of running expenses, the Force's vehicles were simply great value, depreciation costing the police authority, at most, (the Ford Zephyrs) approx. £15 per month. (NB The two Zephyrs and the Anglia were part-exchanged for £1545 – no individual values were detailed).

Above, left: *Joe Richardson and Dick Cowen on BSA m/cycles.* **Right:** *Irving Lyon and John Lennox with new Triumph 650cc bikes.*

Below: *clockwise from top left, the Force's first motor vehicle, a 'Black Maria', HH247, converted from a redundant ambulance, used to ferry prisoners between the police station and the courts and operated by police-firemen (pictured outside Spring Gardens Lane Fire Station). A Vauxhall Velox; PCs Norman Jackson and Shaw Milligan pictured with Humber Hawk cars outside the Citadel Station awaiting the arrival of HRH The Princess Margaret, 1951. CHH 857 was Chief Constable Lakeman's private car; a Morris Isis; A Morris Commercial ambulance similar to that used by the Force Coroner's Officer.*

Above: *PC Norman Jackson again, carrying out running repairs to a Humber patrol car. The Force made full use of any skills that were 'freely' available; Morris Commercial ambulance similar to that used by the Force Coroner's Officer. Vauxhall Velox and Morris Isis vehicles (photographs are not of the Force cars) were used for traffic patrols.*

Left: *Advance notification of the proposed movement of abnormal loads, together with a full description and details of the route were required by law to be sent to every police force along the proposed routes, thereby providing each force the opportunity to vary routes and times to suit local traffic conditions. Several hundred of these notices were received at the city police headquarters every year. Thus it was that, during the daylight hours, traffic officers spent much of their duty time, perhaps for the whole of an eight-hour shift, escorting abnormal loads. Frequently, by the time an abnormal load had been collected from the north city boundary and guided to the south, another would be waiting to be escorted in the opposite direction, and vice versa.*

Boring, one could be forgiven for thinking, but absolutely necessary, not only for road safety, but simply because such vehicles would never have been able to negotiate city centre traffic and other obstacles. It was on this sort of duty that the motor cycles came into their own. The pictures show some examples of huge vehicles negotiating city centre streets.

Top: *a Wrekin Roadways vehicle in London Road, passing Durranhill Road and the Harraby Inn.*

Centre: *a McKelvie vehicle hauling a gas tank, 120-foot long, 13'6" wide and weighing 100 tons northwards along Rickergate past police headquarters and the Civic Centre.*

Bottom: *a 100-foot long, 80-ton vehicle carrying a storage tank for the Scottish Gas Board passes Marks and Spencer's store in English Street and turns down towards Scotch Street.*

Pictures of some early traffic accidents:
Top left: *exchange names and addresses?* **Top right:** *a crash on Rickergate Brow does not seem to excite the interest of bystanders.*
Centre left: *The aftermath of a crash involving two lorries on London Road in March 1937.* **Centre right:** *1928, local children gather at the scene of an accident in Botchergate where a lorry has crashed into a shop.*
Above: *the Kingstown bus crashes into the railings at Bridgewater Road in February 1925. The onlooking city policeman keeps a discreet distance from the activity - a pocket-book entry sufficient to mark off this incident?*

Left: the civic opening of the 1965 Road Safety Week. A parade of vintage cars and trucks, with a number of decorated floats, is led off through the city centre by the band of the Border Regiment.

Left: During the latter years of the Force, Sergeant John Walker was the city's Road Safety Officer. His involvement in the city's schools teaching road safety, the 'Tufty Club,' and supervising cycling proficiency, together with his high profile role in promoting higher standards of performance and care from drivers and pedestrians, brought him into contact with most of the population, not to mention all branches of the media. He was probably the most photographed bobby in the city, frequently appearing in the local newspapers and, in his time, one of the best known policemen in Carlisle. Pictured above, in 1967, with a parrot borrowed from a local hairdresser, he captures the attention of pupils at Ashley Street Junior School.

Above: *Open Day, Police Headquarters, c1967.*

Right: *Sergeants Arnold Middleton and John Walker at an exhibition in the Marklet Hall, c1967.*

Right: *The City Mayor, Councillor Jim Smith, presenting Cycling Proficiency Awards to two local children.*

Below: *at Inglewood Junior School, Harraby, with CoCo the Clown from the famous Bertram Mills Circus which was performing in the town. Sgt. Walker asked if he would help get the Road Safety message across to the children and he was only too happy to oblige;*

Above right: *PC 'Dixie' Dean, remembering that he must take into custody anyone carrying a bag of 'swag', arrests a bearded old man only to find that it is the ubiquitous Sergeant Walker again, this time on his rounds distributing Christmas 'goodies' to schoolchildren, 1963.*

196

Timeline for use of motor vehicles in the force

1920 Oct 12 - Watch Committee require Chief Constable to report on the question of obtaining a motor prison van for police use.

Oct 18 - Chief Constable reports that the cost of converting the horse-drawn prison van onto the old motor ambulance chassis would be £10, and the cost of replacing the motor ambulance £600.

1924 Chief Constable granted an allowance of six gallons of petrol per month to enable him to use his vehicle for police purposes.

1925 Nov 24 - Chief Constable instructed to arrange for road accident victims, corpses and injured persons, to be removed from the scenes by motor vehicle.

1926 Nov 30 - Old ambulance [horse-drawn] to be converted into a prison van for police use at cost of £17. Old van sold for £3.10s.

1928 Jan 28 - Police boat reported to be *'dilapidated'* and in urgent need of replacement.

1947 Dec 16 - Two Humber Hawk saloon cars, CHH 833 and CHH 834, to police spec. and complete with 2-way wireless system supplied by Harrisons Motor Engineers, Cecil Street, Carlisle at a cost of £1827.12s.2d. plus cost of wireless equipment. The manufacturer had earlier decided to discontinue this type of vehicle for police use, but, it seems, they made an exception on this occasion for Carlisle Police.

1950 Oct 31 - Establishment of Force vehicle fleet was 4 cars, 2 vans and 3 motor cycles.

oooOooo

Criminal Investigation

There is a dearth of information about the origins and history of the Force Criminal Investigation Department. In the early days the Chief Officer, himself, investigated indictable offences. The first detective appeared during the tenure of Chief Constable Bent in 1872. However, between them, they made a *'pig's ear'* of a murder enquiry on behalf of Lancaster Police (ibid p86) as a result of which the chief officer was severely reprimanded (following a Watch Committee motion initially requiring him to resign) and the office of detective was abolished. After this fiasco, chief constables continued to have a hands-on role in the investigation of serious offences, no doubt assisted by one or more of their officers. In 1860, photographic apparatus was purchased, quite what usage to which it was put is not on record. The turn of the century saw the re-appearance of detectives. In March 1918, new regulations allowed for the payment of five shillings a week plain clothes allowance and a further two shillings out-of-pocket expenses. In 1919, Andrew Johnston, a Staff Sergeant in the Newcastle upon Tyne City Police, was appointed Superintendent and Deputy Chief Constable. He took charge of crime investigation. The Watch Committee approved the purchase of fingerprinting equipment in April 1923 but it was not until the new police headquarters was occupied in 1941 that the CID was provided with purpose built studio facilities (fingerprints and photographic section), office accommodation and interview rooms.

Unlike in county forces where beat constables enquired into most minor crimes, detective officers in Carlisle investigated every reported crime, those reported to uniform constables being immediately passed to the CID. By the time of integration with Cumberland and Westmorland Constabulary in 1963, the department's strength comprised one detective chief inspector, one detective inspector, 2 detective sergeants, two Scenes of Crime officers, eight detective constables and one Coroner's officer. A uniform constable was engaged as office manager and a cadet was occasionally attached to the department. Two cars and a Scenes of Crime van provided the available transport.

All detective officers were required to attend an initial training course at one of the national Detective Training Schools at Wakefield (West Riding Constabulary), Preston (Lancashire Constabulary) or Birmingham (Birmingham City Police). Advanced courses for senior CID officers were provided at these centres. I attended my initial CID training as a constable at Birmingham and advanced, as detective inspector at Wakefield Central Government (Home Office) facilities included the Forensic Science Laboratory at Preston, Regional Criminal Record Offices at Preston and Wakefield, and later, North West Regional Crime Squad assistance. Unlike many forces, Carlisle City did not utilise the facilities of the Metropolitan Police in major investigations. The Met's involvement was attractive to many forces, since, provided it was called in to assist within forty-eight hours of a murder being discovered, the cost of the investigation would be met from central and not local funds. A protracted investigation could otherwise impose a prohibitive burden on a force budget. Instead an arrangement was in place for Lancashire Constabulary to supply mutual aid, the difference being that whilst the Met would have sent a senior detective and a detective sergeant, Lancashire supplied, in addition, sufficient manpower, equipment and transport to supplement the Carlisle force. Did the Met have greater expertise in the investigation of serious crime? Overall, certainly, given that it policed the capital with a population of over eight million and a correspondingly greater number of crimes, but, so far as relates to the investigating officers, individually, not necessarily so. Lancashire was the country's largest county constabulary and its senior detectives were well experienced investigators. I recall that at the time of the Yorkshire Ripper murders, when there was a cry from the press and others to call in the Met, the head of West Yorkshire CID was reputed to have presided over fifty-two murder investigations in a single year. Few, if any, senior officers from any other force could have matched that. However, one has to remember that, in the times under review here, (pre 1967) most killers, who did not immediately surrender to the police, were identified very quickly, murders being of a local or domestic nature or the perpetrators being known to the victim (straight-races as we detectives called them). Local intelligence built up over many years would point investigators in the direction of likely suspects. Such crimes did not require *'outside'* assistance and so, in most cases, mutual aid arrangements were academic.

The CID 1960 - Back row from left, Detective Constables Bob Sloan, Vic Humphries, Raymond Follows, Bill Wilkie and Ian Shannon. Front row, Detective Sergeant Ronnie Rutherford, Detective Inspector Stanley Armstrong and Detective Constable Bob Wilkinson.

Policewomen.

Female police officers were first introduced onto the streets of Carlisle in the war-time conditions of 1916, which saw an influx of female labour into the city in connection with the Gretna munitions works. It was much later, however, before a permanent women's department was made an integral unit of the force.

Mr. E.H. deSchmid, Chief Constable, in his annual report for the year ending 31 December 1916, wrote:
"During the past few months a number of women have been sworn in for duty in connection with special works situated on the Border [the Gretna Munitions Works]. It has been found necessary to lodge a large number of the girl operatives at hostels in various parts of the city, and it was very desirable that some supervision, apart from that of the regular police force [all male officers] should be exercised over them during the time they were here.

Arrangements were accordingly made for the policewomen to be sworn in for the County of Cumberland and the City of Carlisle, and for some time past a certain number have been employed on patrol work every Saturday afternoon and evening in the main streets, railway station, etc. It is hoped that at an early date a dozen will be permanently quartered in the city and work in connection with the regular force. I see no reason why, if the proper type of woman is forthcoming, they should not be found of the greatest assistance to all police forces for domiciliary visiting among women, inspection of women's lodging houses, patrolling public places where indecency may be found, and in cases of offences against children and young girls, where a woman is most useful in eliciting the facts and separating truth from falsehood, frequently a most difficult thing in cases of this description."

Policewoman Constable 4
Yvonne Harvey
Photographed on duty on Binn's Crossing, c1960.

No records exist as to the identities of these pioneers, whether or not they were local women, experienced in such duties, or borrowed from other forces (doubtful, for there weren't many serving policewomen nationally).

Before these appointments, recognising that since the early days of the war there had been a need to efficiently address numerous complaints about the conduct of young girls on the streets of the city, the chief constable had made use of facilities offered by a national organisation, the *'National Union of Women Workers of Great Britain and Ireland.'* It provided women patrols in proximity to military establishments, and was officially recognised by the Home Office, War Office, Admiralty and Police. Each patrol carried a card signed by the chief constable, wore a stamped armlet with her registered number and the initials NUWW, and, working in pairs, had virtually eradicated the problem in Carlisle in little over a year. By the end of 1917, the city police had an establishment of policewomen comprising one sergeant and eight constables. They occupied a house in Portland Square and regularly patrolled the city's streets, public parks, etc. During their first year of operation, they were instrumental in securing numerous convictions for immorality and had rendered valuable assistance in collecting evidence in several sexual offences, including rape. War-time appointments of female officers were sanctioned, and usually paid for, by the Home Secretary, and were additional to a police force's authorised establishment. When the war ended they were discharged. However, soon afterwards, Miss Mary Faulder, believed to be the city's first full-time policewoman, was appointed. She began as a constable, at a salary of thirty shillings a week, on 1 April 1919 from the position of shorthand/typist/clerk in the Force. Her pay was raised to thirty-five shillings after six months, and rose to a ceiling of forty-five shillings. She combined her duties with the job of assistant to the police matron, Mrs. Elizabeth Johnston, wife of the Superintendent, later Chief Constable, Andrew Johnston, who had recently arrived from Newcastle upon Tyne. Mary Faulder's ability as a clerk/typist was not lost, since, in October 1922, records show that she was granted an allowance of 3/6d (17p) for carrying out such duties. So far as can be ascertained, she was not required to perform regular outside patrol duties.

On 25 November 1919, the Watch Committee, had before it a letter from the Carlisle and District Branch of the National Council for Women asking that, having regard to their services during the war, married women be considered for appointment to the Force as in London and some other cities. The Town Clerk was instructed to reply to the effect that the Force was up to strength and that the Committee could not see its way to appointing more officers. On 22 June 1931, the Watch Committee deferred a decision on a request by the Carlisle Divisional Council for Social and Moral Welfare for the appointment of an additional policewoman. In December 1938, taking note that a new police headquarters was planned, the National Council of Women asked the Watch Committee to appoint two female officers to the city force. In the past such pleas had met with the excuse that lack of facilities in the West Walls station precluded such appointments. This was an opportunity to press the matter once again but, alas, to no avail.

A Home Office Circular brought to the attention of the Watch Committee in October 1939, related to the Women's Auxillary Police Corps and set out details for the employment of female officers in case of war. They would receive no pay in peacetime and even in the event of war they would probably only be engaged on a part-time, unpaid basis - big deal! It's surprising that the Corporation did not take advantage of the unpaid or cheap labour but since Chief Constable Lakeman suggested he didn't need any policewomen, for the moment at least, none were recruited. At the time, 1939, there were only 200 female officers in the UK, none at all in three-quarters of the 183 forces. However, some 3,700 served in the Women's Auxillary Police Corps during the war years. One of the country's first policewomen was Miss Barbara Mary Denis de Vitre. She joined Sheffield City Police in 1928, later serving in Cairo City Police, Leicester and Kent, becoming Staff Officer to H.M. Inspectors of Constabulary and finally Assistant HMI. She visited Carlisle to advise the Chief Constable and Watch Committee on the formation of a Policewomen's Branch in the city Force. In May 1944, the Secretary of State gave consideration to the appointment of female officers, especially in areas with large concentrations of servicemen *'whether British or allied'* forces, and he instructed H.M. Inspectors to look into the matter and advise. He proposed that women should be treated as additional to the war-time establishment and that they could be appointed either permanently or temporarily. Their pay would be re-imbursed in full by the Exchequer. HMI Major Egan recommended that Carlisle City Police should have four policewomen and the city's Watch Committee concurred and instructed the chief constable to put the proposal into effect.

Policewoman Constable Mary Smith on patrol with Sergeant Billy Irwin.

passing the Assize Courts [1949]. Mary left the Force in February,1950, just a few months after this picture was taken.

When a permanent establishment of female officers came into being, the *'Policewomen's Branch'* in common with most Forces was quite a separate entity within the City Force dealing mainly with matters associated with women and children. Policewomen's salaries were lower than those of their male counterparts commensurate with their working a 7fi-hour tour of duty (thirty minutes less than male officers), with their longer refreshment break (one hour as opposed to the men's 45 minutes), and with the fact that they did not work between midnight and 8am. However, whilst their pension contributions were also lower, they benefited from higher actuarial values based on the longer life-expectancy of females. Policewomen did not work the city's beat system nor were they employed in specialist departments such as CID and Traffic. Out on patrol, their duties were mainly confined to the city centre where they were additional to the beat men. They also assisted in traffic control, but usually only on pedestrian crossings (which had to be police-controlled to allow traffic to flow without constant interruption) and seldom, if ever, on the principal traffic points such as the top of Botchergate or the top of Warwick Road. Policewomen, although a separate department, were also at the beck and call, and under the supervision of, the male duty inspector. Female police officers enjoyed their own promotion structure, but in Carlisle there was only one above the rank of constable, a policewoman sergeant who was the branch's senior officer. None of the city's policewomen constables achieved promotion. The only sergeant, Thelma Ellis transferred on promotion from Plymouth City Police. The careers of most policewomen were short-lived and the average was about four to five years. Marriage, and raising a family, was the main reason for leaving, and once resignations had taken effect, there was no way back - no maternity leave or job-sharing in those days. In fact, female officers in many forces were required to resign upon marriage, and this rule still stood in all Scottish forces as late as 1965. Later, when husband and wife officers served in the same Force, they were not usually posted to the same station. Those policewomen who did remain in the service, provided they passed the qualifying examinations, (which could not be sat by any officer, male or female, until after the completion of four years service), and especially if they were prepared to transfer to other forces, had better prospects than their male colleagues and could reasonably expect early advancement and a good career.

At the demise of the city force, the female establishment stood at one sergeant and six constables. The strength of Cumberland and Westmorland Constabulary's female establishment doubled upon integration with the city force. Upon the application of Equal Opportunities legislation to the police service, policewomen's departments were fully integrated into the normal workings and female officers' conditions of service, duties and shift-working patterns became identical to those of the men, not always to the satisfaction of the female officers.

oooOooo

Police Cadets

The cadet scheme was designed to develop in young persons aged 16 to 19 wishing to pursue a police career, character, confidence and initiative to widen their education and community awareness and to improve their physique and bearing. It allowed recruits early access to an attractive career that would otherwise be denied them until reaching the age of 19 years, by which time many would have settled into alternative employment. They were not to monopolise appointments to constable rank, the service retaining the principle that recruits should come from a wide variety of occupations, including the military, so as to reflect and bring experience to the service from a fair cross-section of the public. Carlisle City had just four cadets at any one time, all male.

Constable Dick Cowen, Traffic Department, photographed with, from left, Cadets Billy Orr, ?, Gerald Salkeld and Peter Ullyart. All but the unidentified cadet subsequently served in the regular force.

Conditions of entry were much the same as those for the regular force, with the exception that they could be appointed notwithstanding they were below the minimum height provided that they were still growing and likely to achieve the required standard. The emphasis was on training and preparing them for police duties. Although they wore a police uniform (distinguished by blue cap-bands and shoulder 'flashes') they did not perform street duties until they were given a short insight immediately before appointment to the regular force. Cadets were instructed in drill, first aid, physical training, swimming and life-saving, self defence, etc., and they were encouraged to take part in competitive sports. Many attended adventure training courses, for example at Outward Bound Schools, and participated in the Duke of Edinburgh's Award Scheme. They spent time with various community groups such as hospitals, children's homes and the like, and attended colleges of further education where they studied Law, British Constitution and English. All moved around the various departments of the force gaining an insight into specialist duties such as CID, scenes of crime and traffic patrol, along the way also becoming quite proficient at making tea! Carlisle City made no female appointments into the cadet force. Most city cadets were eventually appointed constables. I understand there were a few who did not reach the 5'10" required height for Carlisle City but who made their marks elsewhere where requirements were less stringent. Recruiting to the regular establishment of constables was never a problem for the city force as it was in many others, but nevertheless, the cadet scheme provided a very good source of young men who had been trained and had demonstrated a flair for the job. The appointment, pay and conditions of service of cadets was governed by a set of Police Cadet Regulations.

oooOooo

201

The Special Constabulary

Part-time and unpaid, sometimes known within the service as 'hobby-bobbies', the 'Specials' are an integral part of every police force, engaged, at least in theory, to provide support in times of any emergency that might remove full-time officers from their normal duties. It is not, and never was, intended that they fill in for shortages in the regular establishment.

The Special Constables Act of 1831 provided for members of the public to be sworn-in by Justices of the Peace to act as constables in times of tumult, riot and disorder. In 1831, there were, of course, very few professional police forces, and those that did exist were of insufficient strength to contain the problems of industrial and political unrest of the day. Liverpool, with a population of 250,000 was a classic example with just fifty night watchmen. Carlisle had only twenty-two constables for a city of 30,000 but with the advantage of it being a garrison city the Mayor and/or the Magistrates could call upon the military to assist the civil force. Special constables, drawn from property owners, were often sworn in, even before 1831, sometimes hundreds at any one time, usually after, rather than in preparation for, an event. In Carlisle, in the months leading up to the creation of a permanent police force in 1827, one riot precipitated the appointment of three hundred specials, whilst in July, 1839 nine hundred were sworn in anticipation of trouble with the Chartist movement. On at least two other occasions 200 were sworn. Few of them were true volunteers; all were untrained and, understandably, most were reluctant to face up to hostile crowds. Many would run away at the first sign of trouble. The 1831 Act, with numerous amendments and additions, remained in force until repealed by the Police Act, 1964.

Between these two Acts of Parliament, a major change came about with the outbreak of the Great War of 1914 -18, when many police forces were depleted of their regular constables through enlistment into the armed services. April, 1912 saw the publication of a Home Office Circular to police authorities regarding the appointment of special constables and a 'police reserve' force. Twelve former city policemen volunteered for the 'First Reserve', for which they expected to be paid a retainer of £5 pa. plus, when called upon to do duty, remuneration at the going rates for regular officers of their respective ranks, ie, five shillings a day for constables, six shillings for sergeants and seven shillings for inspectors. They were required to sign an agreement for one year and to attend as often as the Chief Constable deemed necessary for training. When on duty, they were to be treated as part of the regular force and wear the uniform of their respective ranks. For a *'Second Reserve',* twenty-six former military men were considered by the Chief Constable as suitable for appointment until it was discovered that they were either railwaymen or trade unionists (seemingly prohibited from taking up office). Two hundred others were approached to register as *'Specials'* but only seven consented. Employers generally were willing to release men to join but not a single member of the Corporation's workforce volunteered. Some 60% of Carlisle's establishment of constables went to war. The Special Constables Act, 1914 removed restrictions on appointments and gave chief constables authority to appoint 'Specials', not just in times of emergency, but to be used at any time. Thus the Special Constabulary, as we know it today, came about - a force of volunteers, trained to work alongside regular policemen or independently and to carry out the full range of policing duties. The Specials, following the age-old tradition of local peacekeepers before them, were part-time and unpaid but they became an integral part of every UK police force with all the powers of a constable in their particular area and with their own rank structure. One hundred and seventy two Specials were sworn in during the year 1915 to help police Carlisle for the duration of the War. Their presence, on Sundays, allowed regular officers to take a rest-day, a privilege they had not enjoyed since the beginning of the war. By the end of 1916, 101 Specials were serving and for the first time, they were issued with uniforms which, said the Chief Constable, Mr. deSchmid, *'had added to their confidence and efficiency'.* Prior to then, Specials could be identified by a brassard worn on the left arm. A number of the men were promoted to sergeant rank. In the 1918 New Year's Honours list, Special Sergeant H.E. Winter was appointed MBE for his services to the Carlisle Special Constabulary. He was, in fact, chief of the Special Constabulary during the war.

After the war there was clearly a strong and active group of Specials in the city as evidenced by the award of Special Constabulary Long Service Medals to forty-three officers in 1937 and a further forty-four in 1938.

The first post-WW2 promotions in the 'Specials', approved by the Watch Committee on Tuesday, 24 November, 1964, included Sergeant Thomas Robert Jenkins of Vallum House, Burgh Road, Carlisle, to the rank of Inspector and Constable Archibald Crooks of Fairfield Gardens, Carlisle, promoted to Sergeant. Each had served in the Force during the war, Bob Jenkins joining the 'Specials' in 1939 while Archie Crooks had

Special Constables, 1839

A citizen's obligation to respond to a magistrate's directive to attend before them and be sworn-in as a special constable was made clear in a case before Birmingham Magistrates:

"A mistaken notion prevails that persons sworn in as special constables are not amenable to the summary jurisdiction of the magistrates in cases of neglect of duty or refusal to act. A special constable who refused to act was called up yesterday at the public office on warrant, and it was only on his submission and promise to comply in future with the regulations for watching and warding that he was excused a fine. The Magistrates intimated, at the same time, their determination to impose a fine in all similar cases that should hereafter come before them."

Birmingham Journal, August, 1839

Above: *Special Constables leaving West Walls Police Station wearing their sole item of uniform, a brassard on the left arm.*

Top right: *Special Constabulary Long Service Medal, obverse and front.*

Above: *WW1 Specials - believed to be their final march through the city, having completed their WW1 service.*

203

Above: *Outside West Walls Police Station, Constables and Sergeant together with Special Constables, gathered for duty in World War 1. Note the brassard on the left arm.*

Above right: *A Carlisle Special Constabulary cap badge together with annual service clasps issued during World War 1.*

Right: *Special Constable Archie Crooks at 'the centre of things' as the Mayor, Alderman George Routledge, greets HRH the Princess Margaret on 7 August 1951.*

been a War Reserve Constable, afterwards joining the 'Specials' in 1949. Bob Jenkins continued to serve beyond amalgamation and retired as Commandant of Cumbria Special Constabulary.

Under the provisions of Section 16 of the Police Act, 1964, chief constables were authorised to *'hire and fire'* special constables without reference to the police authority. By Section 18 every special constable had to be attested by making a declaration before a Justice of the Peace, whilst Section 19 defined the extent of the specials' jurisdiction. Compared to a regular officer's power to act as a constable throughout the whole of England and Wales, a special's authority was confined to the police area for which he was appointed, thus Carlisle City Specials had authority only within the city boundaries, whilst present-day officers are appointed for the whole of Cumbria. Special Constables Regulations contain conditions of service, including qualifications for appointment, payment of expenses and sick pay where an officer suffers loss of earnings from his normal employment through of injury or disease contracted whilst serving as a police officer. It should be noted that rank in the Special Constabulary confers no authority over regular full-time police officers.

During the Second World War one hundred and fifty specials served in the force but afterwards, numbers in the branch declined and, in my time in the force, little was seen of them on the city's streets. Most who then served were elderly and although their loyalty and public spirited nature could not be faulted, the operational demands of the service were necessarily addressed more to the younger, fitter, regular officers. Specials were deployed on duties such as football matches, supervision at polling stations, shows, exhibitions, etc. The establishment of the Special Constabulary at 31 December 1962 stood at three sergeants and twenty-four constables, a substantial decrease from the forty-two serving at end of the previous year, but, said the Chief Constable, the current officers now are active.

oooOooo

Part Seven - Competitions, sport and leisure
First Aid and Civil Defence

City Police first-aid teams were always very competent at tying narrow bandages and administering the 'kiss of life' and were successful in many local and regional competitions, frequently winning trophies. Of course, every officer was trained to St. John's Ambulance standards and regularly had to undertake instruction from the police surgeon and the Force First Aid trainer and pass theoretical and practical examinations to the satisfaction of a local independent GP. Failure in the exams would mean another course of training. Never the most popular of past-times for most officers!!

Left: *1957, standing, Ken Grainger, Arnold Middleton, Gordon Harling and Jofre Robinson.*

Right: *c1959, standing PC Ken Grainger and Sgt. Arnold Middleton,[Force First Aid Trainer].*

Front row: *Inspector Harold Joffre Robinson, Chief Constable Willie Lakeman and PC Gordon Harling [Coroner's Officer, whose customers were usually beyond first-aid].*

Above: *1962, winning City Police team in the Mayor's Civil Defence competition, PC Ken Grainger, PC Gordon Coupe, PS Arnold Middleton, PC Billy Orr and PC Bill 'Cash'Little. Who was worried about the 'bomb' with people like this about?*

The Force football team played in the Carlisle Thursday League against local works and military teams, the military sides comprising mainly of professional footballers, some of international standard, completing their National Service training in or near the city.

Above: The CID cricket team leaving the hallowed turf of Edenside, c1966.

From left: John Aird, Sandy Ruddick, Vic Humphries, Bob Sloan, Laurie Ingles, Bill Wilkie, Stanley Armstrong, Martin MacAlinden, Ray Follows, Jack Taylor and Ken Grainger.

Above: *1963, Carlisle Thursday League Cup Final. City Police 1 'Bonzo's Cumberland Wrestlers 4.*

Standing, from left: *PC 65 Sandy Bremner MM,,[trainer], PC 86 Brian Henderson, PC 111 Sandy Ruddick, PC 119 Gordon Kendal, PC 114 Dave Beveridge, PC Stan Brown [MOD Police] Cadet Des Sellars.*

Front: *PC 31 Howard Nixon [captain], DS 52 Ray Follows, PC 118 Dave Fordy, PC 34 Jimmy Dunn, PC 121 John Winthrop.*

Above: *Police Athletic Association cup-tie played at Brunton Park. The picture must have been taken before the match since the players have happy faces. They actually lost 11-0, wiping all the smiles away.*
Standing, from left, Sandy Bremner,[trainer] Jimmy Preston, Alex Archibald, Andy 'Tut' Rutherford, Gerry Jenkinson, Gordon Coupe, Des Sellars and John Aird [manager].
Front row, Howard Nixon [captain], Ray Follows, John Winthrop, Peter Ullyart and Bob Wilson.

Below: *1920, City Police athletics team.*

Standing, from left: *PC Vic Todhunter, NK, NK, PC Johnston, J Potts, Joe Roe and Ab Bird,*

Seated: *NK, NK, Insp. Percival, Chief Constable Spence, NK, and PC Jack Norman.*

Above: *Tickets were much sought after for the Force Annual Balls, usually held in the Crown and Mitre Hotel. Local members of parliament, civic leaders, senior members of the legal profession, chief officers of the county police, senior military officers and other VIPs were all invited to attend. As well as being very enjoyable social occasions, monies were raised for charities. The pictures date back to the 1930s but the annual function continued until the demise of the Force, though, by that time, not on such a grand scale.*

Part Eight - Major Awards and Decorations

Queen's Police Medal for Gallantry (posthumous)

PC 33 George William McKinlay Russell.
George Russell was awarded the Queen's Police Medal for Gallantry for his courageous actions during the incident at Oxenholme on 10 February 1965 in which he was shot and killed. A full account of the occurrence is provided elsewhere in this publication.

British Empire Medal

PC 57 Alexander Archibald
Inspector Alfred Harrison
For their part in the Oxenholme Railway Station shooting incident on 10 February 1965, each was awarded the British Empire Medal.

Queen's Gallantry Medal

PS 556 Irving Lyon
PC 347 Malcolm Brough
PC 248 Andrew Gardner
'Sergeant Lyon, Constable Brough and Constable Gardner, acting within the finest spirit of the police service and whilst unarmed, displayed bravery of a very high order and with a complete disregard of their own safety when, after driving at high speeds in the pursuit of a stolen car, they overpowered, disarmed and arrested the two extremely dangerous criminals who had already committed three violent murders that evening'.

Murders at Carstairs, Lanarkshire

Irving Lyon, a native of Egremont, Cumberland, joined Carlisle City Police Force on 16 June 1957 after three years service, as a Sergeant, in the Scots Guards. Most of his military service was spent on ceremonial guard duties and included taking part in Trooping of the Colour parades on two occasions. In the city police, after the mandatory time spent on beat patrols he transferred to the Traffic Department in 1962. Initially he was one of two officers assigned to the newly acquired Triumph Speed Twin motor cycles. In April 1963, he moved to patrol cars and remained so employed until his promotion to sergeant (Road Safety) in 1971. Then came two years as a beat sergeant before returning to the Traffic Branch. During his service, Sergeant Lyon accumulated five commendations from his chief constables.

Though these medals were awarded after amalgamation of the city and county police forces, details are included since Sergeant Lyon was a former city officer who spent all of his police service in Carlisle.

The series of events leading to the award of his Queen's Gallantry Medal took place on 30 November, 1976, and began in Scotland with a prison (hospital) escape and three horrific murders that were quickly followed by a high-speed cross-border car chase culminating in the arrest of the killers in Carlisle.

Carstairs State Hospital, in Lanarkshire, Scotland, is a secure psychiatric hospital housing a number of highly dangerous, psychopathic criminals, including, on the day in question, Thomas McCulloch, and Robert Mone. At the age of 21 years in 1970, McCulloch was ordered to be detained *'without limit of time'* after being charged with a crime of attempted murder. Mone was committed to Carstairs when, as a 19 years old private in the Gordon Highlanders, he was found unfit to plead to charges of murder, rape and assault. During their detention both men had been accorded 'trustee' status which allowed them some freedom of movement in the hospital and its grounds, a liberty which, allegedly, did not have the endorsment of the hospital's branch of the Prison Officers Association. The doubts, fears, frustrations and objections of members of the association at the liberal attitudes and methods of the hospital's management, reported to have been repeatedly aired over a period of five years, were to be vindicated. The security of the hospital also obviously left much to be desired, evidenced by the fact that the two men, whilst employed in the joiners shop, secretly put together an escape kit and a collection of formidable weapons including a weighted rope-ladder, a makeshift 'sword' and scabbard, five knives, a hatchet, and two garrottes made from brass handles and guitar string. They each made themselves a belt with loops in which to carry the knives. Hindsight, of course, is an exact science, but it is clear that the two prisoners had been planning and preparing for an escape for some considerable time and that their scheming and cache of weapons and equipment had gone completely unnoticed by the hospital authorities. Events were to illustrate that despite a background of mental disorder, both inmates had the nous, the determination and the cunning to put their plans into effect, as well as the willingness to kill in the process.

The drama began in the early evening of Tuesday, 30 November 1976. For recreation McCulloch and Mone had for some time been participating in a drama group run by Staff Nurse McLellan. On that particular evening the officer took both men, as well as a third inmate, a double murderer named Ian Simpson, to the hospital's recreational block for a 'remedial period.' A short time later the mutilated bodies of McLellan and Simpson were found in a corridor in the block, the wounds believed to have been inflicted by an axe, a knife and a garden fork. The alarm was raised and it was discovered that McCulloch and Mone had escaped from the hospital using the rope ladder to scramble over the perimeter fence. A large axe, commonly known as a fireman's axe, and indeed kept for fire-fighting purposes, was missing from a safe in Mr. McLellan's office. The officer's keys were also missing. For reasons better known to the hospital's management there was a forty- minute delay in informing the local police of the occurrences.

Once over the fence, using the darkness of the evening to their advantage, the two fugitives set about the next phase of their escape plan - acquiring the means to put some distance between themselves and Carstairs. Each man was dressed partly in nursing officer's uniform. Mone lay on the unlit roadway feigning injury, whilst McCulloch, purporting to be seeking help, flagged down a passing motor car. Fatefully, as that car drew to a standstill, a police patrol car manned by Constables George Taylor and John Gillies of the Strathclyde Police also arrived upon the scene. At that moment in time the two policemen were unaware of an escape from the nearby hospital. Believing matters to be in hand the driver of the first vehicle drove off. PC Taylor left the vehicle and spoke to McCulloch who told him that the man laid on the roadway, Mone, had been struck by a passing vehicle that had failed to stop. The unsuspecting officer moved to examine the 'injured' man and as he did so McCulloch, hidden by the darkness of the evening, followed behind him and struck him a fierce and fatal blow across the head with the blade of the axe. PC Gillies, now out of the police car and coming to the aid of his colleague, was also attacked and in avoiding blows aimed at him he overbalanced and fell into a roadside ditch, becoming immersed up to his chest in oozing mud and water. A few minutes passed before he was able to free himself from his predicament by which time the two fugitives had made off in the police vehicle. They did not get far before losing control and crashing the car into a ditch. Scrambling back onto the roadway they flagged down an approaching vehicle, an old van containing two men. The escapees told the occupants that they were policemen conveying a prisoner to Carstairs when the prisoner had suddenly struck out and caused them to crash. Then, without warning, McCulloch and Mone attacked the two men stabbing them several times before taking possession of their van. However, the escapees being unable to start it, the severely injured driver was dragged to his feet and forced to start it for them. The villains then quit the scene. But once again they made little progress before the vehicle broke down. Abandoning it, they made off on foot shortly reaching Townfoot Farm at Roberton. Much had happened since their escape but they were still barely a dozen miles from Carstairs. At the farm they cut through the telephone cable before subjecting the occupants to a terrifying ordeal lasting some fifteen minutes. Believing that this farmer, like most, would own a firearm, they demanded a shotgun from him. They were mistaken. Providentially there were no guns on the premises. Having so far used their own cunning to their advantage the fugitives then fell for the trickery of a 12 year old girl. The farmer's daughter successfully pleaded to be allowed to use the upstairs toilet, and seizing the opportunity, and unbeknown to the criminals, she telephoned the police from an upstairs room, an action that undoubtedly took a great deal of courage in the circumstances. McCulloch and Mone, oblivious of the girl's telephone call and confident that they had left the family without means of communication, made off in the farmer's Austin Allegro motor car before the arrival of the police. The police, by this time knowing of the escape from, and the murders at, Carstairs, now knew also that the villains were still in the area. Their details and the vehicle they were using was quickly circulated to surrounding forces, including Cumbria. It was not long before the Austin car was spotted travelling south towards Carlisle on the busy A74 road by Dumfries and Galloway Constabulary's traffic patrols. Two Jaguar patrol cars, containing armed officers, gave pursuit as the fleeing killers headed towards the English border.

Sergeant Lyon with Mrs. Lyon at Buckingham Palace.

Cumbria Police, meanwhile, were closely monitoring events across the border and had placed traffic patrol cars in position ready to intercept the fugitives should they cross over into their territory. Sergeant Lyon, together with Constables Malcolm Brough and Andrew Gardner, all unarmed and each in separate patrol cars and in radio contact with one another, waited at Gretna. Shortly before 9pm, they saw the stolen car crossing the Scottish border into England, the Scottish police still in close pursuit. They joined in the chase and as the vehicles reached speeds of 100 mph along the A74 and onto the M6 at Carlisle, they put into effect a plan to force the fugitives off the motorway. Constable Brough passed the target vehicle and as he tried to 'push' it over onto the hard-shoulder the driver made several attempts to pass his vehicle on its nearside. As the chase approached Junction 43 at Rosehill, Constable Brough succeeded in forcing the driver up the slip road where, on reaching the roundabout, the driver having lost control of the car, it crashed into the barriers and a lamp-standard before coming to an abrupt stand-still. Constable Brough was unable, himself, to enter the slip-road having overshot the junction in his efforts to force the target off the motorway, but, and fortunately as it turned out, quickly returned to the scene. Meanwhile, McCulloch and Mone escaped from the wreckage of their vehicle, and were seen, one of them brandishing the fireman's axe above his head, running towards a car that had stopped at the crash scene to help. Their intention was clearly to hi-jack this vehicle and continue their flight. Sergeant Lyon was by this time on foot and giving chase, reaching the car in the nick of time as McCulloch was clambering inside. The sergeant grabbed him and a violent struggle ensued, during which, the sergeant sensed a sudden lunging movement from the criminal's left hand. Acting instinctively, Sergeant Lyon grasped a dagger-type knife by its blade as it was thrust at his body. He managed to retain hold of the weapon during the violent struggle that continued until the arrival on the scene of Constable Brough. The officers overpowered McCulloch, disarmed him, dragged him from the car and handcuffed him. Meanwhile, Constable Gardner was struggling with Mone, who was also partially inside the rear of the car threatening the thunderstruck driver with the axe. The officer managed to disarm him, drag him from the car and arrest him. Whilst the prisoners were held pending their removal to Carlisle Police Station, neither showed any remorse for their evil deeds and went so far as to say that *'another policeman would not be missed'.* They indicated that they had not expected to be taken alive by the police.

On 11 November 1978, at an investiture at Buckingham Palace, Her Majesty Queen Elizabeth II presented Sergeant Lyon, Constable Brough and Constable Gardner each with the Queen's Gallantry Medal. The citation read, *'Sergeant Lyon, Constable Brough and Constable Gardner, acting within the finest spirit of the police service and whilst unarmed, displayed bravery of a very high order and with a complete disregard of their own safety when, after driving at high speeds in the pursuit of a stolen car, they overpowered, disarmed and arrested the two extremely dangerous criminals who had already committed three violent murders that evening'* .

McCulloch and Mone subsequently appeared at the High Court in Edinburgh charged with three counts of murder and three of attempted murder, all of the offences committed in Scotland. The Judge, Lord Dunpark sentenced them to life imprisonment on each count, adding *'these were as desperately brutal murders as have ever been my misfortune to deal with, and for you 'life' means life, the natural life, three times over.'*

Left: *Chief Constable Spence [centre, front] with Superintendent Johnston [himself later Chief Constable] to his left.*

Pictured at Tassell's studio garden on Lowther Street, c1920.

Above: *Pictured inside the Market Hall, in March 1925, at the annual inspection, with the one remaining woman police officer, Mary Faulder, in attendance. Chief Constable Spence is on her right and Superintendent Johston on the far right of the picture.*

Above: *Photographed outside the Rickergate Headquarters, c1950.*

Front row, from left: *Inspectors Tommy Wright and Jack Davidson, Superintendent and Deputy Chief Constable Fred Blacklock, Chief Constable Willie Lakeman, Inspectors Bob Sutcliffe and 'Tiny' Wilson and Sgt Harold Simons.*

Back row: *Sgts John Bushby, Maurice Hendry, James Ballantyne, Roy Harrison [later Chief Constable of Dewsbury Borough and Deputy Chief Constable of West Yorkshire] Tommy Rutherford, Leonard 'Cash' Little and Herbert Boak.*

Part Nine - Major crimes

Fortunately, the citizens of Carlisle are, generally, a peaceable population and the city has never experienced high levels of major crime such as those in many of our large towns today. True, in the early 19th Century, at a time when most of the inhabitants were desperately struggling to survive the abject poverty prevailing in the city and district and when resorting to thieving was almost a necessity of life that could be excused, the incidence of disorder, robberies and petty thieving caused public outrage and contributed much to the formation of a City Police Force. However, after the appearance of a professional police on the streets, good order was quickly restored and maintained over the ensuing years. That Carlisle is a small city and that it had its own dedicated police force was an advantage - officers, especially the detective branch, could often identify perpetrators from their modus operandi, witnesses' descriptions, area of operation, etc. and many criminals often experienced difficulty concealing their activities from the Force. Of course, the town has never been crime free, but there have been relatively few murders and most have been of a family/domestic nature, the killers quickly detected and brought to justice. It is not within the aims of this work to record details of the city's criminal past; there are sufficient publications on offer already. It is true to say, however, that some, probably most, of those publications tend to concentrate on killings that resulted in the offenders having a date with the hangman in the county jail. Not all did. It is clear that, locally at least, there has always been much opposition to the death penalty and a reluctance of juries to accept responsibility for sending offenders to the gallows. The trial of PC Jardine's killer, reported elsewhere in this work, amply illustrated that. A sample of interesting cases follows, not selected because they are the most horrific, but simply because they provide a cross-section of killings investigated by the Force from its early days until its demise and include a drunken brawl, a 'domestic,' an undetected (or was it, was it investigated and prosecuted with sufficient determination? - the reader can decide) a hanging (actually the first person in Britain to be executed under the provisions of the Homicide Act, 1957, a case that created a legal precedent) and finally, a vile, horrible child murder. The murder, in 1965, of city policeman George Russell and the shooting of his colleagues, took place at Oxenholme in the county police area and is recorded separately.

Murder at the Pack Horse Inn

Binge drinking and the relaxation of licensing laws are much blamed for current levels of murder and mayhem in the country. It was ever thus. Drink has always played a predominant part in murders and serious injury crimes. Two examples from 19th Century Carlisle show how a minor argument over a petty matter can quickly escalate into violent attack and death.

The scene is the Pack Horse Inn at Newtown, the time about 9pm on 22 August 1835. Two men John Dixon, a pig gelder aged 63, and Joseph Burney, 30, each the worse for drink and in an argumentative mood, entered the pub and began a silly exchange over who had the price of a pint of ale, three old pence. It mattered not because the landlady, Ann Miller, refused to serve them considering that they had already drunk too much and they were too quarrelsome to remain on her premises. The argument continued, however, and Dixon produced a knife from his pocket and told Burney *"I'll hurt thee before thou goes out."* He put the knife back but then struck Burney in the face with his hand. He made to leave, but Burney followed him into the passageway where a scuffle took place. Burney aimed a couple of blows before the older man grabbed him by his collar and stabbed him in the abdomen. As he left the pub Dixon said, *"I have done his goose now."* The landlord saw Burney bent over and holding his stomach and went to his aid. He was bleeding profusely and Mr. Miller saw that he was seriously hurt, his innards protruding from the wound. He sent for a doctor and the Parish Constable and Overseer of the Poor, Joseph Nixon. The Constable went to Dixon's home and told him why he'd come *"It's a bad job and they could hang me for it,"* said Dixon. He was arrested, and Nixon delivered him to PC Russell of the City Police. Burney was attended by two surgeons but died six days later.

On Wednesday, 23 March 1836, the accused man faced Lord Chief Justice Denman at Cumberland Assizes in Carlisle charged with murder. He wore a woollen nightcap and looked thin and sickly. He pleaded not guilty. A number of witnesses were called to give evidence of Dixon's previous good character. Summing up, the Judge explained to the Grand Jury the difference between murder and manslaughter, with particular reference to the defence of provocation. *"Dixon had produced a knife and told Burney he would hurt him.*

He then deliberately put it into his pocket then struck the deceased as if to provoke him in order to afford an excuse for doing him a mischief and gratifying a revengeful feeling." LCJ Denman appeared set in his mind that this was a case of murder. He said he had seldom come across a case where all the circumstances were more clearly proved, in which there was so little discrepancy and in which all the facts could be so easily reconciled. However, he continued, *"the jury, if they are satisfied that Dixon killed Burney, have to consider whether he had done so in the sudden ebullition of passion and under great excitement of provocation."* There did not appear to be the slightest indication of provocation. The jury retired to consider the evidence, returning within a few minutes to declare Dixon *'not guilty'* of murder, but guilty of manslaughter - a good example of a jury not being prepared to accept responsibility for sending an accused to the gallows.

The Lord Chief Justice addressed the prisoner, *"There would have been no option for me but to condemn you to that death to which you suddenly consigned a fellow creature. The jury has acquitted you of murder, but a more aggravated case of manslaughter never came before a Court of Justice. For the paltry quarrel over sixpence or a shilling you inflicted the grievous injury which produced death. I should not be doing justice were I to allow you to remain in this country. It is necessary to show that the law can and will punish crimes so dangerous to society. The sentence is that you be transported across the seas for the term of your natural life."* And so Caldewgate lost one of its colourful characters!

oooOooo

Despite the wretched living conditions and low incomes in Victorian Carlisle, it is amazing, as it is in modern times, that money could always be found for drink.

A 'domestic' in Shaddongate

In 1880, 39-year old basket-maker John O'Neill lived in a two-room tenement in Broadguards, Shaddongate, with his common-law wife Mary Duffy, a hawker, and her two children by a previous relationship. Drinking to excess was a way of life to them. On 16 November, after an afternoon session in local pubs, they returned home the worse for wear, Duffy at 6pm and O'Neill ten minutes later. The younger of Duffy's two daughters left to stay the night with an aunt. The elder left home at 7pm. It was not unusual for them to see their mother and O'Neill intoxicated, arguing and sometimes coming to blows. At 9.30pm, a neighbour saw O'Neill, *"coming home"* apparently *"fresh of drink."* A short while later, as she was fetching water from a tap in the communal yard, the neighbour heard Duffy screaming. Nothing unusual in that, but she nevertheless called to her husband, her words probably simply a figure of speech, *"There's murder being done!"* They let the matter pass. At 11pm, Duffy's elder daughter returned home. She had to pass through her parent's bedroom to reach her own. As she did so, in the dark, she saw her mother lying on her back on the floor. O'Neill was on the bed, apparently sleeping (it was the only bed the family possessed, the daughters having to sleep on the floor in their bedroom). She thought they had been quarrelling and knowing that O'Neill often refused to allow her mother into the bed she thought no more about what she had seen and retired to her room for the night. O'Neill went for his brother early next morning and told him, *"Mary Duffy's dead."* *"Have you been striking her?"* he asked, (he obviously knew of the volatility of their relationship). O'Neill sat down and cried. The brother called the police. Constable Thomas Watson went to the scene of the crime. He saw the body of Mary Duffy lying at the foot of the stairs. O'Neill told him that he'd gone to bed the previous night and left her. *"She must have tumbled down the stairs,"* he told the officer. The constable, not satisfied with his explanation, arrested him and took him to the police office. Inspector Phillips questioned O'Neill, who said, *"She was the worse for drink and wanted to go out for some more. She ran and I ran after her. She fell downstairs."* *"When did you next see her?"* asked the Inspector. *"This morning,"* he replied. He then changed his story saying that he'd found her dead in bed. The Inspector went to O'Neill's home where he saw Duffy's body, bruised and covered in blood. Chief Constable MacKay, who at one time was head of detectives in Edinburgh and no stranger to such occurrences, was informed and he went and examined the scene and took various forensic samples. A police surgeon examined the body. He found ten abrasions on the deceased's throat - apparently fingernail impressions - bruises all over the body, hair matted in blood and other injuries that he considered may have been caused by boot studs from a kicking. A post-mortem examination revealed

214

the cause of death to be a ruptured liver and internal bleeding, possibly brought about by a man kneeling on the deceased. O'Neill was charged with murder and committed for trial.

At Cumberland Assizes in Carlisle on 18 January, 1881, he faced trial on the lesser charge of manslaughter, based entirely on circumstantial evidence. Prosecuting counsel described the location of the crime as *'the poorest district of the city.'* A neighbour told the court she heard a commotion, but added, as a reason for not suspecting the worst, *"there are a good many houses and gardens and on a Saturday night things generally are all ends up!"* PC Watson told the Court that the couple were well known to him. They frequently quarrelled. Inspector Phillips corroborated the constable but said that O'Neill had not previously been before the courts. The defence barrister argued that there had been no witnesses to the alleged attack on Mary Duffy and, therefore, the accused's explanation that she had fallen down the stairs could not be disputed. *"The case against him should be dismissed,"* he said. The Judge was having none of it. *"Crimes would go unpunished,"* he said, *"if juries required only absolute and direct evidence."* O'Neill was found guilty of manslaughter. Counsel told the Judge that the prosecution had asked for mercy. *"Who is the prosecutor?"* asked the Judge. *"The police,"* he was told. *"Then the recommendation comes to nothing more than we can think for ourselves!"* said the Judge. (Seems he didn't think much of a police opinion!) He told O'Neill, *"You have been found guilty of a very serious offence. Human life must not be tampered with, and a woman's life must not be tampered with and brought to an end under circumstances like this. Without provocation on her part she was brought to an untimely end by the accused. The jury has arrived at the right result. Violence of a most extraordinary kind was used. There was hardly a part of her body that had not been subject to blows and,"* he feared, *"kicks, lacerated wounds on the head and clots of blood, blood on her face, over her clothes, bruises on the lower part of her body and that fatal blow to the chest (pathologist's opinion as to cause of death) all of which must have been brought about by fearful violence."* He noted that O'Neill had been kind to the deceased when not in drunken fits, but he could sentence the prisoner *"to no less than seven years penal servitude."*

oooOooo

Murder of a businessman in West Walls

[Photo by Tassell.
THE PRISONER, ARCHIBALD NORVAL.

Seventy-five year old Alexander Norval, who resided at Corby a few miles from the city, carried on business as a currier from a warehouse premises in West Walls, just a couple of hundred yards from the city's police headquarters. He was assisted by his 38 year-old married son, Archibald, (pictured) who lived with his wife in Sheffield Street, Carlisle. At 12mn on Saturday, 5th November 1910, Constable Foster, going about his patrol and trying doors of business premises on his beat, found the door of Mr. Norval's warehouse closed but, unusually, unlocked. He entered the premises and shone his torch into the total darkness inside. He found the body of Mr. Norval, senior, lying at the foot of an open staircase. There was blood on the head and on the floor close to the body. The officer searched the building and established that there was no-one else inside. All other doors and windows were secured and shuttered. PC Foster returned to the nearby police office to report his discovery.

Enquiries quickly revealed that father and son were two completely different characters. Norval senior was described as being tight-fisted, hard, a man who treated his son with firmness, kept him very short of wages and who would not tolerate him answering back, probably fonder of money than he was of his own people. In contrast, Norval junior was known to spend much of his money on drink and gambling.

PC Foster went to the son's home to report the death of his father. He found him under the influence of drink and asked him to accompany him to the police station. There he was seen by Inspector Turnbull. *"Poor old*

215

dad," he said, *"He was good to me."* He said that he had last seen his father when he left work at 1.10pm and that he expected his father would leave shortly afterwards to go home, catching the 1.50pm train to Wetheral. All three then went to the warehouse where Archibald lit the gas lights. *"There,"* he said, *"that axe* (pointing to an axe close to the body), *"that ought not to be there. We use it upstairs for breaking coal."* The old man's false teeth and his lunchbox were lying on the floor beside the body, the presence of the lunchbox, which was normally kept upstairs during working hours, suggesting that the deceased was probably making his way down the stairs to go home when he met his death. The Inspector asked Archibald to search his father's clothing to establish if anything was missing. He did so and said, *"His wallet and papers are OK."* The police search of the premises led them to conclude that there had been no robbery, no struggle and no signs of intruders having been on the premises. So far as could be ascertained the old man had no quarrel with anyone that might have provoked the attack It was clear that the deceased had had his lunch, upstairs, before setting off to catch the train.

Dr. Lediard carried out a post mortem examination of the body and established that death was due to numerous head injuries and fractures, smashed bones and internal bleeding brought about by two severe blows on the head. In his opinion, the injuries could not have been caused by a fall downstairs, but they could have been sustained by blows from the blunt side of the axe that he had examined at the scene. He estimated the time of death to be not less than ten to twelve hours prior to his examination, which put it back close to the time the son said he last saw his father. Since the old man intended to travel home by train from the Citadel Station, about 15 minutes walk from his workplace, it allowed only twenty-five minutes maximum for a stranger to enter the warehouse, go upstairs, find the axe, follow the old man down the stairs, kill him then escape.

Police Sergeant Seaton, who knew the deceased, saw him and passed the time of day with him in West Walls when he was on his way to work a little after 8am. *"Mr. Norval was very cheerful,"* he said. He saw him again sometime between mid-day and one o'clock when he was in a different temper. *"He snubbed me off,"* said the Sergeant, *"He was very vexed about something."* Two witnesses were traced who saw the son leave the workplace at 1.20pm, ten minutes later than he had told the police and cutting the time available for another assailant to carry out the crime. About that time a railwayman saw him, unusually running, going over Caldew Bridge towards Caldewgate and asked, *"What's up Archie?"* Later in the day, a policeman saw the son on the Sands Fairground at 8.15pm and spoke with him. At 8.30pm, another witness saw him running from the direction of the warehouse along West Walls.

Police enquiries revealed that Archibald had recently visited customers in Scotland collecting from them payment for skins supplied by the family business. It seems he had not paid those monies over to his father. Could that have been the reason that old man Norval was vexed?

On Sunday morning, Detective Inspector Pattinson arrested Archibald Norval on suspicion of murdering his father. He took him to the police station where he interviewed him. *"Alright,"* said the accused, *"I can account for every minute of the day."* He denied that he was responsible for the killing. The DI and PC Rawson (later to be Chief Constable of Swansea Borough and Bradford City Police Forces) took possession of clothing from the prisoner's home address which the constable took to London for forensic examination.

Dr. Wilcox, Home Office Government Analyst found blood on the upper clothing. He travelled to Carlisle and examined the scene of the killing. He found extensive splashing of blood, some thirty to forty drops and concluded that the assailant would be splashed, but only his upper garments, consistent with that on the son's clothing that he had previously examined. He dismissed the prisoner's explanation that the blood was probably from a cut finger, cut when he had been preparing and hanging skins. However, no evidence was produced to identify the blood as that of the deceased man - no DNA in those days! The expert concluded that the blows to the father's head were probably aimed from behind as he descended the stairs.

Archibald Norval was charged with his father's murder and committed for trial. At Cumberland Assizes in Carlisle on 26 January 1915, before Mr. Justice Grantham, the accused pleaded not guilty. The judge and jury visited the crime scene to familiarise themselves with the layout of the premises. After hearing the evidence, the judge told the jury that this was indeed a case of murder, but by whom, he asked. He did not think there was sufficient evidence to say that it was the accused. There might have been the greatest suspicion - the accused was there at about the time of death, he said. *"There was not the slightest suspicion that anyone else had committed the crime, therefore the strongest suspicion was on the accused. But,"* he directed, *"that is not enough to convict."* The jury found Archibald not guilty and he was discharged. The police were not looking for anyone else.

oooOooo

Murder in the corner shop

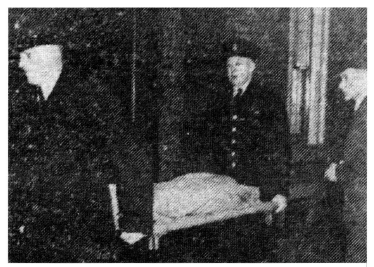

Jane Duckett, a 72 years old spinster, kept a corner shop selling sweets and groceries at the corner of Tait Street and Cecil Street, Carlisle. At mid-day on Sunday, 14 April 1957, a ten year old schoolboy, noticing that, unusually for the time of day, the shop blinds were drawn and the milk was still on the doorstep, drew the matter to the attention of his parents who went to investigate. Peering into the basement through a broken cellar window they saw a body. They called the police. Policewoman Sergeant Thelma Ellis was the first officer on the scene. She found the body of Miss Duckett. There were signs of what were believed to be non-accidental injuries. Faced with a potential protracted major investigation, the Force called in the assistance of Lancashire Constabulary. However, local officers had already begun their enquiries led by Detective Inspector Stanley Blair and a 22-year old man, John Wilson Vickers, living in Aglionby Street, just a short distance from the shop, was questioned. In a search of his lodgings police found a wing mirror stolen from a motor car in a nearby street. He was arrested by Detective Sergeant Stanley Armstrong and charged with the theft of the mirror. That was sufficient reason to hold him in custody whilst enquiries into the murder continued. There was a strong suspicion that Vickers was connected with the killing. Forensic evidence subsequently positively linked Vickers to Miss Duckett's shop and to her murder. He admitted the attack. He said that he kicked in

Top: *A policeman stands guard outside the shop in Tait Street.*

Above: *Constables Val Clark and Shaw Millican remove the body from the murder scene to the mortuary under the watchful eyes of Detective Inspector Stanley Blair.*

a window and entered the shop to look for money but was disturbed as he searched the cellar by the old lady descending the steps and asking *"What's going on here?"* He struck her three or four blows and she fell to the floor. He left her where she fell and went off to search her bedroom. Unable to find any cash he left the premises. He thought Miss Duckett might be unconscious when he left, but, he said, he did not think she was dead *"I am sorry I did this"*, Vickers said, *"I only meant to get some money. I panicked. I had tried before to get into the cellar. I stopped that time and I should have stopped on Sunday night."* He was charged with killing the old lady in the furtherance of theft, a new offence under the recently enacted Homicide Act, 1957. This Act followed a period of suspension of capital punishment while Parliament considered its total abolition. In the event, The Homicide Act did not abolish the death penalty but restricted it to only five categories of murder, including that with which Vickers was charged.

*Miss Jane Duckett,
the murdered shopkeeper.*

On Thursday, 23 May 1957, Vickers was tried at Cumberland Assizes in Carlisle. His counsel asked the jury to bring in a finding of guilt to a charge of manslaughter, (an alternative charge usually contained in a murder indictment). *"The damage inflicted upon Miss Duckett was slight to moderately slight"* he said. (Which planet do these people come from; since when was death considered to be "slight damage?") *"She had moved herself after the attack in an attempt to mount the cellar steps but had died from shock. I ask not for Vickers' liberty, but for his life."* Vickers was found guilty of capital murder, Mr. Justice Hinchcliffe telling him, *"upon evidence which left no room for doubt. The sentence of the Court on you is that you suffer death in the manner authorised by law."*

An appeal against conviction was dismissed by the Court of Appeal on 5 July 1957 but a second appeal, raising a point of law under the new Act, was allowed. This second appeal, before Lord Chief Justice Goddard and four Appeal Judges, was based on the interpretation of the word 'malice' contained in the charge of murder - 'unlawfully and maliciously did kill.' Vickers' counsel argued that the doctrine of 'constructive' malice had been abolished by the new Act and he challenged the trial judge's summing up to the jury when he told them *"there being no 'express' malice, if Vickers caused the injured person grievous bodily harm with intent to do so, and death ensued, that was murder."* The Attorney General submitted that an intention to kill or cause grievous bodily harm would provide the necessary malice to prove murder; equally, knowledge that the action would be likely to result in death or grievous bodily harm was sufficient. The Court upheld the conviction and, dismissing the Appeal, Goddard, LCJ, said there was complete unanimity on the Bench. He rejected an application to further appeal to the House of Lords. The Home Secretary, Mr. R.A.B. Butler, announced that he was unable to find grounds for recommending a reprieve. The Press reported that those Members of Parliament who had favoured abolition of hanging, most of the Labour Party and about thirty Conservatives, were shocked. They had firmly believed that the new Act had effectively abolished hangings. The Howard League for Penal Reform stated, *"The intended execution of John Vickers inevitably underlines the doubtful moral basis of the new Homicide Act. Whatever the legality of hanging a 22-year old youth who did not, in the opinion of the Court, intend to kill, while criminals who deliberately poison or strangle are automatically exempt from the death penalty, ordinary people will find it hard to see the justice behind the law."* The National Council for Civil Liberties asked the Home Secretary to reconsider his decision in view of the fact that the point of law had not been decided by the highest court in the land, the House of Lords. All to no avail. John Vickers was hanged at Durham Jail on 23 July 1957, the first person to be executed under the provisions of the Homicide Act of 1957 and the first killer to be hanged for two years. The Prison Chaplain said, *"He went as if he was looking forward to something. He said he knew he had done wrong and he wanted it this way because he deserved it. He was ready to take his medicine."* The 'stated case', Crown-v-Vickers 1957, thus became the law on the interpretation of the word 'malice'. The arguments as to what its correct interpretation ought to have been raged on for years after the Vickers' case.

A dubious distinction for the City of Carlisle - not only was the first person to be hanged under the Homicide Act a local criminal but so also was the last. John Walby, also known as Gwynn Owen Evans, grew up in the city, was well known to the city police and on record for criminal activity in the town. He was one of the last two persons to be executed in the UK, when, on 13 August 1964, he and Peter Anthony Allen were hanged simultaneously, but in separate prisons, (Evans in Strangeways, Manchester and Allen in Walton, Liverpool) for the murder of John Allen West at Seaton, Workington.

oooOooo

Horrific child murder

At 10.40pm, on Monday, 12 August 1963, Thomas Allen Bell of 22 Charles Street, Carlisle, walked into the police station in Rickergate with his stepson, 23 year-old William James Berwick and reported that his eight-year old daughter, Maureen Bell, was missing from home. (I was on duty in the police station at the time). She had left home with a small puppy belonging to Berwick and was last seen in Close Street shortly before 3pm. Mr. Bell had been at work, returning home after 10pm to find his daughter missing. Likely places where she might be were quickly checked, he said, with negative result, before he set off to inform the police. Details of the child were circulated to patrolmen and to surrounding police forces. It should be noted that there was no motorway around the city in 1963 and that the heavy volume, day and night, of traffic on the busy A6/A7 north/south highway, had to pass through the city centre, amongst other streets, along Botchergate and London Road. The child's home lay just off London Road, and one of the early police fears was that she may have been picked up by a passing motorist. Given that she had been missing for over seven hours, it was considered that by the time the police were informed of her disappearance, she could have been many miles away from the city. There was also serious concern that her disappearance had not been reported earlier. It was most unusual, if not suspicious, for such a young child to be missing so long before alerting the police. From the outset, the enquiry was treated as a potential murder enquiry. Searches and enquiries continued throughout the night without result. Early on Tuesday morning, six hundred people, including Berwick, Civil Defence volunteers and the Territorial Army, joined one hundred police officers to carry out extensive searches throughout the city. Fifty detectives, as well as conducting interviews of family, neighbours and friends, were assisted by the city firemen to enter and search unoccupied properties in the area surrounding Charles Street and Close Street. Policewomen questioned children in the neighbourhood. No trace of the child was found. Just before 6am on Wednesday, 14 August, a resident of Charles Street popped out of his front door to check the time from the large clock on the front of the City General Hospital at the end of the street, before he set off for work. In a lane leading into the rear yard of houses in Charles Street, he saw what he thought might be a body. He dashed to the police pillar in Fusehill Street and reported his discovery. I took that call. I despatched a traffic patrol car and kept the caller in conversation. The patrol car was alongside him within two minutes. He took the constables to the lane where they found the body of the missing child. The lower part of her body was naked and there was evidence of a violent attack. The victim's body and clothing were wet. The paving surrounding it was quite dry. It was almost

219

certainly the case that she had not been murdered in that alleyway and that the body had been dumped there by the killer. Had she been taken from the city as previously considered, murdered elsewhere then the body returned to the area where she was last seen? It was a distinct possibility since many motorists, lorry drivers and others, used the A6 road frequently. There were also many transport lodgings, used by long-distance lorry drivers, in the Charles Street/ London Road area. A full-scale murder hunt began.

Left: *police and firemen search empty houses in the area where Maureen Bell disappeared.*

Right: *PW Sergeant Thelma Ellis and PW Eileen Robinson seeking information from local children.*

Chief Constable Williamson called in mutual aid from the Lancashire Constabulary, the largest force in the North West. It was usual for the City Force and Cumberland and Westmorland Constabulary to seek help from Lancashire rather than from Scotland Yard. The only advantage of having the Yard called in was that, provided they were called within forty-eight hours of a reported murder, the cost of the enquiry would be met from central funds. The Met would, however, have sent a detective chief superintendent and a detective sergeant. Lancashire, on the other hand, would send a full investigation team together with sufficient transport and equipment to meet the demands of the enquiry. Detective Superintendent Harold Prescott arrived in Carlisle with his team and announced, *"Someone in this vicinity is hiding or shielding a sexual maniac."*

A post-mortem examination was carried out on the body by Dr. Stephen Faulds, Home Office and local pathologist at the Cumberland Infirmary in Carlisle. He found bruises to the head and legs, haemorrhages of the brain and concussion caused prior to death. There were bruises on the throat, consistent with being grabbed by fingers and pressure applied, ligature marks on the neck and marks on the back caused by a blow with a sharp instrument, a 5-inch knife, struck downwards. Death was caused by this wound. There was evidence of a serious sexual assault. The pathologist estimated that death occurred sometime between 3pm and 4.30pm on 12 August. Traces of a white powder, flecked green, and birdseed were found on and removed from the body.

Soon after the discovery of the body, William James Berwick, the victim's step-brother, attempted to commit suicide by gassing. He was found and taken to hospital where he recovered. He told detectives that the child had been in his house with the puppy. *"She fell off the couch and the knife blade went into her back,"* he said. His house was searched - it had already been searched soon after Maureen went missing - and a bloodstained mattress

Detective Sergeant Ronnie Rutherford and PC Bobby Robinson escort Berwick from City Police Headquarters after his remand in custody to HM Prison Durham.

220

was found. A packet of a washing powder, Fairy Snow, a new product available only in Carlisle where it was undergoing market trials, was a significant find. A detailed examination revealed loose floorboards in the scullery and when removed, stagnant water in the cavity below. Forensic tests established that the body had lain in that cavity. Traces of charred paper and ash were found both on the body and in the cavity. Traces of Fairy Snow washing powder were found on the body, bedclothes and in the cavity. Berwick continued to deny killing the child. *"Give me the truth drug,"* he demanded. *"All this is a dream. Something tells me I've done something wrong. It was an accident. She fell off the couch onto it. I didn't rape her and I didn't kill her."* He agreed that he had placed the body on the bed and then hid it in the cavity. He said that he didn't know what to do. He contemplated dumping the victim in the River Petteril, but it was daylight and there were too many people about. He concealed the knife in the nearby hospital grounds. He went to bed as usual but got up during the night and carried the body towards the hospital where he intended to leave it, but it slipped from his hands. He heard the sound of someone approaching and in panic went into the alleyway where he left the body. He then made up his mind to kill himself and he wrote a note to his wife.

Despite his denials, Berwick was charged with the murder of his step-sister and appeared at Cumberland Assizes in Carlisle on 3 October 1963. He pleaded not guilty and was represented by Miss Rose Heilbron, QC, one of the country's foremost lawyers. Prosecuting, Mr. Cantley, QC, said *"this was not an accident, it was deliberate murder of this eight year old girl, a case of vile lust leading to an attack on the little girl. Her head injuries were inflicted before death, there was evidence of sexual interference and there were no cuts in her clothing. Had it been an accident,"* he said, *"Berwick could easily have got help; the child's mother was only 120 yards away and the hospital was just at the end of the street."* Miss Heilbron asked Dr. Faulds if the wounds on the neck could have been caused during the post-mortem examination. Was this an attack on the pathologist's skills, an attempt perhaps to discredit his evidence? Mr. Cantley intervened. *"Doctor Faulds, have you kept a record of the number of post-mortems you have performed?"* *"Yes,"* the expert promptly responded, *"Ten thousand in Carlisle, and others when I first started out in Glasgow forty years ago."* *"Then I suppose you know what to look for by now."* The jury found the prisoner's explanation too incredible to be true and found him guilty as charged. He was sentenced to life imprisonment, the only sentence allowed by law.

oooOooo

Being in The Right Place at the Right Time

There follows a story of a dramatic arrest that was carried out near Carlisle in 1995, after the City Police had become part of the Cumbria Force. The criminals involved decided to carry out a robbery at Aspatria on a day when, unfortunately for them, there were probably more armed officers in Cumbria than ever before.

Police Segeant Mark Sindle then of the Northern Tactical Support Group (now retired) tells the dramatic story:

The armed guarding of the Carlisle Crown Court in the case of Michael Austin 1995 was a long complicated operation which put a considerable strain on the resources of Cumbria Police. The officers involved were mainly drawn from the Tactical Support Group and Operational Support, spending long, cold hours on rotation at various points around the Court, with the considerable strain of the safe handling of the weapons. One of the Observation points was the top of the tower of St Georges Church which was reached by ladders lashed together inside the tower – not for the faint hearted! Whilst on observations on the tower it was discovered that at least one of the four steeples was loose and in danger of falling due to the centre rod corroding. All four steeples had then to be removed for safety by crane.

On Thursday 23 February 1995 Michael Austin was found guilty of conspiracy to commit murder and was taken in a high speed convoy of armed police officers to H.M.P. Durham. I was the officer who had been handcuffed to the prisoner during the transfer to Durham Prison. Following what had been several arduous weeks for all the officers concerned, we were all starting to relax a little on the return having handed over the prisoner safely, without incident, and having been thanked by the Chief Inspector in charge of the operation.

Then as we were passing Brampton, some 8 miles east of Carlisle we received information that, following an armed robbery in Aspatria, west of the city, a police officer had been shot and wounded in Carlisle.

The convoy picked up speed and we all regrouped and rearmed at Rosehill, Junc. 43 M6, on the outskirts of the Carlisle. The convoy then star burst to strategic locations. The patrol car I was in was sent to the Golden Fleece, Junc. 42, M6 interchange. On the way we were informed that the red Saab, in which the two wanted suspects were now believed to be travelling, had been seen by the police spotter plane, in the Wetheral area, 4 miles east of Junc. 42.

The scene outside Carlisle's Parkfield Nursery after the shoooting yesterday.

We travelled at high speed through the villages of Scotby and Wetheral. We then received information that the suspects had been seen to stop by the police spotter plane and had high-jacked a grey Nissan car. They were now a short distance ahead of us making for Warwick Bridge village. We were travelling at high speed as we passed the people in a lay by who had had their Nissan car high jacked and who were standing next to the abandoned Saab. They were unaware that we already know what had taken place and they waved frantically as we passed.

I remember thinking that those people were not going to be happy having just been high-jacked and then being passed by a speeding police car that refused to stop.

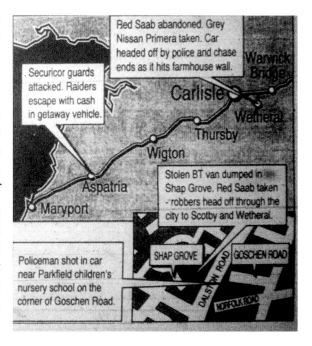

A police contingent was already set up at Warwick Bridge. The grey Nissan car tried to turn into a farmyard just before the village, lost control and crashed into a wall. The suspects then ran from the crashed car and jumped over a wall at the rear of the farm into a very muddy, slurry filled field. We followed them. The suspects were met by the sight of a line of heavily armed police officers walking down the field towards them from the direction of Warwick Bridge. With us behind them, and with more police officers arriving at the farm it must have been a pretty daunting and frightening moment for the suspects. who quickly gave themselves up. They were arrested and placed in police vehicles and taken to Carlisle police station smelling highly of farmyard slurry!

We were elated that the operation had ended so successfully and thankful that our wounded college PC Craig Simth was likely to make a full recovery.

Part Ten - Carlisle's New Police Station

On Thursday, 21 May, 2009, the city's new police station, (to give it its correct title, Northern Division Basic Command Unit Headquarters) built on a commanding site at Durranhill to replace the former Rickergate building, was officially opened by Councillor Reg Watson, OBE, Chairman of Cumbria Police Authority. A light and modern working environment combined with state of the art facilities, the building is a world away from previous police accommodation in the city and has already been identified as a model for police buildings in other parts of the county and country.

Above: *the plaque commemorating the official opening of the new station is displayed in the atrium.*

Right: *the public reception area and enquiry office.*

Above: *the main entrance - revolving doors provide access to the reception area.*

Above right: *this portrait of Sir Robert Peel, the founder of the modern police service, was handed down through generations of his family and presented to Cumbria Police in 1999 by a descendant, Annie Peel, specifically to be displayed in Carlisle Police Station. It hangs in the new public enquiry office.*

Above right: *two pictures of the front aspect of the main building; the station yard and custody suite and staff car park; a view from the ground floor of the atrium.*

Above: *the roof garden , a view from the first floor of the atrium and part of the cell complex in the custody suite.*

And finally, George Carlton

Constable No. 45, Sergeant No.15, Carlisle City Police, later Sergeant in Cumbria Constabulary.

Whenever a former Carlisle City policeman admits to his service in the Force, almost without exception the first question he is asked is, *"Did you know George Carlton?"* It is a question posed by complete strangers and by people not old enough to have known George themselves. Of course we all knew him, it wasn't a big Force and we all knew each other. I knew him long before I joined the Force since my brother, Bill, worked in the same shift group as George. The next question would be, *"Did you work with him?"* Every-one, it seems, is eager to have a first-hand account of experiences with the man who, it seems, achieved almost legendary status. How often we hear the public use the term, *"The police could do with a few George Carltons."*

George Carlton was the first post-war recruit to the Force in June 1946. He became known and respected by everyone in the city. His was a no-nonsense approach to policing and stories of his exploits, some true, some exaggerated and some pure fantasy, abound. If only half of

George, in the uniform of Cumbria Constabulary

the tales were true George would have been matched with Cassius Clay and would have earned more money in the ring than he ever did as a policeman. A Coldstream Guards sergeant who saw much active service during the war and a super-fit athlete and sprinter, he was afraid of no-one, as many of the local *'hard men'* found to their cost. None of them *'pushed their luck'* with George, in fact, nobody trifled with *'Mister Carlton',* as the villains nearly always addressed him, hardly daring the familiarity of using his first name. In short, George Carlton was a good, old-fashioned street patrol bobby, with an aura about him, a bobby who knew all about zero-tolerance policing long before some of the more modern officers re-invented the wheel, and a bobby who did not *'look the other way'* when duty called. Not much crime or disorder took place when he was around. His smart appearance, stature, confidence and reputation commanded respect. But though he attained such elevated status, almost immortality, in the eyes of the public, he really did nothing exceptional to mark him out for such fame. He didn't make any exceptionally newsworthy arrests, nor did he go looking for trouble or fights. He didn't have to. His reputation was sufficient to deter troublemakers. He was no more a maverick than any other. I would say that he wasn't even the hardest cop in the Force. George was a very ordinary man, a family man, a man's man and a policeman's copper, a proud member of the Force, well liked by his colleagues. It was good to know him as a colleague and a friend, and, yes, it was an experience to have him, as a sergeant, accompany you on your bustling city centre beat! George was one of two very experienced constables who showed me around a couple of central beats on my very first duty on the night of 6 June 1959 - an excellent introduction to my police career. Young bobbies saw at first-hand *'respect for the law and for the police'* when they walked out with George.

No history of the Carlisle City Police Force would be complete without mention of George Carlton.

APPENDICES

The following appendices include, in addition to those mentioned elsewhere in this work, details:

(i)   another Carlisle City Police Force - that in Iowa, USA (Appendix 'K'). Remarkably, the motto of the Force is the same as our own - 'Be Just and Fear Not'.

(ii)   a list of former UK police forces (Appendix 'L') that over the years has been reduced to just 43 in England and Wales (that includes just one independent city police force the 'City of London Police') and eight in Scotland.

APPENDIX 'A'   CITIZENS COMMITTEE 1826

Rev. W. Rees	John Dixon	John Forster, Jnr
Henry Pearson, solicitor	Peter Dixon	Thomas Carrick, hatter
G. G. Mounsey, solicitor	William Sowerby	Major Wilde
Silas Saul, solicitor	John Blamire	Mr Longcake
Richard Dixon, solicitor	James Connell	Mr Law
John Blow, solicitor	William Halton	Mr Mounsey
William Dobinson, solicitor	Robert Ashbridge	Mr Lonsdale
Joseph Ferguson, Fisher St	Arthur Graham	

APPENDIX 'B'

8GeoIV, LXXXXVI
[THE CARLISLE POLICE ACT, 1827]

*An Act for Watching, Regulating and Improving the City of Carlisle
and the suburbs thereof, given Royal Assent on 14th June, 1827.*

Section 1.	Mayor, Recorder, Aldermen, resident in the city or within three miles thereof, the Dean and Prebendaries of the Cathedral, together with fifty persons to be elected to be appointed Commissioners of Police for carrying this Act into execution.
Section 2.	No person to be appointed unless he be an occupier of hereditaments [in the city and suburbs] to the clear annual value of £30. No alehouse keeper, innkeeper or victualler or any other person in any way interested or concerned in any contract to be made by virtue of this Act shall be eligible.
Section 3.	Every male person over 21 being in occupation of hereditaments computed at the annual value of £10 shall be eligible to vote at the elections of Commissioners.
Section 4.	Fifty Commissioners of Police to be appointed along with the Mayor, Recorder, Aldermen, Dean and Prebendaries; [16 for Parish of St. Cuthberts Without, 16 for St. Marys Within, 6 for Botchergate, 6 for Rickergate and 6 for Caldewgate].
Section 5.	Fifty Commissioners are to be chosen on the first Thursday in June in every third year following.
Section 7.	Any unqualified person acting as Commissioner to forfeit £40 plus expenses.
Section 8.	Every Commissioner is to swear an oath that he will truly and impartially execute and perform all and every the powers and authority reposed in him under the Act.
Section 9.	The Commissioners are to meet on the last Thursday in June, 1827, to put this Act into execution - at least nine are to be present at meetings.
Section 11.	The Clerk to keep a record of meetings.
Section 12 & 13.	Commissioners' powers and procedures for appointing or dismissing Treasurer and Clerk.
Section 14.	Accounts Books may be inspected by any Commissioner, ratepayer or creditor - Clerk to forfeit £5 for any / each refusal.
Section 15.	Officers are accountable for all matters and all monies on pain of imprisonment for neglect or refusal.
Section 16.	Clerk not to be appointed Treasurer [nor his partner, nor anyone in his employ].
Section 17.	Clerk/Treasurer not to be involved in the prosecution of offenders, but Clerk may also be Clerk to the Justices.
Section 18.	Offence to accept rewards or emoluments.
Section 21.	The Commissioners are empowered to appoint such a number of able-bodied men to be employed as watchmen or patrols, either on foot or on horseback, or as beadles to act as well as for the day as for the night as the Commissioners shall judge necessary. Every watchman, patrol or beadle who shall be guilty of neglect or disobedience shall forfeit any sum not exceeding forty shillings. The Commissioners shall from time to time make orders and regulations for the conduct of the watchmen, etc., and grant rewards or allowances to them, or to any persons assisting them, who may be disabled or hurt in the execution of their duty.

228

Section 22.	Such watchmen shall have the powers to prevent fires and to keep watch and ward …. and to apprehend all felons, malefactors, rogues, vagabonds, vagrants, idle and disorderly persons, disturbers of the public peace, prostitutes, nightwalkers and others who shall be found wandering and misbehaving themselves, and any one Justice shall have the power to commit them to gaol for any time not exceeding two months, or otherwise commit or hold them to bail to be tried in the ordinary course of the law.
Section 23.	The day beadles shall patrol the streets and public places during the hours and times appointed by the Commissioners and apprehend all drunken, riotous and disorderly persons, or persons causing any nuisance, defacing the walls or wilfully obstructing the free passage of any of the said streets or ways, beating and shaking carpets at any time after nine in the morning, playing at any game, setting dogs to fight, or by any other means disturbing good order or the public peace.
Section 24.	All such Watchmen, Patrols or Beadles and also the Superintendent or Superintendents shall be sworn in as constables before they begin to act.
Section 25.	Any victualler, alehouse keeper or other persons selling liquors by retail who may be convicted of harbouring any watchman, patrol or beadle shall forfeit any sum not exceeding forty shillings.
Section 26.	Commissioners shall appoint a certain of their number to a Watch Committee, to manage, suspend or appoint watchmen, patrols or beadles, and they may appoint a superintendent or superintendents.
Section 27.	Watchmen, patrols or beadles who are guilty of neglect or misconduct in the execution of their duty are liable to be prosecuted and imprisoned and kept to hard labour for any time not exceeding three months.
Section 28.	Anyone who assaults or obstructs a watchman, patrol or beadle is liable to a penalty not exceeding forty shillings AND imprisonment with hard labour for any time not exceeding three months.
Section 29 & 30.	List of nuisances / offences [Byelaws]. Fine of £5. Power of arrest found committing.
Section 31.	Mayor to remain Clerk to the Markets.
Section 32.	Public Health nuisances and powers of Commissioners to take action.
Section 33.	Commissioners to provide fire engines in case of fire and to water the roads.
Section 34.	Police watchboxes are property of the Commissioners.
Section 35 & 36.	Powers to hire or to purchase buildings or rooms for a police office - also conveyances.
Section 37 & 38.	Names of streets and numbers of houses to be marked. Offence for anyone to deface them.
Section 39.	Commissioners' powers in relation to spouts, etc, dripping water onto footpaths.
Section 40.	The Commissioners are empowered to raise money for defraying the expenses of obtaining and executing this Act by an assessment on the inhabitants at a rate not exceeding one shilling in the pound upon the rack-rent or value of the premises which they respectively occupy.
Section 41.	The rates are to be signed by so many of the Commissioners as are competent to transact business at meetings under this Act [9] and shall be allowed and confirmed by two Justices of the Peace for the County.
Section 42.	The Collectors of the Police Rate are to be, from time to time, appointed respectively by the several parishes for which they act.
Section 43.	Such Collectors are to be allowed three pence in the pound on all such sums they collect.
Section 44.	Any person as Any person assessed refusing to pay the assessment for seven days after it has been demanded may be distrained on the warrant of any Justice, or Justices, of the Peace for the County.
Section 45.	If such rates are not paid by persons before quitting their houses, and shall not be paid for seven days after demanded at their usual place of abode, they should be liable to distress as at Section 44, such defaulter having been previously summoned before a Justice or Justices of the Peace for the County.
Section 46.	The rates are to be apportioned on persons quitting any houses according to the time they have occupied them.

Section 47.	The Landlord, or any occupier, may be rated for houses let in separate apartments and for houses let for less than ten pounds per year.
Section 48.	It shall be competent for the Commissioners to mitigate or remit the Police Rate in any cases of poverty or inability to pay, but upon proof of any goods having been conveyed away to avoid distress, one or more of the Justices of the Peace for the County may commit the offenders to gaol, to remain at hard labour without bail or mainprize, for any period not exceeding three months.
Section 49 & 50.	Empowered the Commissioners to borrow up to £500 for the purposes of the Act.
Section 51.	All monies raised by virtue of this Act shall be vested in the Commissioners, to be by them applied in defraying the expenses of obtaining this Act, and all other charges incidental to the execution of this Act, and for no other purpose whatever.
Section 52.	Persons summonsed as witnesses who refuse to give evidence - Fine £5
Section 53 & 58.	Justices powers to enforce penalties, recover costs and damages; court procedures.
Section 59.	Appeals, if brought within four calendar months, will lie before the General or Quarter Sessions.
Section 67 & 68.	Nothing herein contained shall extend, alter, lessen or abridge any of the rights, privileges or immunities of the Dean and Chapter, nor release the Corporation from their liability as before the passing of this Act for the expense of protecting the Peace of the City, and finding an adequate number of civil officers for watching and otherwise regulating the same.
Section 69.	The Commissioners have the power to offer rewards for the detection of offenders.
Section 70.	The rights of the City Corporation are reserved in the same manner as those of the Dean and Chapter.

APPENDIX 'C ' - POLICE COMMISSIONERS (1827)

CALDEWGATE
John Blow, Scotch Street, solicitor
John Creighton, Willow Holme, dyer
Arthur Graham, Caldewgate, brewer
Rev. Samuel Hudson, Abbey Street
Edward James, Scotch Street, ironmonger
Edward Routledge, Scotch Street, hatter

RICKERGATE
John Andrew, Rickergate, wine merchant
John Cartmell, Damside, tanner
John Hetherington, Damside, tanner
Rev. Joseph Marshall, Spring Gardens
Thomas Ramsay, Castle Street, druggist
Edward Rowland, Eden Street, gentleman
Thomas Stordy, George Street, currier

ST. CUTHBERT'S WITHOUT
Robert Ashbridge, English Street, grocer
John Beck, English Street, Draper
Thomas Carrick, English Street, hat manufacturer
William Carrick, Lowther Street, gentleman
John Connell, Scotch Street, saddler
Dr. Elliott, English Street
Dr. Heysham, St. Cuthberts Lane
Thomas Hunton, The Crescent, manufacturer
William Jackson, English Street, fishmonger
William Martindale, English Street, druggist
Daniel Pattinson, Damside, brewer
Joseph Railton, Scotch Street, draper
William Robinson, English Street, solicitor
Charles Thurnam, English Street, bookseller
Thomas Wyllie, English Street, flax dresser

BOTCHERGATE
John Blow, Scotch Street, solicitor
David Carrick, Scotch Street, banker
William Dalston, Botchergate, ironfounder
William Graham, Botchergate, farmer
Thomas Halton, English Street, brewer
John Slater, Cotton Mill

The result for **ST. MARY'S WITHIN** was announced at a later date, the successful candidates being:
Robert Backhouse
John Blamire
Ellwood Brockbank
John Cockburn
James Connell
Joseph Ferguson
John Fowler
Gustavus Gale
Richard Law
G.G.Mounsey, solicitor
G.S. Mounsey
Henry Pearson
George Saul
Silas Saul, solicitor
George Waugh
John Wilson

APPENDIX 'D' FIRST CORPORATION WATCH COMMITTEE, JULY 1827

Dr. John HEYSHAM, St. Cuthberts Lane
Rev Samuel HUDSON, Abbey Street
Messrs. Silas SAUL, Solicitor
George WAUGH
Joseph FERGUSON
John COCKBURN
James CONNELL
John CONNELL, Saddler, Scotch Street
John BLOW, Solicitor, Scotch Street
Henry PEARSON, Solicitor
John ANDREW, Wine Merchant, Rickergate
John BLAMIRE,

APPENDIX 'E' - FIRST POLICE OFFICERS (1827)

Superintendent and Chief Officer Benjamin Batty

(The twenty-one 'stout men')

George BLAIR	Edward HEWARD	John RIGG
Samuel BROMFIELD	John HEWSON	James SIDDON
William CORRIGHAM	Robert HOWE	John SOWERBY
James DUNGLINSON	William MAINE	Robert STORROW
Robert GIBSON	John NICHOLSON	William SUNDERLAND
John GRAHAM	Joseph NIXSON	Robert WALKER
Michael HENDERSON	James RIGG	John WRIGHT

APPENDIX 'F' - CHIEF CONSTABLES

Chief officer	From	To	Previous Force	Reason for Leaving	Subsequent Appointment
BATTY	03.02.1827	09.03.1831	Manor of Manchester [Beadle]	Dismissed	Manor of Manchester [Beadle]
BROWN	10.03.1831	16.10.1839	None [Prison Service]	Resigned	
GRAHAM	17.10.1839	26.09.1844	London Metropolitan, Liverpool City	Resigned	
SABBAGE	27.09.1844	21.01.1857	London Metropolitan	Transferred	Superintendent [Ch.Con] Newcastle City
BENT	22.01.1857	17.07.1873	London Metropolitan	Ill-health [died 03.08.1873]	
HEMINGWAY	21.08.1873	03.08.1876	Birkenhead Borough	Transferred	Ch.Con. Cardiff City
MacKAY	19.08.1876	11.08.1904	London Metropolitan Midlothian and Linlithgow	Retired	
HILL	12.08.1904	07.01.1913	Edinburgh City and Kilmarnock [Ch.Con]	Compulsorily retired by the Watch Committee	Ch. Con. Edmonton City, Ch. Con.Assimiboia Municipality, Winnipeg, both in Canada
ECKFORD [Superintendent	08.01.1913	01.05.1913	Lanarkshire [PC]	[Acting Chief Constable only]	
DeSCHMID [SPENCE]	02.05.1913	30.11.1928	Nottingham City, Devon County, Exeter City [Ch.Con]	Retired	
WILSON	01.12.1928	30.11.1929	Cardiff City	Transferred	Ch. Con. Plymouth City Ch. Con. Liverpool City
JOHNSTON	01.12.1929	31.08.1938	Newcastle City	Ill-health	
LAKEMAN	01.09.1938	15.11.1961	Plymouth City	Retired	
WILLIAMSON	16.11.1961	31.03.1967	Manchester City	Amalgamation	Ch.Con. Cumberland, Westmorland & Carlisle, Ch. Con. Cumbria, HM Inspector of Constabulary [Crime]

APPENDIX 'G' - CITY POLICING, 1 JANUARY, 1836

(upon the implementation of the Municipal Corporations Act, 1835)

FIRST WATCH COMMITTEE

Robert Bendle	Thomas C Heysham
Richard Brown	Thomas Hunton
Alexander Cockburn	Richard Pattinson
James Connell	William Richardson
James Connell*	Thomas Scarrow
George Dixon	William Sowerby
William Harvey	William Weir
John Hetherington	

OFFICERS OF THE COMMITTEE

Chairman	George Gill Mounsey, Mayor
Clerk	James Willoughby
Treasurer	The City Treasurer

* NB. Two gentlemen named James Connell are listed in official records. This is probably an error. Amongst the former Police Commissioners were a James and a John Connell.

POLICE OFFICERS

Superintendent and Chief Officer: Robert Brown.
Night Constable and Deputy Chief Officer: Jonathan Fisher (wef. 18 February 1836).

Day Constables: John Bird and Thomas Russell.

Night patrol:

Richard Barnfather	Andrew Holliday
Thomas Cail	John Irving
Edward Ewart	George Laird
John Foster	David Robinson
George Graham	Robert Robinson
John Hewson	Robert Storrow

John Hewson and Robert Storrow are the only positively identified survivors from the original (1827) police. However, in those far off times, it was not unusual for names to be erroneously recorded. It is therefore possible that Edward Ewart and George Graham were the Edward Heward the John Graham of 1827,

At the time of amalgamation in 1967, the establishment of the force had grown to 149 officers, an increase of just 133 over a period of 140 years, (less than one officer per annum).

ESTIMATED ANNUAL EXPENDITURE, 1836

One Superintendent	£1.10s.0d (£1.50) per week	£78.0s.0d (£78.00)
One Night-Constable	£1.1s.0d (£1.05) per week	£54.12s.0d (£54.60p)
Two day-men	16shillings (80p) per week each	£83.4s.0d (£83.20p)
Twelve night patrolmen	13 shillings (65p) per week each	£405.12s.0d (£405.60p)
Clothing		£30.0s.0d (£30.00)
Rent for Police Office		£40.0s.0d (£40.00)
Taxes		£5.0s.0d (£5.00)
Clerk and incidentals		£80.0s.0d (£80.00)
Total		£776.8s.0d (£776.40) (£14.93 per week)

APPENDIX 'H' - RULES AND REGULATIONS 1844

Rules and Regulations.

1.   To enable police officers to discharge their duties efficiently, and to prevent mistakes and blunders, it is necessary that they should make themselves well acquainted with the inhabitants of the town and their respective businesses and callings; and that they should be sober, steady and attentive in their conduct; civil and respectful in their demeanour; and cleanly and orderly in their appearance. They should at all times endeavour to possess a perfect command of temper, not allowing themselves to be irritated into a display of passion by threats or abuse, or ill language; and to discharge their duty in a quiet but determined manner avoiding violence and unnecessary harshness to persons in their custody. By such conduct they will at all times be able to secure the aid of well disposed persons who may happen to be present and obtain the confidence and respect of their employers.

2.   No officer shall be suffered to remain on the police establishment who is found intoxicated while on duty.

3.   Officers when on duty are strictly cautioned against stopping to talk together when they meet on their beats; they are merely to exchange a word and pass on; they are also strictly forbidden to enter into conversation with other persons on the street, except on matters relative to their duty. Disobedience to these orders will be punished.

4.   They are strictly forbidden to carry sticks or umbrellas in their hands when on duty.

5.   The particular attention of officers is called to the fact that the greater number of robberies are effected by entering from Backyards, Gardens, Areas and through uninhabited houses to the premises intended to be robbed, and they are directed to examine all such places in their respective beats with the utmost care and vigilance to satisfy themselves that persons are not therein concealed waiting the opportunity to carry their unlawful designs into effect.

6.   Each officer should see every part of his beat in the time allowed and he will be expected to do so regularly so that persons requiring the assistance of an officer may, by remaining in one spot for a certain time, be sure of meeting with one.

7.   The regularity of moving through his beat shall not however prevent his remaining at any particular place where his presence may be necessary in order to observe the conduct of any suspected person or for any other good reason, but he will be required to satisfy his sergeant or superior officer that there was sufficient cause for any delay or irregularity in keeping time which may thus arise, and he must attend at the appointed time to make a report to his sergeant of anything requiring notice.

8.   Officers are not to refuse to give their assistance for the protection of persons or property near their own beats if called upon in any case requiring immediate attention, but the officer is always to return as soon as possible to his own beat.

9.   Officers are not to go into public houses at night to order the Landlord to close their houses or interfere in any other manner with the management or regulation of the House, but if disorderly conduct is observed in any Public House a notice is to be given to the Sergeant who will report the case to the proper authorities.

10.   Any officer reported for endeavouring to conceal his number or refusing to shew or tell it when properly asked, will be punished. The officer who is doing his duty with propriety can have no good reason for concealment.

11.   Should it be proved against any officer that he had been guilty of receiving drink or money from any person who has been brought by him before the Magistrates upon any charge, he will be considered wholly unfit for his situation as a police officer.

12.   Every officer to keep and deliver up his clothing in a proper state of repair.

13.   The clothing to be inspected weekly by the Superintendent who is empowered to order such repairs as he may think necessary at the expense of the officer.

14.   Whenever any officer of the establishment shall have to attend at any place other than Carlisle as a witness, he must give a detailed account of his expenses and a statement of the sum received by him for attendance.

15.   Officers of this establishment are forbidden to communicate with any Attorney relative to persons in custody charged with Felony unless directed so to do by the examining Magistrate, or at the request of the prisoner, on pain of dismissal.

16.   Previous to any article being obtained for the use of the Police Office, an order for the same signed by the Chairman, one of the Inspectors for the week, or the Chairman of a sub-committee must be obtained. Officers are directed not to apply to any other member of the Watch Committee than those named for their signature to orders.

17.   Every officer to be furnished with a copy of these Rules and Regulations and to produce it once a week and the whole to be read over monthly in the presence of the Superintendent.

For a first offence, the Superintendent would impose a fine of 2/6d [12½d], the same for a second offence but only if the defaulter's character as a police officer was good, otherwise to be reported to the Watch Committee; five shillings [25p] for a third offence and cautioned if of good character, and, finally, for a fourth offence, whatever his character, to be reported to the Watch Committee.

APPENDIX ' I ' - THE LAST CITY POLICE OFFICERS

Serving on 31 August 1963 - last to hold Carlisle City Police warrant cards and shoulder numbers

CHIEF CONSTABLE
Frank Williamson

**SUPERINTENDENT and DEPUTY
CHIEF CONSTABLE**
Clarence Sutcliffe

CHIEF INSPECTORS
Donald Roy [CID]
Stanley Blair

INSPECTORS
Stanley Armstrong [CID]
Arnold Coulthard [Traffic]
John Bushby
Harold Simons
Harold Robinson
George Beck
Tom Farmer
Bob Dewsnap
[District Police Training Centre, Bruche,
Warrington]

	Sergeants
1.	Joe Tinnion [Chief Clerk]
2.	Alec Gelley
3.	Jimmy Hetherington
4.	Arnold Middleton
5.	John Brown [?]
6.	Ronnie Rutherford
7.	John Walker [Traffic]
8.	Eddie Mason
9.	Clarry 'Dusty' Smith
10.	Tommy 'Doctor' Dawes
11.	Dick Cowen
12.	John Aird
13.	Tommy Bowerbank
14.	Bob Wilkinson
15.	George Carlton
16.	George Kerr
17	Ian Shannon
18.	Jim Kerr

	Constables
19.	Charlie Stevens
20.	Stan Brown [Traffic}
21.	John Lennox [Traffic]
22.	Vacant
23.	Norman Robinson [CID]
24.	Lyall Milton
25.	John Sharp
26.	Bill Wilkie
27.	George Townsend
28.	Alec McCall
29.	Peter Ullyart [Traffic]
30.	Keith Goodman [Traffic]
31.	Howard Nixon
32.	Mike Thomas [CID - SoCO]
33.	George Russell [Traffic]
34.	Jimmy Dunn [Jnr}

35.	George Dalton
36.	Gordon Coupe
37.	Bobby Taylor
38.	Sid Monk
39.	Billy Mitchell
40.	Harold Armstrong [Traffic]
41.	Jim Crawford
42.	Kenny Darling
43.	Jimmy Dunn Snr. [CID]
44.	Roger Milburn [CID]
45.	Bob Wilson
46.	Chris Gibbons [Enquiry Office]
47.	Dennis Mattinson
48.	Jim Johnston
49.	Tom 'Nobby' Clark
50.	Lenny Hodgson
51.	David Pullen [Traffic]
52.	Raymond Follows [CID]
53.	Bob Postlethwaite
54.	Laurie Inglis [CID - SoCO]
55.	Bob Foster [Traffic]
56.	Irving Lyon [Traffic]
57.	Alec Archibald
58.	Jimmy Preston [CID]
59.	Joe Richardson [Traffic]
60.	John Howarth
61.	Dennis Graham
62.	Bob Sloan [CID - SoCO]
63.	Brian Tingey
64.	Con Allen
65.	Alec Bremner
66.	John Bardgett
67.	Val Clarke [Traffic]
68.	Andy Lowrie
69.	Bill Little
70.	Sid Peel
71.	Vic Humphries
72.	Arthur Adamson
73.	Brian Firth
74.	Frank McCormick
75.	Harry Kennedy [Inf.Room]
76.	Ian Scott
77.	Bob Lowther [CID]
78.	John Singleton-Browne [Traffic]
79.	Ken Grainger [CID Clerk]
80.	John Wilkinson
81.	Brian Deane
82.	Bobby Robinson
83.	Jack Watmuff
84.	Brian Patterson
85.	Ian Kitchen
86.	Brian Henderson [Traffic]
87.	Bill Kennedy
88.	Drew Graham

89.	Arthur Ferry [Enquiry Office]
90.	Billy Davidson
91.	Peter Firth
92.	Eddie Day
93.	Les Brown
94.	Andy Rutherford [CID]
95.	Brian Watson [Admin]
96.	Billy Orr
97.	Billy Rogerson
98.	Ted Wilkinson
99.	Derek Graham
100.	Martin MacAlindon
101.	Goff Metcalfe
102.	Eric Rice
103.	Roy Wadeson
104.	Gerry 'Slim' Congreve
105.	Spencer Stockdale [Dog]
106	Howard Long
107.	Jim Keenan
108.	Jack Caird [Coroner's Officer]
109.	Ian Dobbie
110.	Brian Dunn
111.	Sandy Ruddick
112.	Eddie Lloyd
113.	Mike Coleman
114.	Dave Beverage
115.	Alan Shields
116.	Mike Newstead
117.	Peter Bradley
118.	Dave Fordy
119.	Gordon Kendal
120.	Peter O'Donnell
121.	John Winthrop
122.	Andy Pretswell
123.	Tom Atkinson

	Policewomen
1.	Thelma Ellis [Sergeant]
2.	Merle Dixon
3.	Jennifer Watson
4.	Yvonne Harvey
5.	Eileen Robinson
6.	Elizabeth Campbell

The Watch Committee introduced new rules for its governance of the Force, including:

* Two Inspectors to be appointed on rota from all members.
* Inspectors to attend the Police Office at 10am every day to examine reports and books.
* Inspectors to have the power to suspend any policeman guilty of a breach of duty until the next Watch Committee meeting.
* Inspectors may order summonses to be issued in respect of Bye-law offences.
* Vacancies in the Force to remain until one week has elapsed. No promises of support for individuals to be given by any member until all applications have been fully examined. Appointments to the Force to be by the votes of the majority, including the casting vote of the Chairman.
* When it is necessary to examine [formally question] an officer, it will be by the Chairman in the first instance; no other member will be allowed to speak until the Chairman is finished. Reprimands and/or verbal instructions to come from the Chairman only.

APPENDIX 'J' - FORCE VEHICLES

Date acquired	Date of disposal	Vehicle	Regd Number	Cost £	Sold £
		Black Maria motor van	HH 247		£3/10/-
Nov 1935	1939	MG Magnette		£345	
Dec 1937		Triumph 16		£313	
1939	Feb 1952	Wolseley	FKF 522		£240
1941	Feb 1951	M/cycle	CAO 762		nil
1941	June 1953	Rudge M/cycle	AHH 50		?
1941	Feb 1951	M/cycle	BHH 748		nil
1941		M/cycle			?
		Austin [CID]	BHH 549		
	Feb 1952	Morris van [GP]	CS 4353		£60
Dec 1947	Oct 1952	Humber Hawk	CHH 833	£914	£406
Dec 1947	Oct 1952	Humber Hawk	CHH 834	£914	£325
Aug 1950	1959	Bedford 10cwt van [GP]	EHH 141	£407	£100
Nov 1951	1958	Vauxhall Velox	FHH	£849	
	1958	Vauxhall Velox	FHH		
June 1953	April 1960	Austin A40 [CID]	FHH 855	£673	£255
June 1957	April 1962	BSA 250cc m/cycle [Beat work]		£160	
June 1957	April 1962	BSA 250cc m/cycle [Beat work]		£160	
1959		Ford Thames 10cwt van [GP]	OHH	£485	
1958	April 1960	Morris Isis	JHH 170		£310
1958		Austin Westminster	KHH 484		
April 1960	April 1962	Ford Zephyr 6	THH 92	£869	£515
April 1960	April 1962	Ford Zephyr 6	THH 93	£869	£515
April 1960	April 1962	Ford Anglia [CID]	THH 94		£515
April 1960	April 1962	Ford Prefect [CID]	RHH 467	£616	£355
April 1962	1964	Morris Minor Traveller [CID]	VHH409	£782	
April 1962	1964	Morris Oxford	VHH410	£954	
April 1962	1964	Morris Oxford [CID]	VHH411	£954	
April 1962	1964	Morris Oxford	VHH412	£954	
1963?		Austin A35 van {SoCO]			
1963?	1965	Morris ambulance [Coroner's Officer]			
June 1963		Austin J4 van [patrol]	YHH 8	£570	
June 1963		Triumph 650 Speed Twin m/cycle	XHH 956	£286	
June 1963		Triumph 650 Speed Twin m/cycle	XHH 957	£286	

POLICE DEPARTMENT

**Chief of Police
Jason Doll**

DEPARTMENT MOTTO

The department motto, **"Be Just and Fear Not"**, symbolizes the department's values on how we respond to our citizens of Carlisle. Ethics and Integrity are our core value the Carlisle Police Department and it's employees. The mission of the Carlisle Police Department is to serve the community and provide safety and improve the quality of life while we strive for excellence.

"Fairness, equality, justice, and the highest standards of ethics are our guiding principles in executing our duties and obligations." - Jason Doll

"Respect from the public cannot be bought, it can only be earned." - Jason Doll

OUR VALUES

LOYALTY
We care about the people and the communities we serve.
We are proud of the Department and the services we provide.
We serve with pride and devotion to keep the community safe.

INTEGRITY
We respect the rights and dignity of all people.
We are committed to honesty and ethical behavior in all our actions.
We accept individual responsibility and accountability for our actions and decisions.
We maintain the trust of the community through honesty, compassion and fairness.

FAIRNESS
We are dedicated to protecting the rights of all people.
We believe all people deserve impartial and effective service from the Department.
We are committed to fairness, strength, respect, and compassion with the people we serve.

EXCELLENCE

We are committed to excellence in the service we provide.
We committed to the highest standards of personal and professional conduct.
We are committed to excellence in our personal performance and professionalism.

HISTORY OF THE
CARLISLE POLICE DEPARTMENT PATCH

The Carlisle Police Department (Carlisle, Iowa, United States of America) patch was researched and designed in 1986.

The community name, "Carlisle," was used as the central theme for the design because a police department is, and should be, a direct reflection of the community it represents. The investigation revealed origin of the city's name was traced back to descendants from Carlisle, UK who named their new home after the one they had left.

The Library of Congress in the United States returned search results that traced the name "Carlisle" back to its origin in the UK as being the name of the Carlisle family. The search results included a picture of the Carlisle family coat of arms with a shield under which was a banner bearing the motto:

"BE JUST AND FEAR NOT."

The Carlisle Police Department adopted this motto on the patch. The motto, "Be Just and Fear Not" admonishes the officers of the department to always "Be Just" in the exercise of their authority and in their dealings with the people that they are sworn to serve, and from whom that authority is derived. The motto, which dates back to medieval times, is a "double edged sword" that also reminds the public that should they "Be Just" in their dealings with their fellow man, they should "Fear Not" the police department.

The patch was designed with only black, gray, and white and was intended to look sharp and professional on the uniform.
The symbolism of the patch has meaning.

Five Stars: The five stars represent the officers and their five start work ethics.

1851: This is the year the town of Carlisle, Warren County, Iowa, was established by its founder Jeremiah Church after a flood had wiped out the previous settlement of Dudley, Iowa, east of now present Carlisle.

Shield: The shield is divided into quadrants representing time in the life of the community.

The white upper quadrant represents the good times in the community's past. It represents the commitment to family, friendship, and faith that contributed to the growth and success of the community. These are the desire for the community and the department's firm commitment to maintain it.

The dark upper quadrant represents the dark and difficult times of the community's past. It represents not only the hardships, struggle and losses of the frontier community but also the strength and commitment that as been required to insure it's survival through time.

The lower white corner represents the good times ahead and the future of the community as long as we remain committed to those values upon which the community was built.

The lower dark quadrant is a reminder that difficult times may lay ahead and that our strength and commitment may be needed again to see the community through and insure it's continuation.

Olive Branch: The olive branch is the symbol of peace and represents the peace that we desire for the community and the department's firm commitment to maintain it.

APPENDIX 'L' FORMER UK POLICE FORCES
Information from the website of Wikipedia

There are currently over 50 police forces operating in the United Kingdom. See List of police forces in the United Kingdom for these. The following forces are no longer in existence:

Former England and Wales forces
Cumberland Constabulary and Westmorland Constabulary merged very early

Abolished before 1946
Abingdon Borough Police, to Berkshire
Andover Borough Police (1846, to Hampshire)
Banbury Borough Police, to Oxfordshire
Barnstaple Borough Police (1921, to Devon)
Basingstoke Borough Police (1889, to Hampshire)
Berwick upon Tweed Police (1921, to Northumberland)
Bideford Borough Police (1889, to Devon)
Bodmin Borough Police (1865, to Cornwall)
Bradninch Borough Police (1865, to Devon)
Buckingham Borough Police, to Buckinghamshire
Chipping Norton Borough Police, to Oxfordshire
Deal Borough Police (1889, to Kent)
Devonport Borough Police (1914, to Plymouth)
Dover Borough Police (1943, to Kent)
Falmouth Borough Police (1889, to Cornwall)
Faversham Borough Police (1889, to Kent)
Folkestone Borough Police (1943, to Kent)
Helston Borough Police (1889, to Cornwall)
Henley Borough Police, to Oxfordshire
Hertford Borough Police (1889, to Hertfordshire)
Hanley Borough Police (1910, to Stoke-on-Trent Borough Police)
Honiton Borough Police; (to Devon County)
Hythe Borough Police (1889, to Kent)
Isles of Scilly Police (1947, to Cornwall)
Launceston Borough Police (1883, to Cornwall)
Liskeard Borough Police (1877, to Cornwall)
Lymington Borough Police (1852, to Hampshire)
Maidstone Borough Police (1943, to Kent)
Maidenhead Borough Police, to Berkshire
Margate Borough Police (1943, to Kent)
Monmouth Borough Police (1881, to Monmouthshire)
Newbury Borough Police (1875, to Berkshire)
Newport Borough Police (1890, to Isle of Wight)
Okehampton Borough Police (1860, to Devon)
Penryn Borough Police (1889, to Cornwall)
Ramsgate Borough Police (1943, to Kent)
Rochester City Police (1943, to Kent)
Romsey Borough Police (1865, to Hampshire)
Ryde Borough Police (1922, to Isle of Wight)
Sandwich Borough Police (1889, to Kent)
South Molton Borough Police (1877, to Devon)
Stratford-upon-Avon Borough Police (1889, to Warwickshire)
Stonehouse District Police (1914)
St Ives Borough Police (1889, to Hertfordshire)
Tavistock Borough Police (1856, to Devon)
Tenterden Borough Police (1889, to Kent)
Tiverton Borough Police (1943, to Devon)
Torrington Borough Police (1870,
             then again from 1878-1886, to Devon)
Torquay Borough Police (1870, to Devon)
Totnes Borough Police (1884, to Devon)
Tunbridge Wells Police Force (1943, to Kent)
Truro City Police (1921, to Cornwall)
Wallingford Borough Police, to Berkshire
Wantage Borough Police, to Berkshire
Warwick Borough Police (1875, to Warwickshire)
Winchester City Police (1942, to Hampshire Joint)

Wolborough Borough Police (1859)

Abolished under the Police Act 1946

Non-county borough forces

Accrington Borough Police; to Lancashire Constabulary
Ashton-under-Lyne Borough Police; to Lancashire Constabulary
Bacup Borough Police; to Lancashire Constabulary
Bedford Borough Police; to Bedfordshire Constabulary
Boston Borough Police; to Lincolnshire Constabulary
Carmarthen Borough Police; to Carmarthenshire Constabulary
Chepping Wycombe Borough Police; to Buckinghamshire Constabulary
Chesterfield Borough Police; to Derbyshire Constabulary
Clitheroe Borough Police; to Lancashire Constabulary
Colchester Borough Police; to Essex Constabulary
Congleton Borough Police; to Cheshire Constabulary
Glossop Borough Police; to Derbyshire Constabulary
Grantham Borough Police; to Lincolnshire Constabulary
Hartlepool Borough Police; to Durham Constabulary
Hereford Borough Police; to Herefordshire Constabulary
Hyde Borough Police; to Cheshire Constabulary
Kendal Borough Police; to Cumberland and Westmorland Constabulary
Kidderminster Borough Police; to Worcestershire Constabulary
King's Lynn Borough Police; to Norfolk Constabulary
Lancaster Borough Police; to Lancashire Constabulary
Leamington Spa Borough Police; to Warwickshire Constabulary
Luton Borough Police; to Bedfordshire Constabulary
Macclesfield Borough Police; to Cheshire Constabulary
Neath Borough Police; to Glamorgan Constabulary
Newark Borough Police; to Nottinghamshire Constabulary
Newcastle-under-Lyme Borough Police; to Staffordshire Constabulary
Peterborough City Police; to Peterborough Combined Police Force
Penzance Borough Police; to Cornwall County Constabulary
St. Albans City Police; to Hertfordshire Constabulary
Scarborough Borough Police; to North Riding Constabulary
Shrewsbury Borough Police; to Shropshire Constabulary
Stalybridge Borough Police; to Cheshire Constabulary
Windsor Borough Police; to Berkshire Constabulary

County borough forces

Chester City Police; to Cheshire Constabulary
Canterbury City Police; to Kent Constabulary

County forces

Anglesey Constabulary; to Gwynedd Constabulary
Breconshire Constabulary; to Mid Wales Constabulary
Caernarvonshire Constabulary; to Gwynedd Constabulary
Cardiganshire Constabulary; to Mid Wales Constabulary
Carmarthenshire Constabulary; to Mid Wales Constabulary
Isle of Wight Constabulary; to Hampshire Constabulary
Merionethshire Constabulary; to Gwynedd Constabulary
Montgomeryshire Constabulary; to Mid Wales Constabulary

Radnorshire Constabulary; to Mid Wales Constabulary
Leicestershire Constabulary; to Leicestershire and Rutland
Constabulary
Liberty of Peterborough Constabulary; to Peterborough
Combined Police Force
Rutland Constabulary; to Leicestershire and Rutland Constabulary

Abolished under the Police Act 1964

Borough forces

Bath City Police; to Somerset and Bath Constabulary
Barnsley Borough Police; to West Yorkshire Constabulary
Barrow-in-Furness Borough Police; to Lancashire Constabulary
Birkenhead Borough Police; to Cheshire Constabulary
Blackburn Borough Police; to Lancashire Constabulary
Blackpool Borough Police; to Lancashire Constabulary
Bolton Borough Police; to Lancashire Constabulary
Bootle Borough Police; to Lancashire Constabulary
Bournemouth Borough Police; to Dorset and Bournemouth
Constabulary
Brighton Borough Police; to Sussex Constabulary
Burnley Borough Police; to Lancashire Constabulary
Bury Borough Police; to Lancashire Constabulary
Cambridge City Police; to Mid Anglia Constabulary
Cardiff Borough Police; to South Wales Police

Carlisle City Police; to Cumbria Constabulary

Coventry City Police; to Warwickshire and Coventry Constabulary
Derby Borough Police; to Derby County and Borough Constabulary
Dewsbury Borough Police; to West Yorkshire Constabulary
Doncaster Borough Police; to West Yorkshire Constabulary
Eastbourne Borough Police; to Sussex Constabulary
Gateshead Borough Police; to Durham Constabulary
Great Yarmouth Borough Police; to Norfolk Constabulary
Grimsby Borough Police; to Lincolnshire Constabulary
Hastings Borough Police; to Sussex Constabulary
Halifax Borough Police; to West Yorkshire Constabulary
Huddersfield Borough Police; to West Yorkshire Constabulary
Ipswich Borough Police; to Suffolk Constabulary
Leicester City Police; to Leicester and Rutland Constabulary
Lincoln City Police; to Lincolnshire Constabulary
Liverpool City Police; to Liverpool and Bootle Constabulary
Luton Borough Police (again); to Bedfordshire and Luton Constabulary
Manchester City Police; to Manchester and Salford Police
Merthyr Tydfil Borough Police; to South Wales Constabulary
Middlesbrough Borough Police; to Teesside
Newcastle upon Tyne Borough Police; to Northumberland
Constabulary
Newport Borough Police; to Gwent Police
Northampton Borough Police; to Northampton and County
Constabulary
Norwich City Police; to Norfolk Constabulary
Nottingham City Police; to Nottinghamshire Combined Constabulary
Oldham Borough Police; to Lancashire Constabulary
Oxford City Police; to Thames Valley Constabulary
Plymouth City Police; to Devon and Cornwall Constabulary
Portsmouth Borough Police; to Hampshire Constabulary
Preston Borough Police; to Lancashire Constabulary
Reading Borough Police; to Thames Valley Constabulary
Rochdale Borough Police; to Lancashire Constabulary
Rotherham Borough Police; to Sheffield and Rotherham Constabulary
Salford City Police; to Manchester and Salford Police
Sheffield Borough Police; to Sheffield and Rotherham Constabulary
St Helens Borough Police; to Lancashire Constabulary
Stockport Borough Police; to Cheshire Constabulary
Stoke-on-Trent City Police; to Staffordshire County and
Stoke-on-Trent Constabulary
Southampton City Police; to Hampshire Constabulary
Southend-on-Sea Borough Police; to Essex and Southend-on-Sea
Joint Constabulary

South Shields Borough Police; to Durham Constabulary
Southport Borough Police; to Lancashire Constabulary
Sunderland Borough Police; to Durham Constabulary
Swansea Borough Police; to South Wales Constabulary
Tynemouth Borough Police; to Northumberland Constabulary
Wakefield City Police; to West Yorkshire Constabulary
Wallasey Borough Police; to Cheshire Constabulary
Warrington Borough Police; to Lancashire Constabulary
Wigan Borough Police; to Lancashire Constabulary
Worcester City Police; to West Mercia Constabulary
York City Police; to York and North East Yorkshire Police

County/combined forces

Bedfordshire Constabulary; to Bedfordshire and Luton Constabulary
Berkshire Constabulary; to Thames Valley Constabulary
Buckinghamshire Constabulary; to Thames Valley Constabulary
Cambridgeshire Constabulary (original); to Mid Anglia Constabulary
Carmarthenshire and Cardiganshire Constabulary; to Dyfed-Powys
Constabulary
Cornwall County Constabulary; to Devon and Cornwall Constabulary
Cumberland and Westmorland Constabulary; to Cumbria
Constabulary
Derbyshire Constabulary; to Derby County and Borough
Constabulary
Devon and Exeter Police; to Devon and Cornwall Constabulary
Dorset Constabulary; to Dorset and Bournemouth Constabulary
East Riding Constabulary; to York and North East Yorkshire Police
East Suffolk Constabulary; to Suffolk Constabulary
East Sussex Constabulary; to Sussex Constabulary
Essex Constabulary; to Essex and Southend-on-Sea Joint
Constabulary
Glamorgan Constabulary; to South Wales Constabulary
Herefordshire Constabulary; to West Mercia Constabulary
Huntingdonshire Constabulary; to Mid Anglia Constabulary
Isle of Ely Constabulary; to Mid Anglia Constabulary
Leicestershire and Rutland Constabulary; to Leicester and Rutland
Constabulary
Mid Wales Constabulary; to Dyfed-Powys Constabulary
Monmouthshire Constabulary; to Gwent Constabulary
North Riding Constabulary; to York and North East Yorkshire Police
Northamptonshire Constabulary; to Northampton and County
Constabulary
Northumberland County Constabulary; to Northumberland
Constabulary
Nottinghamshire Constabulary; to Nottinghamshire Combined
Constabulary
Peterborough Combined Police Force; to Mid Anglia Constabulary
Oxfordshire Constabulary; to Thames Valley Constabulary
Shropshire Constabulary; to West Mercia Constabulary
Somerset Constabulary; to Somerset and Bath Constabulary
Staffordshire Constabulary; to Staffordshire County and
Stoke-on-Trent Constabulary
West Riding Constabulary; to West Yorkshire Constabulary
West Suffolk Constabulary; to Suffolk Constabulary
West Sussex Constabulary; to Sussex Constabulary
Warwickshire Constabulary; to Warwickshire and Coventry
Constabulary
Worcestershire Constabulary; to West Mercia Constabulary

Abolished by the Local Government Act 1972

All police forces in England and Wales were abolished and reconstituted at midnight on March 31, 1974/April 1, 1974. This list shows the ones that existed then and their fate

(ignoring minor transfers).

Bedfordshire and Luton Constabulary; reconstituted as Bedfordshire Police
Birmingham City Police; merged into West Midlands Police
Bradford City Police; merged into West Yorkshire Police
Bristol City Police; merged into Avon and Somerset Constabulary
Cheshire Constabulary; reconstituted, areas transferred to Merseyside Police and Greater Manchester Police
Cumbria Constabulary; reconstituted
Derby County and Borough Constabulary; reconstituted as Derbyshire Constabulary
Devon and Cornwall Constabulary; reconstituted
Dorset and Bournemouth Constabulary; reconstituted as Dorset Police
Durham Constabulary; reconstituted, areas transferred to Cleveland Police and Northumbria Police
Dyfed-Powys Constabulary; reconstituted
Essex and Southend-on-Sea Joint Constabulary; reconstituted as Essex Police
Gloucestershire Constabulary; reconstituted, areas transferred to Avon and Somerset Constabulary
Gwent Constabulary; reconstituted
Gwynedd Constabulary; reconstituted as North Wales Police
Hampshire Constabulary; reconstituted, areas transferred to Dorset Police
Hertfordshire Constabulary; reconstituted
Kent Police; reconstituted
Kingston-upon-Hull City Police; merged into Humberside Police
Lancashire Constabulary; reconstituted, areas transferred to Merseyside Police, Greater Manchester Police, Cheshire Constabulary and Cumbria Constabulary
Leeds City Police; merged into West Yorkshire Police
Leicester and Rutland Constabulary; reconstituted as Leicestershire Constabulary
Lincolnshire Constabulary; reconstituted, areas transferred to Humberside Police
Liverpool and Bootle Constabulary; merged into Merseyside Police
Manchester and Salford Police; merged into Greater Manchester Police
Mid-Anglia Constabulary; reconstituted as Cambridgeshire Constabulary
Norfolk Constabulary; reconstituted
Northampton and County Constabulary; reconstituted as Northamptonshire Police
Northumberland Constabulary; merged into Northumbria Police
Nottinghamshire Combined Constabulary; reconstituted as Nottinghamshire Police
Sheffield and Rotherham Constabulary; merged into South Yorkshire Police
Somerset and Bath Constabulary; merged into Avon and Somerset Constabulary
South Wales Constabulary; reconstituted
Staffordshire County and Stoke-on-Trent Constabulary; reconstituted as Staffordshire Police
Suffolk Constabulary; reconstituted
Surrey Constabulary; reconstituted
Sussex Constabulary; reconstituted
Teesside Constabulary; merged into Cleveland Constabulary
Thames Valley Constabulary; reconstituted
Warwickshire and Coventry Constabulary; split between Warwickshire Police and West Midlands Police
West Mercia Constabulary; reconstituted
West Midlands Constabulary; merged into West Midlands Police
West Yorkshire Constabulary; split mainly between West Yorkshire Police, South Yorkshire Police and North Yorkshire Police
Wiltshire Constabulary; reconstituted
York and North East Yorkshire Police; split mainly between North Yorkshire Police, Humberside Police and Cleveland Police

Former Scottish forces

Each police burgh had a police force originally, although many merged in the 19th century.

Abolished 1940's
Aberdeenshire Constabulary
Banffshire Constabulary
Dumfriesshire County Police
Kincardineshire Constabulary
Stewartry of Kirkcudbright Police
Moray and Nairn Constabulary
Wigtownshire County Police

Abolished 1960's
Caithness Constabulary
Orkney Constabulary
Shetland Constabulary

Abolished 1975
Aberdeen City Police
Angus Constabulary
Argyll County Police
Ayrshire Constabulary
Berwick, Roxburgh and Selkirk Constabulary
City of Glasgow Police
Dunbartonshire Constabulary
Dundee City Police
Edinburgh City Police
Inverness Constabulary
Lanarkshire Constabulary
The Lothians and Peebles Constabulary
Northern Constabulary (name retained by its successor after merger)
Perth and Kinross Constabulary
Renfrew & Bute Constabulary
Ross and Sutherland Constabulary
Scottish North Eastern Counties Constabulary
Stirling and Clackmannan Police

APPENDIX M - APPOINTMENTS TO CHIEF OFFICER RANK

11 May 1839, John Bird, who had joined Carlisle Police as a Watchman, was appointed Superintendent and Head Constable of Barnard Castle, County Durham.

27 November 1856, PC. Anderson resigned his appointment in Carlisle to take up office as Superintendent and Head Constable of Hexham, Northumberland.

21 January 1857, Superintendent [Chief Officer] John Sabbage left to take up similar appointment in Newcastle-upon-Tyne City Police. He died in office some ten years later.

3 August 1876, Chief Constable Walter Hemingway left upon his appointment as Chief Constable of Cardiff City Police.

14 November 1929, Chief Constable Archibald Kennedy Wilson left to take up office as Chief Constable of Plymouth City Police. He moved again to the position of Chief Constable of Liverpool City Police with an establishment of over 2,500 men.

27 January 1914, Thomas Rawson, who joined the City Force as a constable and became Second Clerk in Police Office, resigned. Appointed Chief Constable of Swansea Borough Police before transferring to become Chief Constable of Bradford City Police.

1960 Roy Harrison, joined the City Police, PC. 39, in January, 1937, rising to Chief Inspector transferred to Dewsbury Borough Police as Superintendent and Deputy Chief Constable, later becoming Chief Constable of that Force. On its amalgamation with several other Yorkshire Boroughs and the West Riding County Force, Mr. Harrison became Deputy Chief Constable of the newly created West Yorkshire Constabulary.

Tom Farmer, appointed Inspector in the City Police on 1 July 1962 on transfer from Durham Constabulary, moved to South Wales Constabulary on promotion to Superintendent then to West Yorkshire Constabulary as a Chief Superintendent. Appointed Assistant Chief Constable of Durham (c1976), he later became Deputy Chief Constable of that Force.

Donald Roy, appointed DCI on transfer from Preston Borough Police on 3 August 1962, rose to become the city's first Chief Superintendent before transferring to West Yorkshire Constabulary (c1970) as Assistant Chief Constable (Crime). Later he held office as Assistant Chief Constable with responsibility for Bradford District.

1 September 1963, Chief Constable Frank Edgar Williamson, appointed head of the Carlisle City Force on 16 November 1961, became Chief Constable also of Cumberland and Westmorland Constabulary on integration of the three forces. On the formation of Cumbria Constabulary on 1 April 1967 he became its first Chief Constable. He left the Force in 1968 upon his appointment as H.M. Inspector of Constabulary for Crime.

James Kerr, PC.85 in city police, rose to the rank of Chief Superintendent in charge of the Carlisle Division of Cumbria Constabulary before transferring, as Assistant Chief Constable to North Yorkshire Constabulary (c1976). He moved on as Deputy Chief Constable of Lincolnshire Constabulary, becoming Chief Constable of the same force.